The New Political Economy of Southeast Asia

Edited by

Rajah Rasiah

Professor of Technology and Innovation Policy, Faculty of Economics and Administration, University of Malaya, Malaysia, Professorial Fellow, UNU-MERIT, The Netherlands, Senior Research Associate, Sanjaya Lall Centre for Technology and Development, Oxford University, UK

Johannes Dragsbaek Schmidt

Associate Professor in Development and International Relations, Aalborg University, Denmark

Edward Elgar

Cheltenham, UK • Northampton, MA, USA

Published by
Edward Elgar Publishing Limited
The Lypiatts
15 Lansdown Road
Cheltenham
Glos GL50 2JA
UK

Edward Elgar Publishing, Inc.
William Pratt House
9 Dewey Court
Northampton
Massachusetts 01060
USA

A catalogue record for this book
is available from the British Library

Library of Congress Control Number: 2010922146

Mixed Sources
Product group from well-managed
forests and other controlled sources
www.fsc.org Cert no. SA-COC-1565
© 1996 Forest Stewardship Council

ISBN 978 1 84980 265 9

Printed and bound by MPG Books Group, UK

Contents

Contributors

Aekapol Chongvilaivan is Fellow at the Institute of Southeast Asian Studies (ISEAS), Singapore.

Anis Chowdhury is Professor of Economics, University of Western Sydney, Australia, and currently affiliated with the Department of Economic and Social Affairs of the United Nations (UN-DESA) in New York as Senior Economic Affairs Officer.

Sanchita Basu Das is Visiting Fellow and the Lead Researcher for Economic Affairs in the ASEAN Studies Centre at the Institute of Southeast Asian Studies (ISEAS), Singapore.

Chris Dixon is Professor of International Development, Deputy Director and Head of Asia Programme at the Global Policy Institute at London Metropolitan University.

Iyanatul Islam is Professor of International Business at Griffith Business School, Griffith University, Nathan, Australia.

Arthur P.J. Mol is Professor Environmental Policy Department of Social Sciences at Wageningen University, the Netherlands, Director of the Wageningen School. He is also Professor in Environmental Policy at Renmin University, Beijing, China.

Rene Ofreneo is Professor in the School of Labor and Industrial Relations at the University of the Philippines (UP SOLAIR), Manila, Research Consultant at the Asia-Pacific Regional Organization of Union Network International (UNI-APRO) in Singapore and Trustee of the Asia Monitor Centre (AMRC) in Hong Kong.

Rajah Rasiah is Professor of Technology and Innovation Policy in the Faculty of Economics and Administration at the University of Malaya, Malaysia, Professorial Fellow at UNU-MERIT in the Netherlands and Senior Research Associate in the Sanjaya Lall Centre for Technology and Development at Oxford University, UK.

Johannes Dragsbaek Schmidt is Associate Professor in Development and International Relations in the Research Center on Development and International Relations at Aalborg University, Denmark.

David A. Sonnenfeld is Professor and Chair of Environmental Studies at the State University of New York College of Environmental Science and Forestry (SUNY-ESF) in Syracuse, NY.

Peter Wad is Associate Professor in the Department of Intercultural Communication and Management at Copenhagen Business School (CBS) and affiliated to the Centre for Business and Development Studies at CBS, Denmark.

Preface

This book examines an important area of political economy to which not many publications have so far been able to give any convincing account. By taking an interdisciplinary approach on such critical issues as industrialization, economic crisis and reform, inequality, industrial relations, environment, civil society and distributional conflicts and free trade agreements, the book attempts to fill a lacuna in the existing literature on the political economy of Southeast Asia.

The book grew out of dissatisfaction among many scholars that a sufficiently exhaustive account of Southeast Asia that addresses these issues in a political economy and social change perspective has been missing. By limiting the analysis to single countries, existing books tend to miss important influences that drive social political and economic transformation in the region. As a consequence, the Danish Development Agency (Danida) and the Ministry of Foreign Affairs approved funds that led to the hosting of a number of workshops where the components of the book were deliberated and charted.

The book is important reading for both undergraduate and graduate students at universities and colleges across the world who are interested in understanding the social, political and economic transformation of Southeast Asia. It will particularly appeal to those seeking a detailed account of the historical and contemporary issues of social change in the region.

The editors would like to thank colleagues and students at the University of Malaya and Aalborg University for useful comments concerning the themes and problems raised in this book. We are grateful for useful comments from a number of friends, particularly Peter Limqueco, Garry Rodan, Kevin Hewison, Vedi Hadiz and Shaharil Talib. The usual disclaimer applies.

Rajah Rasiah and Johannes Dragbaek Schmidt

1. Introduction

Rajah Rasiah and Johannes Dragsbaek Schmidt

Southeast Asia's unique history, which covers some of the culturally rich nations of the world, has been shaped by both internal and international forces of change. The classical period of Southeast Asian history was marked both by the profound influence of forces external to the region and by a range of indigenous responses. Taken together, they shaped the elements for new forms of state and society, religion and culture, economy and commerce, labour relations and the environment.

The changing contours of colonialization altered the patterns of political authority and economic development, tying the Southeast Asian states to metropolitan powers in the process. Primary commodity production – ranging originally from spices to cultivated sugarcane, coffee, cocoa, coconut, rubber, and mining of tin and later oil – became the cornerstone of the colonial mode of production. Thailand escaped direct colonial rule but got absorbed into the capitalist world economy. Resistance to colonial rule had begun the very moment colonialism started. Although Japanese military intervention in 1941–45 provided the initial escape from colonization as Indonesia declared itself independent from both the Japanese and the Dutch, a larger army opposed to capitalist relations was to play a key role in shaping power relations in Southeast Asia. Communist insurgencies gripped British Malaya and the Philippines while communist forces gained control of Vietnam, Cambodia and Laos from initially the French and subsequently the Americans. It was only after the collapse of the Soviet Union that Vietnam, Laos and Cambodia gradually integrated into the capitalist world economy. Myanmar remains isolated from global economic forces, but its military-ruled economy has begun integrating with the Association of Southeast Asian Nations (ASEAN) since the 1990s.

Decolonization and the formation of independent states in the region heralded a shift in domestic and international politics, the nature of state–society relations, and the pace and direction of economic development. The post-colonial ruling elites in Southeast Asia sought to deal with the legacies of colonialism while at the same time dealing with political challenges that threatened social order. This often turbulent period in the

1

region's history (from 1945 to the early 1970s) was also inscribed by the impact of the Cold War, which dominated the international relations of Southeast Asia until the disintegration of the Soviet Union from 1989. This way the evolution of modern Southeast Asia was profoundly influenced by external and domestic developments. In fact ASEAN was formed in 1967 to strengthen ties among the free market economies to stem the potential political threat of a domino effect from communist Indochina and its impact on internal insurgencies. In addition to the geopolitical concerns to contain and defeat communism, the United States and its allies promoted free market relations in Southeast Asia.

Political alliances changed dramatically when the Cold War ended following the collapse of the Soviet Union as the former command economies of Vietnam, Laos and Cambodia quickly inserted themselves into ASEAN and the regional trade integration process that was begun in 1991, i.e. the ASEAN Free Trade Area (AFTA). Not only have developments involving the AFTA process signalled a shift away from strategic concerns associated with the Cold War to the primacy of national economic interests, but the process has also become an important platform for Southeast Asian countries to confront global governance mechanisms such as the World Trade Organization (WTO) collectively. Strongly connected with China but isolated by the United States and Europe, military-ruled Myanmar also formally obtained membership of ASEAN in 1997.

The integration of the Southeast Asian economies into the world economy, including the transitional economies of Indo-China and Myanmar, saw the introduction of development policies, which was led by capitalist economic accumulation but often with roots embedded in the social fabric of societies in each of the individual economies. As the early history of the region shows, a diverse set of ethnic groups who integrated following several spurts of major in-migration from other parts of Asia with wide-ranging cultures and religions characteristic of the populations of the nations often coloured government policies. Although ethnicity has remained a rallying point for strengthening unity as well as political support, especially in Indonesia and Malaysia, political leaderships in these countries have often relied upon hybrid cultures to achieve winning constituencies.

The transformation from feudalism to industrial capitalism in most of Europe was characterized by widespread factory-based proletarianization, but it also evolved alongside owner-farm crop and livestock farming and the guilds systems that reproduced capitalist relations differently as skilled tradesmen under the guilds system evolved in economies such as Germany, the Netherlands, France, Belgium and Italy, thereby reducing the valorization capacity of the bourgeoisie. Bloody Taylorization as well as the defeat of facism in the Second World War gave rise to successful labour movements and industrial relations that created the welfare state in Europe – though its authority has been increasingly undermined since Thatcher became prime minister in Britain in 1979.

However, the pre-capitalist forms as well as colonial integration in Southeast Asia lacked the productive and later the welfaristic egalitarian dynamics essential to engender the conditions for even capitalist accumulation across the societies. The shift from peasants to proletariats as well as the various other forms it has taken in many parts of Southeast Asia has affected the majority of the people differently. Indeed, premature deindustrialization in the Philippines has continued to support the informalization of labour. The large majority of the populations – both paid workers and informal dwellers – continue to enjoy less representation from governments in most of Southeast Asia than the bourgeoisie. Underemployment and unemployment rates are high in the Philippines, East Timor, Indonesia and Myanmar. Hence, despite the trend improvements shown, poverty and inequality continue to deny a significant section of the population in the region, especially in Indonesia, the Philippines, Vietnam, Cambodia, Laos, East Timor and Myanmar, access to basic amenities.

The formation of nation states demarcated by colonial interests has left behind ethnopolitical divides that have coloured social relations in Malaysia and Indonesia. The national borders of Malaysia and Indonesia were largely defined by the British and the Dutch, particularly following the Anglo-Dutch Treaty in 1824 (Hall, 1981), whereas in Malaysia ethnopolitical tensions have often risen between the Malays, and Chinese and Indians, in addition to differences between the *pribumi* and the Chinese in Indonesia, where severe tensions have also led to separatist movements among the *pribumis* in Acheh and Irian Jaya. The birth of East Timor in 2000 is a direct result of these tensions. Although ethno-pluralism and multi-culturalism have become a dominant idiom and strategy of nation building in most of the countries, vernacular roots to narrow ethnonationalism have created polarized, truncated societies in Malaysia and Indonesia.

Separatist movements have also gripped Thailand, the Philippines and Myanmar. Muslim separatists in the southern Philippines and southern Thailand have cashed in on centralist policies and ethno-religious differences to wage a bloody campaign against government forces. Meanwhile a military dictatorship has kept a tight lid not only on political democracy, but on its ethno-regional differences with their historical roots going deep into British colonialism, with a potentially volatile explosion in the waiting if and when democracy is eventually restored in Myanmar.

Being resource rich, all but Singapore among the Southeast Asian economies began with commodity production as the driver of economic growth. The city state of Singapore embarked on industrialization and service modernization after its exit from the Malaysian pact in 1965. However, with the exception of Brunei, East Timor, Myanmar, Laos and to some extent the Philippines and Indonesia, industrialization has become the engine of growth in the other economies. Manufacturing became the leading sector among the primary and secondary sectors in GDP in Malaysia and Singapore, while it had become very important in Thailand by the 1990s. Indonesia, Malaysia, the Philippines and Thailand largely derived poor results from import-substitution strategies, but achieved rapid manufacturing growth on the back of multinational-driven export-oriented firms. The unprecedented financial crisis of 1997–98 affected Thailand, Indonesia, Malaysia and the Philippines seriously, and its contagion aggravated economic growth rates of the remaining Southeast Asian economies. The nature of integration of the region in the global economy left it vulnerable to the vicissitudes of both currency and capital market volatility. Although Thailand was the epicentre of the crisis, Indonesia faced the worst damage following the political fallout that accompanied the demise of the New Order regime of Suharto. Nevertheless, despite different policy packages implemented by governments, a decade later all the main economies showed signs of a fragile economic recovery, only to be sucked into the global financial crisis, fuelled this time by the housing and banking crash in the United States. Whereas a booming United States' economy assisted quick recovery from the Asian financial crisis, the prime source of economic recession in Southeast Asia has resulted from exactly the opposite effect with a severe deceleration in exports.

Rapid growth and industrialization have also brought consequences on the social relations and environmental landscape of Southeast Asia. The transition from peasantry to capitalist relations has not been smooth, as the inability of some of the governments to generate sufficient numbers of jobs and subsistence wages in the formal labour markets have left significant segments of the populations in squalor. Indonesia and the Philippines, and subsequently Cambodia, Vietnam, Laos and Myanmar, face high levels of unemployment and underemployment. Although absolute poverty levels have fallen, Malaysia and Thailand have faced rising levels of inequality since the 1990s. Income inequality levels in Malaysia, Thailand, Indonesia and Singapore show a zig-zag pattern – increasing initially before falling over long periods and then worsening again from the 1990s (see Rasiah and Ishak, 2001). Indeed in Singapore income inequality has been rapidly rising in a sustained way since the late 1990s, which has prompted the government to introduce some major policy initiatives.

Labour movements – both legally and illegally – have strengthened as well as weakened in the region. Low levels of union densities, authoritarian governments and exposure to casualizing global production networks have reduced the power of trade unions in the region (see Todd and Jomo, 1994; Rasiah and von Hofmann, 1998; Hutchison and Brown, 2001). Co-optation into mainstream politics has helped unions to participate in the development process in Singapore and Vietnam. Early authoritarianism followed by democratization in the Philippines and Indonesia since the fall of Marcos and Suharto in 1986 and 1998 respectively has not given similar representation in the development process. The often intense contestation for representation among rival unions has undermined the position of unions in the electoral process in Indonesia and the Philippines. Trade unions have been isolated from government policy making and hence have remained peripheral to the processes of development in Malaysia and Thailand. Trade unions arc nascent, and their activities remain uncoordinated in Cambodia, Laos and Myanmar.

The overarching influence of state–market coordinates of government policies in early accumulation generally excluded emphasis on the environment. The destruction of forests in Southeast Asia, to support logging, plantation agriculture and housing for profits, has continued unabated. Nevertheless a combination of rising middle-class pressure, international standards imposed on multinational firms operating in the region from 1989 (the Montreal Protocol) and the proliferation of eco-labels has helped bring environmental considerations into government policy making in the region. Until then, domestic efforts to strengthen environmental standards emerged in Indonesia, Malaysia, Thailand and the Philippines, but faced little enforcement. The cross-border movement of haze, particularly from Sumatra in Indonesia to Singapore and peninsular Malaysia, as well as Kalimantan in Indonesia to Sarawak in Malaysia, is a case in point where much talk has translated little into solutions. In addition, industrial emission and cross-border spillover effects of pollution had also become a thorny regional problem by the 1990s.

The economic and security significance of Southeast Asia in the world economy could not be overstated, as the region connects the East and West trade routes through the South China Sea and the Straits of Malacca. American interest in the region has remained paramount. Home to almost 550 million people, Southeast Asia commanded a GNP exceeding $700 billion and was the United States' fifth largest trading partner in 2005. The United States and its allies spent a considerable period of time trying to stem the possible domino effect from communism. Although the threat of communist insurgencies is no longer critical, American political interest in the region has become important again since the emergence of terrorist threats in the southern Philippines, southern Thailand and Indonesia.

   This brief introduction denotes the importance of the region itself but also implicitly shows the need for a careful analysis of political economic change. The next section discusses the main approaches used so far to understand and interpret the political economy of Southeast Asia. Most works have tended to limit analysis to the boundaries of nation states even when discussing globalization issues. This book brings four advantages over previous accounts of the political economy of Southeast Asia. Firstly, the book examines a wider range of socio-economic and political topics that are important to Southeast Asia than those attempted by others. Secondly, by allowing a free hand on the formulation of the political economy approach for the individual chapters the book recognizes the need to examine the various topics differently and hence the preference for a new political economy of Southeast Asia. Thirdly, by extending analysis to at least three nations in the region this book seeks to examine the interrelationships that capture the mediation of global and national interactions and interventions that have acted as the drivers of political and economic change in the region. Fourthly, the book captures the dramatic changes that have taken place in the region since the turn of the millennium. In doing so, this book seeks to complement rather than supplant the important contributions other scholars have made to understanding the political economy of Southeast Asia (notably Limqueco, McFarlane and Odhnoff, 1989; Rodan, Hewison and Robison, 1997, 2006).

THEORY AND SOUTHEAST ASIAN STUDIES

Most studies of economic development in capitalist Southeast Asia have relied on five approaches – the neo-liberal (e.g. World Bank, 1993), the state-capital approach (see Yoshihara, 1988; Jesudason, 1989; Jomo *et al.*, 1997), the classical Marxist approach (e.g. Rasiah, 1988, 1997; Limqueco, McFarlane and Odhnoff, 1989; Rodan, Hewison and Robison, 1997), neo-Marxist approaches (e.g. Jomo, 1986) and structural functionalist and populist approaches (e.g. Kitching, 1982; Budiman, 1990). The first view is synonymous with the tradition of neoclassical economics and has had strong advocacy from the World Bank and the International Monetary Fund (IMF). The second has leanings to the developmental state approach (Johnson, 1982; Amsden, 1989; Evans, 1995), but the articulations capture the reasons behind slow growth and lack of industrial upgrading in most of Southeast Asia. Although the third and fourth line of thought emerged as a critique of the other two approaches, their definitional, relational and epistemological foundation has relied on a critical and a conflict-based perspective of social change. In their overall meta-theoretical vision, these transhistorical and grand social traditions differ considerably, as the first and the second are Weberian, while the latter two belong to the Marxist tradition.[1] The fifth school of thought captures the work of structural functionalist scholars who seem to have sought a simple but popular refuge in arguments to explain problems of capitalist accumulation and the interaction with political development.

Neoclassical

Driven by the belief that, if left alone to natural forces, markets (relative prices) will always clear and that rational economic agents will always optimize (see Lucas, 1978), neoclassical economists argue that efforts must be taken to avoid distortions in the market. Given information imperfections, Hahn (1984) went on to argue that governments should follow market signals to remove rather than introduce distortions to achieve allocative efficiency (Pareto optimality).

This argument has been contested by critics on the grounds that markets on their own will achieve only static efficiency and prevent the appropriation of dynamic gains in efficiency associated with increasing returns, complementarities and structural interdependence (see Kornai, 1962; Kaldor, 1979). Keynes (1936) had argued that economies will achieve equilibrium before full employment can be reached because of market imperfections, which will particularly be severe in developing economies characterized by demand constraints. Markets on their own will also prevent the appropriation of Schumpeterian innovation synergies, as in the absence of rents economic agents would prefer to imitate rather than innovate (see Schumpeter, 1942).

Pointing to the examples of countries faced with import-substitution and corruption (for example, Turkey, India and Pakistan), neoclassical economists responded by claiming that government failures are more severe than market failures and hence that the pendulum had swung permanently toward their side (Krueger, 1983; Sachs and Warner, 1995). Despite the use of interventionist instruments for a long time neoclassical economists had argued that the East Asian economies were more market-than government-driven by simply showing that these economies have been open, export-oriented and characterized by low mean tariffs (see also Belassa, 1982; World Bank, 1993).

Even when the World Bank (1993) conceded on interventionist forays by governments in Northeast Asia, it had argued that Southeast Asian development was driven essentially by market forces. Hill (1996) and Pangestu (1998) on Indonesia and Athukorala and Menon (1999) and Salleh and Sahathevan (1992) on Malaysia argued that liberalization had unleashed a greater allocative role for markets, with the corollary of efficiency-oriented rapid growth and structural change in these economies. Using cost–benefit analysis, Warr (1987a, 1987b, 1989) concluded that the explicit and implicit subsidies provided to firms located in export processing zones merely distorted prices at the peril of dissipation of scarce resources in Malaysia, the Philippines and Thailand. Neoclassical works on Southeast Asia explain economic development on the basis of the increased role of markets. The methodology used to arrive at such a conclusion again relied on openness, liberal financial systems, high trade–GDP ratios and relatively low mean tariffs. This position is taken despite the fact that government in the most advanced country in the region – i.e. Singapore – has intervened selectively to take advantage as well as direct the composition, direction and pace of market development, including integration in global markets (see Rodan, 1989). Rasiah and Ishak (2001) provided evidence to argue that Malaysia has had a mixed experience, with interventions being responsible for both the successful and the unsuccessful experiences of growth and distribution in Malaysia. Rasiah (1998) went further to argue that Indonesia, Malaysia and Thailand have not intervened effectively to provide the institutional change necessary to engender catch-up in manufacturing in these economies.

State-Capital

The state-capital approach tends to examine economic development from the lenses of the role of the state in capital accumulation without addressing class relations. Because interventions successfully transformed Japan, Korea and Taiwan, these countries have been referred to as developmental states (see Johnson, 1982; Amsden, 1989; Wade, 1990; Johnson, Tyson and Zysman 1991; Evans, 1995).

Extending the arguments of Gerschenkron (1962), the state-capital approach examines the nature of interventions by looking at institutional development in the catch-up process. Development planning that takes on the role of governments as the key driver can be traced also to Chakravaty (1969, 1993) and Sen (1999). However, unlike evolutionary economists who do not confine themselves to one single master in driving development (see Nelson and Winter, 1982), state-capital advocates regard the state as the chief architect in the process. Interestingly, Johnson (1982), Fransman (1985), Amsden (1989), Wade (1990) and Amsden and Chu (2003) provide specific examples of state intervention in the processes of learning and innovation in Northeast Asia. Amsden (1989) went as far as to argue that the Korean state 'got relative prices wrong' to stimulate and quicken manufacturing firms' movement toward the technology frontier.

Similar approaches attempting to explain why similar industrial success to that of Northeast Asia has eluded Indonesia and Malaysia argue that the lack of support from the state in these countries has been caused by ethnic factors and misguided neo-liberal instruments or both. Hence, Jesudason (1989) argues that the Bumiputera-dominated government has failed to provide similar support to the predominantly Chinese entrepreneurs. Yoshihara (1988) argued that the Chinese have been reluctant to invest in risky and lumpy businesses on a large scale owing to the fear of ethnic tensions that could arise from indigenous-dominated governments. Jomo *et al.,* (1997) go further to explain the contradictions of government policy to distinguish Southeast Asia from Northeast Asia. Rasiah (1998) argued that the very limited use of Northeast Asian-style interventions had largely been the cause of the lack of upgrading achieved in Indonesia, Malaysia and Thailand. Jomo, Rasiah, Alavi and Jaya Gopal (2003) present firm-level experiences to show cases of productive interventions that assisted the growth of some successful Malaysian firms. Also, whereas governments in Northeast Asia actively raised the share of human capital in their populations, the Southeast Asian economies other than Singapore have continued to face low levels of human capital development (see Rasiah, 2009). The successful use of tariffs and other support successfully assisted oil palm firms in Malaysia to reach the technology frontier (see Jaya Gopal, 1999; Rasiah, 2005).[7] Pasuk and Baker (1994) make the case that unproductive rentier activities alongside liberal policies have restricted rapid growth in Thailand.

The main questions in this regard are: (1) Which factors explain that Southeast Asia was unable to emulate the most important parts of the development strategies pursued by the East Asian NICs? (2) Why have industrial firms in Southeast Asia failed to reach the global technology frontier? (3) Why did Southeast Asia not achieve a shift from low-value-added economic activities to high-value-added activities?

One answer stresses the following historical and contemporary factors which proved to be important in the case of East Asia: (1) the international realm, (2) the creation of an institutional framework of market-favourable conditions structured by the state, and (3) politically determined policies and industrial strategies with a simultaneous emphasis on import-substitution and export orientation and monetary nationalism (high savings and low exchange rates) (Schmidt, 1996: 199). Land and urban reforms, high investments in human development, low levels of inequality and poverty, and the politically determined facilitation of trade to the US market all prepared the way for the evolution of the Japanese miracle, the NICs and later on China's unprecedented high economic growth rates. Furthermore, the first-generation NICs and Japan did not rely on FDI and were able to raise domestic capital accumulation orchestrated by the state.

None of these factors have been visible in Southeast Asian, although Singapore and Malaysia have made attempts to copy the state interventionist parts of the NIC strategy with varying results (Schmidt, 2000).

Classical Marxist

Despite the primacy of economic accumulation, classical Marxist analysis takes an interdisciplinary approach. This approach examines social phenomena from the unity of the three circuits of capital – money, productive and commodity (see Marx, 1956; Warren, 1980; Luxemburg, 2003; see also Jenkins, 1984; Rasiah, 1993). Because Marx was convinced that it is in capitalism that the forces of production reach their highest accumulation and efficiency, the emphasis is laid on technological transformation.

Consistent with Marx (1867), Warren (1980) argued that the nature of capitalist expansion – however destructive and painful – had opened the way for underdeveloped economies to create the conditions to govern and experience capitalist accumulation. Indeed, one can argue that Northeast Asia's successes are examples of governments proactively absorbing technology to reach the catch-up phase. Although labour struggles went undocumented in the work of Johnson (1982), Amsden (1989) and Wade (1990), rapid increases in real wages ensured that standards of living at a larger scale improved.

Robison (1986) and Robison and Hadiz (2004) on Indonesia, Rodan (1989) on Singapore, Hewison (1989) on Thailand, Beresford (1988) on Vietnam, Hutchison and Brown (2001) on the Philippines, and Rasiah (1997) and Rasiah and Ishak (2001) on Malaysia examine the nature of power relations to explain the political economy processes behind accumulation in these economies. Rasiah (1987, 1988, 1996) had argued that global integration, far from causing de-industrialization and de-accumulation, was actually transforming the labour process in the electronics industry in Penang to support upgrading in the 1980s and early 1990s. However, owing to ethnic coloured policies and the lack of proper catch-up interventions the potential synergies had been dissipated by the second half of the 1990s (see Rasiah, 1999). Limqueco and McFarlane (1983) and Limqueco, McFarlane and Odhnoff (1989) discuss the impact of capital-relations on the labour process in Southeast Asia.

Neo-Marxist

Lenin's account of monopoly capital, arising from combining the work of Hilferding (1912) and Bukharin (1929), arguably sowed the seeds for

Baran's (1973) neo-Marxist account of capital accumulation on a world scale. By focusing on the circuits of money and commodity, neo-Marxists are opposed to capitalist organizations from developed countries operating in developing countries owing to their argument that such operations are directed at surplus appropriation in the latter for accumulation in the former. The world systems perspective used by Wallerstein (1979) and his followers allows accumulation in the periphery but only marginally. Because of its appeal, scholars from the developing world have in many cases tended to integrate neo-Marxist accounts with a nationalist ideological flavour. Hence, political, cultural and social dynamics are considered to be adapted or impacted through the channels of integration by capitalist forces from developed countries. The successful examples of Korea and Taiwan are argued by neo-Marxists as driven by the geo-political considerations of the global metropole (the United States in particular) seeking to thwart support for the communist block despite the miserable failure of the American-aligned Philippines.

Using the most incisive account of history to understand the forces of capitalist integration and exploitation, neo-Marxist analysis provides a detailed account of development in latecomer economies (Caldwell, 1968; Elliott, 1978). Indeed, Jomo (1986) provided arguably the most incisive class and nationalist analysis of Malaysia's pre-colonial, colonial and post-colonial history. Constantino (1969, 1982) offered a nationalist account of the Philippines. Pramoedya (1980, 1992) through his novels expounded a similar account of Indonesia, criticizing the role of colonialism and divisive post-colonialist policies (Utrecht, 1972).

The articulation of the nature of integration, and the transition faced by the classes, has been a major strength of neo-Marxist works on Southeast Asia. However, the lack of emphasis on Marx's and Luxemburg's advocacy – in particular on the productive circuit – on the need to endure the pains of integration but with a focus on creating and driving the productive forces of accumulation reduced the capacity for accumulation-oriented policy formulation. If Northeast Asia achieved rapid growth and structural change on the back of largely local firms it was also driven by global integration – access to foreign sources of knowledge through imitation and licensing as well as domestic absorption and development, and exposure to foreign markets that provided the scale, scope and competition (creative destruction). Policy prescriptions of neo-Marxists tended to discourage integration in global markets. Even the transitional economies of Vietnam, Cambodia and Laos have recognized the problems with this and as a consequence have re-integrated into the capitalist system since 1989.

Modernization, Nation Building and Populist Approaches

In contrast to dependency and other critical theory formations, modernization and nation-building theories (Pye, 1962; Geertz, 1963; Pye and Verba, 1965; Huntington, 1968) have had a profound impact on the evolution of studies of political economy in the region. In fact, these structural functionalist theories played a key role in the foundation of the study of Southeast Asia from independence and as prime mover during and after the Vietnam War to construct and rearticulate new regional and national identities. The basic ideas were based on the well-known dualities of backward–advanced, traditional–modern, rural–urban and not least authoritarianism versus democracy. And in many cases they served US foreign policy ambitions in the region. Even today the relative success of Southeast Asia in terms of high economic growth has led to a revision of modernization theory and a celebration of its success (Berger, 2003: 447).

In close connection to modernization and nation building, another set of approaches emerged in the 1980s and 1990s. Although some will argue that these approaches should be seen within a strict political science context, they do have important ramifications on the nexus between politics and economics.

They tried to explain the phenomenon of the importance of populism as a term explaining why various regimes in Southeast Asia can be characterized by their appeal to the will of the people or rather 'against both the established structure of power and the dominant ideas and values of the society. . . . They involve some kind of revolt against the established structure of power in the name of the people' (Canovan, 1999: 3; Laclau, 1977). Personalized politics through populist leadership and with important references to nationalism has re-emerged again and again in the region and thus is a very important social phenomenon which has been reflected in the literature. Like democracy itself, populism in various forms has ebbed and flowed throughout the twentieth century in the region (Rodan and Hewison, 1996; Rodan and Jayasuriya, 2006) and is important to consider as an explanatory factor which shows how individual politicians, leaders and parties cope with economic stagnation, crisis and the perils of globalization. Thus populism per se is a movement, a moment, and an analytical framework explaining the importance of personalized politics and populist reforms in the region.

Changes in the Political Economy Approaches to Southeast Asian Studies

Drawing from colonial records Marx (1853: 3–4) had argued that social relations in India were reminiscent of European antiquity, and that colonization was a necessary phase to quicken the transformation to industrial capitalism – the transformation of the slave–master relations to bourgeois–proletariat skipping the feudal lord–servant relationship in the process. There is much debate on the impact of colonialism and capitalist integration on India. Bagchi (1982) and Griffin (1979) refer to the phase as 'underdevelopment', and the latter went further to describe it as 'pillaging'. While acknowledging the destructive consequences initially Luxemburg (2001) and later Desai and Kumar (1982) argue that capitalist integration initiated under colonialism provided the conditions for the modernization of the forces of production under capitalism.

The Marxist notion of economic crisis and its different constructs have also produced divergent explications of development in Southeast Asia. Whereas the neo-Marxists, focusing on the circuits of commodity and money, considered that the mid-1980s crisis in Southeast Asia would undermine industrial accumulation, classical Marxists used the uneven and circular nature of capitalist evolution to dismiss such an assertion. Indeed, Rasiah (1988) had provided empirical evidence in the semiconductor industry – which faced a cyclical downturn in 1984–86 – to show a revival in the industry by pointing to rising investment and capital–labour ratios. Similarly the neo-Marxists and populists focused extensively on proving the deleterious effects of the labour process on workers and working conditions in the capitalist economies of Southeast Asia, while classical Marxists researched whether capitalist relations in these economies showed signs of shifting from the low road to industrialization to the high road to industrialization. Pyke and Sengenberger (1992) referred to rampant casualization of workers facing low wages, poor working conditions, low skills and monotonous, regimented and temporary work as the low road to industrialization, and job permanence, high wages, rich working conditions that stimulate skilling, and participation and thinking as the high road to industrialization. Ofreneo (2007) and Henderson and Phillips (2007) provide empirical evidence to argue over the re-transition to the low road to industrialization in the Philippines and Malaysia respectively.

A number of studies have tried to discuss conceptualizations of Marx on the Asiatic mode of production and Oriental despotism, and Weber's concepts of patrimonial bureaucracy. It is intriguing to note the merchantalism on the basis of commodity exchange that existed in Southeast Asia well before the successful supplanting of feudalism with capitalism in Europe (Reid, 1990a, 1990b). The classical Weberian investigation of whether the cultural elements of the Protestant ethic could be found in Islam, Hinduism and Confucianism has also been a recurrent theme. Attempts to link Confucianism with Protestantism extended beyond explications of successful development in Japan, Korea, Taiwan and China, but also the Chinese diaspora in Southeast Asia (see Bolt, 2000). Evaluations of the nature of social relations emerging in East and Southeast Asia often manifested themselves in the investigation of similarities and differences that existed between the West and Asia, and the ways in which each could be conceptually brought into relationship with the other. More specifically, Marx, Weber and their contemporaries tried to explain why industrial capitalism and an industrial bourgeoisie had emerged in Southeast Asia prior to Western intervention (Wertheim, 1995; King, 1996: 171). Why there was a lag to take off by Asia at the time Europe began to take off remains a controversy without closure.

Once some cultural sociologists had linked the so-called Weberian achieve-oriented Protestantism equivalent in Confucianist capitalism following the successful development of Japan, Korea, Taiwan, Hong Kong and Singapore, there began the search to explain Southeast Asia's paradox. The Chinese have also integrated with Southeast Asia, and only cut out from leadership roles in politics in Brunei, Indonesia and Malaysia. Yoshihara (1988) attempted to explain Chinese participation in less risky and small business ventures rather than in dynamic and lumpy industries' enterprises by arguing that the ersatz capitalism they helped promote was a direct response to the uncertainties they faced from native leaderships. Jesudason (1989) had argued that ethnic policies restricted the emergence of a vibrant Chinese bourgeoisie in Malaysia. Several scholars had begun working seriously on the merits of Chinese networks and their impact on capitalist accumulation (see Chirot and Reid, 1997). Gomez and Jomo (1997) examined whether indeed Chinese ethnic networking existed in Malaysia, though the conclusions drawn from shareholder structures did not provide the rigour required to draw accurate conclusions.

There have also been attempts to contrast Southeast Asia's accumulation with that of Japan, Korea and Taiwan and to some extent Singapore (also located in Southeast Asia). Whereas until the financial crisis of 1997–98 the neo-liberal verdict glorified the success of the Southeast Asian economies as being more noteworthy for imitation elsewhere than those of the Northeast Asian economies owing to the apparent role of markets (World Bank, 1993), dirigiste and developmental exponents pointed to the effective use of industrial policy as the reason why the industrial bourgeoisie is deeply rooted in the latter while being shallowly rooted in the former (see Fishlow, Gwin, Haggard, Rodrik and Wade, 1994; Jomo, 1996; Rasiah, 1998). Interestingly, the very neo-liberals who considered Indonesia, Malaysia and Thailand as salutary examples of market-led liberal economies turned against this story to claim that government-led cronyism and corruption accounted for the financial crisis. Although no country in the world has a totally liberal or closed regime, some neo-liberals have continued to point to selected examples of interventions such as quasi-currency pegs as the cause of the Asian financial crisis (see McLeod and Garnaut, 1998). Yet the fact of the matter is that the orderly coordination of trade and investment involving currencies of highly open economies is not viable in the presence of liberal capital markets.[3]

The discipline of political economy has undergone significant changes over the years. Whereas the classical political economists such as Smith (1776), Ricardo (1981), Mill (1844), Marx (1867), List (1885) and Marshall (1890) examined jointly the principles, American economists had detached politics from political economy by the early twentieth century. Subsequently American mainstream scholars, anxious to provide an alternative to the Marxist theoretical approach, switched emphasis from unearthing the root causes of unequal development to examining how capitalism should shape politics, society and culture. Rostow (1960) led among the early American-driven non-communist initiatives to arrest the then overwhelming interest in Marxist thought. The global influence of *pax Americana* has been felt strongly even in Southeast Asia so that political economy has become largely an exercise in public policy and the financial and industrial institutions promoting economic growth in capitalist societies. The basic assumption is that this is a presumptively benign process whereby the neutral state rationally, following Weber, bestows rewards and inflicts punishments on private and public capital in the course of making policy. Thus the logic is that the best person wins, it is only business, nothing personal, but X gets the capital and Y does not. This type of so-called objective social science based on neoclassical theory draws on evolutionary (Darwin, 1859) as well as liberal (Hayek, 1979) fundamentals of a particular polity that enables the development of the best elements in the most optimal way. As mentioned above,[4] it provides one of the foundations of societal evolution within modernization theory, and is based on a static understanding of the socio-economic system that neither recognizes nor appreciates the complexity, non-linearity and open nature of human societies as well as the dynamic forces that drive social change (see Marx, 1867; Schumpeter, 1942; Polanyi, 1957; Nelson and Winter, 1982). North (1994) arguably went far to address how institutions – including political and social – mediate to influence economic outcomes, but his line of argument remained stuck to a stylized model of rational outcomes with markets as the superior institution. Nelson's (2008) evolutionary concept of institutions is preferred here, with its dynamic, non-linear and uneven effects. Markets are seen by Nelson as only one of the many institutions, and the configuration that determines political economy outcomes in particular times and physical spaces cannot be generalized.

The joint influence of political economy factors has certainly been part of Southeast Asian studies, but nevertheless, with the notable exception of the debate over moral versus market-based peasant behavior (Scott, 1976, 1985; Turton, 1984, 1989; Gravers, 1989) and the rather substantive work on capital–state relations,[5] research by Southeast Asianists has been relatively weak and largely failed to address theoretical concerns of international political economy (Doner, 1991: 819). Furthermore, scholars focusing on the region have been preoccupied with modernization, structural functionalism and cultural factors in the study of politics; the predictable consequence has been that Southeast Asian studies in general did not contribute satisfactorily to the general field of international relations (Keyes, 1992: 16).

While each theoretical explanation contributed to the understanding of Southeast Asian development and political economy, these studies have focused on distinct and sometimes narrow subjects with only a limited level of explanatory power (Schmidt, 1997). In the late 1980s some observers noted that Southeast Asia had acquired increasing importance in world affairs, yet the degree and quality of much of the research on the region often did not enable one to address the most important aspects of its current and future development (Taylor and Turton, 1988: 1).[6] Another scholar noted, 'In a region like Southeast Asia, where relevant knowledge about local society is still limited, it is understandable that academics as well as bureaucrats feel that the main task of scholarship is to fill in the blanks rather than to test the framework' (McVey, 1995: 3). As a result, much political economy scholarship on the region has aimed at providing solid workaday examinations without challenging creatively existing theoretical conjectures. For that matter, such questioning may be thought to be not only unnecessary but subversive by those in power (McVey, 1995: 3).[7]

This changed to a considerable degree with the emergence of the Murdoch school (Rodan, Hewison and Robison, 1997, 2006), which saw a new critical scholarship on a whole variety of issues related to the political economy of Southeast Asia. However, in most cases this valuable scholarship was devoted to single-country studies, but with important exceptions some aspects of a more interdisciplinary and transnational nature have also been touched upon, and recently especially after the 1997 financial crisis hit the region international political economy has been incorporated into various contributions (Jaysuriya, 2008).

This book attempts to fill the gaps identified above by investigating the regional aspects of comparative politics and economics and how they have affected various important aspects of development and social change in Southeast Asia, which is done implicitly through an interdisciplinary meta-theoretical perspective of comparative political economy of region-alization. The intention is to shift attention away from an artificial division between state and market, and look at internal and external social agencies and institutions as they evolve along transnational lines. There is an attempt to break with the market–government (dichotomy) debate that observes the supremacy of one over the other. In so doing the authors of the individual chapters have been told to introduce whatever novelty of approach is necessary to give a better political economy account of the region but with a focused analytical perspective on the increased scope, diversity, fluidity and non-conformity of regional and transborder aspects of the political economy of Southeast Asia. Hence, the vantage point taken in each of the subsequent chapters is expected to be different so as to provide the bricks and mortar to construct a coherent political economy story of the region by emphasizing transnational aspects of the evolution of the region. The book is an attempt to complement and in some cases contrast with the burgeoning literature already covering the formal and institutional aspects of Southeast Asian security, diplomacy, and trade-related matters (Macintyre, 1994; Acharya, 1997; Bowles, 2002; Alagappa, 2003) and is thus a new approach focusing on uneven social change and the heterogeneity, pluralistic and multi-dimensional processes in the region. The transnationality of the new political economy in Southeast Asia argues that it is important to examine the heterogeneous linkages and interactions among states, markets and civil society (Hettne, Inotai and Sunkel, 1999/2001; Schulz, Söderbaum and Öjendal, 2001: 2).

The comparative political economy of Southeast Asia advanced in this book is twofold: the first examines how states and markets mediate in the creation and governance of institutions and economic development across the region in the face of local, national and global forces. The second examines the interaction of local, national and global transnational actors and institutions in shaping the political and economic history, civil society, environmental state, industrialization, absolute and relative poverty, and the transition of social relations from pre-capitalist to capitalist forms of production.

ANOMALIES AND PROBLEMS

It is worth introducing a few highly contested accounts of development and social change in Southeast Asia here. Whereas there is now consensus over the rapid development and structural change that has occurred in Japan, Korea and Taiwan, there is still debate over the drivers of growth in Southeast Asia.

Jacobs (1971) found in his comparative study that Japan and Thailand not only had escaped colonialism, but also showed a high degree of cultural homogeneity and a strong national identity. Both countries also prevented direct colonization in identical ways: Japan's system of ministries and agencies came into being well before its political parties, constitution or parliament. Differing from those of the United States, these ministries were not created for civil servants to regulate private agents or to supply jobs for party loyalists, but rather to guide Japan's forced development targeted at checking incipient colonization by Western imperialists (Jacobs, 1971: 3–4). The administrative and bureaucratic praxis was characterized by a vertical administration (Johnson, Tyson and Zysman, 1989: 187). Interestingly, many observers at that time were sure that Thailand would develop while Japan would not (Jacobs, 1971: 4). One intriguing question is of course why did the opposite happen? Japan developed and became an economic superpower and since the 1980s has become second only to the United States. A related question which applies to the other Southeast Asian states as well is whether it is possible to explain this anomaly by focusing on internal factors such as the role of social and political stability, cohesiveness and the strength of the state apparatus or whether external elements such as the indirect influence of colonial powers, and after the Second World War the role of the US and later of Japan itself, should be given more prominence.

The significance of openness and closeness of particular economies has become even more pressing since the 1980s because of the impressive economic growth rates of East Asia over the past 30 years. It is well known that Japan's ascendancy has been nothing short of spectacular. The subsequent growth of the high-productivity, high-wage economies of South Korea, Taiwan, Hong Kong and Singapore prompted an intense debate on whether there is indeed an East Asian growth model. The early explanatory model came in the form of Akamatsu's (1962) flying geese model. Quite apart from its scholastic merits and demerits,[8] this model faded away when Japan experienced an economic slowdown over the period 1989–2002. What is left now is the same old neo-liberal–dirigiste debate, which has continued to attract followers despite their diametrically opposed arguments. The dirigistes have argued that strong governments (the master) have been pivotal to interventions that got relative prices wrong (in relation to factor endowments) in the short run to drive sustained catch-up in Japan, Korea and Taiwan (Johnson, 1982; Fransman, 1985; Deyo, 1987a; Freeman, 1987; Amsden, 1989; Wade, 1990; Chang, 1994; Amsden and Chu, 2003). Market apostles insist that price-distorting interventions are neither possible nor plausible in engendering rapid growth and structural change (Belassa, 1982; World Bank, 1993).

The World Bank (1993) conceded that interventions were indeed rife in the Northeast Asian economies but argued that they will no longer be possible and that the potential for government failure is much more severe than that for market failure so that the so-called market-friendly options assumed by Malaysia, Thailand and Indonesia are better examples to follow. Despite their superior economic endowments at the time policies were implemented to drive economic growth, all three economies have not only recorded far slower growth than the Northeast Asian economies, but also demonstrated little catch-up in manufacturing, which drove Fishlow, Gwin, Haggard, Rodrik and Wade (1994) to state that the World Bank had 'perfected the art of paradigm maintenance'.

Between 1993 and 1998 neo-liberal arguments condemning state intervention as the cause of the slowdown and subsequent crash in Southeast Asia were rife. Using a totally false proposition (see Nelson, 1994; Romer, 1994; Vaitsos, 2003; Rasiah, 2004) – i.e. total factor productivity (TFP) that was estimated originally by Solow (1956) using the growth accounting framework – Young (1994, 1995) had argued that the low TFP growth rates achieved by the East Asian economies (including South Korea, Taiwan and Singapore) simply showed that these economies have grown through factor inputs rather than technical change. Drawing on these findings, Krugman (1994, 1995) had argued that the interventionist policies in the Northeast Asian economies had simply produced Stalinist-type growth through perspiration rather than inspiration – something that cannot be sustained over the long run. The financial crisis of 1997–98 was interpreted by such followers as being the cause of rentier policies that painted governments as corrupt and ill equipped to lead markets. Consistent with Stiglitz's (2000) position, Krugman (1999) was to dramatically shift his opinion to accept Keynesian arguments on financial liberalization of capital and currency (despite the use of the currency peg among Southeast Asian economies) markets as being the cause of the financial crisis that gripped the East Asian economies in 1997–98 (see also Keynes, 1936). UNCTAD (1996) had already warned over the bubble that had grown from rising deficits in trade and debt accounts, which was exposing Korea, Thailand, Indonesia and the Philippines to financial collapse from the late 1980s. Indeed, the Asian financial crisis merely exposed the weaknesses of neo-liberal views as growth rates in the real sectors of Malaysia, Thailand and Indonesia slowed down significantly from the mid-1990s owing to fundamental problems with technological change – though Indonesian growth rates collapsed also because of a political fallout.

Whether through the use of local capital or foreign direct investment, rapid growth in East Asia relied on integration in global markets and value chains driven by transnational corporations. Global markets have also been critical in technology imports – embodied in machinery and equipment, and the tacitness acquired through employment abroad, licences and imitation – to Southeast Asian economies. FDI inflow has traditionally been high in Singapore as well as in Malaysia and has become important in Cambodia, Laos, Vietnam, Indonesia, Thailand and the Philippines since the 1990s. Whereas access to technology enjoyed by local firms via licensing, duplicative imitation and later creative imitation from transnational corporations dominated learning and innovation in Japan, Korea and Taiwan (see Fukasaku, 1992; Kim, 1997), transnational affiliates continue to provide the main external market links to drive manufactured exports in the Southeast Asian economies. As argued earlier, simple market–government dichotomies cannot explain adequately these trends, and hence the book seeks to explain how the different modes of governance – especially government and markets – have mediated effectively and ineffectively to produce the existing political economy outcomes. If pre-capitalist social bonds that evolved under the guilds system have remained important in Europe, old socio-cultural elements as well as new ones (including political) have emerged to co-exist in some cases but integrate in other cases to colour capitalist transformation in Southeast Asia. Pro-Bumiputera policies and Chinese business networks have been significant in Malaysia and Indonesia.

TOWARDS AN INTERDISCIPLINARY APPROACH

There is a long and well-established field of research explaining the political economic determinants behind an understanding of the role of the state and patterns of economic policy making in Japan and the newly industrialized countries, and the interplay of internal and external factors to engender economic growth and welfare. However, this is not the case in the Southeast Asian context, where, in contrast, most scholars have laid emphasis on the role of the markets and explanations of economic growth have been based on narrow political and culturalist conceptualizations drawn from a nation-building perspective.

While interdisciplinary approaches have continued to grow, much of these developments have been limited to specific cases so that the spheres of social upheavals, investment and currency flows and the environment in Southeast Asia have been dominated by narrow disciplinary lenses of analysis. Even if sociology is broadened to include anthropology, political science, economics and history, a recent survey concluded that, in comparison with studies of other regions of the world, the sociological literature on Southeast Asia is not particularly extensive or distinguished, the sociological materials are still patchy and we have not seen the emergence of many strong and distinctive schools of study or important internationally recognized academic programmes in particular universities or institutions (King, 1996: 148). Neither do prospects give cause for optimism. As McVey (1995: 7–8) puts it,

> We can expect that Southeast Asian studies of the future will devote more attention to the urban sector, to labor as well as industry, and also to the media and modern culture. All this implies a larger place for sociology. Until recently, the most promising response has been the rise of political economy as a way of explaining Southeast Asian arrangements not least a variety of approaches based on country studies which have attempted to explain the rise of the middle class as a potent force and also a whole range of issues dealing with industrial strategy, accumulation of capital, and class interests and power.

Interdisciplinary political economy is critical to the questions of how and why development strategies and economic policies in particular localities, nations, regions and countries change. This study complements existing cross-national studies of development strategy and choices from other regions, such as Northeast Asia, Africa and Latin America, by looking at the evolution of strategy over time in the late-industrializing Southeast Asian context. The findings suggest that different mechanisms in the international system have delayed capital accumulation in certain countries in Southeast Asia. Although these economies range across least developed (Cambodia, Laos, Myanmar and East Timor), lower-middle-income countries (Indonesia, the Philippines and Vietnam), upper-middle-income economies (Malaysia and Thailand) and high-income economies (Brunei and Singapore), they expose at the same time a number of important problems and contradictions which cannot be resolved without careful and collective scrutiny. Some of these economies rely almost exclusively on resources (for example, Brunei and East Timor). Myanmar has faced trade sanctions from the United States since 2001. Malaysia is by far the most industrialized if the share of GDP is the measure used, while Singapore enjoyed the highest-value-added manufacturing operations in 2005.

Since the middle of the 1980s most Southeast Asian countries have had a distinctive break with more traditional development strategies towards what is referred to in the literature as liberalism aimed at rationalizing the allocation of resources and reliance on an open export-oriented industrialization (EOI) strategy accompanied by deregulation and privatization of the construction, utilities, service and financial sectors. The mid-1980s was characterized by a global economic crisis – fuelled by third world debt – which affected all the export-oriented economies of Southeast Asia with varying consequences. Both manufacturing (especially electronics) and commodity (including rubber, tin, oil palm and petroleum) prices fell sharply (see Jomo, 1990). Governments in Malaysia, Indonesia, the Philippines and Thailand liberalized their financial markets, devalued their currencies and took on a more aggressive strategy to attract foreign direct investment (FDI) (see Rasiah, 1998). Some of these developments had become unavoidable, as the rising unemployment and a severe balance-of-payments crisis culminated in the International Monetary Fund (IMF) dishing out its usual 'one size fits all' structural adjustment package in the mid-1980s to the Philippines, and in addition to Indonesia, Thailand and Korea following the financial crisis in 1997–98. In some countries, such as Malaysia and Thailand, efficiency arguments were advanced to mask privatization initiatives. Indeed, privatization had become a haven for rent seeking among political elites (see Pasuk and Sungsidh, 1996; Gomez and Jomo, 1997). The comparative political economy framework used in the book is expected to unravel a number of significant aspects of the inter-linkage between the world economy, the state and various opposing actors in the domestic context which have hitherto been overlooked.

While being hard-pressed into quick-fix solutions during moments of crisis, states also have a long-term obligation to deliver a range of services to their people. Hence, the state as one of the main objects of research is a key analytical political economy instrument used in this book (Skockpol, 1985; Jessop, 1990). Whatever the form of the state in Southeast Asia, politics plays a determining role in economic development in creating the conditions for industrialization and setting up external trading and outward investment links. The level and nature of political development also provide the space within which civil societies operate to influence government policy on press freedom, distribution and the environment. The mediation and translation of politics, culture and other societal instruments through institutions and institutional change into economic development were articulated by North (1994) and Nelson and Winter (1982).

The interventionist state was at the heart of successful industrialization in the developed economies of the United Kingdom, the United States, Germany, Australia, Japan, Korea and Taiwan (see Hamilton, 1791; List, 1885; Gerschenkron, 1962; McFarlane, 1981, 1984, 1996; Johnson, 1982; Deyo, 1987a, 1987b; Amsden, 1989; Wade, 1990; Reinert, 1994; Chang, 1994, 2003; Amsden and Chu, 2003). The state in Korea and Taiwan has been characterized by the implementation of a deliberate and coherent industrialization strategy, which required governing the market (Amsden, 1989; Johnson, Tyson and Zysman 1989; Wade 1990). The Japanese prototype of a capitalist developmental state (CDS) as the prime mover of development had its theoretical origins in the German historical school of thought and the practice of latecomers such as the United States and

Germany. This strategy is sometimes referred to as economic national-ism, *handelspolitik* or neo-mercantilism (List, 1885; Johnson, 1982; Foster Carter, 1985; Senghass, 1985). The central pillar in this theory and praxis is not that states intervene in the economy. All states do. Therefore, the interesting research agenda is on how they intervene, and the nature of the politics behind the intervention. Consistent with Gerschenkron (1962), Johnson's (1986, 1987, 1989) analysis of Japan, South Korea and Taiwan constitutes a fruitful contribution to the explanation of the hyper-growth economies, and could prove to be a useful instrument to observe how latecomer economies catch the wave of capitalism to develop against the underdevelopment dictum associated with dependentistas and world system theories. Despite the devastating critique of Palma (1978, 1981), who reduced the dependency approach as one bereft of epistemology, this school has continued to drive populist work. However, this book seeks to examine development and social change from a more holistic perspective to appropriate the synergies political economy as an interdisciplinary field can offer and hence broaches a wider range of topics that include poverty, distribution, the environment and civil society.

The need for other theories to complement the institutionalist approach is clearly demonstrated in the case of Thailand, as for example the inter-national dimension is absent in the narrowly defined concept of the CDS. The explanation of soft authoritarianism and capitalism combined with a developmental elite reigning and creating political stability as well as governing the market through an inherent technocratic and bureaucratic meritocracy has to be, because of its descriptive specification of institu-tional arrangements, combined with a comparative analytical perspective (Wade, 1990: 26; White, 1988).

Southeast Asian countries are extremely diverse and heterogeneous in culture, religion, language, history and geography, but what they share in common is capitalist market economies and post-colonial nation-building projects. They are also faced with the same tasks of dealing with politi-cal succession and economic growth, with the state as the primary actor in international and domestic affairs. However, the important question of capacity versus autonomy of the state has to be left open for further research and empirical falsification (Crone, 1988; Wurfel and Burton, 1990).[9]

Also, social political struggles in Southeast Asia cannot simply be pre-sented as a dichotomy of class struggle using orthodox Marxian lenses, as the distinction between classes, the owners and the workers has trans-formed to many different forms. Marxist analysts have absorbed these changes and hence offer a wide array of options for examining develop-ment and social change. Part of these developments took place even as

Lenin (1948) advanced the role of the vanguard in leading the cause of the proletariats – which also became the basis of the Bolshevik revolution in Russia, which eventually gave birth to the concept of the middle class in Marxist analysis. For a long time Marxist scholars driven by praxis believed in the middle class to bring social change in capitalist economies. It is the failure of the middle class to effect developmental social change that led many neo-Marxist scholars away to join the post-modernist school. Indeed, the problems of defining the middle class – especially the boundaries separating it from the bourgeoisie and the labouring class – have undermined rather than improved Marxist efforts to seek an effective agent of social change.

Another interesting element worthy of mention here that has a relationship with contemporary development theory is the Poulantzas–Miliband debate. Whereas Poulantzas (1973, 1974, 1978) analysed social reproduction using an interdisciplinary framework by examining the economic, social, political and ideological conditions of accumulation and examining the role played by capitalist state institutions on class relations, Miliband (1979) argued that the state is an instrumentalist invention of the capitalist class and political elites to serve their interests. Elements of state autonomy can arise in Poulantzas arguments on the state going a step further than the state-capital developmentalist school to include class relations. Such a postulation also lends weight to Evan's (1995) arguments on captured and autonomous states. However, the overriding effect of class- and elitist-led political leaderships on development in Southeast Asia also reveals the impact of dominant interest groups, which is also consistent with Polanyi's (1957) arguments. Far from taking any one as *sine qua non*, these approaches are used to generate as much as possible a more informed framework for examining Southeast Asian political economy in this book.[10]

The institutional framework of governance in Thailand, Malaysia, Indonesia and the Philippines is heavily influenced by their colonial past (Huynh Cao Tri *et al.,* 1988). Despite the absence of Western colonialism, capitalist integration led to the formation of a colonial-style, centralized, functionally differentiated bureaucracy. The kingdom of Siam adopted certain practices of internal colonialism in order to escape external colonialism (Girling, 1981). This observation can be generalized to some extent, as the Southeast Asian political structures are partly historical and colonial products but also heavily moulded by state elites (Crone, 1988). This cleavage between historically determined modern (state elites) and traditional (colonial) factors in the institutional framework explains, partly, the weak state capacities achieved in these countries (Huynh Cao Tri *et al.,* 1988).

Globalization and the new information technologies are eroding long-standing socio-economic, cultural and political boundaries in East and Southeast Asia. Programmes of economic liberalization and transitions to democracies are transforming the parameters of public policy; and there are significant differences between strata, classes, generations, time and spatial perspectives across the region on the outcome of these basic transformations. These tendencies also open up new avenues for growth and enhanced individual wealth capacities, but also create new forms of unevenness and exclusion.

Democratization and decentralization might lead to greater demands for public welfare provisions and renewed challenges to the nation state to meet these demands.

What is clear is that Southeast Asia can best be understood as a historical product both of long-standing regional dynamics and of the specificities of the distinctive political economies that constitute it. Obviously, some of these processes of change have been subjected to considerable scholarly scrutiny. But these developments have so far been examined in a fairly circumscribed manner: the rich historical studies of the region offer either accounts of a particular period or synoptic surveys (Hall, 1981; Reid, 1990a, 1990b, 2000; SarDesai, 1997); international relations scholarship has largely been concerned with security issues and the character of formal regional institutions (Acharya, 2000; Beeson, 2002); and, political science and political economy texts have mainly focused on domestic-level studies of the contemporary dynamics of change (Rodan, Hewison and Robison, 2001; Funston, 2002; MacIntyre, 2002). At present, there exists no work that brings together in a single textbook the different dimensions that explain the political economy of Southeast Asia using interdisciplinary lenses. This book seeks to fill this void with contributions from experts who have a research and publication record consistent with interdisciplinary approaches. All chapters seek to cover the region as a whole, with a historical backdrop to locate the analysis.

The main aim of the regimes in the region has historically been to strengthen or retain political and social stability to sustain improvements in the standards of living of the people. However, efforts to expand elitist accumulation, illegal migration and logging, human and drug trafficking, and even piracy involve vested interests, including the military and economic activities that lead to environmental damage, and are some of the immediate security problems the region has been encountering.

Far from introducing a multiplicity of disciplines loosely without any cohesion in a shell, this book seeks to use the lenses available from them to examine development and social change in Southeast Asia. Trying to understand political economy in an interdisciplinary perspective rather than confining analysis to particular disciplines is in itself a satisfactory theoretical edifice. Interdisciplinarity is readily identified by the conjoining of the names of more than one discipline, such as anthropology, sociology, politics and economics. It is the failure of single disciplines to explain social phenomena effectively that has driven scholars of common disciplines to more holistic and cross-fertilizing interdisciplinary approaches. Nevertheless, interdisciplinary approaches have been unavoidably constrained by the core disciplines individual analysts have been exposed to.

Methodologically, comparative political economy analysis is often employed with selected slices of the national contingent historical paths as units of comparison. What is new and what is provoking is the argument that the dichotomy in development theory between the modernization and dependency or inter-dependency traditions is claimed to build on an artificial confrontation between the Weberian and Marxist approaches to political economy, which in fact might complement rather than conflict with each other. As we have argued earlier, wide divisions exist even within Marxist approaches (see Jenkins, 1986; Rasiah, 1988, 1995).

In reality what is happening is far more complex. A body of studies has grown combining comparative historical method with insights of radical political economy, which has provided a cogent attack on a variety of substantive issues. These interdisciplinary approaches are eclectic in their methodology, but share a number of characteristics that have distinguished them from earlier works: (1) the realization that political and economic development cannot be fruitfully examined in isolation from each other; (2) showing sensitivity to international factors (without determination); (3) consideration for historical and national contingency; and (4) application of a comparative framework (Evans and Stephens, 1988/89: 713–14). These studies neither offer a theoretical paradigm in the strict sense of a set of axiomatic relationships that constitute a sequence of testable propositions nor can be used to generate universal predictions of developmental outcomes. This new eclectic political economy shares some working hypotheses about the likely political and economic consequences of different patterns of interaction between states and classes. It also shares common assumptions about what problems are most central to the study of development and social change, and what factors should be taken into account in order to understand social outcomes (Evans and Stephens, 1988: 740).

Besides the inspiration from both Karl Marx and Max Weber, the ontology of this approach builds to a large degree on such scholars as Gerschenkron (1962), Polanyi (1957) and Moore ([1967] 1981), and shares the assumptions linking economic models and political forms, classes of varying strengths coming together in coalitions, compromises and conflicts. This approach suggests analysing the historical specificity of economic development models in accordance with the evolution of the world system, state strength as a variable, and the state as a historical actor but embedded in the domestic context and to varying degrees dependent on external factors beyond the jurisdiction of classes and state managers. All these suppositions are important themes to varying degrees in these authors' contributions.[11]

Dependency and world system theories also influenced the new comparative political economy framework, especially at the methodological and conceptual levels suggested by Frank (1967), Baran (1973), Wallerstein (1974, 1979) and Amin (2004). These theories built their argumentation around historical case studies that included an integrated examination of local and international actors. At both local and international levels, they emphasized interests rather than norms and values, economic and political structures rather than cultural patterns. Taking into consideration the historical structural approach and associated dependency of Cardoso and Faletto (1979), the importance of class alliances and conflicts that cross national boundaries is clear. The new element, however, is the non-deterministic influence of the international context in shaping these alliances and conflicts within national boundaries (Evans and Stephens, 1988/89: 719). Although a non-reductionist perspective is a necessary point of departure, regulating relations with the external world has been a persistent theme of any late-industrializing state. The state as the gatekeeper between intrasocietal and extrasocietal flows of activity is a most important criterion in any assessment of its strength. The state is strong to the degree that it is capable of acting autonomously and enjoys the capability to check clientelist and foreign pressures.

ARGUMENTS OF THE BOOK

Proceeding to the next step in analysing the correlates of development and social change in Southeast Asia, the interdisciplinary political economy framework adopted in this book considers the socio-economic character of government elites, and their relations with the capitalist class, foreign capital and the other classes. Previous writings on political development in Southeast Asia only partially explained this problematic (Anderson, 1972 on Indonesia; Wilson, 1962; Riggs, 1966; and Siffin, 1966 on Thailand; Lande, 1965; and Wurfel, 1959 on the Philippines; and Milne, 1978 on Malaysia).[12] Jomo (1986) offered arguably the most impressive class account available on Malaysian development, but the central arguments have tended to understate the significance of capitalist transformation.

Jesudason (1989) and Yoshihara (1989) provided an excellent explanation of why the entrepreneurial Chinese failed to make the transition to the technology frontier in Malaysia and Southeast Asia respectively, but their instruments have been overly confined to ethnic lenses. Gomez (2002) attempted an antithesis to their arguments by claiming that Chinese business networks have not been a dominant feature of capitalist accumulation in Malaysia, but his methodology of examining shareholder structure failed to provide the rigour required to dismiss the presence of ethnic networking.

By far the most convincing account of the political economy of Southeast Asia appears in Rodan, Hewison and Robison (1997), though it originally underestimated the external environment for domestic accumulation, did not examine social change at a cross-regional level and also did not specifically take into account the inner contradictions within labour and other categories situated in the rural and urban sectors. However, recent work, especially after the financial crisis, has made important contributions covering these issues thoroughly (Robison, 2006; Hewison and Robison, 2006; Rodan, Hewison and Robison, 2006). Limqueco, McFarlane and Odhnoff (1989) fill this gap, though their coverage is spatially limited owing to the obvious paucity of data. Nevertheless, to a large extent Limqueco, McFarlane and Odhnoff (1989) and Rodan, Hewison and Robison (1997) approach the problem using some of the best instruments of political economy, but examine six countries individually and regional relations in three other chapters. Limqueco, McFarlane and Odhnoff (1989) complement this with a rich account of the labour process in Southeast Asia. This book does not seek to supplant their very rich work. Instead it aims to provide an alternative but complementary way of examining the topics. This book approaches the problem by taking Southeast Asia as a whole as the unit of analysis and attempts to examine each political economy question by examining the nature of interface, integration and interrelations it has had within and with the rest of the global capitalist economy. By doing so, this volume seeks to capture the impact of global political economy forces on the political economy of the Southeast Asian economies.

Although each individual country in the region has a specifically defined government and has in place electoral processes or other machinery that keeps or appoints governments, and hence it enjoys the autonomy to absorb or counter global forces, the nature of investment, trade and currency flows on the one hand, and regional alliances, social and cultural intercourse, and movement of labour and people show that the region is very much integrated, suggesting that the causes and consequences of a number of economic, social and political upheavals are broader in nature. Hence, an attempt to examine these issues through the lenses of

Southeast Asia rather than its component countries is expected to offer a complementary picture to what already exists on Southeast Asia's political economy.

As a number of scholars have also shown, using a radical political economy perspective helps the understanding of some key dimensions of economic development in Southeast Asia. On the one hand, favourable coalitions supporting export-oriented industrial development policies were able to contain, suppress or outmanoeuvre other groups opposed to such policies and have been used to explain the success of the newly industrializing economies, including Singapore (Deyo, 1987a, 1987b, 1989; Haggard and Chen, 1987). Something similar happened in Southeast Asia since the 1960s, where peasant organizations, the working classes and trade unions have been excluded from effective political action, but that was not the case for the business sector, at least in the Thai context (Schmidt, 1997). Empirical information from workers (Limqueco, McFarlane and Odhnoff, 1989; Hadiz, 1997; Hutchison and Brown, 2001) provided an impressive account of the impact of capitalist integration on the labour process in Southeast Asia.

Instead of exploring the similarities and differences between Southeast Asia and Northeast Asia, this volume seeks to build a political economy of the former purely from the vantage point of its evolution. Economic nationalism, and its ideological legacies, has constituted a far more significant political constraint upon governments in Southeast Asia than in the Northeast Asian economies, regarding both the importance of foreign capital and most strikingly the economic role of the Southeast Asian Chinese minorities (Mackie, 1988). In short, the role of the state in Southeast Asia has included both an accumulation function and a legitimation function (Linqueco, McFarlane and Odhnoff, 1989), but whether this is sustainable or not is a matter of investigation, and especially in terms of autonomy, capacity and welfare; in other words, it is an empirical question.

This book builds upon the contribution and tradition of this comparative political economy approach and in particular on the analysis of the politics of alliance, which form the basis of policy making in developing countries. However, the concept of associated dependent development has to be combined with explanations of how the international political economy interacts with and influences economic policy formulation and policy making in latecomer economies. On the other hand, two more concepts (descriptive and Weberian) have to be elaborated. One is related to the institutional perspective, and the other to the question of capacity versus autonomy of the developmental state.[13]

Therefore, the outcomes of economic policy making in Southeast Asia are to a certain degree a function both of internal class constellations and of the workings of foreign capital, technology and markets. Trade alone does not show sufficiently the differences between Southeast Asia and Northeast Asia, as most of the countries are heavily immersed in export-oriented manufacturing. Unlike Japan, Korea and Taiwan where the prime source of foreign technology came in the form of imports, licensing and imitation from multinational corporations, the Southeast Asian economies have relied much more on the direct operations of multinational corporations (or FDI). Hence, the Southeast Asian economies have been dependent on FDI, while the Northeast Asian economies of Japan, Korea and Taiwan have not.

The volume addresses the typical focus on the transformation of Southeast Asian economies from reliance on the primary sectors of agriculture and mining to industry, as well as the effects of development policy on poverty and inequality, industrial relations practices, economic and political crises, the environment, civil society space and regional trade alliances. The volume examines the emergence of new social and political pressures from industrialization without much technological progress, more complex crises, the use of sophisticated instruments in the labour process and increased awareness of the environment.

These considerations must be complemented with a regional and trans-border focus on transnational actors and institutions and policy issues and problems which have a wider impact on spatial configurations.

STRUCTURE OF THE BOOK

Following this introductory chapter, the subsequent chapters examine the different dimensions of development and social change using an integrated political economy approach. Like all fields in the social sciences where subjective elements prevent the adoption of a common-path-dependent approach, each chapter is presented using what the authors deem as the right framework for capturing development and social change in the most effective way.

Rajah Rasiah examines in Chapter 2 industrial promotion initiatives and industrialization. Focusing on the countries of Indonesia, Malaysia, Philippines and Thailand, the chapter argues that eclectic industrial policies targeted at promoting industrialization and attracting transnational corporations helped the countries generate industrial investment and employment, but the lack of focus on technological upgrading has left the countries entrenched in low-end, low-value-added activities.

In Chapter 3 Chris Dixon reviews the extent of the recovery from the

1997 financial crisis. It is stressed that the Bretton Woods institutions saw the crisis as internal in origin rather than rooted in the operation of capital at the global scale. Policy prescriptions stressed liberalization, particularly of foreign ownership regulation, and reform of corporate governance. The overall aim was the 'Westernization' of Southeast Asian business and regulatory systems. It is argued that, while there has been some significant liberalization of foreign ownership and a degree of corporate reform, the distinctive Southeast Asian business systems remain largely intact. The question is whether unreformed and still heavily protected Southeast Asian business can in the long run retain its dynamism. China has become an increasingly important driver of regional growth and integration, a situation many of the Southeast Asian countries are far from comfortable with.

Anis Chowdhury and Iyanatul Islam examine in Chapter 4 the inequality experiences of a group of Southeast Asian economies with the question of whether they were really worthy exemplars of 'shared growth'. Focusing on Indonesia, Malaysia, the Philippines and Thailand, which are diverse both regionally and ethnically, the chapter provides a historical account of inequality trends in these countries and concludes with an assessment of horizontal inequality as well as its political and social ramifications.

In Chapter 5 Rene Ofreneo and Peter Wad show how the uneven and relatively weak industrial relations (IR) and labour market institutions and conditions have shaped the accumulation process in the region, especially in economies depending on transnational corporations (TNCs). Ofreneo and Wad explore the relationship between TNCs and labour unions, with a specific focus on export economic zones (EEZs). They show that there are areas where the unions have managed to survive and remain viable despite the anti-union environment in the region, and they propose a wider collaboration between labour and civil society in order to strengthen bargaining and a popular base of the labour movement.

David A. Sonnenfeld and Arthur P.J. Mol investigate in Chapter 6 the environmental impacts of recent urban and industrial development in five Southeast Asian countries, and compare successes and failures of environmental policy making and reform in those countries. The chapter investigates the extent to which recent economic development in these countries has been accompanied by environmental improvements and/or deteriorations, and identifies sites of improved environmental performance. Using available and newly gathered data, the chapter draws substantive and methodological conclusions on the political economy of urban and industrial environmental reform in Southeast Asia, and sets out an agenda for future studies in the region and more generally.

In Chapter 7 Johannes Dragsbaek Schmidt focuses on the competing

theoretical definitions and assumptions about civil society, democratization and social change. The chapter then explores the attempts by civil
society actors to affect conflicts over resources and distribution of welfare
in Southeast Asia; the third section focuses on the conflictual relationship
between civil society organizations (CSOs) and the state and various types
of regulations, laws and contractual relationships, and finally the need
for social reform is emphasized as one important type of social resistance
against the downsizing of the social and public sector's provision of collective goods.

Sanchita Basu Das and Aekapol Chongvilaivan in Chapter 8 examine
the political economy rationale behind the proliferation of free trade
agreements (FTAs) in six Southeast Asian countries, namely Indonesia,
Malaysia, the Philippines, Singapore, Thailand and Vietnam. The authors
recognize the potential benefits that can emerge from the elimination
of tariff and non-tariff barriers and its positive impact on intra-regional
trade and foreign direct investment (FDI), but also argue that burgeoning FTAs remain rather patchy and may ultimately become a stumbling
block to deeper and wider economic integration, particularly the ASEAN
Economic Community (AEC) and East Asia Integration (ASEAN plus
China, Japan and Korea).

NOTES

1. See the discussion of the relationship between these perspectives in the introduction of Henderson and Appelbaum (1992).
2. However, interventions in automotives and steel have not been directed at creative glo-bally competitive firms and hence the unproductive rents involved have dissipated eco-nomic efficiency in Indonesia and Malaysia. Liberal policies have attracted large-scale electronics assembly to Malaysia, the Philippines, Thailand, Indonesia and Vietnam, but the lack of productive interventions has restricted upgrading in these countries.
3. Keynes (1936) had argued that liberal capital and currency markets would be disastrous to economies.
4. Hayek's (1979) emphasis on democracy must, however, be recognized as important.
5. This approach is what we have choosen to dubb the 'Murdoch school', which bases its theoretical and empirical analysis on Ralph Miliband's conceptualization of state–capital relations.
6. One simple explanation refers to the institutional and political constraints and histori-cal circumstances of sociological inquiry in the region (King, 1996).
7. However, since the student uprising in 1973 Thailand has been the exception that confirms the rule. It remains intellectually the most stimulating case in the region, and Thai critical discourse has to a considerable degree been shaped by indigenous and not foreign analysis (McVey, 1995: 4).
8. Using the flying geese model, Kojima (1975) had argued that Japan's foreign direct investment was trade creating while that of the United States was trade diverting. Ozawa (1995) also used this framework to examine Japan's trade and investment syner-gies in East Asia. While acknowledging the powerful investment and trade flows that

have absorbed and driven growth rates among the lower-order wedges in the flight of geese, Gore (1996), Rowthorn (1996) and Rasiah (1998) argued otherwise, making the point that technological discontinuities and crisis have allowed particular sectors in the lower-order countries to skip certain phases or leapfrog over higher-order wedges of geese (countries).

9. Thus to be precise we do not intend to pursue the concept of the autonomous state (*beamtemstaat*), but to explore the nature of the state and its relationship with social groups, forces, actors and institutions at the domestic as well as the international level.

10. Conner's (1973) account to differentiate capitalist ownership in corporations to distinguish the directors who effectively control the means of production from the shareholders who own them is an illuminating example in understanding capitalist accumulation in industrial capitalism.

11. This proposition indicates that this book is an attempt to complement the view of the state-capital approach of the Murdoch school which sees capitalist power stemming from the very indispensability of the capitalist class as the machine that drives the economy. In this sense the capitalists exert a veto power over the state, whose leaders, although exercising a degree of autonomy, must always consider the consequences of policies which threaten the flow of investment (Hewison, 1989: Ch. 1 and 212–13; Robison, 1992: 87).

12. It was these works which established the basic parameters within which most subsequent political analysis has been conducted, although in some cases those studies have been modified by important later works, such as Crouch (1978, 1984) and Girling (1981).

13. Capacity and autonomy indicate that the state formulates and pursues its own goals. However, these concepts require a specific kind of sensitivity, because the state's autonomy from society is not a fixed structural feature. Rather it changes according to situational variations. Therefore, state autonomy, along with the actions and decisions by political elites and policy makers, should be probed historically and case by case. Likewise the capacity of the state means the ability to formulate and implement policy along predictable lines (Skocpol, 1985: 9). Thus analysing the state in relation to socio-economic contexts is also testing state capacity. The capacity of the state includes various aspects, and will be conceptualized in Chapters 2 and 3. Here it is enough to mention that, in a Weberian framework, it would include everything from military and financial (i.e. fiscal) resources to a skilled and highly motivated bureaucracy, the strength of legitimacy and authority of political leadership, and historical and geopolitical location in the world context. The capacities of the state mean the ability of the state to implement goals, especially over the actual or potential opposition of powerful social groups or in the face of recalcitrant socio-economic circumstances (Skocpol, 1985: 9).

REFERENCES

Acharya, A. (1997), 'Sovereignty, non-intervention and regionalism', Canadian Consortium for Asia Pacific Security paper no. 15, Toronto and Yale Universities.

Acharya, A. (2000), *The Quest for Identity: International Relations of Southeast Asia*, Oxford: Oxford University Press.

Akamatsu, K. (1962), 'A historical pattern of economic growth in developing countries', *Journal of Developing Economies*, **1**(1): 3–25.

Alagappa, M. (ed.) (2003), *Asian Security Order: Instrumental and Normative Features*, Stanford, CA: Stanford University Press.

Amin, S. (2004), *Obsolescent Capitalism: Contemporary Politics and Global Disorder*, London: Zed Books.
Amsden, A.O. (1989), *Asia's Next Giant: South Korea and Late Industrialization*, New York: Oxford University Press.
Amsden, A. and W.W. Chu (2003), *Beyond Late Development: Taiwan's Upgrading Policies*, Cambridge, MA: MIT Press.
Anderson, B. (1972), *The Idea of Power in Indonesian Culture: Culture and Politics in Indonesia*, Ithaca, NY: Cornell University Press.
Athukorala, P. and J. Menon (1999), 'Outward orientation and economic development in Malaysia', *World Economy*, **22**(8): 1119–39.
Bagchi, A.K. (1982), *Political Economy of Underdevelopment*, Cambridge: Cambridge University Press.
Baran, P. (1973), 'Political economy of backwardness', in C.K. Wilber (ed.), *Political Economy of Development and Underdevelopment*, New York: Random House.
Beeson, M. (2002), 'Theorising institutional change in East Asia', in M. Beeson (ed.), *Reconfiguring East Asia: Regional Institutions and Organisations after the Crisis*, London: Curzon Press.
Belassa, B. (1982), *Development Strategies in Semi-Industrial Economies*, Baltimore, MD: Johns Hopkins University Press.
Beresford, M. (1988), *Vietnam: Politics, Economics, and Society*, London: Pinter.
Berger, M.T. (2003), 'Decolonisation, modernisation and nation-building: political development theory and the appeal of communism in southeast Asia, 1945–1975', *Journal of Southeast Asian Studies*, **34**(3), (October): 421–48.
Bolt, P.J. (2000), *China and Southeast Asia's Ethnic Chinese: State and Diaspora in Contemporary Asia*, Westport, CT: Praeger.
Bowles, P. (2002), 'Asia's post-crisis regionalism: bringing the state back in, keeping the (United) States out', *Review of International Political Economy*, **9**(2).
Budiman, Arief (1990), *State and Civil Society in Indonesia*, Clayton, VIC: Centre of Southeast Asian Studies, Monash University.
Bukharin, N. (1929), *Imperialism and the World Economy*, London: International Publishers.
Caldwell, M. (1968), *Indonesia*, London: Oxford University Press.
Canovan, M. (1999), 'Trust the people! Populism and the two faces of democracy', *Political Studies*, **47**.
Cardoso, F.H. and E. Faletto (1979), *Dependency and Development in Latin America* (English translation by Marjory Marringly Urquidi), Berkeley and Los Angeles, CA: University of California Press; published 1969 as *Dependencia y desarrollo en América Latina*, Mexico City: Siglo XXI.
Chakravaty, S. (1969), *Capital and Development Planning*, Cambridge, MA: MIT Press.
Chakravaty, S. (1993), *Development Planning: The Indian Experience*, New York: Oxford University Press.
Chang, H.J. (1994), *The Political Economy of Industrial Policy*, New York: St. Martin's Press.
Chang, H.J. (2003) *Kicking Away the Ladder*, London: Anthem Press.
Chirot, D. and A. Reid (eds) (1997), *Essential Outsiders: Chinese and Jews in the Modern Transformation of Southeast Asia and Europe*, Seattle, WA: Washington University Press.

Conner, J.O. (1973), *The Fiscal Crisis of the State*, New York: St Martins.
Constantino, R. (1969), *The Making of a Filipino: a Study of Philippine Colonial Politics*, Quezon City, Philippines: Malaya Books.
Constantino, R. (1982), *The Miseducation of the Filipino*, Quezon City, Philippines: Foundation for Nationalistic Studies.
Crone, D.K. (1988), 'State, social elites, and government capacity in Southeast Asia', *World Politics*, **40**(2).
Crouch, H. (1978), *The Army and Politics in Indonesia*, Ithaca, NY: Cornell University Press.
Crouch, H. (1984), *Domestic Political Structures and Regional Economic Co-operation*, Singapore: ISEAS.
Darwin, C. (1859), *On the Origin of Species by Means of Natural Selection*, London: J. Murray.
Desai, M. and D. Kumar (1982), *Cambridge History of India*, Cambridge: Cambridge University Press.
Deyo, F. (1987a), 'Coalitions, institutions, and linkage-sequencing – toward a strategic capacity model of East Asian development', in F.C. Deyo (ed.), *The Political Economy of the New Asian Industrialism*, Ithaca, NY: Cornell University Press.
Deyo, F. (1987b), 'State and labor: modes of political exclusion in East Asian development', in F.C. Deyo (ed.), *The Political Economy of the New Asian Industrialism*, Ithaca, NY: Cornell University Press.
Deyo, F. (1989), *Beneath the Miracle: Labor, Subordination in the New Asian Industrialism*, Berkeley, CA: University of California Press.
Doner, R. (1991), *Driving a Bargain: Automobile Industrialization and Japanese Firms in Southeast Asia*, Berkeley, CA: University of California Press.
Elliott, D. (1978), *Thailand: Origins of Military Rule*, London: Zed Press.
Evans, P. (1995), *Embedded Autonomy: States and Industrial Transformation*, Princeton, NJ: Princeton University Press.
Evans, P. and J.D. Stephens (1988), 'Development and the world economy', in N.J. Smelser (ed.), *Handbook of Sociology*, Newbury Park, CA: Sage.
Evans, P. and J.D. Stephens (1988/89), 'Studying development since the sixties: the emergence of a new political economy', *Theory and Society*, **17**(5), special issue on Breaking Boundaries: Social Theory and the Sixties.
Fishlow, A., C. Gwin, S. Haggard, D. Rodrik and R. Wade (1994), *Miracle or Design: Lessons from the East Asian Experience*, Washington, DC: Overseas Development Council.
Foster Carter, A. (1985), 'Friederich List lives!', *Economy and Development*, September–October.
Frank, A.G. (1967), *Capitalism and Underdevelopment in Latin America: Historical Studies of Chile and Brazil*, New York: Monthly Review Press.
Fransman, M. (1985), 'International competitiveness, technical change and the state: the machine tool industries in Taiwan and Japan', *World Development*, **14**(12): 1375–96.
Freeman, G. (1987), *Technology, Policy and Economic Performance: Lessons from Japan*, London: Pinter.
Fukasaku, Y. (1992), *Technology Development in Pre-War Japan: Mitsubishi Nagasaki Shipyard*, London: Routledge.
Funston, J. (2002), *Government and Politics in South-East Asia*, London: Zed Press.

Geertz, C.J. (1963), *Peddlers and Princes: Social Development and Economic Change in Two Indonesian Towns*, Chicago, IL: University of Chicago Press.
Gerschenkron, A. (1962), *Economic Backwardness in Historical Perspective*, Cambridge, MA: Belknap Press.
Girling, J.L.S. (1981), *Thailand: Society and Politics*, Ithaca, NY: Cornell University Press.
Gomez, E.T. (2002), 'Political business in Malaysia: party factionalism, corporate development, and economic crisis', in E.T. Gomez (ed.), *Political Business in East Asia*, London: Routledge.
Gomez, T. and Jomo, K.S. (1997), *Malaysia's Political Economy: Politics, Patronage and Profits*, Cambridge: Cambridge University Press.
Gopal, Jaya (1999), 'Malaysia's palm oil refining industry: policy, growth, technical change and competitiveness', in K.S. Jomo, G. Felker and R. Rasiah (eds), *Industrial Technology Development in Malaysia: Industry and Firm Studies*, London: Routledge.
Gore, C. (1996), 'Methodological nationalism and the misunderstanding of East Asian industrialization', UNCTAD discussion papers, 111, United Nations Conference for Trade and Development, Geneva.
Gravers, M. (1989), 'The debate on "everyday forms of peasant resistance": a critique', in M. Gravers, P. Wad, V. Brun and A. Kalland (eds), *Southeast Asia between Autocracy and Democracy*, Aarhus, Denmark: Nordic Association for Southeast Asian Studies and Aarhus University Press.
Griffin, K. (1979), 'Underdevelopment in history', in C.K. Wilber (ed.), *The Political Economy of Development and Underdevelopment*, London: Random House.
Hadiz, V. (1997), *Workers and the State in New Order Indonesia*, London: Routledge.
Haggard, S. and Tun-Jen Chen (1987), 'State strategies and foreign capital in the Gang of Four', in F.C. Deyo (ed.), *The Political Economy of the New Asian Industrialism*, Ithaca, NY: Cornell University Press.
Hahn, F. (1984), *Equilibrium and Macroeconomics*, Oxford: Basil Blackwell.
Hall, D.G.E. (1981), *A History of South-East Asia*, Basingstoke: Macmillan.
Hamilton, A. (1791), 'Report on manufactures', 5 December, www.oberlin.edu/~gkornbl/Hist258/ReportMfres.html, downloaded on 13 December 2005.
Hayek, F. (1979), *Law, Legislation and Liberty: The Political Order of a Free People*, Chicago, IL: University of Chicago Press.
Henderson, J. and R.P. Appelbaum (1992), *States and Development in the Asian Pacific Rim*, Newbury Park, CA: Sage.
Henderson, J. and R. Phillips (2007), 'Unintended consequences: social policy, state institutions and the "stalling" of the Malaysian industrialisation project', *Economy and Society*, **36**(1): 78–102.
Hettne, B., A. Inotai and O. Sunkel (eds) (1999/2001), *Studies in the New Regionalism*, vols I–V, London: Macmillan.
Hewison, K. (1989), *Bankers and Bureaucrats: Capital and the Role of State in Thailand*, monograph series 34, Yale University Southeast Asian Studies, New Haven, CT: Yale Center for International and Area Studies.
Hewison, K. and R. Robison (eds) (2006), *East Asia and the Trials of Neo-Liberalism*, London: Routledge.
Hilferding, R. (1912), *Finance Capital*, Moscow: Progress Publishers.

Hill, H. (1996), *The Indonesian Economy since 1966: Southeast Asia's Emerging Giant*, Cambridge: Cambridge University Press.

Huntington, S.P. (1968), *Political Order in Changing Societies*, New Haven, CT: Yale University Press.

Hutchison, J. and A. Brown (eds) (2001), *Organising Labour in Globalising Asia*, London: Routledge.

Huynh Cao Tri *et al.* (eds) (1988), *Participative Administration and Endogenous Development*, Brussels: International Institute of Administrative Sciences and UNESCO.

Jacobs, N. (1971), *Modernization Without Development*, New York: Praeger.

Jayasuriya, Kanishka (2008), *Asian Regional Governance: Crisis and Change*, London: Routledge.

Jenkins, R. (1984), *Transnational Corporations and Industrial Transformation in Latin America*, New York: St. Martin's Press.

Jenkins, R. (1986), *Transnational Corporations and the Latin American Automobile Industry*, Basingstoke: Palgrave Macmillan.

Jessop, B. (1990), *State Theory: Putting Capitalist States in Their Place*, Cambridge: Polity Press.

Jesudason, J. (1989), *Ethnicity and the Economy: The State, Chinese Business and Multinationals in Malaysia*, Singapore: Oxford University Press.

Johnson, C. (1982), *MITI and the Japanese Miracle*, Stanford, CA: Stanford University Press.

Johnson, C. (1986), 'The nonsocialist NICs: East Asia', *International Organization*, **40**(2), Spring.

Johnson, C. (1987), 'Political institutions and economic performance: the government business relationship in Japan, South Korea and Taiwan', in F.C. Deyo (ed.), *The Political Economy of the New Asian Industrialism*, Ithaca, NY: Cornell University Press.

Johnson, C. (1989), 'The democratization of South Korea: what role does economic development play?', in *Copenhagen Papers in East and Southeast Asian Studies*, The Modernization Process in East Asia: Economic, Political, and Cultural Perspectives, no. 4, Copenhagen: University of Copenhagen, Museum Tusculanums Press.

Johnson, C., Laura D'Andrea Tyson and John Zysman (eds) (1989), *The Politics of Productivity: The Real Story of Why Japan Works*, Cambridge, MA: Ballinger Publishing Co.

Johnson, C., L. Tyson and J. Zysman (1991), *Politics and Productivity: The Real Story of Why Japan Works*, New York: HarperCollins.

Jomo, K.S. (1986), *A Question of Class: Capital, the State and Uneven Development in Malaya*, Singapore: Oxford University Press.

Jomo, K.S. (1990), *Growth and Structural Change in the Malaysian Economy*, Basingstoke: Macmillan.

Jomo, K.S. (1996), *Southeast Asia's Misunderstood Miracle*, Boulder, CO: Westview.

Jomo, K.S., Y.C. Chen, B.C. Folk, I. Ul-Haque, P. Pasuk, B. Simatupang and M. Tateishi (1997), *Southeast Asia's Misunderstood Miracle: Industrial Policy and Economic Development in Thailand, Malaysia and Indonesia*, Boulder, CO: Westview.

Jomo, K.S., R. Rasiah, R. Alavi and Jaya Gopal (2003), 'Industrial policy and the emergence of internationally competitive manufacturing firms in Malaysia', in K.S. Jomo and Ken Togo (eds), *Manufacturing Competitiveness: How Internationally Competitive National Firms and Industries Developed in East Asia*, London: Routledge.

Kaldor, N. (1979), 'Equilibrium theory and growth theory', in M. Boskin (ed.), *Economics and Human Welfare: Essays in Honor of Tibor Scitovsky*, New York: Academic Press.

Keyes, C.F. (1992), 'A conference at Wingspread and rethinking Southeast Asian studies', in C. Hirschman, C.F. Keyes and K. Hutterer (eds), *Southeast Asian Studies in the Balance: Reflections from America*, Ann Arbor, MI: Association for Asian Studies.

Keynes, J.M. (1936), *The General Theory of Employment, Interest and Money*, London: Macmillan.

Kim, L. (1997), *Imitation to Innovation: The Dynamics of Korea's Technological Learning*, Cambridge, MA: Harvard Business School Press.

King, V.T. (1996), 'Sociology', in M. Halib and T. Huxley (eds), *An Introduction to Southeast Asian Studies*, Tauris Academic Studies, London: I.B. Tauris.

Kitching, Gavin (1982), *Development and Underdevelopment in Historical Perspective*, London: Methuen.

Kojima, K. (1975), 'International trade and foreign investment: substitute or complement', *Hitotsubashi Journal of Economics*, **16**(1): 1–12.

Krueger, A. (1983), *Trade and Employment in Developing Countries*, Chicago, IL: University of Chicago Press.

Krugman, P. (1994), 'The myth of Asia's miracle', *Foreign Affairs*, **73**(6).

Krugman, P. (1995), *The Age of Diminished Expectations*, Cambridge, MA: MIT Press.

Krugman, P. (1999), *The Return of Depression Economics*, New York: Norton.

Laclau, E. (1977), 'Towards a theory of populism', in E. Laclau (ed.), *Politics and Ideology in Marxist Theory*, London: New Left Books.

Lande, C. (1965), *Leaders, Factions and Parties: The Structure of Philippines Politics*, Yale Southeast Asia Studies Monograph Series no. 6, New Haven, CT: Yale University Press.

Lenin, V. (1948), *Imperialism: The Highest Stage of Capitalism*, London: Lawrence & Wishart.

Limqueco, P. and B. McFarlane (eds) (1983), *Neo-Marxist Theories of Development*, London: Croom Helm.

Limqueco, P., B. McFarlane and J. Odhnoff (1989), *Labour and Industry in ASEAN*, Manila: Journal of Contemporary Asia Press.

List, F. (1885), *The National System of Political Economy*, London: Longman.

Lucas, R. (1978), 'Asset prices in an exchange economy', *Econometrica*, **46**(6): 1429–45.

Luxemburg, R. (2003), *The Accumulation of Capital*, London: Routledge.

MacIntyre, A. (ed.) (1994), *Business and Government in Industrialising Asia*, Sydney, NSW: Allen & Unwin.

MacIntyre, A. (2002), *The Power of Institutions: Political Architecture and Governance*, Ithaca, NY: Cornell University Press.

Mackie, J.A.C. (1988), 'Economic growth in the ASEAN region: the political underpinnings', in H. Hughes (ed.), *Achieving Industrialization*, Cambridge: Cambridge University Press.

Marshall, A. (1890), *Principles of Economics*, London: Macmillan.

Marx, K. (1853), 'The British rule in India', *New York Daily Tribune*, 10 June.

Marx, K. (1867), *Capital: The Process of Production of Capital*, vol I, Moscow: Progress Publishers.

Marx, K. (1956), *Capital: The Process of Circulation of Capital*, vol II, Moscow: Progress Publishers.

McFarlane, B. (1981), *Australian Capitalism in Boom and Depression*, Sydney, NSW: APCD Publishers.

McFarlane, B. (1984), 'Australian postwar economic policy, 1947–1953', in J. Merrit and A. Cuthoys (eds), *Australia's First Cold War*, London: Allen & Unwin.

McFarlane, B. (1996), 'Michal Kalecki and the political economy of the Third World', in J.E. King (ed.), *An Alternative Macroeconomic Theory: The Kaleckian Model and Post-Keynesian Economics*, Boston, MA: Kluwer.

McLeod, R.H. and R. Garnaut (1998), *East Asia in Crisis: From Being a Miracle to Needing One*, London: Routledge.

McVey, R. (1995), 'Change and continuity in Southeast Asian studies', *Journal of Southeast Asian Studies*, **26**(1) (March).

Miliband, R. (1979), *The State in Capitalist Society*, London: Allen & Unwin.

Mill, J.S. (1844), 'Unsettled questions of political economy', in J.M. Robson (ed.), *Collected Works*, vol 4, Toronto, ON: Toronto University Press.

Milne, R.S. (1978), *Politics and Government in Malaysia*, Singapore: Federal Publications.

Moore, B. ([1967] 1981), *Social Origins of Dictatorship and Democracy: Lord and Peasant in the Making of the Modern World*, Boston, MA: Beacon Press.

Nelson, R. (1994), What has been the matter with neoclassical growth theory?' in G. Silberger and L. Soete (eds), *The Economics of Growth und Technical Change: Technologies, Nations, Agents*, Aldershot, UK and Brookfield, VT, USA: Edward Elgar.

Nelson, R. (2008), 'Economic development from the perspective of evolutionary theory', *Oxford Development Studies*, **36**(1): 9–21.

Nelson, R. and S. Winter (1982), *An Evolutionary Theory of Economic Change*, Cambridge: Cambridge University Press.

North, D. (1994), 'Economic performance through time', *American Economic Review*, **84**(3): 359–68.

Ofreneo, R. (2007), 'Arrested development: multinationals, TRIMs and the Philippines' automotive industry', *Asia Pacific Business Review*, **12**(2): 131–47.

Ozawa, T. (1995), 'The Flying Geese paradigm of FDI, economic development and shifts in competitiveness', background paper submitted to United Nations Conference for Trade and Development.

Palma, G. (1978), 'Dependency: a formal theory of underdevelopment or methodology for the analysis of concrete situations of underdevelopment?', *World Development*, **6**(7–8): 881–924.

Palma, G. (1981), 'Dependency and development: a critical overview', in D. Seers (ed.), *Dependency Theory: A Critical Reassessment*, London: Frances Pinter.

Pangestu, M. (1998), 'More misery ahead', *Far Eastern Economic Review*, 19 February, 52–3.

Pasuk Phongpaichit and C. Baker (1994), *Thailand: Economy and Politics*, Oxford: Oxford University Press.

Pasuk, P. and P. Sungsidh (1996), *Corruption and Democracy in Thailand*, Chiengmai, Thailand: Silkworm Books.

Polanyi, K. (1957), *The Great Transformation*, New York: Octagon.

Poulantzas, N. (1973), *Political Power and Social Classes*, London: Sheed and Ward.
Poulantzas, N. (1974), 'The internationalization of capitalist relations and the nation state', *Economy and Society*, **3**(2): 145–79.
Poulantzas, N. (1978), *State, Power, Socialism*, London: Verso.
Pramoedya, A.T. (1980), *Bumi Manusia*, Jakarta: Hasta Mitra.
Pramoedya, A.T. (1992), *House of Glass*, Ringwood: Penguin.
Pye, Lucian W. (1962), *Politics, Personality, and Nation Building: Burma's Search for Identity*, New Haven, CT: Yale University Press.
Pye, Lucian W. and Sidney Verba (eds) (1965), *Political Culture and Political Development*, Studies in Political Development, Princeton, NJ: Princeton University Press.
Pyke, F. and W. Sengenberger (1992), *Industrial Districts and Local Economic Regeneration*, Geneva: International Labour Organization.
Rasiah, R. (1987), 'Pembahagian Kerja Antarabangsa: Industri Separa Konduktor di Pulau Pinang', master's thesis approved by Science University of Malaysia, published by Malaysian Social Science Association, Kuala Lumpur, in 1993.
Rasiah, R. (1988), 'The semiconductor industry in Penang: implications for the new international Division of labour theories', *Journal of Contemporary Asia*, **18**(1): 24–46.
Rasiah, R. (1993), *Pembahagian Kerja Antarabangsa: Industri Separa Konduktor di Pulau Pinang*, Kuala Lumpur: Malaysian Social Science Association.
Rasiah, R. (1995), *Foreign Capital and Industrialization in Malaysia*, Basingstoke: Macmillan.
Rasiah, R. (1996), 'Institutions and innovations: moving up the technology ladder in the electronics industry in Malaysia', *Industry and Innovation*, **3**(2).
Rasiah, R. (1997), 'Class, ethnicity and economic development in Malaysia', in G. Rodan, R. Robison and K. Hewison (eds), *Political Economy of Southeast Asia*, Sydney, NSW: Oxford University Press.
Rasiah, R. (1998), 'The export manufacturing experience of Indonesia, Malaysia and Thailand: Lessons for Africa', United Nations Conference for Trade and Development discussion paper 137, Geneva.
Rasiah, R. (1999), 'Malaysia's national innovation system', in Jomo, K.S. and G. Felker (eds), *Technology, Competitiveness and the State*, London: Routledge.
Rasiah, R. (2004), *Foreign Firms, Technological Capabilities and Economic Performance: Evidence from Africa, Asia and Latin America*, Cheltenham, UK and Northampton, MA, USA: Edward Elgar.
Rasiah, R. (2005), 'Trade-related investment liberalization: the Malaysian experience', *Global Economic Review*, **34**(4): 453–71.
Rasiah, R. (2009), 'Growth and slowdown in the electronics industry in Southeast Asia', *Journal of Asia Pacific Economy*, **14**(2): 123–37.
Rasiah, R. and N. von Hofmann (1998), *Workers on the Brink: Unions, Crisis and Exclusion in Southeast Asia*, Singapore: Friedrich-Ebert Stiftung.
Rasiah, R. and S. Ishak (2001), 'Markets, government and Malaysia's new economic policy', *Cambridge Journal of Economics*, **25**(1): 57–78.
Reid, A. (1990a), *Southeast Asia in the Age of Commerce, 1450–1680: Crisis and Expansion*, New Haven, CT: Yale University Press.
Reid, A. (1990b), *Southeast Asia in the Age of Commerce, 1450–1680: The Lands below the Winds*, New Haven, CT: Yale University Press.
Reid, A. (ed.) (2000), *Sojourners and Settlers: Histories of Southeast Asia and the*

Chinese, Sydney, Allen & Unwin, 1996; Honolulu: University of Hawai'i Press, 2001; Italian translation 2000.

Reinert, E. (1994), 'Catching up from way behind: a Third World perspective on First World history', in J. Fagerberg, B. Verspagen and N. von Tunzelmann (eds), *The Dynamics of Technology, Trade and Growth*, Aldershot: Ashgate.

Ricardo, D. ([1817] 1981), *On the Principles of Political Economy and Taxation*, Cambridge: Cambridge University Press.

Riggs, F.W. (1966), *Thailand: The Modernization of a Bureaucratic Polity*, Honolulu, HI: East–West Center Press.

Robison, R. (1986), *Indonesia: The Rise of Capital*, London: Allen & Unwin.

Robison, R. (1992), 'Industrialization and the economic and political development of capital: the case of Indonesia', in R. McVey (ed.), *Southeast Asian Capitalists*, Cornell Southeast Asia Program, Ithaca, NY: Cornell University Press.

Robison, R. (ed.) (2006), *The Neoliberal Revolution: Forging the Market State*, London, Palgrave.

Robison, R. and V.R. Hadiz (2004), *Reorganising Power in Indonesia: The Politics of Oligarchy in an Age of Markets*, London: RoutledgeCurzon.

Rodan, Garry (1989), *The Political Economy of Singapore's Industrialization: National State and International Capital*, London: Macmillan.

Rodan, G. and K. Hewison (1996), 'The ebb and flow of civil society and the decline of the left in Southeast Asia', in G. Rodan (ed.), *Political Oppositions in Industrialising Asia*, London: Routledge.

Rodan, G. and K. Jayasuriya (2006), 'Conflict and the new political participation in Southeast Asia', Murdoch University Asia Research Centre working paper no. 129, Perth, Australia.

Rodan G., K. Hewison and R. Robison (1997), *Political Economy of Southeast Asia*, Melbourne, VIC: Cambridge University Press.

Rodan, G., K. Hewison and R. Robison (eds) (2001), *The Political Economy of South-East Asia: Conflict, Crises, and Change*, Melbourne, VIC: Oxford University Press.

Rodan, G., K. Hewison and R. Robison (2006), *The Political Economy of South-East Asia: Markets, Power and Contestation*, Melbourne, VIC: Oxford University Press.

Romer, P.M. (1994), 'The origins of endogenous growth', *Journal of Economic Perspectives*, **8**(1): 3–22.

Rostow, W.W. (1960), *The Stages of Economic Growth: A Non-Communist Manifesto*, Cambridge: Cambridge University Press.

Rowthorn, R. (1996), 'East Asian development: the flying geese paradigm reconsidered', background paper submitted to United Nations Conference for Trade and Development, Geneva.

Sachs, J. and A. Warner (1995), 'Economic reform and the process of global integration', in W.C. Brainard and G.L. Perry (eds), *Brookings Papers on Economic Activity*, Washington, DC: Brookings Institution.

Salleh, I. and M. Sahathevan (1992), 'Growth, equity and structural transformation in Malaysia: role of the public sector', mimeo prepared for the World Bank Workshop on the Role of Government and East Asian Success, Washington, DC.

SarDesai, D.R. (1997), *Southeast Asia: Past and Present*, Boulder, CO: Westview Press.

Schmidt, J.D. (1996), 'Models of dirigisme in East Asia: perspectives for Eastern

Europe', in J. Hersh, and J.D. Schmidt (eds), *The Aftermath of 'Real Existing Socialism' in Eastern Europe, Vol. 1: Between Western Europe and East Asia*, London and New York: St Martin's Press and Macmillan.

Schmidt, J.D. (1997), 'The challenge from Southeast Asia: between equity and growth', in C. Dixon, and D. Drakakis-Smith (eds), *Uneven Development in South East Asia*, Aldershot: Ashgate.

Schmidt, J.D. (2000), 'Globalization, democratization, and labor social welfare in Thailand', in J.D. Schmidt, and J. Hersh (eds), *Globalization and Social Change*, London: Routledge.

Schumpeter, J. (1942), *Capitalism, Socialism and Democracy*, New York: Harper & Row.

Scott, J.C. (1976), *The Moral Economy of the Peasant: Rebellion and Subsistence in Southeast Asia*, New Haven, CT: Yale University Press.

Scott, J.C. (1985), *Everyday Forms of Peasant Resistance*, New Haven, CT: Yale University Press.

Sen, A. (1999), *Development as Freedom*, New York: Random House.

Senghass, D. (1985), *The European Experience*, Leamington Spa: Berg.

Siffin, W.J. (1966), *The Thai Bureaucracy: Institutional Change and Development*, Honolulu, HI: East–West Center Press.

Skocpol, T. (1985), 'Bringing the state back in: strategies of analysis in current research', in P. Evans, D. Rueschemeyer and T. Skocpol (eds), *Bringing the State Back In*, Cambridge: Cambridge University Press.

Smith, A. (1776), *The Wealth of Nations*, London: Strahan and Cadell.

Solow, R. (1956), 'A contribution to the theory of economic growth', *Quarterly Journal of Economics*, **70**: 65–94.

Stiglitz, J. (2000), 'Capital market liberalization, economic growth, and instability', *World Development*, **28**(6): 1075–86.

Taylor, J.G. and A. Turton (eds) (1988), *Sociology of 'Developing Societies': Southeast Asia*, New York: Monthly Review Press.

Todd, P. and K.S. Jomo (1994), *Trade Unions and the State in Peninsular Malaysia*, Kuala Lumpur: Oxford University Press.

Turton, A. (1984), 'Limits of ideological domination and the formation of social consciousness', in S. Tanabe and A. Turton (eds), *History and Peasant Consciousness in Southeast Asia*, Senri ethnological studies no. 14, Osaka, Japan: National Museum of Ethnology.

Turton, A. (1989), 'Local powers and rural differentiation', in G. Hart, A. Turton and B. White (eds), *Agrarian Transformations: Local Processes and the State in Southeast Asia*, Berkeley, CA: University of California Press.

United Nations Conference for Trade and Development (UNCTAD) (1996), *Trade and Development Report*, Geneva: UNCTAD.

Utrecht, E. (1972), 'The Indonesian army as an instrument of repression', *Journal of Contemporary Asia*, **2**(1): 56–67.

Vaitsos, C. (2003), 'Growth theories revisited: enduring questions with changing answers', Intech discussion paper no. 9, UNU-INTECH, Maastricht, Netherlands.

Wade, R. (1990), *Governing the Market*, Princeton, NJ: Princeton University Press.

Wallerstein, I. (1974), *The Modern World-System: Mercantilism and the Consolidation of the European World-Economy, 1600–1750*, New York: Academic Press.

Wallerstein, I. (1979), *The Capitalist World Economy*, Cambridge: Cambridge University Press.

Warr, P. (1987a), 'Export promotion via industrial enclaves: the Philippines' Bataan Export Processing Zone', *Journal of Development Studies*, **23**(1): 220–42.

Warr, P. (1987b), 'Malaysia's industrial enclaves: benefits and costs', *Developing Economies*, **25**(1): 30–55.

Warr, P. (1989), 'Export processing zones: the economics of enclave manufacturing', *World Bank Research Observer*, **4**(1): 65–88.

Warren, B. (1980), *Imperialism: Pioneer of Capitalism*, London: New Left Books.

Wertheim, W.F. (1995), 'The contribution of Weberian sociology to studies of Southeast Asia', *Journal of Southeast Asian Studies*, **26**(1), March.

White, G. (ed.) (1988), *Developmental States in East Asia*, London: Macmillan/ Institute of Development Studies, University of Sussex.

Wilson, D.A. (1962), *Politics in Thailand*, Ithaca, NY: Cornell University Press.

World Bank (1993), *The East Asian Miracle, Economic Growth and Public Policy*, New York: Oxford University Press.

Wurfel, D. (1959), 'The Philippines', in G.M. Kahin (ed.), *Government and Politics in Southeast Asia*, Ithaca, NY: Cornell University Press.

Wurfel, D. and B. Burton (eds) (1990), *The Political Economy of Foreign Policy in Southeast Asia*, London: Macmillan.

Yoshihara, K. (1988), *The Rise of Ersatz Capitalism in Southeast Asia*, Kuala Lumpur: Oxford University Press.

Yoshihara, K. (1989), *The Rise of Ersatz Capitalism in Southeast Asia*, Singapore: Oxford University Press.

Young, A. (1994), 'Lessons from the East Asian NICs: a contrarian view', *European Economic Review*, **38**(3/4): 964–73.

Young, A. (1995), 'The tyranny of numbers: confronting the statistical realities of the East Asian growth experience', *Quarterly Journal of Economics*, **110**(3): 641–80.

2. Industrialization in the second-tier NIEs

Rajah Rasiah[1]

Southeast Asia's market economies have recorded substantial manufacturing growth, particularly since the 1990s, driven by export-orientation from 1965 in Singapore, 1971 in Malaysia, 1980 in Thailand, 1986 in Indonesia and 1995 in the Philippines. Since the work of Hamilton (1983) and subsequently Deyo (1985), Amsden (1989), Wade (1990) and Chang (1994), there has been a rise in statist accounts of rapid industrialization in East Asia. Analyses of Southeast Asia, however, have differed starkly. The World Bank (1993) credited liberal policies as being the springboard of successful industrialization in Southeast Asia, while Doner (1991), Jomo (1996), Rasiah and Ishak (2001), Rasiah (2003), and Lauridsen (2008) argue that an eclectic combination of interventionist and liberal policies has characterized Southeast Asian industrialization, with mixed results.

Given the rising tide of opposition to protection and subsidies, especially with the formation of the World Trade Organization (WTO), these accounts of Malaysia, Thailand and Indonesia have led to perceptions that they offer better examples than South Korea and Taiwan. Also, unlike the resource-poor Northeast Asian first-tier newly industrialized economies (NIEs), the second-tier Southeast Asian NIEs are major exporters of primary commodities and as a consequence to some offer useful lessons about the relevance of resource endowments for economic growth (World Bank, 1993).

Doubts have also been raised over trade theory and market-friendly explanations of growth. If Amsden's (1989), Chang's (2003) and Reinert's (2007) argument on the need for actively 'getting relative prices wrong' is important for quickening industrial catch-up, then accounts to follow existing relative prices gradually using market-friendly policies will not provide the desired stimulus for achieving rapid industrialization. Fishlow *et al.* (1996) provided an incisive critique of World Bank (1993) for 'masking' the technological and material development distance achieved by the more interventionist Northeast Asian economies compared to the less interventionist Southeast Asian second-tier economies. Despite the specificity that characterizes any country or locality and hence makes the experiences of each of the East and Southeast Asian countries different (see Perkins, 1994; Morrissey and Nelson, 1998), it is obvious that firms in Japan, Korea and Taiwan have moved up the technology ladder more swiftly to participate in designing and R&D activities on the back of more robust industrial policy than firms in the second-tier Southeast Asian NIEs (see Rasiah, 2003).

This chapter takes a closer look at the industrialization experiences of Indonesia, Malaysia, the Philippines and Thailand with a view to explaining the political economy forces driving growth and structural transformation. Singapore was dropped only because of widespread coverage given to the success of the East Asian NIEs in which it is a component member. Brunei, Cambodia, East Timor, Laos, Myanmar and Vietnam were excluded because of either the insignificance of manufacturing in their GDP or the growth in its significance only from the late 1980s. The rest of the chapter is organized as follows. The next section discusses the importance of industry in the four economies. The subsequent section reviews the main accounts of industrialization, followed by a section on the drivers of industrial growth and structural change in the economies. The final section finishes with the conclusions.

GROWTH AND STRUCTURAL CHANGE

Southeast Asia is essentially a sub-continent noted in history for the busy Malacca Straits, where East–West trade and sailing dominated economic activities in the region. There were pockets of small-scale processing – largely for consumption – of dried spices, handcraft, metalworking and quarrying. However, none of these activities other than dried spices reached large-scale operations. Early modern manufacturing emerged in commercial processing of plantation goods such as coconut oil, rubber sheets, coffee, smelting of tin and other minerals, and engineering. At the heart of the debate is the macroeconomic environment of rapid manufactured export growth and structural change and the specific factors that have stimulated structural change and manufacturing growth in Southeast Asia's second-tier NIEs. Unlike the first-tier East Asian NIEs, the second-tier Southeast Asian NIEs enjoyed fairly strong resource endowments when rapid industrialization took off.

From initial specialization in agricultural and mining commodities Southeast Asia began to focus strongly on stimulating industrialization. Whereas commodity diversification helped these countries to reduce the impact of falling terms of trade that characterized typical developing economies that focused on just one or two products (Rasiah, Osman and Alavi, 2000), the shift to industrialization can be argued to be the prime engine of growth in the market economies of Southeast Asia. This section discusses the extent of industrial transformation to justify why a careful analysis of it is critical to understanding development and change in the region.

Manufacturing gradually displaced the primary sectors as the prime engine of growth in all four economies. In export-oriented plantation agriculture (particularly rubber, oil palm and sugarcane), timber and minerals (especially oil and tin) accounted for much of the export volume originating from Indonesia, Malaysia, the Philippines and Thailand. Malaysia, as a result, enjoyed an exports/GDP ratio of 56.2 per cent in 1960. As primary commodity prices fell, the overall export proportion of GDP gradually fell to 35.7 per cent in 1972, before rising rapidly as export-oriented manufacturing expanded. This rise was complemented by increases in commodity prices in the second half of the 1970s. Rapid manufacturing expansion pushed up the exports/GDP ratio to 89.9 per cent in 1994. Indonesia and Thailand, however, initially faced low export shares owing to strong biases introduced against exports to support state enterprises from 1945. Indonesia and Thailand had export/GDP shares of 4.2 per cent and 17.5 per cent in 1965 and 1960 respectively, which rose to 29.0 and 22.3 per cent respectively in 1974. Both economies have since experienced a trend rise in export shares, initially dominated by agriculture, timber, tin, oil and gas. Manufactured exports became important from the second half of the 1980s. As manufactured exports expanded, Indonesia's exports/GDP ratio rose to over 24 per cent from 1987, and that of Thailand to over 34 per cent from 1988. It is noteworthy that these economies did not allow falling commodity prices to reduce exports, and thereby averted long-term balance-of-payments crises until the 1990s.

Benefiting from early participation in import-substitution policies, the Philippines was the earliest to show a high share of industry in GDP. In 1960 the Philippines' share of industry in GDP was 28 per cent, when it was less than 20 per cent in the other market economies of Southeast Asia (see Table 2.1). However, by 1990 the Philippines' share had fallen to the lowest among these economies. Indonesia (42 per cent) followed by Malaysia (41 per cent) enjoyed the highest share in 1980. Industrialization became most dominant in Malaysia from 1990, accounting for over half of GDP since 2000.

Among the five Southeast Asian market economies, Indonesia, the Philippines and Singapore have also experienced deindustrialization over the period 1960–2007 (see Table 2.1). Industry's share in GDP in Indonesia declined from 42 per cent in 1980 to 39 per cent in 1990. A similar decline

Table 2.1   Share of industry in gross domestic product, 1960–2007 (%)

	1960	1970	1980	1990	2000	2007
Indonesia	15	19	42	39	46	47
Malaysia	19	27	41	42	51	51
Philippines	28	32	39	34	32	31
Thailand	19	25	29	37	42	44

Source: http://ddp-ext.worldbank.org/ext/DDPQQ/showReport.do?method=showReport, downloaded on 11 February 2009.

Table 2.2   Share of manufactured exports in total exports, 1990–2007

	US$ billions			National share (%)	
	1990	2000	2007	2000	2007
Indonesia	9	37	49	57	41
Malaysia	16	79	125	80	71
Philippines	6	35	44	87	86
Thailand	15	52	117	75	76

Source: WTO (2007).

took place in the Philippines and Singapore from 39 and 38 per cent in 1980 to 31 per cent each in 2007. Whereas industrialization's share in Indonesia has since 2000 enjoyed significant expansion, the shares in the Philippines and Singapore have continued to decline.

The share of manufactured exports in total exports in the four Southeast Asian market economies is also highly significant (see Table 2.2). Manufactured exports expanded sharply over the period 1990–2000. While the expansion continued strongly over the period 2000–07, the share of manufactured exports in overall exports fell significantly in Indonesia and Malaysia and slightly in the Philippines in the same period. It will be examined in the next section if this relative fall in the face of continued growth in manufactured exports suggests the onset of positive deindustrialization.

While foreign direct investment has been important for export expansion, the sub-sectors bolstering manufactured exports have differed slightly in these economies. High-tech exports accounted for 1, 38 and 21 per cent respectively of exports from Indonesia, Malaysia and Thailand in 1990. The commensurate export percentages from these countries rose to 7, 46 and 24 per cent in 1995 and 16, 60 and 33 per cent in 2000 (see Table 2.3).

Table 2.3　Share of high-tech exports, 1990–2006

	1990	1995	2000	2006
Indonesia	1	7	16	13
Malaysia	38	46	60	54
Philippines	0	35	73	68
Thailand	21	24	33	27

Source: http://ddp-ext.worldbank.org/ext/DDPQQ/showReport.do?method=showReport, downloaded on 11 February 2009.

The commensurate shares fell to 13, 54 and 27 per cent respectively in 2006. From zero in 1990, high-tech exports in overall exports from the Philippines rose to 35 per cent in 1995 and 73 per cent in 2000 before falling to 68 per cent in 2006.

Textiles, garments and footwear as well as plywood have been the prime export components in Indonesia, contributing 38.4 and 18.6 per cent respectively of overall manufactured exports in 1991 (computed from Hill, 1996: Table 8.3). Textiles and clothing, and food have been Thailand's main manufactured exports, accounting for 27.9 and 21.3 per cent respectively of total manufactured exports in 1985. In 1993, the share of textiles and garments in overall manufactured exports fell to 21.3 per cent, while that of electric/electronics rose to 18.8 per cent (see Rasiah, 2003: Table 11). Malaysia's electric/electronics industry – dominated by foreign ownership – remained labour-intensive until the mid-1980s, but has since become increasingly technology-intensive. Microelectronics assembly and tests, in particular, have become highly skill-intensive (Rasiah, 1996b). Despite being resource-intensive, Indonesia's and Thailand's textile, garment and footwear industries rely on imported inputs and are highly labour-intensive. Indeed, within manufacturing, the key non-resource-based export-oriented industries such as electronics and textiles and garments have also been highly import-dependent, whether ownership has been foreign or local. Of these industries, only electronics is foreign-dominated in Indonesia and Thailand. In the former, the shares of foreign ownership in the textile, garment and footwear industries in 1988 were only 24.8, 1.8 and 12.9 per cent respectively (Hill, 1996: Table 8.3). Resource-based export-oriented industries in these economies, such as Indonesia's plywood, Thailand's food processing and Malaysia's oil palm processing industries, are dominated by local owners and are less import-dependent.

Industry has become a key contributor to the four economies, and hence it is important to understand the political economy dynamics of its drivers.

What is also evident from the account above is the slowdown in manufacturing in all four countries since 2000. Several explanations already exist, but all of them contradict in many ways and hence this chapter reviews these accounts critically before providing an integrated political economy account of it.

MAIN ARGUMENTS

Southeast Asia's industrialization has been presented using four major lenses, with little in common over their drivers. The oldest account depicts the region's industrialization as being the result of capitalist domination. The second simply explains the rapid expansion of manufacturing as a result of the pursuit of market-friendly liberal policies. The third takes a similar broad perspective but situates it as an extension of the flying geese framework. The last uses statist assessments to portray it as an eclectic arrangement with the role of the government and international forces combining to set into motion an incomplete set of processes that has driven industrialization but with little technological catch-up.

Imperialist Subordination

All Southeast Asian economics apart from Thailand were colonized by Western powers. Coming in the wake of colonial domination, Leninist accounts of imperialism by Western capital resonated strongly in efforts to engender industrial development in these countries. The success of the Chinese Communist Party (CCP) in unifying China gave confidence to radical communist groups in Indo-China. Similar efforts in Indonesia, Malaysia, the Philippines and Singapore were thwarted by a combination of cavalier British, American and domestic anti-insurgency policies – though the rebellion remained a potent force in Malaysia until the armistice of 1989.[2] American foreign policy dominated the military-backed Suharto government to paralyse any socialist activism in Indonesia. Massive American military aid financed anti-imperial struggles in the Philippines and Indonesia. In addition to the Vietnam War, American military aid and restrictive foreign trade policies were used extensively to destabilize Indo-China and Myanmar.

Lenin (1948) had argued that capitalism had reached a monopoly stage, thereby denying the room for the growth of new capital and newly integrated regions owing to a fall in rivalry between capital, which was a departure from the original work of Marx which stated that industrial capitalism is defined by the continuity of all three circuits of capital and that the primacy of the productive circuit differentiated it from other modes of production. Like Marx (1976), Luxemburg (1967) had also argued that 'however destabilising the period of incorporation was it was necessary to create the conditions for accumulation in new regions'. Baran (1973) and subsequent works with long historical roots in the Latin American dependency school (e.g. Dos Santos, 1970; Furtado, 1973; Sunkel, 1989), which was articulated and championed by Frank (1969, 1979) and Amin (1974, 2004), waged this debate using structural explanations. Similar works but with added dynamics of unequal exchange were advanced by Emmanuel (1972) and Wallerstein (1979). Evans (1995), Cardoso (2001) and Frobel, Heinrich and Kreye (1980) discussed the room some economies enjoy to achieve marginalized accumulation (see also Rasiah, 1988).

Whatever the version, followers of this school focused extensively on exchange relations to argue that integration into the capitalist world economy would peripheralize, underdevelop or at most allow highly restricted accumulation in the Southeast Asian economies (see Bello, Kinley and Elinson, 1982; Jomo, 1986; Khor, 1987; Henderson, 1989; Hewison, 1989). The success of Korea, Taiwan, Singapore and Hong Kong is explained as their being marginalized sub-metropoles benefiting from geopolitical strategies by the imperialists. These examples are used as the semi-periphery by Wallerstein (1979) and Henderson (1989). In addition, unlike the earlier arguments à la Latin American dependency school which had originally posited that integration into the capitalist world economy was meant to retain developing economies as primary commodity producers for its processing in developed economies, rising antagonism between capital and labour in the developed economies has been argued subsequently to have led the former to decompose and relocate production in developing locations. Imperial initiatives to absorb Southeast Asian economies into this division of labour were considered to meet the twin objective of undermining the bargaining power of labour in the developed world and absorbing cheap labour abroad to increase valorization. However, these theorists argue that it has only changed 'banana republics into pyjama republics' (Adam, 1975).

Notwithstanding the attraction these theories have especially with the disadvantaged, a number of theoretical problems have undermined their scientific merits. In addition to a lack of consistent empirical evidence, neo-Marxist explications of industrialization in Southeast Asia have been filled with rhetoric rather than reason. Hence, neo-Marxist accounts do not provide a rigorous explanation of industrialization in Southeast Asia. Despite the theoretical flaws that have left these exchange theories open to easy attacks (see Palma, 1981), they have resurfaced in new forms because of their political appeal and whenever serious crises erupt, for example, the

1973–75 and 1979–80 oil crises, the 1985–86 contraction and the 1997–98 financial crisis.

Neo-Liberal

Arguably the most influential explanation of industrial expansion in Southeast Asia is provided by the neo-liberal school. This school simply argues that increased integration into market (price) relationships will provide both the incentive and the discipline to drive resource allocation efficiently. The initial attraction in Southeast Asia for this school came from repressive regimes that often wasted rents appropriated from unproductive and clientelist networks. It is argued that interest groups with a common dislike for rentier domestic political regimes often merged to call for deregulation and democratization.

The most dominant account of manufacturing growth and industrial transformation in Southeast Asia that equates it with liberalization and outward orientation is provided by the World Bank (1993) (see also Garnaut, 1980; Krueger, 1983; Balassa, 1991; Pangestu, 1991; Ismail Salleh and Meyanathan, 1993; Athukorola and Menon, 1999; Hill, 1996, 1999). Using Southeast Asia as the empirical platform, the World Bank (1993) argued that other developing countries must adopt its liberal stance to promote growth and equity on the grounds that interventions were neither possible nor desirable for newer economies because of growing liberalization pressures. This feeling reached arguably its peak in political and academic circles when Krugman (1994) referred to the growth of the East Asian economies as being unsustainable owing to the claim that they had grown through the growth of factor inputs – perspiration as opposed to inspiration. The work of Young (1994) that placed the total factor productivity (TFP) growth rates of Korea, Taiwan and Singapore below those of even Egypt, Syria and Pakistan became the evidence to make this point.[3]

However, once it became clear, even to Krugman (1998), that the Keynesian explanation of external shocks from uncontrolled fluid capital flows formed the basis of the crisis, neo-liberal arguments about the successful development of Southeast Asian economies became less tenable. As Khan (1989) and Chang (1994) have argued, corruption and rent seeking merely provide shallow excuses for explaining crises, and there is little rigorously comparable evidence to seek a positive correlation between the so-called 'clean bureaucracies' and economic development. Moreover, the Schumpeterian rent has often figured positively as a carrot to stimulate new growth through innovations. Finally, as Amsden (1989), Rodan (1989), Wade (1990), Chang (1994) and Rasiah and Ishak (2001) have shown, government failures did not deter governments in Korea, Taiwan, Singapore and Malaysia from intervening to support creative ventures. At the time industrial expansion took place, the political regimes in these economies enjoyed sufficient autonomy to intervene in the interest of stimulating industrial progress. The Singapore government enjoyed arguably the greatest insulation from clientelist interests and hence has demonstrated the greatest flexibility to shift policy directions to correct adverse consequences.

The political economy of industrial policy has been one of the most intensely contested development issues between the various schools of thought. Although in his pioneering work Smith (1776) had discussed the significance of industrial policy and increasing returns when reversing the dictum between markets and the division of labour, neoclassical works have largely argued in favour of leaving allocative decisions to relative factor endowment prices. Whereas some neoclassical economists have accepted that manufacturing is important to attract investment and create jobs, the focus remains tied to relative prices, starting with simple natural resource processing and specialization in the labour-intensive stages or tasks of manufacturing.

Flying Geese

A related but quite different view considers the industrial expansion pattern of the second-tier NIEs of Southeast Asia as being a consequence of being sucked into Akamatsu's (1962) flying geese model, with Southeast Asia forming the second follow-up group behind the first follow-up wedge of first-tier Asian NIEs in a sequential process that has been led by the leading goose, Japan (Naya, 1997). This pattern is assumed to have spread to other economies in Southeast Asia. Articulations of industrial transformation involving this model refer to Malaysia, the Philippines, Indonesia and Thailand as the third gaggle of geese following the developmental path defined by Japan. Such a model also assumes that regional economies are unlikely to generate synergic effects in sites far from their borders.

However, this approach has also come under intense criticisms. The sequencing and followship argument reminiscent of flying geese approaches fails to account for the possibility of some economies falling behind. The weak and sick geese even in the animal flock either fall behind or disappear. Also, the flying geese exponents did not examine in detail the specific factors that have stimulated rapid export growth. Work by Gore (1994), Rowthorn (1996) and Bernard and Ravenhill (1995) questions its relevance for explaining East Asian growth and structural change. Prevailing evidence of economic growth and structural change in East and Southeast

Asia at most support such an approach only in a superficial sense. Detailed assessments do not show patterns of structural sequencing, either through deliberate government policies beginning with imports, followed by production for the domestic market, and substituting with exports later, or driven by changes in relative prices (see Rasiah, 1998a).

Where governments intervene, the industries that lose competitiveness in a superior wedge of geese need not fall out to a following wedge of geese if successful interventions stimulate upgrading to higher-value-added activities. Rapid and sustained transformation to support a quick catch-up takes place. For example, Korea's Samsung is currently the leading firm in the manufacture of dynamic random access memories (DRAMs), while Taiwan Semiconductor Manufacturing Corporation (TSMC) is the leading firm in the manufacture of logic technologies. Both firms have also overtaken Renesas (the remnant of Hitachi Semiconductor), which is currently the lead firm in the flying geese model's leading goose, i.e. Japan.

Flying geese proponents have also offered little empirical support to the pattern of foreign direct investment in Southeast Asia. Rasiah (1995: Chapter 2) points out the lack of careful firm-level scrutiny of foreign firms relocating from Japan as evidence of structural patterns across economies in East Asia. Internal pressures (for example, from rising costs), external demand (for example, access to foreign markets) and the specific advantages of particular host sites have been crucial to the relocation of foreign investment into Southeast Asia.

By defining industries in static terms, the flying geese model fails to take account of technical change within industries so that the proliferation of advanced materials, manufacturing and systems technologies reduces the need for certain industries to fall out to following wedges of geese. For example, Taiwan's textile industry has upgraded to high-tech polymers for high-value-added filament manufacturing, while steel manufacturing continues to absorb both process and material improvements so that it continues to operate on a large scale in the country (see Lee, 2009).

Dirigiste

Recognizing the importance of collective action problems in the allocation and distribution of resources, and the differences between private and social efficiency, *dirigiste* expositions argue that accumulation in Korea (Amsden, 1989; Chang, 1994), Taiwan (Wade, 1990; Mathews, 2002) and Singapore (Rodan, 1989; Mathews, 2002) was possible only because the state played a critical role in directing industrialization.

The successful development of Japan, Korea and Taiwan on the back of industrial policy and strong state intervention offered the *dirigiste* school considerable support as other developing economies sought the details to engender similar development paths in their own countries (see Deyo, 1987). Malaysia's prime minister over the period 1981 until 2004, i.e. Mahathir Mohamad, began his first term with inter alia launching the Look East policy to emulate their successes (Jomo, 1990).

However, *dirigiste* arguments that lack discussion on the role of intermediary organizations in strengthening the relationship between markets and government face problems. Some works have even gone overboard to depict Thailand's rapid growth as having been driven by strong state intervention (see for example Amsden, 1995). The eclectic and unfocused nature of political and economic governance in Indonesia, Malaysia, the Philippines and Thailand had sub-optimal consequences (see Pasuk and Baker, 1995; Jomo *et al*, 1996; Rasiah, 1998a; Ofreneo, 2008). Lauridsen (2004) and Busser (2008) also provided evidence from automotive manufacturing over the failure of Thai firms to upgrade to the higher-value-added activities of designing and R&D.

Although these accounts provide interesting analyses and conclusions on how Southeast Asian market economies have evolved, the last appears the most convincing in providing a political economy account of industrialization in Southeast Asia. Neo-liberals viewed the golden years of growth achieved by these economies in 1986–96 as being driven by liberalization and a greater role for markets, whilst the 1997–98 financial crisis was seen by this school as being the result of corrupt *dirigisme*. State interventionists viewed the limited growth achieved in the golden years as being a consequence of specific market-augmenting state interventions. The crisis of 1997–98 is viewed by them as being the consequence of unbridled liberalization, which exposed them to external shocks. Neo-Marxists argue not only that the growth achieved in these economies was marginal but that, because of increased integration in an exploitative capitalist system, it could not be sustained. This chapter seeks to make a fresh and open assessment of the evolution of industrialization in the Southeast Asian market economies to explain the forces that have unfolded and shaped these processes.

INDUSTRIALIZATION EFFORTS

This section attempts to unravel the forces that unleashed the shift towards manufacturing in the second-tier Southeast Asian NIEs. Whereas nationalist interests promoted import-substitution manufacturing, the shift towards export manufacturing was spearheaded by a confluence of: (1) global capitalist interests to stimulate job creation as a means to alleviate poverty so as to check the domino effect expected from the fall of Indo-China to communism in the 1970s; (2) global multilateral organizations such as the UNIDO and the World Bank using multinationals as a vehicle to promote export processing zones in Southeast Asia; and (3) domestic bureaucrats interested in the development of national capitalists as well as those seeking export-orientation to provide the scale and efficiency effects for rapid growth and structural change. Such a strategy also had the support of multinationals seeking to relocate labour-intensive stages to reduce production costs and to appropriate tax incentives (Lim, 1978; Scibberas, 1978). Despite frequent *coup d'états* in Thailand and the heightened insurgency in the Philippines in the 1970s and 1980s, governments in these countries supported industrialization as a vehicle to achieve development. Narrow clientelist interests manifesting by class (the Philippines) and by ethnicity (Malaysia and Indonesia) clouded the instruments used to promote local capital. For brevity the evaluation of industrialization drivers in this section is undertaken by import-substitution (IS) and export-orientation (EO) phases.

Unlike the resource-poor first-tier East Asian NIEs, the second-tier Southeast Asian NIEs enjoyed substantial natural resources. Industrialization in these countries started to grow in processing and engineering support for the mining and agricultural industries (see Allen and Donnithorne, 1957; Thoburn, 1977), which intensified during the wartime disruptions that took place in 1914–18. Industrialization intensified again during 1939–45, but Japanese participation in manufacturing from 1941 was reversed once the war ended (see Rasiah, 1994a). However, it was not until the 1950s and 1960s that Indonesia, Malaysia, the Philippines and Thailand embarked on proactive industrialization. Because of independence in 1898, the Philippines had the earliest participation in IS industrialization. Protection from imports stimulated sugar processing, and consumption goods manufacturing.

The IS sector evolved largely independently of the EO sector in all four countries. In labour-intensive industries such as textile and garment making, local firms, which had initially evolved under the IS regime, began to export, but only as subcontractors to foreign firms that controlled brand names, designs and markets. In fact, IS has been a major source of policy errors in these economies. It is thus useful to explain the specific nature of IS promotion pursued in the latter economies to highlight their differences from typical infant industry promotions reminiscent of structuralist arguments (see Lewis, 1955; Kaldor, 1957; Myrdal, 1957).[4]

Import-Substitution

Despite the differences, common problems afflicted IS activities in the four Southeast Asian second-tier NIEs. IS was operated independently of

EO, was not targeted to create the conditions for EO's take-off and faced little or no performance standards. Hence, despite the different timings of launch, the consequences of IS in all these countries have not been dismal.

Indonesia

During Sukarno's regime, state-owned manufacturing enterprises enjoyed favourable access to subsidies, credit and foreign exchange. Strong anti-foreign sentiments, including anti-local Chinese feelings, limited state support to indigenous-owned private business. Contradictions among the communist party, the bourgeoisie and the military precipitated the end of the Sukarno government (Robison, 1987: 17). Following the demise of the populist-nationalist experiment, Suharto's New Order government liberalized foreign exchange controls, as cumbersome multiple exchange rate mechanisms were streamlined (Palmer, 1978: 36–43). The extent of government failure suggested that any kind of liberalization was for the better. The state began abolishing subsidies to state-owned enterprises and started promoting the private sector, which grew following the introduction of incentives. The lessening of protection in the domestic economy obviously undermined several firms, reflected by the slight fall in the share of manufacturing in GDP from 12 per cent in 1960 to 10 per cent in 1970. Primary commodity exports re-emerged strongly, propelled by foreign aid – particularly from the United States and later from Japan – which helped reduce the high inflation and balance-of-payments deficits that plagued Indonesia in the late 1960s.[5] Foreign investment was liberally promoted, though various weaknesses – including corrupt customs officials and ineffective coordination of infrastructural and administrative facilities – gradually undermined the inflow of FDI.[6] Thus, the share of FDI in gross domestic investment remained low in the 1970s.[7]

Under Indonesia's first five-year plan (Repelita I: 1969/70–1973/74), the state stimulated large-scale, but labour-intensive, resource-based import-substitution (IS) industries. IS became stronger under the Repelita II (1974/75–1978/79), and, following growing anti-foreigner sentiments, manifested in the January 1974 anti-Tanaka riots, tighter controls on foreign capital were imposed.[8] Ethnic Chinese Indonesian capital developed largely in alliance with the politically connected *pribumi* interests (Robison, 1987) favoured by national development policies. Unlike most IS experiences, the Indonesian state also encouraged exports to generate foreign exchange. The subsequent five-year plans increasingly promoted labour-intensive exports. Indonesia saw a serious struggle between statist nationalists, led by the director of Pertamina, and more liberal technocrats working in the National Economic Planning Board (Bappenas). With its enormous oil revenue,[9] Pertamina's management had the means to award contracts and concessions for the development of IS industries (for example, Krakatau steel mill). When Pertamina's massive indebtedness was disclosed in 1975–76, the balance of power shifted. Rapid industrial capital formation through alliances linked to oil revenue-related concessions sustained support for the nationalists over the Bappenas liberals. The promoted IS industries included liquefied natural gas, oil refining, metals, petrochemicals, fertilizers and machine tools (Gray, 1982). Large-scale undertakings in manufacturing, such as liquefied natural gas and petrochemicals, were dominated by state-controlled corporations. Habibie's grandiose high-technology projects later expanded the state's involvement in heavy industries, including aircraft making from the 1980s. Hence, manufacturing grew slowly so that the GDP share of manufacturing grew to only 13 per cent in 1980. Manufactured exports accounted for only 2.3 per cent of exports in 1980 (see Rasiah, 2003: Table 7).

There was a reduction of tariffs in 1979, while export-oriented subsidies were introduced from 1978, but the emphasis on IS industrialization continued until the mid-1980s. The IS policies hardly involved performance standards, gradual reduction of protection and eventual export-orientation. Global recession, bureaucratic inefficiency (including opaque and corrupt practices) and policies biased against exports continued to stifle manufactured export expansion in the early 1980s. Tariff and non-tariff barriers to shield IS industries were, in fact, raised in 1983. As a consequence, the export-oriented (EO) sector grew little until 1986. The situation was worsened by vague foreign investment policies and cumbersome customs and administrative controls. Quantitative restrictions imposed in 1982 required imports of certain merchandise to be handled by approved importers. By the time the EO strategy took off in 1986, 28 per cent of total imported items, 26 per cent of import value and 31 per cent of value added were restricted under this system (Pangestu, 1993: 12).[10]

Indonesian capital, especially state-owned enterprises, thus dominated the manufacturing sector of Indonesian-controlled firms. *Pribumi*, Chinese and state ownership shares were 11, 22 and 62 per cent respectively in 1981. Ownership in foreign-controlled joint ventures in 1981 was 9 per cent state, 13 per cent *pribumi*, 10 per cent Chinese and 68 per cent foreign (Balassa, 1991: 125). IS industrial promotion in Indonesia lacked screening, monitoring, technology appraisal and time-bound performance standards. While the IS sector was the main source of manufacturing growth in Indonesia until the mid-1980s, Indonesian IS promotion differed substantially from that of South Korea and Taiwan. Lack of emphasis on performance standards and competitiveness resulted in heavy, dead-weight rent losses. The IS sector not only failed to push technology to greater frontiers, but also sapped rents unproductively. Nevertheless, some local IS firms improved owing to their production experience, and subsequently participated in export-oriented subcontracting, especially garment making, but only in simple, low-value-added manufacturing activities for foreign companies.

After Suharto took power, the liberalization that followed allowed the emergence of private manufacturing enterprises. Considerable primary commodity exports – particularly oil – helped keep the balance-of-payments deficit down. The state had resumed IS policies in the 1970s to spawn local industry and reduce imports. IS development was, however, constrained by rent dissipation by powerful interest groups enjoying privileged control of much of the heavy industry. With political protection and oil revenues, most state-supported IS industries were under little pressure to perform. The IS sector not only created disincentives against exports in resource allocation, but also offered no strategy for technological development. These enterprises expanded exports only when provided with export incentives (such as subsidized credit refinancing and export abatement allowances) and corporate tax holidays for exporting firms from the late 1980s. Also, where politicians and the army-led bureaucracy were involved, significant leakage took place against protection, as their proxies and cronies often smuggled in and out various goods. IS industrialization nonetheless helped generate capabilities in light and resource industries, which subsequently facilitated subcontracting for export, albeit only in simple, low-value manufacturing.

Malaysia
The Malaysian government began industrial promotion with the enactment of the Pioneer Industries Ordinance in 1958 after independence in 1957. The government offered pioneer status incentives, which exempted firms from corporate taxes for periods of five to ten years. Intervention during the IS phase was limited to tariffs on imported final goods and tax holidays for new industrial enterprises. There was no ownership regulation and industry prioritization. Hence, unlike in Indonesia and Thailand, the freedom to fully own their enterprises, regardless of size, was initially mainly enjoyed by foreign and ethnic Chinese capital. Pioneer firms were protected from unions. Thus, foreign firms relocated operations in Malaysia to circumvent tariffs, enjoy tax holidays and increase domestic market shares. Given the small internal market, industrial growth slowed down after the period 1958–60. The share of manufacturing in GDP, thus, stayed at around 9 per cent between 1960 and 1965. There was no emphasis on targeting, technology appraisal and performance standards.

In 1968 emphasis shifted to export-orientation when the Investment

Incentives Act was enacted. As it gradually lost the earlier incentives, the IS sector continued alongside the EO sector, but declined in importance. The manufactured exports sector was initially dominated by resource processing industries, which, given their proximity to resource supplies, usually enjoyed clear static comparative advantage over other processors further afield. Thus, other metals (particularly smelted tin) accounted for 65.8 per cent of manufactured exports in 1968 (see Rasiah, 2003: Table 10). The absence of dynamic industrial policy instruments limited the evolution of large-scale metal and rubber using intermediate and final goods manufacturing, despite the imposition of export taxes on off-estate and off-mine processed exports.[11]

As noted earlier, Malaysia enjoyed high savings and very low inflation until the first oil crisis struck in 1973. There was, however, little effort to channel the high savings into supporting local infant industries during the early years of IS industrialization. Instead, foreign companies relocated final 'screwdriver' activities in Malaysia to capture the protected market. However, saturation of the small domestic market militated against considerable expansion. With little pressure or incentive to enhance efficiency, e.g. through gradual exposure to external competition, the IS sector hardly expanded. Sluggish labour absorption by the sector exacerbated unemployment, contributing to growing ethno-populism and related political tensions in the country that culminated in the ethnic riots of 13 May 1969.

Following the promulgation of the Industrial Co-ordination Act (ICA) in 1975, ethnic ownership requirements were imposed on manufacturing firms depending on size and market orientation. Licensing was required for firms with equity of over RM250,000 and employment size of 25 or more. The Minister of Trade and Industry often enforced the 30 per cent Bumiputera equity condition before approving applications for manufacturing licences. Since export-oriented companies were exempted from the legislation, there was no export disincentive. The registration floor was subsequently raised a few times; since 1986 it has remained at RM2.5 million equity and 75 or more employees. The neglect of efforts to promote technology development, institutional support and gradual exposure to competition left IS policy moribund. Given the ICA's emphasis on ethnic redistribution, ownership of IS industries generally became dominated by local capital. Beverages and tobacco were clear exceptions, as foreign capital continued to own more than 60 per cent of the combined equity capital. While tariffs were continued, albeit in a declining trend, the government did not renew financial incentives to IS firms. Restrictive conditions on companies enjoying tax holidays hindered the development of inter-firm linkages between foreign and IS firms. The

regulations required the orderly movement of goods to and from the free
trade zones (FTZs) and licensed manufacturing warehouses (LMWs) to
minimize tariff evasion rather than linkage development. Thus, IS firms
benefited relatively little from the export-oriented activities of foreign
firms. Domestic industry, thus, gradually became peripheral to export-
oriented manufacturing. The accumulated experience of some local IS
enterprises nevertheless facilitated their subsequent involvement in export-
oriented subcontracting – especially in knitting, garment making and
wood-based products. However, their participation was limited to simple
original equipment manufacturing (OEM) activities, which restricted their
capacity to export to low-value-added activities, while higher-value-added
chains were controlled by foreign firms.

From 1981, following the introduction of the Heavy Industries
Corporation of Malaysia (HICOM), state-controlled joint ventures with
foreign capital began to invest in heavy industries. For example, Kedah
Cement, Perwaja Steel and Proton all launched in the early 1980s and
experienced heavy losses following a sharp fall in domestic demand in the
mid-1980s. Except for Perwaja,[12] which made a loss of RM2.9 billion in
1995, the others have made substantial profits, mainly rents from tariffs
and quotas (Rasiah, 1995; Rokiah Alavi, 1996). Proton embarked on
export promotion. While heavily subsidized credit and high tariffs were
key to Proton's profits, ineffective rent management, including the apparent lack of performance standards, limited efficiency gains. After growth
of exports in the period 1986–93, when they reached a high of 19.3 per cent
of sales, they fell to 12.4 per cent in 1995. Within the domestic economy,
Proton's prices continued to rise, until the financial slump of 1997 forced
price cuts, while protective tariffs remained high (Rasiah, 1997). Hence,
while Proton's profits have soared since 1989, they have largely been due
to the high tariffs paid by other vehicle imports or Malaysian-assembled
vehicles.

IS industrialization in Malaysia has been characterized by government
failures. Except for tariffs on final consumption goods, the phase between
1958 and 1967 resembled laissez-faireism. There was little real emphasis on
developing infant industries, and institutional support for such development was minimal. Ethnic redistribution requirements were imposed on
IS firms from 1975. Some analysts believe these measures enhanced stability and thus helped to sustain growth (Rasiah and Ishak, 1994), although
they stifled non-Bumiputera SMI growth. From 1981, a second round of
IS minimally involved state-led heavy industries. As in the earlier phase,
IS continued to operate without effective institutional support or emphasis
on technology management and competition. Some labour- and resource-
intensive sub-sectors such as garment making and wood-based products,

nevertheless, gradually developed to become international export subcontractors, but only in simple OEM activities.

The Philippines
The lack of natural oil reserves and the remains of colonial as well as wartime destruction delayed efforts to build infrastructure and restore economic development in the Philippines. Nevertheless, as Ofreneo *et al.* (2006: 14) noted, organized manufacturing grew by 10 per cent per annum in the 1950s to reach 12.7 per cent of GDP in 1962. A combination of American and Sino-Filipino capital started processing, assembly and packaging activities in this period. Colgate, Coca-Cola, Procter & Gamble, Union Carbide, Carnation and United Laboratories were among the big companies that relocated operations in this period. The landed bourgeoisie, led by people such as Lopezes, Aranetas and Ledesmas, took advantage of the protection to expand into manufacturing.

Despite the expansion in value added, manufacturing under import-substitution in the Philippines failed to achieve significant levels of catch-up. Firstly, the government focused only on stimulating investments in manufacturing with incentives and protection without a clear strategy of promoting technological catch-up. Secondly, the imposition of tariffs on final goods encouraged considerable imports of materials and capital goods with little exports, thereby aggravating the balance of payments. If Korea sought to overcome its balance-of-payments and external debt problems in 1976 following a fourfold rise in oil prices in 1973–75 by imposing export performance standards on the heavy industries that were started in 1970, President Diosdado Macapagal managed a US$300 million aid from the International Monetary Fund (IMF). Hence, while Korea continued with its stable exchange rate regime, subsidized credit for preferred industrialists and a dynamic set of technology absorption and catch-up strategies, the Philippines was forced to float its peso and remove import and foreign exchange controls. As the liberalization aggravated further the balance-of-payments problems, the government raised tariffs to as high as 200 per cent on some items (Ofreneo, 2008: 15). IMF pressure again forced the government to devalue the peso in 1969–70.

Pro-American policies did not help, as increased liberalization on one hand, rising protection on the other hand where crony interests were dominant and a general disregard for poverty alleviation generated considerable opposition to the government. With domestic initiatives seemingly incapable of resolving the threat of poverty as it translated into communism, the government sought external support by seeking export-oriented industrialization from the early 1970s. However, export-orientation began with import-substitution industrialization (ISI) remaining dominant outside export processing zones.

ISI continued in the Philippines throughout the Marcos regime and only fell in significance from the mid-1980s following the takeover by the populist government of Corazon Aquino. Particularly the rich, both the landlord class and Chinese businessmen, began to grow as they fed on the IS rents (Billig, 2003; Hutchinson, 2007). A number of family conglomerates expanded to appropriate monopoly rents from the domestic economy (Carroll, 1965; Power and Sicat, 1971; Hutchcroft, 1994a, 1994b). Sugar processing and tobacco manufacturing in particular had remained protected under Marcos, though the lack of technical change left domestic consumers to absorb prices significantly higher than world prices. Both Aquino and Ramos sought to liberalize the economy, and hence these industries were either wiped out or contracted sharply as competition rose, particularly during the government of Ramos. The trade regime in the Philippines became even more liberal as tariffs fell under the common effective preferential tariff programme following the imposition of the ASEAN Free Trade Area process. The World Trade Organization accelerated the process as the Philippines became a signatory to the liberalization process initiated (see Ofreneo, 2003).

Hence, a combination of misguided IS efforts, which created an oligarchy whose conglomerates drove an inefficient domestic sector, which not only had a knock-on effect on domestic prices but also prevented quality improvements, as well as the reliance on heavy imports of materials and capital machinery and equipment, undermined the balance of payments of the Philippines. The balance-of-payments crisis forced the Philippine government to seek assistance from the IMF, which was accompanied by stringent conditions to liberalize. Forced deregulation marginalized the rentier operations of the conglomerates, which began to face stiff competition from imports and rising import prices as the peso fell in value.

Thailand

The Thai government started venturing into consumer and intermediate goods manufacturing after the Second World War. Considerable abuse of rents led to a shift in state emphasis, beginning in the late 1950s, away from manufacturing to infrastructure development. Investments in energy, transportation and communications helped construct an environment conducive for private firms to emerge and develop. The creation of the Board of Investment (BOI) and the enactment of the Promotion of Investment Act in 1960 stimulated private manufacturing investment. The government appears to have followed World Bank (1959) advice, which, inter alia, prescribed the improvement of infrastructure, promotion of private enterprises (e.g. through provision of low-interest credit), promotion of IS industries and rational development planning. The state stringently avoided competing against and nationalizing private business (Hewison, 1985: 279). Among other things, five-year development plans, starting from 1961–66, have continuously emphasized industrial development. State-led mobilization of the financial sector was launched with the reorganization of the financial and banking sector in 1959. The state offered subsidized credit to approved investors. Loans, at low or no interest, were extended to promote private investment. The Industrial Finance Corporation of Thailand (IFCT), formed in 1959, enjoyed state support and participation by Thai and foreign banks (Hewison, 1985: 282–373) which largely funded big businesses. Agricultural exports were given major importance in the first development plan, but industrialization – with particular emphasis on private IS industries – was strongly promoted as well. The government reduced its role in infrastructure development and in promotion of private industrial initiatives with credit support and tariffs. Government intervention, thus, had a pro-private sector bias. Unlike the case in Malaysia and Indonesia, the private sector in Thailand has had greater influence over the allocation of contracts and rents.

From a brief flirtation with indigenization in the 1950s, the state's focus shifted to the broad promotion of national capital from the 1960s. Irrespective of ethnic background, Thai capital began to receive state support. Industrial promotion was complemented by state efforts to limit labour organization, which restricted the cost of labour.[13] Although this draconian strategy adversely affected workers, it attracted both local and foreign investors. Thus, although no explicit industrial master plans were drawn up, the Thai state consciously sought to expand the share of manufacturing and industry in the economy through the promotion of private firms. The first and second five-year plans, lasting until 1971, emphasized the development of IS industries, albeit without clear targeting. Tariffs on final goods were raised, while export taxes were levied to meet domestic demand. There was no emphasis on technological screening, monitoring and promotion. In addition, the promotion of private IS firms appeared as a decisive way to overcome the weaknesses that afflicted state-owned enterprises. The anti-export biases and lack of effective institutional support restricted expansion so that the share of manufactures in overall exports was 7.1 per cent in 1961 and 13.3 per cent in 1971, while manufacturing's share of GDP was 13 and 16 per cent respectively in the years 1960 and 1970. Thai-controlled resource-intensive food and jewellery industries dominated manufactured exports in the 1960s (see Rasiah, 2003: Table 11). Textiles and clothing – including exports, thanks to the Multi-Fibre Arrangement (MFA) privileges – also became a major export.

IS – the main source of growth in Thailand until 1979 – helped spawn several industries, but also increased costs. Tariffs raised the costs of capital goods and intermediate inputs, and were only clumsily offset by investment promotion concessions tied to exports (Pasuk and Baker, 1995: 144–5). While certain IS industries flourished, for example textiles, related export disincentives discouraged exports (Narongchai, 1973a, 1973b). The IS phase was characterized not only by falling consumer good imports, but also by sharply rising capital and intermediate good imports. The latter did not result in the eventual development of domestic capabilities in the manufacture of intermediate and capital goods and therefore, as in Indonesia and Malaysia, did not facilitate their exports.

During the IS phase, buoyant agricultural performance helped subsidize expansion of the protected manufacturing sector. However, prolonged protection without substantial manufactured exports began to increase the trade deficit – causing a serious drain on commodity exports. The need for foreign exchange and reduction of the trade deficit led to the introduction of EO industrialization from 1972. The third development plan propounded promotion of both EO and IS industrialization. Unlike the case in Malaysia, FDI was less important in Thailand's IS phase. Malaysia's colonial past, with strong foreign capital participation, contrasts with its reduced presence in Thailand. Direct foreign investment constituted only 2.1–4.2 per cent of overall gross fixed capital formation in the Thai economy in the period 1960–71 (Hewison, 1987: Table 3.3). The decline of indigenization policies from the late 1950s allowed ethnic Chinese capital to expand production into IS activities. Several such firms eventually managed to gain international export subcontracting capabilities (Rock, 1996), but only in simple and low-value-added OEM activities that relied on low wages and foreign-controlled market niches.

Ethnic considerations and subsequent ethnic-biased policies limited political support to emerging domestic industrial capital in Indonesia from 1945 and in Malaysia from 1971. In Thailand, however, the abandonment of such policies from the late 1950s allowed greater participation by Thai industrial capital, which has been dominated by ethnic Chinese. Swelling trade deficits in Thailand and Indonesia, and growing socio-economic problems in Malaysia were instrumental in the reduction of emphasis on IS strategies. Only in Malaysia and Indonesia, where state ownership is still important, has IS remained important. Even in these economies, export-orientation has become the main engine of growth. Unlike the dynamic experiences of Japan, South Korea and Taiwan, IS in Malaysia, Indonesia and Thailand lacked effective governance to raise infant industries' technological capabilities and eventually face international competition. In Malaysia, liberal ownership regulations and lack of effective discipline and institutionalization of the risks to non-Bumiputera firms in the early years removed 'creative destruction' of local firms to enter IS activities. Subsidies and tariffs were offered that did not demand discipline from firms nor develop complementary institutions that would spur them to success. After some early expansion in all three economies, growth of IS industries slowed down until the emergence of the export-oriented sector, which helped expand consumer demand. The protected sector has continued in Indonesia, Malaysia and Thailand, but with few structural links among them. In Indonesia and Malaysia, a massive injection of state capital has helped expand heavy industries. So far there is little evidence to suggest that these ventures are emulating the Northeast Asian experiences of eventually achieving international competitiveness. Nonetheless, the IS sector in all three economies has helped generate some local capabilities in light, low-value-added labour- and resource-intensive activities such as wood and garments, to facilitate their participation in international export subcontracting. The lack of both institutional development and emphasis on technological deepening has, however, limited their involve ment to low-value-added and OEM activities. Thus, although the IS phase generated some local export capabilities, poor governance has limited technological deepening, which will not be sustainable in the long run as unit costs rise further.

SHIFT TO MANUFACTURED EXPORTS

Export-oriented industrialization in Indonesia, Malaysia, the Philippines and Thailand involved considerable state promotion and subsidies. As Thailand has no officially acknowledged industrial policy, its industrial sector has by far been the most liberal of the four, though government intervention has been crucial for its industrialization. Malaysia's industrial drive from the early 1970s was led by firms new to the country. Foreign capital has dominated all the leading non-resource-based EO manufacturing sectors in Malaysia. Once the Philippines' preoccupation with IS industrialization ended, by the end of the Marcos regime, export-orientation manufacturing was promoted largely through liberal investment instruments. In Indonesia and Thailand, though, domestic capital has dominated resource-based industries. Selective promotion, influenced by resource endowments, helped achieve substantial exports of plywood and timber products from Indonesia, palm oil and timber products from Malaysia, and food and jewellery from Thailand. Apart from these resource-based industries, whose value addition has not usually been very technology-intensive, foreign capital has generally dominated most other manufactured export sectors. Participation by domestic enterprises in non-resource-based products was largely limited to low-value-added assembly and processing activities, with designs and markets mainly controlled by foreign firms. Substantial export promotion, with credit and tax subsidies, has helped domestic firms become subcontractors. Such exports expanded – especially since 1986 – and by the 1990s production costs for such activities had escalated. There was also no effective regulatory framework to restrict capital flows to speculative and other undesirable investments. Employment and investment were the objectives of the initial export-oriented manufacturing thrusts in Indonesia, Malaysia, the Philippines and Thailand. However, given its significant factor endowments and lack of institutional development, FDI expanded generally in labour- and resource-intensive industries.

As noted earlier, IS did not create the conditions for EO in the second-tier NIEs, unlike in the first-tier East Asian NIEs. In South Korea and Taiwan, IS helped spawn widespread domestic export capabilities through extensive credit financing, and government regulated and subsidized loans to support the development of domestic capabilities, but also strictly enforced stringent performance standards (Amsden, 1989; Wade, 1990; Chang, 1994). Either the latter was absent or there was no link between the two in Indonesia, Malaysia, the Philippines and Thailand. The initial IS phases in the second-tier NIEs were characterized by incoherent strategies with little emphasis on the development of domestic technological capabilities for eventual international competitiveness. Export-orientation in these economies, thus, did not arise as a follow-up phase in their development trajectories. Instead, it appeared as an attempt to alleviate pressing socio-economic problems that the IS phase had failed to resolve. The IS sector coexisted alongside the EO sector in Malaysia, with little structural link between the two. Indonesia experienced a similar situation until the collapse of Suharto in 1998, after which import-substitution was gradually ended. External developments and the flow of foreign direct investment largely accounted for export expansion, albeit from low-value-added manufacturing, which largely relocated to the Southeast Asian second-tier NIEs because of favourable domestic political economy conditions. Growing demand, generated by EO manufacturing, helped stimulate growth in the IS sectors eventually, which grew as GDP expanded.

Export-oriented industries were grafted alongside the existing IS sector in Malaysia without any systematic efforts to develop linkages between the two. Agencies such as the World Bank (IBRD), Asia Productivity Centre, United Nations Industrial Development Organization (UNIDO) and Asian Development Bank (ADB) were instrumental in the emergence of export processing zones in all three economies. Indonesia adopted the EO strategy in 1986, primarily because of falling export revenues as primary commodity prices nose-dived. Malaysia's EO industrialization began with the Investment Incentives Act (IIA) in 1968, but only got going after the free trade zones (FTZs) were opened in 1972. It took some time for the first major wave of EO manufacturing firms to relocate production in Malaysia. The special zones and incentives helped reduce infrastructural problems and offset the risks associated with relocating to unproven sites. Thailand's EO industrialization was first launched with initiatives in the mid-1970s, but took off from around 1979.

The relocation of transnational corporations to Southeast Asia involved two massive spurts in the periods 1969–74 and 1986–93 respectively. The first period was driven primarily by transnational efforts to seek relatively sympathetic governments, relatively cheap and non-unionized labour, tax holidays, politically stable sites and good infrastructure (see Lim, 1978; Rasiah, 1987). Also important was the market access to North America and Europe the Southeast Asian NIEs enjoyed from Generalized System of Preferences (GSP) privileges and MFA quotas. Singapore, the Philippines and Malaysia were the favourite investment sites in Southeast Asia in the first period. Singapore had abandoned IS completely in 1967 after seceding from Malaysia in 1965, while the Philippines and Malaysia launched export processing zones in the early 1970s alongside existing IS manufacturing. The regulatory frameworks in Thailand and Indonesia remained highly IS-oriented in this period so that EO firms locating there enjoyed little advantage over the other more EO-oriented ASEAN economies. In addition, anti-foreign capital sentiments discouraged investment flows to Indonesia in the 1970s. Unlike Malaysia and the Philippines, which offered liberal ownership conditions, especially for exporting firms, Indonesia and Thailand generally allowed only joint ventures in the 1970s. Transnational companies, thus, preferred to relocate labour-intensive assembly operations to Malaysia and the Philippines in the 1970s. However, political instability had undermined the Philippines' attractiveness by the late 1970s. Rising wages and other costs, space scarcity and deliberate state policy to promote higher-value-added manufacturing operations drove labour-intensive firms away from Singapore from the late 1970s (Rasiah, 1987; Henderson, 1990). Thus, Malaysia became the most attractive site for labour-intensive manufacturing activities in the early 1980s. In the period 1972–85, electric/electronics and textiles and garments, both labour-intensive manufacturing activities dominated by foreign ownership, grew to account for 63.3 per cent of manufactured exports and over 30 per cent of manufacturing value added. Much of this expansion involved massive imports of intermediate and capital goods.

The second period was characterized by massive relocation of foreign direct investment from Japan and the first-tier East Asian NIEs. The Plaza Accord of 1985, appreciation of their currencies, withdrawal of the GSP privileges in 1988 and rising trade barriers encouraged relocation of their export-oriented manufacturing activities. Indonesia, Malaysia and Thailand were important beneficiaries of this current. All three countries tuned their promotional policies to better attract FDI in EO manufacturing. Growing human resource scarcities and infrastructural bottlenecks in the major industrial locations began scaling down Malaysia's attractiveness as a low-cost production site from the late 1980s and early 1990s. Instead, Indonesia, Thailand and the Philippines have become important.

In some foreign-dominated export processing industries, a regional division of labour emerged from the 1970s until the late 1980s. In electronics manufacturing, for example, high-value-added and regional customization activities were located in Singapore. Before its protracted political crisis worsened, the Philippines had a similar status to Malaysia in the early 1970s. Under the MFA, individual country quotas have been important in the textile and garment making industries, and foreign production has hence been fairly equally spread among these economies (Rasiah, 1990). Rising costs in preferred locations, that is, Malaysia, did not drive away foreign investors in electronics assembly operations to cheaper cost sites elsewhere. While experience, administrative efficiency and customs coordination have been important, the continued presence of assembly and test operations in Malaysia since the late 1980s has also been due to the changing dynamics of production driven by competition and technological evolution. Automation and in-house skill deepening have become necessary to sustain miniaturization in the microelectronics industry. Highly labour-intensive, low-value-added activities such as printed circuit board (PCB) and audio assembly were partly relocated to Indonesia. Where such assembly has involved higher-value-added functions or operations, as with semiconductors, the enterprises have opted to automate production rather than relocate. In textiles and garment manufacturing, the MFA has also limited the extent of relocation from Malaysia to cheaper cost sites. The impending removal of such quotas under the WTO is likely to encourage relocation to cheaper sites that enjoy large labour reserves, such as in China and India.

The unprecedented volume of foreign capital inflows in the second half of the 1980s and early 1990s, as well as increased efforts by host governments to attract them, intensified international and inter-regional rivalries and inter-firm rivalries to secure maximum advantage from incentives and other conditions. Serious labour and land shortages and infrastructural bottlenecks impelled Singapore to initiate regional cooperation strategies that would upgrade as the high-value-added technology and services apex of the Singapore–Johore–Riau (SIJORI) growth triangle (Low and Tan, 1996). Similar cross-border regional initiatives have sprung up in other parts of the Southeast Asian region. Growing regional cooperation has also helped Southeast Asian governments to coordinate their strategies vis-à-vis transnationals and to limit the bargaining power of the latter resulting from 'beggar thy neighbour' policies.

Controls on operations by foreign capital were gradually reduced and subsidies enhanced to further promote export-oriented manufacturing operations in all three economies. Laws on labour and industrial relations were tightened to restrict workers' wages, working conditions and mobility. Draconian labour legislation was introduced to control labour and limit unions (Robison, 1986; Rasiah, 1987, 1995; Jomo and Todd, 1994; Sungsidh, 1995). In Malaysia, for example, only enterprise unions have been allowed in the electronics industry and that too from 1989 (Rasiah, 1996a).[14] Many labour leaders and activists have been threatened or even eliminated in Thailand and Indonesia (Sungsidh, 1995; Rasiah and Chua, 1997). Clearly, interventionist labour policies to promote export growth have undermined the bargaining power of workers. Therefore, real wages grew little in these economies in the initial stages; on average they fell by 1.2 per cent annually in Malaysia in the period 1963–73 before growing at 2.0 per cent per annum in the period 1971–81 (Rasiah, 1994a: Table 10). Thailand saw real wage growth of 2.0 per cent per annum in the period 1973–81. Real wages began to grow faster only from the second half of the 1980s, largely owing to labour shortages in key industrial locations and in skilled work categories. Real wages in Indonesia grew on average by 3.4 per cent in 1983–89, in Malaysia by 3.5 per cent in 1980–88 and in Thailand by 2.8 per cent in 1981–89.

Indonesia

As noted earlier, IS dominated manufacturing activities in Indonesia until the mid-1980s. High oil prices in the period 1973–82 gave the state the financial muscle to invest heavily in industrial infrastructure. Industrial growth, however, began slowing down from the end of the 1970s despite further oil price rises. Incentives to export began to emerge towards the end of the 1970s, though the government continued to prioritize IS until the mid-1980s. From the late 1970s, a dual strategy of IS and EO industrialization began to evolve, but without much connection between the two. Export subsidies were introduced in November 1978 to offset tariffs and taxes on imported inputs and overcome the high costs of protected domestic inputs (Balassa, 1991: 122). Export credits followed in January 1982 under preferential credit schemes, which were phased out from March

1985; in April 1986, they were replaced by duty drawbacks on raw material and machinery imports used in manufacturing for export. Firms exporting at least 85 per cent of production were exempted from domestic content requirements from May 1986. Firms with lower export/output percentages were allowed duty drawbacks on imported raw materials and machinery if import prices were lower than domestic supplies. The cumbersome certification process, however, made this scheme unpopular. The list of products involving export bans, licences and quotas was reduced sharply in 1987.

The highest tariffs for most products fell from 225 to 60 per cent, while the number of tariff lines was reduced from 25 to 11 in March 1985. Measures were taken to offer total duty drawback on inputs for exporters in May 1986. From the end of 1987, other anti-export biases were gradually eliminated (Tjiptoherijanto, 1993: Table 5). Also, a Swiss firm replaced customs officials to control the import and export of goods, simplifying duty controls and eliminating unproductive rent seeking.[15] Corrupt practices in Indonesia's customs department were virtually eliminated by Presidential Instruction No. 4 (Pangestu, 1993: 13); as a consequence, holding and inspection periods decreased by several weeks. Such reductions in customs processing time and in wasteful rents also reduced uncertainties and costs. Thus, private business obviously helped reduce government failures that had inhibited the effective coordination of production and distribution. The government gave back jurisdiction to the Customs Department on 1 May 1997, which some business interests claim has undermined earlier improvements achieved on cargo handling.[16] A revamped Customs Department can, of course, enhance bureaucratic efficiency, but, if the old practices return, they can slow things down, raise costs and create uncertainties. Meanwhile, many firms have begun stocking up inventories in response, raising holding and other such costs.

Textiles, garments, footwear and wood-based products were among the early export-oriented activities that grew rapidly in Indonesia from the late 1970s. Some Japanese and East Asian NIE companies relocated production to Indonesia to benefit from the country's MFA quotas. However, foreign equity ownership in Indonesia has been relatively low owing to uncertain ownership regulations (though they improved in the second half of the 1980s), and the preference of Indonesian firms to serve as putting-out subcontractors. The labour intensity and low technical content of many textiles, garments and wood-based products favoured relocation to Indonesia because of its abundant labour supply, low wages and natural resource endowments. A ban on log exports in the mid-1980s helped wood-based production (especially of plywood), adding low-value-added downstream activities to the timber value-added chain. Indonesia's output of over 50 per cent of the world's plywood has ensured some leverage in sustaining external demand. The share of plywood in overall manufactured exports grew from 10.8 per cent in 1980 to 37.1 per cent in 1986 (computed from Rasiah, 2003: Table 9). Owing to the low-value-added content of its production, limits to the sustainability of timber supply and similar promotion of downstream activities in competing economies through controls on log exports from the late 1980s, Indonesia's plywood manufacturing expansion has been overshadowed by the growth in textile and garment exports since the second half of the 1980s. Thus, the share of plywood in overall manufactured exports dropped to 18.4 per cent in 1991. Primarily Indonesian export-oriented resource-based firms began to expand into export processing ventures. The share of textiles, garments and footwear in overall manufactured exports rose from 22.7 per cent in 1980 to 27.3 per cent in 1986 and 38.6 per cent in 1991 (computed from Rasiah, 2003: Table 9), much of which was dominated by foreign-operated joint ventures and Indonesian subcontractors performing low-value-added activities.

Although emphasis on export-oriented manufacturing began in 1978, it has only become important since the second half of the 1980s, when oil and agricultural commodity prices had fallen sharply. Active deregulation began in 1983 with the service sector, especially banking and education. Bapeksta was formed in that year to undertake export promotion (APDC, 1987), with new incentives as one of its major promotional instruments. Export processing zones, export credits, duty drawbacks (on imported inputs and machinery) and tax holidays helped attract foreign investment. A combination of foreign labour-intensive firms seeking cheaper workers and third country market access, and domestic policy reforms helped stimulate EO manufacturing from the second half of the 1980s. Consequently the share of manufactures in total exports grew from 2.3 per cent in 1980 to 47.3 per cent in 1992 (see Rasiah, 2003: Table 5).

The trade reform package of 1988 allowed imports of steel and plastic raw materials, which had previously been produced and supplied by state monopolies. However, the government left control of steel imports to the state-owned steel maker, and of polystyrene and polyethylene to a state-owned trading firm so that only demand in excess of domestic production could be imported. Tariff ceilings on most imported products were reduced to 40 per cent in 1990. However, opposition by the politically well connected has constrained some reforms. For example, the automobile sector experienced increased tariffs from 1990 to protect production by joint ventures involving the president's family.

Gradual ownership liberalization from the early 1980s led to a fall in the share of state-owned enterprises among manufacturing enterprises, from 28 per cent in 1975 to 20 per cent in 1983 (Balassa, 1991: 125). State-owned enterprises have been primarily concentrated in heavy industries:

oil refineries, petrochemicals, fertilizers, steel, aluminium and aeroplanes. In addition, state ownership has dominated in cement, basic chemicals, capital goods and shipbuilding. The promotion of *pribumi* business led to the introduction of the Small Investment Credit and Permanent Working Capital Credit schemes, and the reservation of a long list of items for procurement to *pribumi* businesses. It is unclear if the liberalization efforts from the 1980s have actually facilitated achieving international competitiveness.

Some heavy industry ventures have been profitable owing to heavy tariff protection. Interviews suggest that the protected automobile industry, with its high prices, is far from achieving international competitiveness. There has nevertheless been a rise in Indonesian component suppliers, with some even exporting to neighbouring countries (Doner, 1991). However, it appears that the component industry, which has benefited from foreign technology, has not gone beyond simple and OEM activities. These firms lack institutional support to progress to higher-value activities, e.g. design and direct marketing.[17] Ownership deregulation in manufacturing became more pronounced from 1986. Domestic equity requirements in high-risk export-oriented firms were lowered to 5 per cent from the 20 per cent previously required, while others were given a five-year grace period to achieve the 20 per cent Indonesian equity ownership requirement. The share of exports in output, initially set at 80 per cent to qualify for these generous equity conditions, was later reduced to 60 per cent (Pangestu, 1993: 16). Companies locating in Batam, which operates as an export processing zone, are allowed full foreign equity ownership. Firms exporting all output have been exempted from the 5 per cent divestment required over the five years. The divestment requirement for other firms was set at 51 per cent over 15 years. Foreign firms could be licensed for an additional 30 years. Investment licensing was further relaxed in 1987. The elimination of the requirement for approval for capacity expansion of less than 30 per cent and for diversification to related product lines has helped reduce red tape. Private institutions, including foreign concerns, have been allowed to set up industrial estates since 1989. These initiatives suggest a shift in ownership gradually to private concerns and reduced bias against foreign capital.

The mid-1980s also experienced three devaluations, most recently in September 1986, which amounted to a massive 50 per cent fall in the value of the rupiah. Unlike in the past when a fixed exchange rate policy was pursued after devaluation, from 1988 the government has depreciated the rupiah by around 5 per cent annually to stabilize Indonesia's real effective exchange rate (Pangestu, 1993: 14). Coming just after the Plaza Accord of 1985, the rupiah's devaluation of 1986 appeared more significant than the 50 per cent devaluations in 1978 and 1983. The appreciation of the yen, won and Singapore and Taiwan dollars further lowered the costs of production and exports from Indonesia. Currency appreciation and rising trade barriers in developed economies against exports from Japan and the East Asian NIEs pushed manufacturing operations out from these economies. Indonesia became an important recipient of such foreign capital and of related international subcontracting opportunities. The share of FDI in total domestic investment, which had initially fallen from 4.6 per cent in 1971–75 to 1.0 per cent in 1981–85, rose again to 4.5 per cent in 1991–93 (see Rasiah, 2003: Table 2). The more advanced transnational corporate operations in Singapore and, to a lesser extent, Malaysia helped generate demand for the location of lower-end, labour-intensive stages of production, with the promotion of growth triangles boosting such operations in Indonesia. Hence, the shift in policy emphasis to export-orientation, along with increased FDI, helped to sharply expand the contribution of manufacturing to the economy. The share of manufacturing in GDP rose to 22 per cent in 1993 (see Rasiah, 2003: Table 3), while manufactures accounted for 47.3 per cent of overall exports in 1992 (see Rasiah, 2003: Table 5).

Despite the increase in foreign direct investment, the share of foreign equity ownership in the manufacturing sector has remained well below half in all industries. The highest sectoral share of foreign equity control in 1988 still remained below 40 per cent of total equity – paper products (39.7 per cent), other chemicals (38.6 per cent) and non-electrical machinery (37.1 per cent) (Hill, 1996: Table 8.4).[18] These shares probably rose in the 1990s, following the exhaustion of labour reserves in Malaysia's key industrial zones. Also, the foreign share of manufacturing is likely to be much higher owing to commercial arrangements (see Hill, 1996: 165).

Overall economic reform has attracted more foreign capital and reduced the creation and appropriation of unproductive rents but has yet to provide the impetus for rapid technological catch-up. Regional production strategies by transnational corporations have driven a rise in exports of automotive products, with Indonesia's contribution to global exports rising from 0.01 per cent in 1990 to 0.06 per cent in 2000 and 0.17 per cent in 2006 (WTO, 2007: Appendix Table 11.54). However, Indonesia's contribution to global electronics exports fell from 0.8 per cent in 2000 to 0.4 per cent in 2006 (WTO, Appendix Table 11.64). Indonesia's contribution to global clothing exports also fell from 2.4 per cent in 2000 to 1.8 per cent in 2006 (WTO, 2007: Appendix Table 11.64).

Policy reforms to promote export-oriented manufacturing in Indonesia have focused primarily on direct instruments to attract foreign investment and stimulate exports. There has been little emphasis on institutional development to create the requisite capabilities for structural deepening – such

as human resource development, technology absorption and development and performance assessment. Deregulation – rather than improved
financial and educational (including training) services – appears to have
further reduced the potential for expanding institutional support. Indeed,
in Indonesia, no institutions exist to vet, monitor and appraise technology
transfer agreements. Although rapid export-led growth has contributed
to a steady rise in manufacturing and GDP, the lack of institutions to
enable technological deepening and of stronger linkages with the domestic
economy limits the potential for higher productivity, especially adversely
affecting competitiveness. Consequently, Indonesian enterprises are still
largely limited to simple processing activities, with the most advanced
firms using OEM capabilities to produce for transnational companies.

Malaysia

Export promotion in Malaysia began following the enactment of the
Investment Incentives Act in 1968, but accelerated after the opening of
the FTZs. Investment incentives have been particularly important in
Malaysia. Forty-eight per cent of the manufacturing investment projects
approved by the Malaysian Industrial Development Authority (MIDA)
in the period 1980–90 consisted of granted investment incentives (Ismail
Salleh, 1995: 49). Unlike Indonesia and Thailand, Malaysia has never
imposed restrictions on manufactured exports. Export taxes have been
levied only on primary – agricultural and mineral – products. Exporting
firms, however, faced indirect barriers in the form of incentives going to IS
firms in the 1960s and to state-sponsored heavy industries since the 1980s.
The FTZ Act removed all tariffs and customs controls involving export
processing companies located in the FTZs.[19] Where individual firms have
a preferred location outside FTZs, similar incentives have been granted
under the Licensed Manufacturing Warehouse (LMW) arrangements.
Pioneer Status (PS) and the Investment Tax Allowance (ITA) have been
among the most generous incentives given to enterprises operating in these
zones. PS offered tax holidays for a period of five to ten years. The PS and
ITA together accounted for 98 per cent of all incentives granted to the
manufacturing sector in the period 1980–90 (Ismail Salleh, 1995: 49). The
government has also offered several other export-promotion incentives.
The export credit insurance and export credit refinancing schemes – both
of which effectively subsidized export credit – were launched in 1977 to
stimulate exports.

In the 1970s, firms were also offered locational, labour utilization and
accelerated depreciation allowances. From 1986, following the enactment
of the Promotion of Investment Act (PIA), these incentives were scrapped,

but the PIA offered an array of other lucrative incentives to encourage exports. Amendments to the PIA in 1988 scaled down incentives for firms engaged in 'non-strategic' activities, and increased emphasis on training and research and development. Tax exemptions for firms granted PS and the ITA were reduced to 70 per cent of taxable income for firms exporting not less than 80 per cent of production. Strategic investors, however, could apply for total tax exemptions. With the PIA, the government also offered double deductions on taxable income from approved exports, until this programme was scrapped in the mid-1990s. These export incentives were instrumental in boosting Malaysian business exports in conjunction with international subcontracting, which has gradually declined following their elimination.

The government also introduced several non-tariff instruments to promote exports. The export insurance and refinancing schemes were launched in 1977. By the end of 1989, the insurance scheme had 192 policies valued at RM1.12 billion, with 26.7 per cent declared (Ismail Salleh, 1995: 52). A revamp in 1988 allowed extensions to the insurance scheme to cover commercial bank losses against loans, advances to exporters and suppliers. The export credit refinancing scheme offered subsidized credit, both pre- and post-shipment. Handled by Bank Negara, it has offered easy access to credit at preferential rates for firms with high value added and local content.[20] Pre-shipment financing grew at an average annual rate of 68 per cent to reach RM13.9 billion in 1989. The volume of exports refinanced under the export credit refinancing scheme rose from 3 per cent in 1977 to 22.5 per cent in 1989 (Ismail Salleh, 1995: 54).

Malaysia also devalued the ringgit and reoriented its incentives structure to attract the second wave of export-oriented foreign direct investment from the mid-1980s. The mid-1980s recession and rising foreign debt (accumulated as a result of increased government spending from the early 1980s, including a grandiose heavy industrialization programme) induced the government to offer generous financial incentives as part of the enactment of the Promotion of Investment Act in 1986. Good infrastructure, the successful export manufacturing experience of the 1970s and early 1980s, large reserves of unemployed labour, especially in the mid- and late 1980s, and political stability made Malaysia an attractive site for the second wave of foreign direct investment. Thus, the foreign share of manufacturing fixed assets rose from 35 per cent in 1985 to 50 per cent in 1990, with the share of foreign capital in the electric/electronics industry reaching 91 per cent in 1994.

Ownership regulations in Malaysia were far more liberal during the IS phase in the 1960s than from the mid-1970s, as national control of equity was not yet a priority. Ethnic ownership conditions were imposed after the introduction of the New Economic Policy (NEP), and in the manufacturing sector with the promulgation of the Industrial Co-ordination Act (ICA) in 1975. Firms with paid-up capital of RM250,000 and 25 or more employees were required to be licensed by the Ministry of Trade and Industry (now MITI). Ethnic ownership conditions were waived for enterprises exporting 80 per cent or more of their output. Export-oriented foreign firms, thus, faced no ownership requirements, while ethnic employment regulations were generally not strictly enforced. In fact, the government has generally only advised foreign firms applying to renew their incentives to absorb more Bumiputeras to reflect the national ethnic population structure (Rasiah, 1994b).

The ICA has particularly stifled Malaysian non-Bumiputera capital, which has to have 30 per cent Bumiputera equity to qualify for a licence. Given the limited Bumiputera capital in the 1970s, many non-Bumiputera capitalists had to virtually give away stock at heavy discounts to meet this condition. Foreign capital in the IS sector gradually experienced shifts in ownership. The ICA allowed only 30 per cent foreign ownership of equity for fully domestically oriented firms. But since the Act was enforced with substantial discretion by the Minister of Trade and Industry, several non-Bumiputera enterprises operated without meeting these conditions. In the case of beverages and tobacco, Bumiputera equity ownership requirements in alcoholic breweries were relaxed because of Muslim reservations. Foreign ownership of fixed assets in the beverage and tobacco industry exceeded 60 per cent in the period 1968–93 (Rasiah, 1997: Table 5.3). Several firms have also avoided licensing by declaring lower equity levels and expanding their liabilities instead.

The equity level for companies exempt from the ownership condition was raised in 1979 and again in 1985, and in 1986 when it was defined at RM2.5 million following the Promotion of Investment Act. By the late 1980s, a growing Bumiputera bourgeoisie meant that non-Bumiputera-controlled firms could now expect some contributions from their prospective Bumiputera partners. Bumiputera partners could also provide valuable connections and business options, making such partnerships more mutually lucrative (Yoshihara, 1988; Rasiah, 1995: Chapter 6). Also, a number of non-Bumiputera enterprises managed to obtain special waivers to operate without meeting ICA conditions, with some even successfully obtaining tax incentives. Sharing equity with Bumiputera interests seems to have been quite lucrative for several non-Bumiputera firms. Export-oriented foreign capital continued to enjoy total equity control. Ownership conditions for foreign export-oriented enterprises have, thus, remained very liberal in Malaysia. For some Malaysian firms, deregulation facilitated capacity expansion. Small and medium-scale enterprises in

Penang, with political links to the Gerakan-led Penang state government, have managed to attract capital from some leading Bumiputera holding companies (Rasiah, 1997). The Malaysian Technology Development Corporation (MTDC), formed by the government in 1993, began capitalization and promotion drives to support potentially successful high-technology exporters (Rasiah, 1996c).

Given the official policy emphasis and the nature of process technologies associated with export processing and assembly operations, Malaysia's manufacturing sector was dominated by highly labour-intensive activities between 1972 and the late 1980s. The share of electric/electronics, as well as textiles and clothing in manufacturing value added, grew from 8.1 per cent and 6.0 per cent respectively in 1973 to 22.5 per cent and 6.7 per cent respectively in 1990 (see Rasiah, 2004: Table 8). The corresponding shares in manufactured exports rose from 0.7 per cent and 1.4 per cent respectively in 1968 to 50.5 per cent and 8.8 per cent respectively in 1990 (see Rasiah, 2003: Table 9). It was only in the 1990s that the share of labour-intensive textile and clothing exports began to fall, declining to 5.1 per cent in 1995. The switch to automated production in electronics helped raise the share of electronics exports to 67.5 per cent in 1995. Consequently, resource-based industries, which accounted for much of manufactured exports from Malaysia in 1968, declined gradually in significance. The shares of other metals and food in total manufactured exports fell from 65.8 per cent and 17.5 per cent in 1968 to 2.5 per cent and 1.8 per cent respectively in 1995. The dramatic fall in exports of other metals was precipitated by declining tin reserves, rising production costs and the emergence of new low-cost producers such as Brazil and China (Jomo, 1990). Despite the domination of non-resource-based technology-intensive exports (for example electronics), Malaysia's manufactured exports have also experienced considerable expansion in capital-intensive resource processing (for example in palm oil processing), with the entire manufacturing value chain located within the country. Much of the rest of manufacturing in Malaysia is confined to low-value-added processing and assembly activities. The vast majority of these industries did not evolve from IS to EO, as in Northeast Asia.

Manufacturing in the western corridor of Malaysia became more skill- and technology-intensive from the late 1980s owing to changing production dynamics and labour shortages. Microelectronics assembly became increasingly automated and skill-intensive from the second half of the 1980s following changes in production technology (Rasiah, 1996a). Rising skill emphasis in consumer and industrial electronics and textiles followed the exhaustion of labour in the key industrial locations of Penang, Kelang Valley, Johore, Seremban and Malacca. Although some firms relocated to East Malaysia and Indonesia, the bulk of them have remained in the congested locations. Thus, escalating production costs from the second half of the 1980s have not substantially altered the composition of manufacturing. Instead, electronics assembly has expanded further its share in overall manufactured exports in the 1990s. Rising wage costs and labour scarcity, in the face of limited transformation in training and technology generating institutions, has led to an enlargement of the labour-intensive workforce through labour imports, primarily from Indonesia and Bangladesh.

The lack of rapid technological catch-up policies led to a slowdown in manufacturing growth from 2000. Key manufacturing industries have faced a slowdown or a fall in trade performance and productivity since 2000. The share of manufacturing in GDP fell from 30.9 per cent in 2000 to 30.1 per cent in 2007 (Rasiah, 2008). Malaysia's contribution to global electronics components export fell from 5.4 per cent in 2000 to 4.7 per cent in 2006 (WTO, 2007: Appendix Table 11.64). Malaysia's contribution to global clothing exports fell from 1.2 per cent in 1990 to 0.9 per cent in 2006 (WTO, 2007: Appendix Table 11.64). Despite the enormous subsidy enjoyed by Malaysian companies, exports of automotive products rose only from 0.05 per cent in 2000 to 0.09 per cent in 2006 (WTO, 2007: Appendix Table 11.54). Average annual manufacturing labour productivity fell by -1.4 per cent over the period 2000–05 (Rasiah, 2008). While the 2008–10 global financial crisis is expected to force the further contraction of manufactured exports from Malaysia, its slowdown since 2000 has already been established as structural rather than cyclical, arising from a lack of upgrading. Hence, unless the organizations entrusted with the role of stimulating technological upgrading are forced to coordinate better their activities through the enforcement of performance standards and the utilization of managers with tacit knowledge gained working in more successful enterprises and organizations, Malaysia is likely to face premature deindustrialization.

The machine tool industry servicing foreign electronics firms in Penang gained international competitiveness in low-value-added activities through strong technology transfer from foreign clients, through both employee transfers and market and technology support (Rasiah, 1995, 1997). Apart from the strong coordination role of the local Penang government, the lack of effective institutional support facilities has constrained its participation to simple and OEM manufacturing activities.[21] Hence, if the Northeast Asian infants negotiated the daunting technology trajectory effectively to reach the top, these potentially capable firms remain in low-value-added niches.

The resource-based oil palm processing industry, which is at the technology frontier, has clearly enjoyed substantial promotional benefits to raise exports and technology development. A rich resource supply has obviously offered a natural comparative advantage to the industry.[22] However, not only was the oil palm industry non-native to Malaysia, but its technological advancement has been influenced strongly by selective taxation and subsidies, for example duty on crude palm oil exports and exemptions on processed palm oil to promote technology development into higher-value-added activities (Gopal, 1996). Clearly, a combination of resource endowments and state support facilitated the growth of palm oil processing in Malaysia.

It can be seen that Malaysia's success in stimulating export manufacturing was influenced by both external and internal factors. Domestic factors included incentives (financial and non-financial), administrative and customs coordination, infrastructure development and political stability. The extent of proactive industrial policy initiatives was generally limited to sweeteners, indirect subsidies (for example, tariff and tax holidays and subsidized land and utilities) and coordinational activities, and controls on labour organization initiatives to block the free movement of labour's relative prices, which were distortionary but coordinated alongside bargaining initiatives with foreign firms. Since the prime drivers of export participation were transnational firms – which accounted for 70 per cent of manufactured exports in 1990 (Ramstetter, 1991, 1998) – the room for government failure was reduced. The lack of institutional support facilities, however, has restricted the complementary development of the indirect agents that support technological upgrading to sustain competitiveness in export markets. Foreign firms continue to access innovation capabilities from abroad but suffer from the lack of operational human resource in the country. Local firms lack technological capabilities; hence their operations have been characterized primarily by simple OEM activities. Only a handful of local firms participate in original design manufacturing and even that with limited capacity to penetrate foreign markets. The only exception is in downstream oil palm products (Gopal, 1996). To overcome these weaknesses and to enable a shift to higher-value-added activities, the government has begun efforts to enhance the ancillary structure, through more proactive governance and coordination from the private sector to improve institutional support in the country (see the next section).

The Philippines

Export-oriented industrialization in the Philippines can be traced to two major phases: the first was introduced by Ferdinand Marcos following the declaration of martial law in 1972, and the second was pushed by Fidel

Ramos from the late 1980s. The first was dominated by an alliance of technocrats, cronies, and the military with Western support. This alliance sought on the one hand to meet American interests to stop the surge in support for communism and on the other hand for Marcos to maintain his leadership by enjoying American military support.

By absorbing the IMF and World Bank prescriptions, the government sought to provide basic infrastructure and a liberal environment (including tariff- and tax-free operations) for multinationals to relocate assembly operations to generate jobs. However, Marcos maintained protection for cronies so that a dual regime of import-substitution and export-orientation with no link between the two evolved in the country à la Malaysia. Just as in the import-substitution sector no dynamic policy was put in place to stimulate technology absorption and catch-up.

However, because only a few countries enjoyed political stability in the region and a labour force capable of conversing in English, the Philippines managed to rival Singapore and Malaysia to attract significant numbers of flagship firms in the early 1970s. Intel was one of the firms to relocate in Manila to assemble memory chips. Because the Philippines was poor and faced severe balance-of-payments and debt problems, the government created export processing zones near airports and sea routes where fairly good basic infrastructure was provided to attract foreign multinationals.

The oil crisis of 1973–75, high inflation, and unemployment and under-employment levels had undermined security severely by the late 1970s. Hence, export-oriented manufacturing had fizzled out by the late 1970s. It was not until civil order was restored from the late 1980s that export-orientation resumed expansion again. In addition, the IMF's structural adjustment package of the 1980s forced the Philippines to liberalize further the economy. The peso was again devalued. Under Macapagal and later Marcos, their cronies engaged in sugar, tobacco and other inward-oriented industries began to lose protection from 1986 (Ofreneo *et al.*, 2006: 16).

As the repressive regime of Marcos ended, and democracy ushered in the Aquino and later Ramos governments, support for the left began to vanish in the Philippines. The collapse of the Soviet Union in 1989 eventually left the communists with little international leadership. The exposure of previously protected heavy industries such as metal manufacturing and automotive assembly to external competition debilitated a catch-up. The use of non-tariff barriers and regional production strategies adopted particularly by Japanese multinational firms such as Toyota has helped support automotive assembly without significant technological catch-up in global value chains (see Ofreneo, 2008). Resource endowments have sustained metal manufacturing, but the failure to upgrade has stifled the industry from participating in higher-value-added activities (see Rasiah and Ofreneo, 2009).

Although unemployment levels have remained high, greater political stability did help the governments of Ramos and later Estrada and Arroyo to expand export-oriented manufacturing in the Philippines. From a mere 7 per cent in 1970, export processing and assembly jumped to 60 per cent of overall exports in 1985 (Montes, 1989: 71). Electronics rose most sharply, as its contribution to overall national exports grew to 63.2 per cent in 2000 before falling to 55.4 per cent in 2006 (WTO, 2007: Appendix Table 11.37). Also, the Philippines' share of global electronics exports rose from 0.6 per cent in 1990 to 2.6 per cent in 2000 before falling to 1.8 per cent in 2006 (WTO, 2007: Appendix Table 11.37).

However, since the focus was on job creation rather than upgrading, multinationals have simply remained confined to assembly, processing, packaging and outsourcing activities in the Philippines. An abundant labour supply and low wages have remained the main attraction for export-oriented activities, particularly in electronics manufacturing. As with Indonesia, Malaysia and Thailand, garment manufacturing, however, has contracted following the removal of the Multi-Fibre Arrangement quotas in 2004. China and the least developed countries have increasingly raised their share of global exports in garment exports (see Ofreneo, 2009). The Philippines' share of global garment exports fell from 1.6 per cent in 1990 to 1.3 per cent in 2000 before falling to 0.8 per cent in 2006 (WTO, 2007: Appendix Table 11.64). Also, the share of garment exports in national exports fell from 6.4 per cent in 2000 to 5.5 per cent in 2006.

Political and legislative changes that took place under Corazon Aquino were instrumental in Ramos's subsequent pursuit of export-oriented industrialization as unproductive rentier monopolies were dismantled. However, the lack of focus on industrial deepening became obvious when Estrada and subsequently Arroyo failed to introduce institutional change to stimulate technological catch-up. Whereas Aquino and Ramos responded to populist support because the emphasis was only on popular democratization à la neo-liberal framework, the instruments necessary for driving increasing returns and technological catch-up activities to support sustained job creation and wage rises were overlooked. Despite enjoying more stability and foreign exchange, the Estrada and Arroyo regimes did not explicitly stimulate technological upgrading. Hence, the fruits of integration into export markets – through connecting with global value chains – were simply lost when the pressures of competition demanded a transition in production technology to higher-value-added activities.

Thailand

The Board of Investment's emphasis on manufacturing in Thailand began to change in the early 1970s. The emphasis on IS had restricted export expansion so that the exports/GDP ratio in Thailand was low even in the 1970s. Export-orientation began in 1972 with the enactment of the Investment Promotion Act. Industries placed on the investment promotion list were eligible to apply for tariff and tax exemptions, and guarantees for the free transfer of profits internationally and against nationalization and competition from state-owned firms (Warr, 1993: 38). However, a combination of factors caused Thailand to be generally bypassed by foreign capital in the 1970s,[23] including its cumbersome certification process and the lead then enjoyed by Malaysia and the Philippines due to their government's greater commitment to attracting foreign capital, their labour force's proficiency in English, and their relatively better infrastructure. Nonetheless, textile and garment firms from Japan and Hong Kong, in particular, began relocating substantially from the early 1970s, to access quotas allocated in the United States and Western Europe. The Philippines began to lose its advantage from the late 1970s, as political instability became a serious problem. Escalating costs and spatial limits eliminated Singapore as a competitor for labour-intensive investments from 1979. Thus, from the 1980s Thailand became Malaysia's main rival for labour-intensive export-oriented firms (Rasiah, 1994b).

A number of resource-intensive EO firms in Thailand started operations as IS firms. Jewellery, food processing and some garment firms initially evolved through import protection. While jewellery and food processing have gained international competitiveness through their resource support, garment firms have operated as subcontractors to international firms that dictate the designs and control the markets. These firms have been operating simple OEM and low-value-added manufacturing.

Completely foreign-owned and joint venture firms began to expand operations in Thailand from the 1960s, supplying the domestic market as well as exporting. American firms preferred to own their firms completely, while the majority of Japanese firms formed joint ventures with local capital. Much of the foreign capital expanded in textile weaving operations to access the local market and quotas in developed economies; Toray, Teijin and Kanebo established 12 factories in Thailand in the period 1963–71 (Pasuk and Baker, 1995: 138). Growing competition from foreign investment incited local businessmen to oppose this foreign encroachment. As a result, the state became less willing to offer tax and tariff holidays to attract foreign capital in the 1970s. Although the BOI promoted EO, import tariffs contributed 30 per cent of total domestic tax revenue in 1971 (Pasuk and Baker, 1995: 145). Between 1974 and 1981, tariffs on 19 products fell, but those of another 54 rose. The effective rate of protection (ERP) between the years 1970 and 1980 doubled.

The saturation of the domestic market and a rise in the trade deficit due primarily to falling agricultural commodity prices influenced a shift to export-orientation from the late 1970s, albeit limited to the reduction of export taxes and adjustments to reduce anti-export biases. The current account deficit increased from 1.5 per cent in 1970–74 to 5.1 and 4.3 per cent respectively in the periods 1975–80 and 1981–86 (Pasuk and Baker, 1995: Table 5.1). The government responded by shifting emphasis aggressively towards export promotion from the mid-1980s. The baht devaluation in 1984, and its ensuing conversion to a managed float, caused it to depreciate by 34.7 per cent in the period 1984–87 (Pasuk and Baker, 1995: 150). Import duties on inputs and machinery used in export manufacturing were reduced in 1985. Many export taxes were scrapped. Export subsidies were introduced in 1986, and business taxes reduced to remove anti-export biases in labour-intensive exports. Special promotions intensified to attract export-oriented foreign investment, including trade and investment missions abroad. From 1986, the BOI allowed even non-American, completely export-oriented foreign manufacturing firms to own 100 per cent equity. Export processing zones were revitalized, and export-oriented manufacturing firms exporting less than 100 per cent were exempted from paying a huge slice of taxable income. Included among the specially promoted industries was agro-processing, which was given tax (corporate, value added and export) breaks ranging from three to seven years, duty drawback on machinery and material inputs, and subsidized power and transport rates (Hewison, 1989; Suehiro, 1992).

Local state efforts to stimulate export-oriented foreign manufacturing coincided with favourable external developments. Like the Indonesian and Malaysian economies, the Thai economy benefited from pressures that drove several manufacturing firms to relocate operations out of Japan and the Asian NIEs. Large-scale relocation of labour-intensive operations and cheapening exports helped stimulate rapid growth in Thailand. Manufactured exports grew by around six times in the period 1985–91. GDP grew at an average annual rate exceeding 10 per cent in the period 1988–90. The strongest growth was recorded in Japanese-dominated manufacturing industries. Machinery, electrical machinery, automobiles (mainly parts) and leather recorded average annual growth rates of 34.4, 26.0, 24.7 and 21.1 per cent respectively (Pasuk and Baker, 1995: Table 5.6). The export to value-added ratios of these industries were 96.6, 74.3, 1.3 and 176.9 per cent respectively in 1988 (Somsak, 1993: Table 3.11). Of these industries, only automobiles has been an IS industry with negligible amounts of exports. Increasing deregulation in this industry, however, is expected to gradually shift its trade orientation. The implementation of AFTA and the still high tariffs in the other main car markets in Southeast Asia are likely to enhance Thailand's emerging role as an export base for foreign transnationals.

The favourable external circumstances and the shift in trade policy towards export promotion expanded manufactured exports sharply. The share of manufactured exports in total exports rose from 35.8 per cent in 1981 to 49.4, 74.7 and 80.4 per cent respectively in the years 1985, 1990 and 1993 (Pasuk and Baker, 1995: Table 5.9). In manufacturing, the share of labour-intensive, low-technology exports grew from 41.3 per cent in 1981 to 43.4 per cent in 1985, before falling gradually to 34.2 per cent in 1993 as medium-technology industries began to expand from the second half of the 1980s. The share of the latter – consisting of machinery, electric and electronic devices – in total manufacturing grew from 14.4 and 14.3 per cent in 1981 and 1985 respectively, to 29.6 and 37.4 per cent in 1990 and 1993 respectively. Of the medium-technology industries in Thailand, electric and electronics, which are predominantly in the labour-intensive assembly stages of production, together contributed 35.2 per cent of manufactured exports in 1993. The overall share of labour-intensive exports in manufactured exports, thus, rose from 55.6 per cent in 1981 to 57.4 and 70.3 per cent respectively in 1985 and 1990, falling slightly to 69.4 per cent in 1993. Textiles were the prime export of Thailand in 1991, contributing 22 per cent of total manufactured exports, but were overtaken by electric and electronics in 1993.

However, the performance of export manufacturing began to face problems as firms from China, Vietnam and other countries began to expand exports in the global market. The share of manufactured exports in overall exports thus fell to 75.3 per cent in 2006 (WTO, 2007: Appendix Table 11.37). Electronics exports from Thailand grew only from 1.9 per cent in 2000 to 2.0 per cent in 2006 (WTO, 2007: Appendix Table 11.54). Thailand's contribution to global garment exports fell from 2.6 per cent in 1990 to 1.9 per cent in 2000 and 1.4 per cent in 2006 (WTO, 2007: Appendix Table 11.64). Unlike the experience of the more developed economies where a relative fall in exports has been led by the relocation of national firms to take advantage of cheaper wage costs abroad while upgrading domestically, the relocation out of export-oriented firms from Thailand has been dominated by foreign multinationals seeking lower wage costs abroad without significant upgrading domestically.

On paper the automobile industry looks successful. Thailand's share of global automotive exports has risen from 0.03 per cent in 1990 to 0.42 per cent in 2000 and 0.97 per cent in 2006 following the massive promotion of the country as the production base and gateway for Southeast Asia and other countries with good trading relations. However, the automobile industry has not developed enough capability to sustain a significant expansion in value added. Much of the exports come from foreign-owned firms that service the plans of multinational corporations (Kamaruding, 1999b; Rasiah, 2001; Lauridsen, 2004; Busser, 2008). Its limited success, however, owes much to effective state–business coordination. Earlier IS policies were instrumental in the expansion of joint ventures and component suppliers in the country. Even when the state deregulated the industry, state–business coordination continued to shape the development of the industry – including support for suppliers and worker training programmes (Doner, 1991). Astra, for example, which developed while benefiting from strong links with foreign assemblers in Thailand, has gained regional competitiveness in vehicle components manufacturing. The industry, however, does not indicate much expansion of exports in the long term, as its participation so far has been confined to low-value-added assembly activities for foreign firms accessing the domestic market (Kamaruding, 1999). Like its Indonesian counterpart it does not have capacity in design and R&D support, nor control over marketing activities (see Lauridsen, 2004; Busser, 2008).

Despite their specificity, the experiences of all four countries show considerable similarity. Industrial widening has taken place in these countries, but the weak focus on technology has prevented them from enjoying technological catch-up à la Japan, Korea and Taiwan. There were no technology transfer agreements between foreign and local firms in Indonesia and the Philippines, while those put in place in Malaysia and Thailand lacked the dynamism, screening and appraisal mechanism to ensure significant levels of technological upgrading in the country. The number of technology transfer agreements in the manufacturing sector in Malaysia rose from 144 in 1975–77 to a total of 2224 agreements by 1993 (Rasiah, 1996a: Table 7). The share of fees involving technology transfer agreements in GDP in Thailand rose from 0.08 per cent in 1972 to 0.14 per cent in 1980 and 0.30 per cent in 1989 (Kamaruding, 1994: Table 5). However, institution building to facilitate effective technology absorption and local development has been weak. Also, none of them have secured effective mechanisms to manage technology transfer. In Japan, South Korea and Taiwan, governments established institutions to vet *ex ante* (assisting local licensees to strike favourable bargains with foreign licensors), monitor rigorously and appraise *ex post* to quicken absorption and development of promoted local capabilities (Johnson, 1982; Fransman, 1985; Amsden, 1989; Wade, 1990; Chang, 1994). Similar governance mechanisms do not exist in Indonesia, Malaysia and Thailand. Malaysia began technology transfer agreements in 1975 and promoted high-technology activities from 1988, but such efforts heightened from 1990, when the Action Plan for Industrial Technology Development (APITD) was launched. Its screening process – owing to a lack of proficient technocrats and the eclectic nature of planning – failed to integrate technology transfer agreements with local capability building (Anuwar Ali, 1992; Rasiah, 1996b, 1997). Indonesia, the Philippines and Thailand similarly have yet to install proper screening, monitoring and appraisal mechanisms to ensure effective technology absorption from technology transfer agreements (Kamaruding, 1994, 1999; Sirigar, 1995).

CONCLUSIONS AND IMPLICATIONS

By most standards, the second-tier Southeast Asian NIEs have achieved rapid industrialization with value added and export shares in GDP and overall exports exceeding those of industrialized countries. However, much of this has occurred in low-value-added goods, with foreign multinationals dominating the most sophisticated activities. As can be seen from the foregoing discussion, governments in Indonesia, Malaysia, the Philippines and Thailand – whether through explicit policy declarations or otherwise – have pursued industrial policies. The extent of government interventions, however, has varied. Except for the earlier IS experience in Malaysia until 1980, the IS sectors have generally been dominated by far more extensive state involvement than the EO sectors. Import-substitution generally failed because of misapplication and the lack of performance controls. The shift to export-orientation became a necessity largely owing to the failure of import-substitution and the prevailing socio-economic and political circumstances in these economies. In Indonesia, the Philippines and Thailand, rising trade deficits reached critical levels. EO was grafted on to IS without proper structural sequencing and thus generally evolved without much link with import-replacing production activities. EO was also introduced during periods when foreign capital was looking for off-shore locations with attractive incentives. Malaysia and the Philippines were the first of the three to launch export-oriented manufacturing (1972), followed by Thailand (1976–80) and Indonesia (1984–86). Despite the contraction in the late 1970s and early 1980s, export-oriented manufacturing became important again in the Philippines from the late 1980s. Hence, the share of manufactured exports in overall exports has been highest in Malaysia and the Philippines, and lowest in Indonesia.

All four economies have enjoyed political stability and relatively good infrastructure, at least from the 1990s through the financial crisis of 1997–98 tore Indonesia politically until 2000. In addition, pro-business legislation, such as guarantees against nationalization, free profits repatriation, movement of goods and services, and tight controls on unions, worker boycotts and labour organizations have helped make these countries a haven for export-oriented firms. Both industrial strategies – IS and EO – faced serious institutional limitations. At least in the initial period, EO was characterized by privileged benefits such as tax holidays, controls on labour organization and subsidized access to infrastructure. Government failure was less apparent in the EO regime owing to its reduced coordination role, which was more specifically to approve investments, allocate resources, offer incentives, and coordinate fiscal policies and customs. Established transnationals with developed external access to technology and markets helped shield the state from the burden of financing local capability building. The lack of effective institutional development – during both IS and EO – restricted the development of local capabilities. Thus, local firms' operations have largely been limited to simple and OEM activities for the export market. Most local exporting firms function as international export subcontractors. The lack of institution building to effectively coordinate growth and structural change has continued to hinder their capacity to sustain a shift to higher productivity sectors. Hence, while IS helped spawn some local capabilities, it has been limited to low-value-added simple and OEM activities where the higher-value-added activities of design and marketing have remained in the hands of foreign firms. It is only in the resource-based plywood (Indonesia), food and jewellery (Thailand) and palm oil (Malaysia) industries that these economies have achieved international competitiveness. While these industries can serve as important building blocks, resource limitations require wider and deeper structural transformation to sustain long-term growth.

Resource endowments were favourably used to avoid serious balance-of-payment problems in Malaysia and to expand manufactured exports initially. As import-dependent manufacturing expanded and production costs began to rise sharply (exacerbated by massive imports for the construction and services sectors in the 1990s), these economies began to experience serious savings–investment gaps, current account deficits and short-term debt. The lack of institutional development to stimulate structural upgrading has confined much export expansion to low-value-added activity, even that involving technology-intensive industries. Malaysia attempted to overcome these problems in the 1990s, but eclectic strategies reduced its potential for long-term solutions. Both Malaysia and Thailand have relied on foreign labour to reduce wage rises, inadvertently delaying structural deepening.

Unlike the case in the first-tier East Asian NIEs, IS industrialization has played a very small role in the development of export capabilities of national firms in the second-tier Southeast Asian NIEs. The modest success has been restricted to labour-intensive activities. Even here, local firms participate only in low-value-added assembly and processing activities. Serious government failures afflicted the initial IS phases. The lack of vetting, monitoring and emphasis on performance standards stifled the growth of competitiveness in both state-supported and private IS initiatives. State-owned ventures in Indonesia, Malaysia and Thailand experienced serious failure. Subsequent efforts to stimulate private IS firms, especially in resource-intensive industries, gained success only in narrow markets, for example food and jewellery in Thailand. This failure can be attributed to a lack of dynamic industrial strategies. Instead of offering rents to enterprises in return for stiff performance standards, and supporting technological upgrading through strong institution building, governments generally concentrated on raising tariffs and banning exports. The second-tier Southeast Asian NIEs' experiences suggest IS paths that ought not to be copied by others.

Foreign multinationals through both full and partial ownership have played a major role in export expansion in these economies. Whereas foreign capital has traditionally been important in Malaysia and the Philippines, its role has become increasingly important from the 1980s and 1990s respectively in Thailand and Indonesia. Political stability, fairly good infrastructure, less bureaucratic red tape, a business-friendly approach and incentives were instrumental in making Malaysia and to a lesser extent Thailand an attractive site for foreign firms to relocate labour-intensive, low-value-added activities. The provision of similar infrastructure and incentives in export processing zones has also attracted strong foreign capital inflows into the Philippines and Indonesia.

The pattern of change in the composition of manufactured exports cannot be explained by neoclassical free trade or simple market-friendly arguments. Considerable state involvement was necessary to attract and support firms in promoting export-oriented activities. Financial incentives – based on employment, investment, export and, in the case of Malaysia since the 1980s, technological criteria – were instrumental, at least in the initial years, in attracting FDI, which has been the backbone of manufactured exports in the second-tier Southeast Asian NIEs. Export expansion proved far more successful because of the operations of enterprises at the technology frontier, which generally located only low-value-added assembly and test operations in these countries. Unlike IS firms, EO firms faced fewer problems of government failure, as they enjoyed sophisticated capabilities and being foreign-owned were already integrated in external markets.

It could, of course, be argued that a significant share of incentives in Southeast Asia may have been redundant and may therefore have unnecessarily dissipated rents (Warr, 1986; Rasiah, 1992). However, the competition among states to attract enterprises has been so intense that it is difficult to write off incentives as irrelevant. Several firms actually noted being influenced to relocate in these economies to benefit from among other factors tax differentials or holidays. Textile and garment firms also considered the MFA regulations as important in their decisions to relocate to these economies. More importantly, the suppression of labour organization fettered the influence of labour in wage bargaining. The promotion of export manufacturing reached such proportions that non-resource manufactures (especially electric/electronics and textiles and garments) accounted for the bulk of manufactured exports in Malaysia from the 1970s, in Thailand from 1980s and in Indonesia from the late 1980s. Since the specific needs of foreign firms vary, effective strategies should involve screening tactics and individual approaches to eliminate uncertainties and link incentives usefully. Singapore and, to a lesser extent, the Penang government in Malaysia have done well in this regard.

Given the low import requirements and static comparative advantages associated with resource-based industries, the success of Indonesia's plywood (at least initially), Thailand's food and jewellery and Malaysia's oil palm industries serves as a good example for emulation. The growth of resource-intensive industries received a boost from a ban on log exports, raw materials availability, and the imposition of export taxes on crude palm oil respectively. These controls and incentives to export and upgrade technologically helped Indonesia, Malaysia and Thailand expand the real value of resource-intensive manufactured exports. As with other export manufactures, resource-based industries have enjoyed strong support from all three governments. Selective interventions obviously distorted relative prices, both in the allocation of resources and in the coordination of production and distribution.

The performance of private local enterprises engaged in non-resource exports has fallen far short of standards achieved by their counterparts in the first-tier East Asian NIEs. While EO has increased through subcontracting activities, the lack of institutional development threatens to restrict its sustainability in the long run, as firms are generally entrenched in import-dependent simple low-value-added OEM activities. Their inability to integrate vertically in the face of rising costs has restricted their capacity to sustain first-tier expansion. Development of local capabilities hinged largely on foreign investment. Similarly, subcontracted activities for exports involving textiles and garments were heavily dependent on foreign capital because of market control by the brand holders (see

Gereffi, 2003). Domestic firms – both local and foreign-owned – can be promoted more effectively if only the governments of the four countries strengthen their institutional support facilities in coordination with stakeholder interests. Systematic promotion of institutions and complementary linkage industries would help economies avoid the burgeoning current account deficits plaguing the second-tier Southeast Asian NIEs.

While government failures have been significant, they cannot be explained by neoclassical arguments. It is true that protectionist practices to support state-owned private firms – especially biases against exports and, in Indonesia, controls on equity – restricted export growth. However, the removal of such obstacles and the stimulation of export growth also depended on the state coordinating industrial strategies with private businesses, from the second half of the 1980s. Especially in Malaysia and Thailand, consultative committees for state–business coordination, involving captains of industry and government officials, became important fora for the formulation and implementation of industrial projects. Also, prioritization distorted relative prices so that export-oriented enterprises generating high investment and employment enjoyed special incentives in Malaysia from the late 1960s. Even if export subsidies helped correct earlier distortions created in Indonesia and Thailand, the state actively selected favoured sectors, and has been the principal agent in coordinating subsidy allocation and implementation. Tax holidays encouraged businesses to internalize transactions to reduce tax liability. All 85 of the 96 foreign firms operating in FTZs and LMWs interviewed in 1995 reported this as an important consideration in the relocation of production activities in Malaysia.[24]

Weak institutions in the second-tier Southeast Asian NIEs have reduced their potential role for offering positive lessons. Some of the conditions and policies that buttressed the rapid development of the first-tier East Asian NIEs have been lacking in the second-tier Southeast Asian NIEs. Indonesia, Malaysia and Thailand have not sufficiently developed the requisite manpower or constructively implemented proactive technology governance that accelerates catching up. These factors, together with their scant emphasis on performance standards and eventual exposure to external competition, have limited firms generally to simple and OEM activities, during both IS and EO phases. The capacity of firms to expand operations in activities undergoing rapid technical change (for example, electronics) will thus be limited.[25] Malaysia – the country which is furthest from the low-cost end of manufacturing – launched plans in the 1990s to help raise value added in key export and strategic manufactures. However, much will depend on institutional support for the movement of enterprises towards the technology frontier. Thailand and later Indonesia will likewise be better prepared to avert such problems if similar initiatives are undertaken now.

The evidence is also clear that structural change in the second-tier Southeast Asian NIEs has differed considerably from that of the first-tier East Asian NIEs. Not only did primary commodities help generate the lion's share of foreign exchange during early growth, which drove early manufacturing in the former, but subsequent expansion in the four economies has also differed. Wood products and textiles and garments dominated Indonesian manufactured exports, electric/electronics became the main growth sub-sector in Malaysia and the Philippines, and textiles, garments, food and jewellery became the main export generators in Thailand. The second-tier Southeast Asian NIEs were not supported by strong domestic expansion. Unlike the case in the first-tier East Asian NIEs, there is no concrete evidence of successful forays into heavy industries in the second-tier Southeast Asian NIEs. The external pressures that pushed FDI from Japan and later the East Asian NIEs to the second-tier NIEs were not just consequences of rising costs, or responses to deliberate government policies to engender structural sequencing. Indeed, the evidence suggests equally important influences stemming from the need to access developed markets (e.g. textiles and garments). Also, skill-intensive automated electronics assembly and test operations expanded in Malaysia from the mid-1980s, despite high levels of unemployment, in the period 1984–87. In Japan and the first-tier East Asian NIEs, industrial policy effectively generated internationally competitive manufacturers, which propelled industrial growth. With the exception of some resource-intensive industries – such as palm oil, jewellery, food and plywood processing – foreign-capital-accessing primarily foreign innovative sources have generally accounted for rapid growth in export manufacturing in the second-tier Southeast Asian NIEs. Also, much of the expansion in the second-tier Southeast Asian NIEs has been in low-value-added segments of export manufacturing when compared to the first-tier East Asian NIEs, which experienced substantial integration into higher-value-added chains.

Overall, industrialization in the second-tier NIEs has failed to produce firms that have managed to move to the technology frontier. Much of the innovative activities have been confined to lower production costs by quickening throughput time and lowering defects, and raising logistics coordination to lower delivery times. The expansion of such activities in China has reduced the capacity of locations in the Southeast Asian second-tier NIEs to raise value added. Except for resource processing in which natural endowments matter, the existing policies for most other manufacturing industries do not appear capable of stimulating rapid increases in value added in the years to come. Export manufacturing in all four countries has expanded sharply, especially in the 1980s and 1990s. However, rapid growth has not been matched by commensurate structural deepening so that foreign affiliates continue to dominate export manufacturing. These economies have experienced substantial structural broadening or diversification within manufacturing operations, which has helped raise investment and employment opportunities. Resource endowments and an institutional framework to strengthen basic infrastructure, provide political stability and provide support from efficient bureaucracies, especially in export processing zones, have proved effective in attracting significant FDI-based industrialization. However, industrial deepening in these countries would require a strong focus on upgrading and local enterprise development policies. Indeed, the key export manufacturing sectors have faced a slowdown in all four countries owing to rising wage costs and a lack of development in the embedding high-tech infrastructure.

Unlike the dirigiste approach employed by the first-tier East Asian NIEs, technology management in the second-tier Southeast Asian NIEs has been liberal. Governments have hardly dictated allocation, production and distribution of resources directly related to technology imports, utilization and development. Liberal state policy on technology in these economies has been due to a lack of effective governance rather than a pursuance of the Marshallian marginal tenets that firms operate as passive recipients of exogenously evolving technologies. It has been established by neo-Schumpeterians that firms actively shape the technology frontier, and that the accumulation of technology by latecomers follows a sequence dominated by technology imports and learning (Nelson and Winter, 1977; Rosenberg, 1982; Freeman, 1994; Kozul-Wright, 1995). Adaptations and developments are critical in pushing latecomers towards the technology frontier. Of the four countries, Malaysia had the most profound national industrial policies to support industrialization. Support for industry, including particular sectors, has ranged from extensive in Indonesia to ad hoc and industry-driven in Thailand. However, whatever the nature of industrial policy adopted, none of the four countries had a systematic appraisal mechanism à la Japan, Korea and Taiwan to support technological catch-up in local firms.

Structural transformation towards higher productivity sectors inevitably requires complementary developments in human resource capabilities. Given imperfections associated with labour markets, especially training and education that involves long gestation periods, and information asymmetries that typify underdeveloped markets, there is a strong need to stimulate state–business collaboration in creating and coordinating institutions to generate manpower for technological upgrading. In Japan, Taiwan and South Korea, the proportion of engineers and R&D scientists and technicians rose when these professions were offered strong incentives to expand. Indonesia, Malaysia and Thailand lack such a manpower base to facilitate a smooth transition to high-technology manufacturing. The share of technology-related human resource in Indonesia, Malaysia and Thailand has been substantially lower than that of the NIEs and developed economies. For example, Indonesia and Thailand had only 12 scientists and one technologist per thousand people in the period 1986–90 (see Rasiah, 2003: Table 12). Malaysia had four R&D scientists and technologists per thousand people in the period 1986–90, while Thailand had two. Malaysia launched several initiatives in the 1990s to redress these deficiencies (Malaysia, 1990, 1994), but institutional initiatives in these economies, in general, have not been able to significantly enhance export competitiveness.

While governments intervened extensively in Japan, South Korea and Taiwan (such as in catching up and frontier R&D activities), conditions imposed (for example, export targets) ensured that unsuccessful enterprises did not continue to sap rents for too long. Thus, such performance standards effectively eliminated under-performers over the long term. Hence, rents have been critical for the emergence of many latecomers (for example Hitachi, Mitsubishi, Hyundai and Acer) (see Freeman, 1987; Amsden, 1989; Wade, 1990; Fukasaku, 1992; Scherer, 1992). If the first-tier East Asian NIEs introduced institutions to minimize rent abuse, the second-tier NIEs generally lack performance standards and institutions to manage them. Instead, they have qualifying standards to access incentives, for example investment and employment levels and industrial classification, and other incentives to access tax breaks, including export credit and refinancing loans at subsidized rates.[26] Export targets for local firms accessing rents – which were so important in South Korea (Amsden, 1989) – have hardly been used in the second-tier Southeast Asian NIEs. Indonesia, the Philippines and Thailand succumbed to liberalization pressures. As protection seems unlimited, the heavy industries of Malaysia and Indonesia have not been exposed to external competition. Official unwillingness to expose domestic firms to the discipline of the external market suggests that such industries have not achieved export capabilities even in the long term.

Significant value-added chains in the three economies extend to foreign economies. Meanwhile, high imports have aggravated current accounts and reduced domestic spin-offs. The most export-oriented industries in these economies – i.e. electronics and textiles – have very weak linkages with the domestic economy (Rasiah, 1995). Only resource-based industries show strong linkages, but this is mainly due to material supplies, while capital goods almost entirely still come from abroad. Malaysian enterprises have not developed adequate technological capabilities to increase their participation in foreign firms' value-added chains. Industrial policies in these economies have generally not attempted to strengthen the capacity of local firms to take greater advantage of official domestic content stipulations. Only a few domestic suppliers have developed strong supply capacities, for example machine tool firms in Penang, Malaysia, and automotive component supplier firms in Indonesia, Malaysia, the Philippines and Thailand (see Rasiah, 2009; Rasiah and Amin, 2010; Sadoi, forthcoming). The achievements of such enterprises owe little to industrial policy, apart from attracting transnationals. As noted earlier, the lack of institutional support has limited their role to low-value-added assembly and OEM activities (Busser, 2008; Lauridsen, 2008; Ofreneo, 2008; Rasiah, 2009). Hence, for example, the export intensity of the transport equipment output of Malaysia fell from 42 per cent in 1990 to 40 per cent in 1995 and 17 per cent in 2005 (Rasiah, 2008: 9).

The slow development of institutional facilities to support technological upgrading and more effective coordination does not mean that unfettered liberalization is the solution. Instead, critical review and enhancement of industrial policy should widen their focus to include better institutional support and greater coordination with private firms. Liberalization, especially tariff deregulation, seemed inevitable in these economies, given the roles of the World Trade Organization, Asia-Pacific Economic Cooperation (APEC) and the ASEAN Free Trade Area. Industrial policy initiatives – including subsidies to support institutional development, for example human resource training and R&D development – will continue to distinguish successful developers. Subsidies for such institutional development activities are not disallowed by the WTO. Further liberalization may be desirable to overcome government failures and to minimize rent abuse.

NOTES

1. Comments from Kevin Hewison, K.S. Jomo, Richard Kozul-Wright, Gerald Helleiner, Akuyz Yilmaz, Peter Limqueco, Gary Rodan and Ajit Singh are gratefully acknowledged.
2. The Malaysian Communist Party agreed to disband, stop their struggle and drop their demand for political recognition in return for the Malaysian government accepting them into Malaysian society.
3. Interestingly the United States and Japan, arguably technologically the most advanced countries in the world, recorded annual average TFP growth rates over the period 1970–85 even lower than those of Korea and Taiwan (see Young, 1994).
4. Krugman (1989) had shown the role of IS in EO promotion.
5. The inflation rate was 600 per cent in 1966.
6. Many firms pulled out of operations in Java after several years of operation.
7. Much of the FDI went to resource-based activities such as oil and gas mining.

8. Hill (1996) also noted that political restrictions on ownership of capital often meant that foreign ownership was understated.

9. Rising oil revenue from the massive 2.5 times price increase helped keep the debt service ratio within the 20 per cent limit set by the state (Pangestu, 1993: 11).

10. Some of the major administrative requirements under this scheme included licences: (a) to import; (b) to become sole distributors for particular brands; (c) for the import of certain items such as steel, scrap metal and tin plate, limited to producers in Indonesia; and (d) for goods manufactured by state-owned firms, e.g. polystyrene and polyethylene (Pangestu, 1993: 12).

11. Minor value-adding activities involving metals and plantation agriculture emerged in Malaysia to manufacture tin cans and slippers for the Asian market.

12. The Malaysian steel maker Perwaja Steel has continued to operate for more than ten years despite accumulating huge losses. Even Proton, which has been recording profits since 1989, has enjoyed high protection. Initiatives involving steel and aircraft production in Indonesia have not approached international competitiveness.

13. After legalizing unions in 1956, the Thai government banned them in 1958, though only 82 strikes were reported in the period 1958–68 (Hewison, 1985: 284).

14. Even so, workers in several firms have faced management pressure to either disband or limit their roles.

15. The word 'unproductive' here is used to distinguish them from the productive Schumpeterian rents. Using Marshall's (1930) definition, a rent exists whenever the transactions rate is lower (to purchasers) or higher (to sellers) than the market-clearing rate (i.e. opportunity costs). Since scale economies as well as risky and uncertain innovative activities involve rents, it becomes necessary to distinguish them (see Khan, 1989; Rasiah, 1997).

16. Based on interviews by the author.

17. Based on interviews by the author in 1997.

18. Eighteen foreign and Malaysian transnationals with subsidiaries in Malaysia and Indonesia reported that serious customs irregularities had frustrated their expansion plans in Indonesia (based on interviews by the author in 1993).

19. The Free Trade Zones were renamed Free Industrial Zones in the early 1990s following the redefinition of exports and imports that no longer included movement of merchandise and services involving FTZs as international trade.

20. The criteria for approval in 1993 were 20 per cent value added and 30 per cent domestic content. Crude rubber, vegetable oils and textile products have been excluded from the criteria. Pre-shipment conditions also require 80 per cent of export value or 70 per cent of the value of eligible exports (Ismail Salleh, 1995: 53).

21. Six firms reported having ODM capability, but not the requisite market potential to support production (Rasiah, 1998b).

22. Malaysia is the world's chief exporter of palm oil.

23. Based on interviews conducted by the author with nine foreign transnationals having subsidiaries in Malaysia, Thailand and the Philippines in 1990.

24. In an earlier interview conducted in 1990, a German firm noted that it preferred to transfer its profits to Malaysia so that the bulk of them would be subject to a value added tax of 14 per cent rather than a German corporate tax of 56 per cent (according to author interviews in 1990). Similarly, an American company executive showed the author the company's income statement for 1990, in which it had recorded its highest profits in 1985, when it had, in fact, recorded overall losses. What the firm had done was to record profits in its subsidiary in Malaysia, where it had enjoyed a tax holiday in 1990.

25. A number of local export subcontractors in the garment and knitting industries in Malaysia and Thailand have shifted operations to property development following the scrapping of export incentives and rising labour costs. Others have relied on imported foreign labour.

26. Export subsidies in these economies have been scaled down substantially since 1995, necessitated by deregulation required by the WTO and the AFTA process.

REFERENCES

Adam, G. (1975), 'Multinational corporations and worldwide sourcing', in H. Radice (ed.), *International Firms and Modern Imperialism*, Harmondsworth: Penguin.

Akamatsu, Kenichi (1962), 'A historical pattern of economic growth in developing countries', *Developing Economies*, **1**(1): 3–25.

Allen, G.C. and A.G. Donnithorne (1957), *Western Enterprise in Indonesia and Malaya*, London: Allen & Unwin.

Amin, S. (1974), 'Growth is not development', mimeo, Dakar.

Amin, S. (2004), *Obsolescent Capitalism: Contemporary Politics and Global Disorder*, London: Zed Books

Amsden, Alice (1989), *Asia's Next Giant: South Korea and Late Industrialization*, New York: Oxford University Press.

Amsden, Alice H. (1995), 'Like the rest: Southeast Asia's late industrialization', *Journal of International Development*, **7**(5): 791–9.

Anuwar Ali (1992), *Malaysian Industrialization: The Quest for Technology*, Kuala Lumpur: Oxford University Press.

APDC (1987), *Business and Investment Environment in Indonesia*, Kuala Lumpur: Asia-Pacific Development Centre.

Athukorola, P. and J. Menon (1999), 'Outward orientation and economic development in Malaysia', *World Economy*, **22**(8): 1119–39.

Balassa, Bela (1991), *Economic Policies in the Pacific Area Developing Countries*, London: Macmillan.

Baran, P. (1973), 'Political economy of backwardness', in C.K. Wilber (ed.), *Political Economy of Development and Underdevelopment*, New York: Random House.

Bello, W., D. Kinley and E. Elinson (1982), *Development Debacle: The World Bank in the Philippines*, San Francisco, CA: Institute for Food and Development Policy.

Bernard, Mitchell and John Ravenhill (1995), 'Beyond product cycles and flying geese: regionalization, hierarchy and industrialization in East Asia', *World Politics*, **47**(2): 171–209.

Billig, M.S. (2003), *Barons, Brokers, and Buyers: The Institutions and Cultures of Philippines Sugar*, Manila: Ateneo de Manila University Press.

Busser, R. (2008), '"Detroit of the East"? Industrial upgrading, Japanese car producers and the development of the automotive industry in Thailand', *Asia Pacific Business Review*, **14**(1): 29–45.

Cardoso, F.H. (2001), *Charting a New Course: The Politics of Globalization and Social Transformation*, New York: Rowman & Littlefield.

Carroll, J. (1965), *The Filipino Manufacturing Entrepreneur: Agent and Product of Change*, Ithaca, NY: Cornell University Press.

Chang, H.J. (1994), *The Political Economy of Industrial Policy*, London: Macmillan.

Chang, H.J. (2003), *Kicking Away the Ladder*, London: Anthem Press.

Deyo, F. (1985), *The Political Economy of the New Asian Industrialism*, Ithaca, NY: Cornell University Press.

Deyo, F. (ed.) (1987), *The Political Economy of New Asian Industrialism*, Ithaca, NY: Cornell University Press.

Doner, R.F. (1991), *Driving a Bargain: Automobile Industrialization and Japanese Firms in Southeast Asia*, Berkeley, CA: University of California Press.

Dos Santos, T. (1970), 'The structure of dependence', *American Economic Review*, **60**: 231–6.

Emmanuel, A. (1972), *Unequal Exchange: A Study in the Imperialism of Trade*, New York: Monthly Review Press.

Evans, P. (1995), *Embedded Autonomy: States and Industrial Transformation*, Princeton, NJ: Princeton University Press.

Fishlow, A., C. Gwin, S. Haggard and D. Rodrik (1996), *Miracle or Design? Lessons from the East Asian Experience*, New York: Overseas Development Council.

Frank, A.G. (1969), *Latin America: Underdevelopment or Revolution*, New York: Monthly Review Press.

Frank, A.G. (1979), *Dependent Accumulation and Underdevelopment*, London: Macmillan.

Fransman, Manfred (1985), 'International competitiveness, technical change and the state: the machine tool industries in Taiwan and Japan', *World Development*, **14**(12): 1375–96.

Freeman, Chris (1987), *Technology Policy and Economic Policy: Lessons for Japan*, London: Frances Pinter.

Freeman, Chris (1994), 'Conceptualising Technical Change', *Cambridge Journal of Economics*, **18**(1).

Frobel, F., J. Heinrich and O. Kreye (1980), *The New International Division of Labour*, Cambridge: Cambridge University Press.

Fukasaku, Y. (1992), *Technology Development in Pre-War Japan: Mitsubishi Nagasaki Shipyard*, London: Routledge.

Furtado, C. (1973), 'The structure of external dependence', in C.K. Wilber (ed.), *Political Economy of Development and Underdevelopment*, New York: Random House

Garnaut, Ross (1980), *ASEAN in a Changing Pacific and World Economy*, Canberra: Australian National University Press.

Gereffi, G. (2003), 'The international competitiveness of Asian economies in the global apparel commodity chain', *International Journal of Business and Society*, **4**(2): 71–110.

Gopal, Jaya (1996), 'Malaysia's palm oil refining industry: policy, growth, technical change and competitiveness', Proceedings of the 1996 PORIM International Palm Oil Congress, Kuala Lumpur, 23-25 September.

Gore, Charles (1994), 'Development strategy in East Asian newly industrializing economies: the experience of post-war Japan, 1953–73', UNCTAD discussion paper no. 92, Geneva.

Gray, P.H. (1982), 'Survey of recent developments', *Bulletin of Indonesian Economic Studies*, **18**(3): 1–51.

Hamilton, C. (1983), 'Capitalist industrialization in East Asia's four Little Tigers', *Journal of Contemporary Asia*, **13**(1): 35–73.

Henderson, J. (1989), *Globalisation of High Technology Production*, London: Routledge.

Henderson, Jeffrey (1990), *Globalisation of High Technology Production*, London: Routledge.

Hewison, Kevin (1985), 'The state and capitalist development in Thailand', in Richard Higgott and Richard Robison (eds), *Southeast Asia: Essays in the Political Economy of Structural Change*, London: Routledge & Kegan Paul.

Hewison, Kevin (1987), 'National interests and economic downturn: Thailand', in Richard Robison, Kevin Hewison and Richard Higgott (eds), *South East*

Asia in the 1980s: The Politics of Economic Crisis, Sydney, NSW: Allen & Unwin.

Hewison, Kevin (1989), *Bankers and Bureaucrats: Capital and the Role of the State in Thailand*, New Haven, CT: Yale Center for International and Area Studies.

Hill, Hal (1996), *The Indonesian Economy since 1966: Southeast Asia's Emerging Giant*, Cambridge: Cambridge University Press.

Hill, H. (1999), 'Indonesia's microeconomic policy challenges: industry policy, competition policy, and small–medium enterprises', *Indonesian Quarterly*, **27**(1): 22–33.

Hutchcroft, P. (1994a), 'Booty capitalism: business–government relations in the Philippines', in A. MacIntyre (ed.), *Business and Government in Industrialising Asia*, Sydney, NSW: Allen & Unwin, pp. 216–43.

Hutchcroft, P. (1994b), 'The state, civil society and foreign actors: the policies of Philippine industrialization', *Contemporary Southeast Asia*, **16**(2): 157–77.

Hutchinson, J. (2007), 'Poverty of poverty in the Philippines', in G. Rodan, K. Hewison and R. Robison (eds), *The Political Economy of South-East Asia*, Melbourne, VIC: Oxford University Press.

Ismail Salleh (1995). 'Non-tariff incentive policies', in K. Vijayakumari (ed.), *Managing Industrial Transformation in Malaysia*, Kuala Lumpur: Institute of Strategic and International Studies.

Ismail Salleh and Sahathevan Meyanathan (1993), 'Malaysia: growth, equity and structural transformation', World Bank occasional paper, Washington, DC.

Johnson, Chalmers (1982), *MITI and the Japanese Miracle*, Stanford, CA: Stanford University Press.

Jomo, K.S. (1986), *A Question of Class*, Singapore: Oxford University Press.

Jomo, K.S. (1990), *Growth and Structural Change in the Malaysian Economy*, London: Macmillan.

Jomo, K.S. (1996), *Southeast Asia's Misunderstood Miracle*, Boulder, CO: Westview.

Jomo, K.S. and Patricia Todd (1994), *Trade Unions and the State in Peninsular Malaysia*, Kuala Lumpur: Oxford University Press.

Jomo, K.S., Y.C. Chen, B.C. Folk, I. Ul-Haque, P. Pasuk, B. Simatupang and M. Tateishi (1997), *Southeast Asia's Misunderstood Miracle: Industrial Policy and Economic Development in Thailand, Malaysia and Indonesia*, Boulder, CO: Westview.

Kaldor, Nicholas (1957), 'A model of economic growth', *Economic Journal*, **67**: 591–624.

Kamaruding, A.S. (1994), 'Thailand: industrialization through foreign technology', Lund University Economics Faculty minor field study working paper no. 54, Lund, Sweden.

Kamaruding, A.S. (1999), 'Promoting industrial and technological development under contrasting industrial policies: the automobile industries in Malaysia and Thailand', in K.S. Jomo, G. Felker and Rajah Rasiah (eds), *Industrial Technology Development in Malaysia*, London: Routledge.

Khan, Mushtaq (1989), 'Clientelism, corruption and the capitalist state: a study of Korea and Bangladesh', Ph.D. thesis at University of Cambridge, Cambridge.

Khor, M.K.P. (1987), *The Malaysian Economy in Decline*, Penang, Malaysia: Consumer Association of Penang.

Kozul-Wright, Z. (1995), 'The role of the firm in the innovation process', UNCTAD discussion paper no. 98, Geneva.

Krueger, A.O. (1983), *Trade and Employment in Developing Countries: Synthesis and Conclusions*, Chicago, IL: Chicago University Press.

Krugman, Paul (1989), 'Import-protection as export promotion: international competition in the presence of oligopoly and economies of scale', in E. Helpman and P. Krugman (eds), *Trade Policy and Market Structure*, Cambridge, MA: MIT Press.

Krugman, P. (1994), 'The myth of Asia's miracle', *Foreign Affairs*, **73**(6).

Krugman, P. (1998), *The Accidental Theorist*, New York: Norton.

Lauridsen, S.L. (2004), 'Foreign direct investment, linkage formation and supplier development in Thailand during the 1990s: the role of state governance', *European Journal of Development Research*, **16**(3): 561–86.

Lauridsen, S.L. (2008), *State, Institutions and Industrial Development: Industrial Deepening and Upgrading Policies in Taiwan and Thailand Compared*, Aachen, Germany: Shaker Verlag.

Lee, I.C.C. (2009), 'Industrial policy and structural change in Taiwan's textile and garment industry', *Journal of Contemporary Asia*, **39**(4): 512–29.

Lenin, V. (1948), *Imperialism: The Highest Stage of Capitalism*, London: Lawrence & Wishart.

Lewis, W.A. (1955), *The Theory of Economic Growth*, London: Allen & Unwin.

Lim, Linda (1978), 'Multinational firms and manufacturing for export in less-developed countries: the case of the electronics industry in Malaysia and Singapore', Ph.D. thesis at University of Michigan, Ann Arbor.

Low, Linda and S. Tan (1996), 'Growth triangles and labor in Southeast Asia', in Rajah Rasiah and N.V. Hofmann (eds), *Liberalization and Labor*, Singapore: Friedrich-Ebert Stiftung.

Luxemburg, R. (2003), *The Accumulation of Capital*, London: Routledge.

Malaysia (1990), *The Second Outline Perspective Plan, 1991–2000* (OPP2), Kuala Lumpur: Government Printers.

Malaysia (1994), *Mid-Term Review of the Sixth Malaysia Plan, 1991–1995*, Kuala Lumpur: Government Printers.

Marshall, Alfred (1930), *Industry and Trade*, London: Macmillan.

Marx, K. (1976), *Capital: A Critical Analysis of Capitalist Production*, London: Lawrence & Wishart.

Mathews, J.A. (2002), *Dragon Multinational: A New Model for Global Growth*, New York: Oxford University Press.

Montes, M.F. (1989), 'Philippine structural adjustments, 1970–1987', in M.F. Montes and S. Hideyoshi (eds), *Philippine Macroeconomic Perspective: Development and Policies*, Tokyo: Institute for Developing Economies, pp. 45–90.

Morrissey, O. and D. Nelson (1998), 'East Asian economic performance: miracle or just a pleasant surprise?', www.tulane.edu/~dnelson/NelsonArticles/MorrisseyNelsonWE1.pdf, pp. 855–79, downloaded on 4 April 2009.

Myrdal, Gunnar (1957), *Economic Theory and Underdeveloped Regions*, New York: Methuen.

Narongchai Akrasanee (1973a), 'The manufacturing sector in Thailand: a study of growth, import-substitution and effective protection, 1960–1969', Ph.D. thesis at Johns Hopkins University, Baltimore, MD.

Narongchai Akrasanee (1973b), 'Growth and structural change in the manufacturing sector in Thailand, 1960–1969', *Developing Economies*, **11**(4).

Naya, S. (1997), 'AFTA and Asian-Pacific economic relations', in I. Kazuhiro (ed.), *Economic Relations and Developments in Asia and Pacific: Collected*

Papers of International Cooperation Studies, Kobe, Japan: Research Institute for Economics and Business Administration, Kobe University.

Nelson, Richard and Sidney Winter (1977), 'In search of a useful theory of innovation', *Research Policy*, **6**: 36–76.

Ofreneo, R. (2003), 'TRIMS and the automobile industry in the Philippines', *Technology Policy Brief*, **2**(1): 4–5.

Ofreneo, R. (2008), 'Arrested development: multinationals, TRIMs and the Philippines' automotive industry', *Asia Pacific Business Review*, **14**(1): 65–84.

Ofreneo, R. (2009), 'Development choices for Philippine textiles and garments in the post-MFA era', *Journal of Contemporary Asia*, **39**(4): 543–61.

Ofreneo, Rene, Mars Mendoza, Ember Cruz and Errol Ramos (2006), *Nationalist Development Agenda: A Roadmap for Economic Revival, Growth and Sustainability*, Quezon City, Philippines: Fair Trade Alliance.

Palma, G. (1981), 'Dependency and development: a critical overview', in D. Seers (ed.), *Dependency Theory: A Critical Reassessment*, London: Frances Pinter.

Palmer, Ingrid (1978), *The Indonesian Economy Since 1965*, London: Frank Cass.

Pangestu, Mari (1991), 'Managing economic policy reforms in Indonesia', in Sylvia Ostry (ed.), *Authority and Academic Scribblers: The Role of Research in East Asian Policy Reforms*, San Francisco, CA: International Center for Economic Development.

Pangestu, Mari (1993), 'Indonesia: from dutch disease to manufactured exports', processed.

Pasuk, Phongpaichit and Chris Baker (1995), *Thailand: Economy and Politics*, Kuala Lumpur: Oxford University Press.

Perkins, D. (1994), 'There are at least three models of East Asian development', *World Development*, **22**(4): 655–62.

Power, J. and G. Sicat (1971), *The Philippines: Industrialization and Trade Policies*, New York: Oxford University Press.

Ramstetter, Eric (1991), *Direct Foreign Investment and Structural Change in the Asia-Pacific Region*, Boulder, CO: Westview.

Ramstetter, Eric (1998), 'Measuring the size of foreign multinationals in the Asia-Pacific', in G. Thompson (ed.), *Economic Dynamism in the Asia Pacific*, London: Routledge.

Rasiah, Rajah (1987), *Pembahagian Kerja Antarabangsa*, Kuala Lumpur: Malaysian Social Science Association.

Rasiah, Rajah (1988), 'The semiconductor industry in Penang: implications for NIDL theories', *Journal of Contemporary Asia*, **18**(1): 24–46.

Rasiah, Rajah (1990), 'Relocation of the electronics, textile and garment industries in Malaysia', processed.

Rasiah, Rajah (1992), 'Foreign manufacturing investment in Malaysia', *Economic Bulletin for Asia Pacific*, **63**(1): 63–77.

Rasiah, Rajah (1994a), 'Flexible production systems and local machine tool subcontracting: electronics transnationals in Malaysia', *Cambridge Journal of Economics*, **18**(3).

Rasiah, Rajah (1994b), 'Capitalist industrialization in ASEAN', *Journal of Contemporary Asia*, **24**(2): 197–216.

Rasiah, Rajah (1995), *Foreign Capital and Industrialization in Malaysia*, London: Macmillan.

Rasiah, Rajah (1996a), 'Manufacturing as engine of growth and industrialisation in Malaysia', *Managerial Finance*, **9**(2): 79–102.

Rasiah, Rajah (1996b), 'Changing dimensions of the labour process in the electronics industry in Malaysia', *Asia Pacific Viewpoint*, **37**(1): 21–38.

Rasiah, R. (1996c), 'Institutions and innovations: moving towards the technology frontier in the electronics industry in Malaysia', *Industry and Innovation*, **3**(2): 79–102.

Rasiah, Rajah (1997), 'Class, ethnicity and economic development in Malaysia', in R. Robison, Garry Rodan and Kevin Hewison (eds), *The Political Economy of Southeast Asia*, Melbourne, VIC: Oxford University Press.

Rasiah, Rajah (1998a), 'The Malaysian financial crisis', *Journal of Asia Pacific Economy*, **3**(3).

Rasiah, Rajah (1998b), 'Explaining manufactured export expansion in Indonesia, Malaysia and Thailand', UNCTAD discussion paper no. 137, Geneva.

Rasiah, Rajah (2001), 'Liberalization and the car industry in SEA-4', *International Journal of Business and Society*, **2**(1): 1–19.

Rasiah, Rajah (2003), 'The export manufacturing experience of Indonesia, Malaysia and Thailand', in Jomo, K.S. (ed.), *Southeast Asia's Paper Tigers*, London: Routledge.

Rasiah, Rajah (2004), 'Technological capabilities in East and Southeast Asian electronics firms: does network strength matter?', *Oxford Development Studies*, **32**(3): 433–54.

Rasiah, Rajah (2008), 'Drivers of growth and poverty reduction in Malaysia: government policy, export manufacturing and foreign direct investment', *Malaysian Journal of Economic Studies*, **45**(1): 21–44.

Rasiah, Rajah (2009), 'Growth and slowdown in the electronics industry in Southeast Asia', *Journal of the Asia Pacific Economy*, **14**(2): 123–37.

Rasiah, Rajah and Ishak Shari (1994), 'Malaysia's new economic policy in retrospect', in H.M. Dahlan, Hamzah Jusoh, A.Y. Hing and J.H. Ong (eds), *Asia in the Global System*, Bangi, Malaysia: UKM Press.

Rasiah, Rajah and T.C. Chua (1997), 'Structural change and trade unionism in Southeast Asia', report to the Friedrich-Ebert Stiftung, Singapore.

Rasiah, Rajah and S. Ishak (2001), 'Market, government and Malaysia's new economic policy', *Cambridge Journal of Economics*, **25**(1): 57–78.

Rasiah, Rajah and R. Ofreneo (2009), 'The dynamics of textile and garment manufacturing in Asia', *Journal of Contemporary Asia*, **39**(4): 501–11.

Rasiah, Rajah and A.S. Amin (2010), 'Ownership and technological capabilities in Indonesia's automotive sector', *Journal of the Asia Pacific Economy*, **15**(3): 288–300.

Rasiah, Rajah, R. Osman and R. Alavi (2000), 'Changing dimensions of Malaysian trade', *International Journal of Business and Society*, **1**(1): 1–29.

Reinert, E. (2007), *How Rich Countries Got Rich . . . and Why Poor Countries Stay Poor*, London: Constable.

Robison, Richard (1986), *Indonesia: The Rise of Capital*, Sydney, NSW: Allen & Unwin.

Robison, Richard (1987), 'After the gold rush: the politics of economic restructuring in Indonesia in the 1980s', in Richard Robison, Kevin Hewison and Richard Higgott (eds), *South East Asia in the 1980s: The Politics of Economic Crisis*, Sydney, NSW: Allen & Unwin.

Rock, Michael (1996), 'Thai development: if rent seeking is so pervasive, why is development performance so good?', paper presented at the conference Rents and Development, Kuala Lumpur, 16-18 June.

Rodan, G. (1989), *The Political Economy of Singapore's Industrialization*, London: Macmillan.
Rokiah Alavi (1996), *Import Substitution Industrialisation: Infant Industries in Malaysia*, London: Routledge.
Rosenberg, Nathan (1982), *Inside the Black Box*, Cambridge: Cambridge University Press.
Rowthorn, Robert (1996), 'Beyond the flying geese', processed, UNCTAD, Geneva.
Sadoi, Y. (forthcoming), 'Technological capabilities of automobile parts suppliers in Thailand', *Journal of the Asia Pacific Economy*.
Scherer, F. (1992), *International High Technology Competition*, Cambridge, MA: Harvard University Press.
Sirigar, M.G. (1995), 'Indonesia', in A.B. Supapol (ed.), *Transnational Corporations and Backward Linkages in Asian Electronics Industries*, New York: United Nations.
Smith, A. (1776), *The Wealth of the Nations*, London: Strahan and Cadell.
Somsak, T. (1993), 'Manufacturing', in Peter Warr (ed.), *The Thai Economy in Transition*, Cambridge: Cambridge University Press.
Suehiro, Akira (1992), 'Capitalist development in post-war Thailand: commercial bankers, industrial elite and agribusiness groups', in Ruth McVey (ed.), *Southeast Asian Capitalists*, Ithaca, NY: South East Asia Program, Cornell University.
Sungsidh, P. (1995), *Economic Development and Labour Issues in Thailand*, Bonn, Germany; Friedrich-Ebert Stiftung.
Sunkel, O. (1989), 'Structuralism, dependency and institutionalism: an exploration of common ground and disparities', *Journal of Economic Issues*, **23**(2): 519–33.
Thoburn, J. (1977), *Primary Commodity Exports and Economic Development: Theory, Evidence, and a Study of Malaysia*, London: John Wiley.
Tjiptoherijanto, P. (1993), 'Macroeconomic policy and export promotion: a case of Indonesia in the context of Asean', *Ekonomi dan Keuangan Indonesia*, **41**(2): 199–210.
Wade, Robert (1990), *Governing the Market*, Princeton, NJ: Princeton University Press.
Wallerstein, I. (1979), *The Capitalist World Economy*, Cambridge: Cambridge University Press.
Warr, Peter (1986), 'Malaysia's industrial enclaves: benefits and costs', in T.G. McGee (ed.), *Industrialization and Labour Force Processes: A Case Study of Peninsular Malaysia*, Canberra: The Australian National University.
Warr, Peter (ed.) (1993), *The Thai Economy in Transition*, Cambridge: Cambridge University Press.
World Bank (1959), *A Public Development Program for Thailand*, Baltimore, MD: World Bank.
World Bank (1993), *The East Asian Miracle: Economic Growth and Public Policy*, New York: Oxford University Press.
WTO (2007), *International Trade Statistics*, Geneva: World Trade Organization.
Yoshihara, Kunio (1988), *The Rise of Ersatz Capitalism in South-East Asia*, Singapore: Oxford University Press.
Young, Alvyn (1994), 'Lessons from the East Asian NICs: a contrarian view', *European Economic Review*, **38**(3/4): 964–73.

3. The 1997 economic crisis, reform and Southeast Asian growth

Chris Dixon

INTRODUCTION

The Southeast Asian economies made a slow recovery from the 1997 crisis. Between 1997 and 2001 growth was, compared to 1991–96, generally low and extremely uneven throughout the region, with two years (1998 and 2001) of negative growth for most of the economies. There was also a general disruption of regional trade and investment flows, with a significant reduction in intra-regional flows, particularly with East Asia. Despite this, the region as a whole and most of the major economies experienced a significant increase in foreign direct investment (FDI). The general expansion of FDI continued into 2002–06 with the growth of GDP and export earnings returning to near pre-crisis levels, before generally declining in the wake of the 2007–09 global financial crisis (Tables 3.1, 3.2 and 3.3).

The recovery was associated with some significant changes, notably: the increased role of China in regional growth and integration; changes in the composition of FDI and its sources, with a striking increase in the contribution of mergers and acquisitions (M&A), and a decline in the East Asian share of inflows; and some important changes in the relative positions of some of the economies. Of the latter, particular interest has focused on the Philippines, so long an exception to the regional 'miracle', which achieved growth levels near to those of Malaysia, and Vietnam growing almost as fast as China. However, despite the general appearance of a Southeast Asian recovery since 2001, growth remains much more uncertain and uneven than was the case during 1991–96, with question marks over long-term prospects. This is particularly the case for Indonesia and Thailand (see for example ADB, 2007; Booth, 2009).

For the Bretton Woods institutions and most commentators, the slow recovery and uncertain outlook rest on the inability or unwillingness of governments to tackle the internal problems that caused the crisis and adjustment to a globalized world, and the challenges posed by China and India. The solution to both the internal and the external issues is generally

Table 3.1   Annual average percentage rates of growth of GDP

	1961–70	1971–80	1981–90	1991–96	1997–2001	2002–06	2002	2003	2004	2005	2006	2007	2008
Indonesia	3.9	7.6	6.1	7.0	−0.2	5.0	4.4	4.7	5.1	5.6	5.4	6.3	6.1
Malaysia	6.5	7.8	5.3	8.6	4.7	5.6	4.1	5.5	7.2	5.2	5.9	6.1	4.6
Philippines	5.1	6.3	1.0	2.9	3.6	5.2	4.4	4.9	6.2	5.0	5.5	7.1	3.9
Singapore	8.8	8.5	6.6	7.5	4.9	6.1	4.0	2.9	8.7	6.4	8.4	7.8	1.1
Thailand	8.4	7.2	7.3	7.8	0.8	5.6	5.3	7.1	6.3	4.5	4.6	4.9	2.6
Vietnam	N/A	N/A	4.6	8.4	6.1	7.7	7.1	7.3	7.8	8.4	7.7	8.5	6.2
Hong Kong	10.0	9.3	7.1	5.0	2.8	5.6	1.8	3.2	8.6	7.5	6.8	6.3	2.3
South Korea	8.6	9.5	9.7	6.7	4.3	4.8	7.0	3.1	4.7	4.0	5.1	5.1	2.2
Taiwan	9.2	9.7	10.2	6.3	4.2	4.4	4.2	3.4	6.1	4.0	4.3	5.7	0.6
China	N/A	5.8	9.2	10.0	7.8	10.0	9.1	10.0	10.2	10.2	10.5	13.0	9.0

N/A not available.

Source: World Bank, Tables, various issues; IMF, World economic database, http://www.imf.org/external/ns/cs.aspx?id=28.

Table 3.2 Growth of export value for the major Southeast and East Asian economies (%)

	1971–80	1981–90	1991–96	1997–2001	2002–06	2001	2002	2003	2004	2005	2006	2007	2008
Indonesia	39.6	2.1	11.6	3.3	10.2	–9.1	3.0	5.0	10.4	22.9	9.3	13.2	20.1
Malaysia	25.3	9.5	18.9	2.7	14.3	–10.4	6.0	6.5	26.5	12.0	20.6	12.1	13.1
Philippines	19.6	5.2	17.1	1.8	7.2	–17.9	11.7	1.4	9.5	0.5	13.3	6.5	–2.9
Singapore	30.1	12.1	14.8	0.9	17.8	–11.6	2.8	15.2	36.4	15.6	18.8	10.2	8.6
Thailand	22.9	14.9	16.3	2.5	15.1	–5.9	4.6	18.2	19.8	14.5	18.2	26.3	13.9
Vietnam	N/A	N/A	20.9	16.0	21.5	4.5	9.5	22.1	31.4	22.5	21.8	30.4	27.9
Hong Kong	22.2	15.2	14.4	0.2	9.7	–6.0	5.3	11.2	11.2	11.6	9.3	8.5	6.1
South Korea	34.2	14.1	14.8	3.7	15.0	–12.8	8.0	19.1	31.1	12.3	4.3	13.7	14.2
Taiwan	29.4	13.7	10.5	3.0	18.0	–15.6	10.2	20.0	29.6	9.7	20.3	9.8	4.4
China	19.3	15.8	18.5	12.3	29.7	7.0	22.2	34.8	35.4	29.0	27.2	25.7	16.8

N/A not available.

Source: IMF, *Direction of Trade Statistics Yearbook*, various issues.

Table 3.3 FDI net inflows (US$m)

	Annual average 1980–85	Annual average 1986–90	Annual average 1991–96	Annual average 1997–2001	Annual average 2002–06	2002	2003	2004	2005	2006	2007	2008
Brunei	–	–	210	619.6	1093.4	1035	3375	334	289	434	260	239
Cambodia	–	–	99	187.6	186.6	54	84	131	381	483	867	815
Indonesia	200	600	2985	–933.2	3066.6	145	–597	1892	8337	4914	6928	7919
Laos	–	–	53	48.2	105.8	25	19	17	281	187	324	228
Malaysia	1100	1240	5436	3454.8	4065.2	3203	2474	4624	3965	6060	8491	8023
Myanmar	–	28	256	453.4	222.4	191	291	251	236	428	258	283
Philippines	–	480	1226	1252.8	1432.0	1792	491	688	1854	2921	2916	1520
Singapore	1300	3420	6856	13909.0	15047.2	5822	10376	19828	15004	27680	31550	22725
Thailand	300	1200	1964	4975.0	5486.6	947	1952	5862	8957	9715	11328	10091
Vietnam	–	30	1217	1672.0	1727.2	1200	1450	1650	2021	2315	6739	8050
SE Asia	2900	6998	20302	25639.2	32433.0	14414	19915	35277	41325	55137	69661	59893
Developing economies	18655	39850	80302	233463.1	261189.3	168350	189442	323288	355484	448312	620210	735094
World	58545	187244	289700	892756.4	705946.8	651188	559576	742143	945795	1461074	1978838	1697353
SE Asia/ Developing economies %	15.5	17.6	25.2	11.0	12.4	8.6	10.5	10.9	11.6	12.3	11.2	8.1
SE Asia/ World %	5.0	3.7	7.0	2.9	4.6	2.2	3.6	4.8	4.4	3.8	3.5	3.5

– zero or near zero.

Source: UNCTAD, *Foreign Investment Yearbook*, various issues; IMF, *Balance of Payments Yearbook*, various issues.

seen as further liberalization and regulatory reform. It is not that there have not been developments in these areas, but that these are not considered sufficient to ensure the continued recovery or insulate from further crisis (see for example ABD, 2005: 39–40, 2007: 15–16; Barton, 2007).[1]

These broadly neo-liberal views of the Southeast Asian economies reflect the general tendency to see the crisis as internal in origin, diverting attention from the operation of capital at the global scale (see for example comments in Glen and Singh, 2004). They also closely follow the conditions attached to the IMF rescue packages for Indonesia and Thailand. The IMF demanded rapid and far-reaching liberalization that would open economies to the forces of economic globalization. Particular emphasis was given to the removal of restrictions on foreign ownership, and related reform of corporate governance.[2] Increased foreign ownership was seen as critical to the restructuring and 'cleaning up' of the corporate sectors – tasks that unaided were considered beyond the ability of the government or business community (Zhan and Ozan, 2001). Foreign ownership was expected to bring modern business practices, improve corporate governance, increase efficiency, raise productivity, increase competition and accelerate economic recovery (Mody and Negishi, 2000: 7–9). The overall aim was a general 'Westernization' of Southeast Asian business and its regulation and as such has been very extensively criticized in terms of the possibly adverse impact on the economies concerned (see for example Bello, Cunningham and Li Kheng Poh, 1998: 51–2; Bullard, 2002: 149–51).

Well before 1997 the barriers to foreign ownership in Southeast Asia had become a major issue for trading partners, the Bretton Woods institutions and international investors as a whole. Indeed, the prominance given to liberalization of ownership in the IMF conditionalities led to accusations that this was serving the interests of international business rather than those of the Southeast Asia economies. While this should be seen as a coincidence of interest rather than a conspiracy (Wade and Veneroso, 1998: 11–12), the response of the Bretton Woods institutions and the USA to the crisis brought home to the Southeast Asian economies that the privileged position that they had enjoyed during the Cold War had ended. Geopolitics had been replaced by geo-economics:

> With the end of the Cold War the world had been made safe for capitalism. Under this situation American sensitivities changed and there were demands for free access to the Asian economies. Almost overnight the Asian economies ceased to be the showpiece of capitalism in the Third World and became directly at odds with American (in particular) interests and ideology.
> (Chang Noi, 'Don't write off the Asian economic model just yet', *The Nation*, 19 August 1998: A5)

Under these radically changed regional and global circumstances, the Southeast Asian economies are facing some serious challenges. They have reaped very considerable benefits from economic globalization, while continuing to shield significant parts of their economies from its direct impact. Since 1997 there has been some significant opening of the Southeast Asian economies, particularly with respect to foreign ownership. However, as is argued below, while this has served to increase trade and investment flows, very significant levels of protection remain. This has contributed to the continuation of the very distinctive Southeast Asian business forms with their high levels of social capital and close links with the state. As in the pre-crisis period, such protection of the domestic sector is coming under increasing pressure from major trading partners, the international institutions, and domestic elements that favour fuller engagement with the forces of economic globalization. There is here the broader question of whether continuing protectionism is compatible with sustained economic recovery, given that Southeast Asian growth remains closely tied to trade and investment flows, particularly with East Asia.

PRE-CRISIS GROWTH, REGIONAL INTEGRATION AND LIBERALIZATION

The pre-1997 patterns of growth were rooted in the position that Southeast Asia occupied during the Cold War, with pro-Western countries in the region receiving high levels of assistance, privileged access to markets and comparatively generous and gentle treatment by the Bretton Woods institutions. The latter was particularly evident during the crises of the early 1980s (Dixon, 1995: 213–16). The Southeast Asian economies (with the exception of the Philippines) came rapidly out of their crises with little of the hardline structural adjustment or debt overhang experienced by much of Latin America and Sub-Saharan Africa. Southeast Asian recovery was closely associated with major changes in industrial production in Japan, South Korea and Taiwan (and, within the region, Singapore). This involved the shedding and exporting of a wide range of processes that were variously low-tech, polluting or seeking 'third market' locations. The associated large-scale export of capital was facilitated by the liberalization of financial regimes in South Korea and Taiwan (Urata, 2001: 418–25). Southeast Asia was to be the major beneficiary of these changes. Thus, from the mid-1980s rapid economic growth in the region centred on the export of manufactured goods and high levels of FDI (Munakat, 2006: 169–70). Under these conditions there was rapid expansion of Southeast Asian domestic business, which generally remained both highly protected and closely connected with the state.

By 1996 Southeast Asia had become a key part of a broader Pacific Asia trade, investment and production complex. Under this, Pacific Asian economies increasingly traded and invested within the region (Urata, 2001). Behind the increasingly complex flows lay a series of nested regional divisions of labour (RDLs), rooted in differential labour costs and exemplified by the regional production systems of regional and extra-regionally based TNCs (Dixon, 1998: 130–1). From the mid-1980s large numbers of East Asian companies became 'transnational' on a Pacific Asia regional basis. This was accompanied within Southeast Asia by Singapore's 'second industrial revolution', the related export of capital and the establishment of the city-state as a conduit for regional and extra-regional trade and investment and as a highly attractive location for the headquarters of regionally organized TNCs. The latter included increasingly large numbers of extra-regional firms as Pacific Asia became a major focus for FDI. The resultant regional production system was far more extensive than in other regions, with strikingly high levels of disaggregated production, and related intra-regional and intra-industry flows (Gill *et al.*, 2007: 82–3, 86–7). Thus, unlike other major components of the global system, trade and investment flows move in parallel (Gill *et al.*, 2007: 87).

For most of the Southeast Asian economies, the result was a high level of dependence on the export of manufactured goods, and trade and FDI flows from East Asia (Japan and increasingly the NIEs) and, within the region, Singapore. The pattern of FDI and manufacturing export-led growth started in Thailand,[3] spreading to Malaysia, Indonesia, the Philippines (where the economy began to emerge from a long period of recession and recurrent crisis) and Vietnam (which was rapidly re-engaging with the regional and global economies).[4] These developments were from the late 1980s supported by some significant liberalization of Southeast Asian trade and financial regimes, though it is important not to see this as either externally imposed or the driving force of growth. In the financial sector, Indonesia had removed most controls on cross-border flows in 1970 (Booth, 2007: 8), while in Thailand the establishment of an almost free capital regime and the Bangkok International Banking Facility (BIBF) in 1992–93 was heavily promoted by influential elements of domestic capital (Pasuk Phongpaichit and Baker, 1995: 345–64; Dixon, 2001: 56; Booth, 2007: 8). In Thailand, liberalization tended to follow the rapid growth and increased trade and investment flows rather than lead them (Dixon, 1999: 122).

Overall, while there was significant pre-1997 liberalization, this left much of Southeast Asian business surprisingly well insulated from many aspects of globalization, while facilitating access to markets and international capital. This was particularly the case with such sectors as banking, reflecting views of their importance to the domestic economy as well as established political influence. Most significantly, foreign ownership of domestic companies remained heavily restricted throughout the region.[5]

SOUTHEAST ASIAN BUSINESS

The 1997 crisis drew attention to the form and practice of Southeast Asian business, areas that had previously been very largely ignored by commentators. It can be argued that Southeast Asian business had performed extremely well prior to the mid-1990s, with failures being absorbed by the dense business networks, high rates of economic growth, buoyant export markets and large amounts of foreign capital. However, many weak sectors had been highly protected from both international and domestic competition, and repeated failures of financial institutions necessitated significant state intervention. In Thailand the state intervened 32 times between 1983 and 1996 in order to support individual institutions (see Ammar Siamwalla, 2001: 7–10). These recurrent crises were indicative of the weakness of central regulation and banking practices that no government had been able, or perhaps willing, to confront. Despite this, the state was always able to contain the crisis and maintain the stability of the system as a whole. There is perhaps more robustness in the business systems and the capacity of the states to effectively intervene under conditions of rapid growth and structural change than has been generally acknowledged. However, it could also be argued that the knowledge that the state would intervene gave the financial institutions little incentive to adopt more prudent lending practices.[6]

Since 1997 what Woo-Cumings (2001) has termed the 'Southeast Asian Chinese business model' has been blamed by the Bretton Woods institutions for corporate sector problems in Indonesia and Thailand (Booth, 2009: 4). Particular attention focused on the tendency for even large Southeast Asian corporations to be family controlled, with a lack of clear separation between ownership and management, and having close links with banks.

In 1997 the percentage of listed company equity held by major family groups was: Indonesia 67.3; Malaysia 42.6; the Philippines 46.4; Singapore 44.8; and Thailand 51.9 (Claessons *et al.*, 1998, cited by Nam, Kang and Kim, 2001: 95). In Indonesia, 16 large family-controlled conglomerates, including several banks, owned 70 per cent of the Jakarta Stock Exchange equity (Indonesia Capital Markets, *Annual Report*, 1997). These figures almost certainly underestimate the concentration of corporate control in family hands, which was extended formally through the use of pyramid structures, cross-holdings and deviations from one-share-one-vote rules (Claessens, Djankov and Lang, 1999: 3). Informally, the extended kinship system further concentrates effective control, while facilitating the coordination of activities and business operations. Overall, this type of business form involves high levels of social capital with companies deeply embedded in dense and complex networks (Crawford, 2000).[7]

All of the above factors are involved in, and reinforced by, the tendency for groupings of companies to cluster around family-controlled banks. Indeed, some have described the banks as operating as 'family treasuries' (Hewison, 2000: 203). In Indonesia, the Salim group, which in 1995 controlled 17 per cent of the Jakarta Stock Exchange equity, centred on the Bank Central Asia, Indonesia's then largest private commercial bank (Brown, 2000: 250–57). A very similar pattern of bank-centred groups had also developed in Thailand (Muscat, 1994: 114–17; Pasuk Phongpaichit and Baker, 1995: 122; Jansen, 1997: 55–65). Such banks provided the majority of funding for the linked companies, which in turn dominated the banks' lending activities. A study of Indonesian banks concluded that, in 1995, 42 of them had lent over 50 per cent of their loans to linked companies (McLeod and Garnaut, 1998: 295). The close linkages with the banks enabled companies to raise large amounts of capital at short notice without recourse to the markets or even Anglo-American-style business plans.[8] Thus, the concentration of ownership was not diluted by share issues, and capitalization levels remained low.[9] For the critics of the Southeast Asian corporate sector, this ability to bypass the 'discipline' of the markets encouraged the sort of unsound lending (and borrowing) that lay at the heart of the 1997 crisis.[10] In contrast, advocates stress that the ability to raise finance through the banks at short notice was central to the successful manner in which companies operated in a flexible, opportunist and market-adaptive manner in 'highly charged' political environments (Crawford, 2000; Woo-Cumings, 2001: 5–6).

Suehiro and Nateneapha Wailerdsak (2004: 91) concluded from a detailed study of Thai family firms that:

> The persistence of all family firms should not be considered as the consequence of the supposed incapacity of Thai or other local entrepreneurs to understand and adopt managerial models of the American modern industrial corporation. Instead, the enduring presence of this particular form of business organisation, especially specialized family business and modern family conglomerates, can be seen as an alternative demonstration of its efficiency and rationality against a defined institutional framework rather than a failure.

More generally, Woo-Cumings (2001: 2) has suggested that Southeast Asian Chinese business practice remains efficient and adaptive enough to need little reform. She further stressed that reform of these structures and practices not only has proved extremely difficult, but if successful might well seriously damage both the resilience and the dynamism of the domestically owned business sectors in much of Southeast Asia. Others have considered that reforms will merely get rid of the traditional strengths of the system without correcting the perceived structural weaknesses (Sin, 2002: 18, 31; Sin and Chang, 2002). Against such views, Regnier (2000: 17) concluded that the Thai–Chinese family business structure worked extremely effectively until the changed conditions of the 1980s. Subsequently, it has become increasingly a barrier to expansion, raising productivity and enhancing competitiveness. Scott (1997) has suggested that the need for personal links limits expansion unless there is a strong and supportive state sector. Certainly the very large corporations and business groups that had developed in Southeast Asia by the mid-1990s had done so under generally highly protected conditions. However, a large number had come to successfully operate transnationally in Southeast Asia and Pacific Asia as a whole, though it could be argued that this generally involved extending operations through personal links into other generally favoured 'Chinese-Asian' business communities.[11] Thus, there is still a question mark over the ability of Southeast Asian business to operate under open and highly globalized conditions.[12]

THE LIBERALIZATION OF FOREIGN OWNERSHIP

Since 1997 there has been significant liberalization of foreign ownership regulations in all the major Southeast Asian economies except Vietnam. In Indonesia and Thailand the reforms were a direct result of IMF conditionalities attached to the 'rescue packages'; elsewhere the relaxation of controls was generally part of wider responses to falling trade, investment and growth.

As may be seen from Table 3.4, prior to the 1997 crisis only in the Philippines and Singapore were there comparatively liberal foreign ownership situations. Elsewhere, where foreign ownership *was* permitted, it was generally either limited to non-controlling levels or confined to various export and other priority sectors under the jurisdiction of such bodies as the Thai Board of Investment (BOI) and the Indonesia Capital Investment Coordinating Board (BKPM).

In 1997 Thailand had the most restrictive foreign ownership regulations in the region, and the IMF demands for rapid reform were opposed by some key elements of the Thai political, bureaucratic and judicial systems (Dixon, 2006: 24). Such opposition also had some considerable popular

Table 3.4   Limits on foreign ownership in 1997

Indonesia	Up to 49% of listed companies; not permitted for unlisted companies; exclusion from such areas as downstream oil and gas, banking and insurance; requirement that most foreign activity had to involve JVs or other forms of cooperation
Malaysia	Generally limited to 30% of equity; stipulation that 30% of shares must be held by *bumiputra*; exclusion from areas deemed in the national interest, e.g. banking, insurance and motor vehicles, and those involving ownership of land
Philippines	100% ownership permitted, but excluded from mass media, telecommunications, retailing, public utilities, resource exploitation, including mining and inshore fishing; limited to 30% in advertising, 40% where land ownership is involved or the enterprise is small,* and 60% in banking
Singapore	Foreign ownership restricted in: media, legal and other professional services, marketing, residential property ownership, banking (40%), insurance (20%); banking approval of the Monetary Authority or holdings of 5% or more; listed companies deemed to be in the national interest limited, e.g. 27.5% for Singapore Airlines
Thailand	Full foreign ownership effectively excluded from all areas under the 1972 Alien Business Law; banking and finance limited to 25%; minority ownership excluded from a wide range of areas, including agriculture and any involving ownership of land

Note: * Defined as less than US$200,000 capitalization in 2003.

Source.   Dixon (2006: 20).

and often highly emotive support (Dixon, 2004: 61; Glassman, 2001a: 142, 2001b). Former prime minister Chavalit Yongchaiyudh saw allowing foreign ownership as 'more difficult for us because we have never been colonised before' (cited in *Far Eastern Economic Review*, 27 December 1998: 13). Despite this, and in accord with the agreement reached with the IMF in mid-August 1997, some immediate moves were made to liberalize foreign ownership. These included permitting majority stakes in the distressed financial sector (*Bangkok Post*, 12 November 1997) and in Thai companies operating under the BOI promotion scheme (*Bangkok Post*, 23 February 1998; Freshfields, 2001). These and other ad hoc measures implemented during 1998 and 1999 rapidly opened the Thai economy and were brought together in the Foreign Business Act, which became effective on 4 March 2000.

While much of the Thai economy had been rapidly opened, foreign participation continued to be limited for some activities on the grounds of national security, cultural consideration, environmental issues, Thai nationals not being considered ready to compete with foreigners and other 'special reasons' (Piyanuj Ratprasatporn and Kobkit Thienpreecha, 2002: 2, 15–19; Freshfields, 2004). These areas included the media, farming, fishing and real estate, domestic transport, mining, sugar refining, rice milling, engineering, architecture services, most construction, tourist services, low-level wholesaling and retailing, insurance, telecommunications, accountancy, law and some brokerage services (EIU, 2003a: 16). In addition, there are various indirect barriers to foreign control. The restrictions on direct purchase of real estate can sometimes prevent foreign investors from acquiring majority control, and anti-trust laws can effectively block acquisitions that would result in a dominant market position. However, the relaxing of controls was sufficient to engender a major surge in acquisitions-related FDI during 1998–2001 (see the section 'Investment since 1997').

While the liberalization of foreign ownership and its result have been most dramatic in Thailand, there were also some far-reaching changes in Indonesia. However, these were very much slower to be implemented, with, as in Thailand, considerable resistance at all levels in the system. There was no effective liberalization until 2000, when most of the economy was opened to full foreign ownership (Jayasuriya and Rosser, 2001: 245; Robison, 2001: 120; EIU, 2003b; Freshfields, 2004). The limits on foreign ownership of listed companies were raised to 100 per cent and 85 per cent for unlisted companies. Particularly significant was the opening of the insurance and banking sectors (see Freshfields, 2001: 15). However, in most cases involving majority ownership, official permission remains necessary and foreign participation remains restricted in a number of key areas, notably the downstream oil and gas sector. In addition, the government reserves the right to veto any transfer of equity to foreign owners if judged 'undesirable' (EIU, 2007a: 17). Thus, while there has been substantial liberalization of foreign ownership restrictions, some significant obstacles remain in place, and approval processes continue to be slow – a situation reinforced by official attitudes, including those of the judiciary (Kawai, 2000: 294–5, 325). Overall, as in the pre-reform period, foreign entry and operation are still often made extremely difficult by the intricate web of laws and regulations, coupled with vague administrative guidance, bureaucratic fiat and related delays. However, as in Thailand, the reduced controls were sufficient to promote a major expansion of acquisitions-related FDI (see the section 'Investment since 1997').

Before the 1997 crisis, Malaysia was, after Singapore, the economy most heavily dependent on FDI[13] and that allowed fully owned foreign companies to operate in the export sector with some of the fewest restrictions in the region (Ito, 2001: 66; Jomo, 2001: 496). However, foreign companies could not acquire controlling interests in Malaysian registered companies, and the state exercised considerable discretionary powers over individual investments (EIU, 2004b: 15). In the wake of the 1997 crisis, Malaysia rejected IMF assistance, reimposed controls over cross-border financial movements, and implemented a programme of support for the domestic corporate and banking sectors (see for example Athukorala, 2000; Torres, 2004).

Under these more nationalistic policies it was perhaps not surprising that there were no immediate moves to reduce the restrictions on foreign ownership. However, with falling growth and investment some restrictions were lifted. The limit on telecommunications was raised to 49 per cent (but to be reviewed on a case-by-case basis), the limit on real estate was raised to 50 per cent, and from mid-1998 100 per cent foreign ownership of new manufacturing projects was permitted, except in areas where local companies were deemed to be well established (EIU, 2004c: 15). More significantly, in May 2003 there was a general relaxation of the 30 per cent limit on foreign equity holding in local firms (see Table 3.4), but approval had to be obtained from the Foreign Investment Committee for acquisitions involving 15 per cent or more (EIU, 2007b: 24). However, the 30 per cent *bumiputra* requirement remained in force (EIU, 2004c: 15). In addition, approval processes can be lengthy, and investors seeking to make acquisitions or mergers must prove that these would not be against the national interest and would provide net economic benefit to Malaysia (EIU, 2003c: 29; Freshfields, 2001: 33, 2004: 36; UNCTAD, 2000: 147, Box V4).

In the Philippines the comparatively liberal foreign ownership situation has seen only limited further relaxation of controls. While a significant number of proposals have been advanced, these have generally failed to be implemented, owing to opposition in the Congress, related vested interests and significant popular support (EIU, 2003a: 10, 12–13). A major exception was the liberalization of the banking sector. From May 2000, foreign interests were permitted to acquire 100 per cent of local banks. However, this is limited in practice by the stipulation that not more than 30 per cent of total domestic banking assets can be foreign owned. The liberal foreign ownership situation in the Philippines, however, has continued to be seriously compromised by complex rules and procedures, weak enforcement of regulations, limited reform of corporate governance, and the overall difficulties involved in rapidly concluding M&A arrangements (Kawai, 2000: 307; Abrenica and Llando, 2003: 276–7; EIU, 2003a: 16).

In Singapore, with the 1997 crisis, the government opted to further liberalize the financial regime (Lim, 2002: 29–30). Some new areas were opened to foreign activity (but not full ownership), for example the state-controlled superannuation funds, and ownership restrictions have been relaxed for the domestic telecommunications, law, medicine and banking sectors (Jayasuriya and Rosser, 2001: 248–9, 252; Rodan, 2001: 155, 157). While the government removed the 40 per cent ceiling on foreign owner-ship of local banks, the approval of the Monetary Authority of Singapore is required, and it has stated that it is not prepared to approve any foreign acquisition of a local bank (Freshfields, 2001: 50, 2004: 54). A similar position was adopted following the removal of the 20 per cent ceiling on foreign ownership of finance companies (EIU, 2004a: 17). Overall, while much more significant than in the Philippines, post-1997 liberalization in Singapore has also been limited. However, both before and after the 1997 crisis, Singapore had by far the most open position on foreign ownership in Southeast Asia and the clearest and simplest M&A procedure (EIU, 2004a: 17–18; Freshfields, 2004: 59).

By 2003, while there had been significant liberalization of foreign own-ership in most of Southeast Asia, some major barriers remained. These were reinforced by the lack or ineffectiveness of reform in other areas. Most notably, outside of Singapore, the cumbersome (and protracted) bankruptcy procedures limit the numbers of distressed assets that become available for purchase. This has been a problem particularly in Indonesia and Thailand despite the relatively large volume of foreign purchases that have taken place since 1997 (Robison, 2001: 123; World Bank, 2005: 32, Section 5). In Thailand, reforms of the bankruptcy laws, initially praised by the World Bank, have proved largely ineffective in speeding up the process in the face of the partiality of the judiciary, bureaucratic obstruc-tion and close personal networks (World Bank, 2001: 10–11, 42–3).

Again, outside of Singapore, the legal framework for M&A remains weak, with complex and demanding procedures that frequently differ markedly from Western practice (Brimble, 2002: 20; EIU, 2003a: 17–18, 43–4; Freshfields, 2004: 88–93). Serious problems result for buyers from regulations that, for example, prevent the forced buyout of minority shareholders while enabling them to block measures such as de-listing, even in the face of 75 per cent control and articles of association that place limits on foreign ownership (for examples see Freshfields, 2001, 2004).[14] It is not that these types of barriers to takeovers and mergers are uncommon outside Southeast Asia, but, in combination with still often limited trans-parency, there are real dangers of 'poisoned pills' hidden in apparently attractive deals. In this context, the lack of transparency extends beyond hidden agreements, undisclosed share ownership and complex articles of association, to include uncertainty over levels of company liabilities.

The persistence of direct and indirect limitations to the extension of foreign ownership continues to be reinforced by general opposition to foreign ownership. This became a key element of increased economic nationalism in the wake of the 1997 crisis. While this was most overt in the case of Malaysian government policy, it has been of considerable importance in Indonesia, Thailand and the Philippines (see for example Glassman, 2001a: 517–24; Kasian Tejapira, 2002; Dixon, 2004: 60–64). However, no matter how liberalized the ownership regulations, reformed the domestic corporate and legal procedures, or acquiescent the system, combinations of low levels of capitalization, the structure of ownership, and a business system that operates to a great extent through close personal links can seriously limit the extension of foreign control and operation.

The low levels of capitalization in much of the Southeast Asian corporate sector (Bartels and Freeman, 2000: 2–3) combine with high levels of family ownership and concentration of shares in a small number of hands to significantly inhibit M&A activity (*Economist*, 2000: 93; Kim, Yun-Hwan, 2000: 21, 28–9; Nam, Kang and Kim, 2001; Kasian Tejapira, 2002: 325; Khan, 2002). It may be that in some areas the strength of family control reduced in the wake of the 1997 crisis (Dixon, 2004: 54; Suehiro and Nateneapha Wailerdsak, 2004: 81). However, in other areas control has increased and many family firms have prospered, expanded and diversified their operations (Suehiro and Natencapha Wailerdsak, 2004: 81). Be that as it may, the interlocking ownership patterns, like that of the Japanese *keiretsu* system, continue to make M&A activity particularly difficult. The situation is further constrained by the existence of large non-traded state sectors and major listed companies in which the state has a controlling interest. In 1997, 40.1 per cent of the share value of traded companies in Singapore was held by the state, and 43.8 per cent in Malaysia (Claessons *et al.*, 1998, cited by Nam, Kang and Kim, 2001: 95).

In addition to the above barriers and disincentives, the Southeast Asian business communities generally hold very negative views of mergers and the disposal of assets (Bartels, 2004: 156). Even under crisis conditions, owners of distressed assets are reluctant to sell if any alternative could be negotiated. Given the limited ability of creditors to force the issue, debtors can often 'wait out' the situation (Dixon, 2004: 58–9), a situation facilitated by deficient bankruptcy procedures and continuing close personal linkages with banks, other businesses and the state.[15] Apart from the general opposition to foreign control noted above, in Thailand the state has given considerable assistance to distressed sectors with the aim of rehabilitating rather than liquidating the assets of companies.[16]

Both before and after the crisis, where mergers occur they are the result of negotiations between key individuals, reflecting the manner in which personal relations have been central to Southeast Asian business operations (Markland, 2001: 2). This tends to militate against purchase by 'outsiders' and renders any form of aggressive M&A extremely rare domestically and even more so cross-border (Nam, Kang and Kim, 2001: 99–100; Rossi and Volpin, 2002: 27).

INVESTMENT SINCE 1997

The sharp decline in growth of GDP and exports that characterized the 1997 crisis was not followed by FDI (Tables 3.1, 3.2 and 3.3). At the regional level, Southeast Asia's share of global inflows declined sharply, but the volume was more than maintained. However, flows have become much more volatile and uneven across the region. Particularly striking is the contrast between the two major economies most seriously affected by the crisis, Indonesia and Thailand. In the former, FDI flows became negative in 1998, and high levels of dis-investment occurred in each year until 2003. The negative balance for the whole period 1998–2003 was the equivalent of 92.1 per cent of the net inflows for 1991–96.

In contrast, Thailand experienced a major surge of FDI during 1998 and 1999, with lower, but still historically high, levels during 2000 and 2001, before FDI declined sharply in 2002. Between 1997 and 2001 net FDI inflows into Thailand were US$24875 million, compared with US$11 784 million in 1991–96 and US$6,000 million in 1986–90 – the periods during which the kingdom was depicted as experiencing a major FDI-driven boom (Dixon, 1995, 1999: 122–38; Jansen, 1997: 147–98; see also the comments below on FDI and gross domestic capital formation (GDCF). The stark contrast between Indonesia's and Thailand's FDI since 1997 has to be seen in terms of the far more uncertain operating conditions that have prevailed in the former (UNCTAD, 2003: 48; EIU, 2004d: 8), the more limited progress made in re-capitalization, and the much slower liberalization of investment and foreign ownership regulations (see the previous section).

Thailand was the most spectacular case of increase during 1997–2001, and Indonesia the only case of flows becoming negative. Of the other economies, only Laos and Malaysia experienced reduced inflows (Table 3.3). The slight fall in FDI flows into Laos reflects the limited and precarious nature of the country's economic growth, marginal attraction for investors and the scale and impact of the crisis.[17] In contrast, Malaysia, despite a 36.5 per cent decline in net inflows, remained, in regional and global terms, a major recipient of FDI. However, given Malaysia's apparently successful weathering of the 1997 crisis, the sharp fall in FDI demands some explanation.[18] It would seem likely that the re-imposition of controls over capital movements played a part, though to nothing like the extent predicted by the IMF and advocates of financial liberalization (see the views cited by Bello, Cunningham and Li Kheng Poh, 1998; Hale, 1998; *Economist*, 1999: 79). Following the imposition of controls, the Heritage Foundation (2001) sharply reduced Malaysia's 'economic freedom' score for FDI, and Welsh (2007: 17) considered that Malaysian policy undermined investor confidence. However, Athukorala (2000: 182–3) found little evidence for the controls being responsible for reduced flows, suggesting they could be explained by combinations of over-capacity in domestic manufacturing and reduced outflows from Japan and Taiwan – responsible for nearly half of Malaysian net inflows – in response to their own domestic problems. Perhaps more importantly, the Malaysian government's support for the corporate sector, banking reform and limited liberalizing of foreign ownership regulations meant that there were fewer distressed assets available to foreign investors and rather less scope for cross-border M&A activity. Only from 2006 does Malaysian FDI exceed pre-crisis levels, and this was accompanied by a significant increase in the level and contribution of M&A.

Despite the decline in Malaysian FDI, its importance relative to GDCF largely recovered in 2002–06 (Table 3.5). However, this reflects both the fall in FDI and the failure of GDCP to recover, relative to GDP, to pre-crisis levels (Table 3.6). There have been similar marked failures of GDCF to recover in the Philippines, Singapore and Thailand. However, in the latter two cases, this has been accompanied by extraordinary increases in FDI. In sharp contrast to all of these, Vietnam, which has experienced a very steep decline in FDI dependence, has experienced a significant increase in foreign investment and a remarkable expansion of GDCF (Tables 3.5 and 3.6).

The changes in the levels and dependence on FDI since 1997 have also been accompanied by marked changes in composition. Prior to the 1997 crisis, while the Southeast Asian economies had been major recipients of FDI, they were limited areas of activity for cross-border M&A (Table 3.7). During the period 1990–96, M&A activity was of significance compared to FDI only in the Philippines and, to a lesser extent, Singapore, reflecting their more liberal foreign ownership regulations (see Table 3.4), reinforced in the case of the Philippines by significant privatization.

During the latter part of 1997 and the early months of 1998, the collapse of large parts of the corporate sector, particularly in Indonesia and Thailand, led to expectations of widespread distressed assets available at 'fire sale' prices, with foreign companies picking up substantial assets at rock-bottom prices (Gilley, 1998; Krugman, 1998; Sender, 1998). In the

Table 3.5 FDI as a percentage of gross domestic capital formation

	Annual average 1991–96	Annual average 1997–2001	Annual average 2002–06	2002	2003	2004	2005	2006	2007	2008
Indonesia	5.8	−8.5	5.3	0.4	−1.3	3.4	12.8	5.6	6.4	5.6
Malaysia	19.3	14.0	16.9	14.5	10.8	19.1	15.2	18.6	20.6	18.4
Philippines	8.5	9.7	8.8	13.3	2.6	4.8	12.6	14.1	13.8	6.2
Singapore	28.8	39.7	58.4	25.1	41.7	77.5	57.6	79.5	78.7	43.8
Thailand	3.7	17.7	11.5	3.3	5.7	14.0	17.5	16.5	17.1	13.5
Vietnam	34.9	22.0	16.1	11.0	11.6	10.6	11.5	12.5	25.5	24.1
Hong Kong	15.9	60.1	71.3	26.4	39.4	96.4	90.4	103.9	130.4	148.8
South Korea	0.8	5.2	2.7	1.9	2.1	4.5	3.0	1.9	0.9	2.8
Taiwan	2.4	4.6	3.7	2.9	0.9	2.8	2.3	10.3	9.6	6.7
China	11.6	11.9	8.4	10.4	8.6	8.0	8.8	8.0	6.0	6.0

Source: UNCTAD, *Foreign Investment Yearbook*, various issues.

Table 3.6   Gross domestic capital formation as a percentage of GDP

	Annual average 1991–96	Annual average 1997–2001	Annual average 2002–06	2002	2003	2004	2005	2006
Indonesia	26.7	19.8	22.1	19.0	19.3	22.4	23.6	24.0
Malaysia	39.8	28.1	21.0	23.2	22.1	20.5	20.0	20.2
Philippines	23.4	20.5	15.5	17.6	16.8	16.1	14.5	13.8
Singapore	35.0	33.7	23.8	25.7	24.9	23.9	22.3	23.1
Thailand	40.5	24.4	26.7	22.8	24.0	26.3	28.9	29.7
Vietnam	22.5	27.4	32.8	31.1	33.4	33.4	33.1	N/A
Hong Kong	29.1	29.0	21.5	22.1	21.2	21.3	20.9	21.5
South Korea	36.8	29.4	29.4	29.1	29.9	29.5	29.3	29.0
Taiwan N/A								
China	34.4	35.7	40.0	46.3	39.2	40.6	41.0	40.8

N/A not available.

Source: UNCTAD, *Foreign Investment Yearbook*, various issues.

Table 3.7 Cross-border M&A by country of selling (US$m)

	Annual average 1987–90	Annual average 1991–96	Annual average 1997–2001	Annual average 2002–06	2002	2003	2004	2005	2006	2007	2008
Brunei	–	–	–	1.0	–	–	5	–	–	–	–
Cambodia	–	–	–	0.2	–	–	1	–	9	6	30
Indonesia	69.7	349.3	1305.4	2681.4	2790	2031	1269	6763	388	1705	2044
Laos	–	1.7	53.7	84.4	266	–	85	71	–	–	–
Malaysia	201.8	333.5	900.6	1094.4	485	84	638	1454	2509	3926	2781
Myanmar	–	3.2	52.0	83.4	–	417	–	–	–	–	–
Philippines	61.0	518.3	2002.8	399.0	544	230	733	328	-134	1165	2621
Singapore	385.0	510.2	2024.6	3323.4	556	1766	1190	5802	2924	7422	14226
Thailand	17.5	183.8	2955.8	1238.0	247	55	1236	338	3771	2372	120
Vietnam	–	1.5	29.0	52.8	6	18	74	–	29	411	859
SE Asia	735.0	1439.1	9364.0	8958.0	4894	4601	5231	14756	9496	17007	22681
Developing economies	4661.3	15916.5	76024.0	71029.3	44532	42130	64747	132708	97525	127670	121367
World	120327.5	155726.5	669167.0	440919.3	369789	296988	380598	716302	635940	1031100	673214
SE Asia/Developing economies %	15.8	9.0	12.3	12.6	11.0	10.9	8.1	11.1	9.7	13.3	18.7
SE Asia/World %	0.6	0.9	1.4	2.0	1.3	1.6	1.4	2.1	1.5	1.6	3.4

– zero or near zero.

Source: UNCTAD, *Foreign Investment Yearbook*, various issues.

Table 3.8   Cross-border M&A as a percentage of FDI

	Annual average 1987–90	Annual average 1991–96	Annual average 1997–2001	Annual Average 2002–06	2007	2008
Brunei	–	0.2	–	–	–	–
Cambodia	–	–	–	–	0.7	3.6
Indonesia	13.8	11.7	*	87.4	24.6	25.8
Laos	–	3.1	110.2	79.9	–	–
Malaysia	21.7	6.1	26.1	26.9	34.5	34.7
Myanmar	–	1.2	11.5	37.5	–	–
Philippines	15.3	42.2	159.9	27.9	40.0	172.4
Singapore	14.7	5.1	14.6	22.1	23.5	62.6
Thailand	1.9	9.4	59.4	22.6	20.9	1.2
Vietnam	–	0.1	1.7	3.1	6.1	10.7
SE Asia	13.7	9.3	36.3	27.6	23.0	37.9
Third world	24.9	27.3	32.6	27.2	20.6	16.5
World	80.4	53.8	75.0	62.5	52.1	39.7

– zero or near zero.
* not meaningful.

Source: Calculated from Tables 3.3 and 3.7.

event, this was tempered by the economic and political disruption, particularly in Indonesia, continuing restrictions on foreign ownership, and the reluctance of many owners to sell. However, as the crisis spread and deepened and foreign ownership regulations were relaxed (see the previous section), cross-border M&A became increasingly common features of Southeast Asia as the region became a new and lucrative hunting ground for purchasers of corporate assets. However, much of the early activity took the form of foreign partners acquiring long-sought majority or full ownership of local joint ventures as this became permitted (*Acquisitions Monthly*, January 1999: 44).

The surge of M&A activity began in the Philippines in 1997, expanding into Thailand from 1998, Singapore from 1999 and Indonesia from 2001. As may be seen from Table 3.8, since 1997 M&A has become a major feature of Southeast Asian FDI – its share rising in 1997–2001 to some four times the 1991–96 level. For the region as a whole it was the surge in M&A that accounted for increased FDI inflows in the wake of the crisis.[19] At the national level this was most spectacularly the case for Thailand.[20]

Since 1997 Southeast Asia has increased its share of global M&A, but the region remains a comparatively small player in M&A, with activity at a very early stage (Table 3.7). However, M&A's share of Southeast Asian FDI has moved very close to that of the third world as a whole (Table 3.8). This may not be a sustainable situation, given the continuing barriers to foreign ownership and operation. In addition, the expansion of cross-border M&A in Southeast Asia since 1997 does not seem to have softened the attitude of policy makers to such activity. Generally it seems to have been regarded as a short-term and unavoidable consequence of the 1997 crisis and its aftermath. Foreign investment is still regarded as principally 'greenfield' (Buckley, 2004: 30; Hill, 2004: 258). In terms of maintaining investment flows, such views may be seriously misplaced. Southeast Asia seems unlikely to regain its attraction for greenfield investment.

Even if M&A continues at its present level, in terms of the growth of domestic economies and production systems, the impact is very different from that of investment in new or extended projects. That is, cross-border M&A links existing capacity to international networks, rather than adding to it.[21] While it can be argued that this *can* lead to new investment, expansion of activity, innovation and efficiency gains, this is far from certain. UNCTAD (2000: xxii–xxviii) concluded from a survey of available material that the short-term impact of M&A is likely on balance to have a more adverse impact on the sectors concerned than greenfield M&A, particularly with respect to the 'crowding out' of domestic operations in the longer term.

There is no clear evidence that increased foreign ownership has in other contexts led to the sort of developments that the IMF and the majority of commentators envisaged for Southeast Asia.[22] To date there is certainly no indication from Southeast Asia that increased foreign ownership is combining with reforms to significantly change the business forms and practice. This may well reflect the early stage of M&A activity in the region, but it may also be that Southeast Asian business remains highly resistant to foreign control and less than conducive to foreign operations. This is certainly the case in the Thai banking sector.

Between 1997 and 2002 Thailand received the largest inflow of M&A in Southeast Asia, 37.5 per cent going into the banking sector. This increased foreign equity holdings in the sector from 9.5 per cent to 38 (Dixon, 2004: 54). However, this only resulted in four of the smaller (more highly capitalized and more distressed) banks passing into majority foreign ownership. These accounted for 5.6 per cent of deposits, 6.2 per cent of the market and 4.7 per cent of assets (Dixon, 2004: 54).[23] Further expansion is inhibited by the ownership pattern and general opposition to foreign control. In addition, the foreign banks have experienced significant operating difficulties and are out-performed by the Thai-controlled banks (*Asian Money*, 2004, XV: 33). They are simply not part of the close-knit and highly personalized banking network, and they are reported to be subject to much greater official scrutiny (EIU, 2003a: 13; Dixon, 2004: 54–5). While there is some evidence to suggest that the foreign banks have played a role in stimulating modernization in terms of forms of credit, the spread of ATMs and on-line banking, it is far less clear whether they have led to a diffusion of international banking practices (Dixon, 2006: 30–31).

The concentration of M&A in the Thai banking sector appears to have been an exception in regional terms – certainly for the financial sector (Hihikawa, 2003: 2). Elsewhere, what evidence there is points to very patchy expansions of foreign control, with no major corporations or groups passing out of local control (Dixon, 2004, 2006).[24] If this is the case, it may well be that the post-1997 expansion of foreign ownership remains too limited and fragmented to have, as yet, any major impact on Southeast Asian business systems. The question is whether, under prevailing conditions, cross-border M&A can continue to the point where major changes do occur. This raises the question of whether changes in the direction of, for example, the Anglo-American model would be in the best interests of Southeast Asian business and society.

REGIONAL INTEGRATION SINCE 1997

Until the 1997 crisis, regional integration between East and Southeast Asia was viewed as both a major advantage for the countries concerned and a significant factor in their rapid economic growth. Indeed, some commentators saw integration as leading to a new dynamic core of the global system that could increasingly 'buck' world trends (Kwan, 1994). Following the crisis there was a decline in the level of intra-regional trade and some questioning of the wisdom of high levels of regional interdependence (Urata, 2001: 453). This was marked by seeking markets outside of Pacific Asia and a proliferation of extra-regional bilateral trade agreements. These were accompanied by some very significant lowering of tariff levels (Table 3.9) and wide-ranging relaxation of controls over FDI (UNCTAD, 2007: 16, 42; World Bank, 2007: 11), of which the foreign ownership changes (see the section 'The liberalization of foreign ownership') are by far the most important.

With the general recovery of trade growth from 2001 (Table 3.2), Southeast Asian trade with East Asia returned to and then exceeded pre-crisis levels (Table 3.10). However, there have been some significant shifts in the patterns and composition of trade. Most strikingly there has been a shift away from Japan and towards China, Taiwan and South Korea. The reduced importance of Japan reflects the slow growth of the economy

Table 3.9   Average unweighted percentage import tariffs

	1996	2000	2007
Indonesia	10.8	7.8	6.6
Malaysia	8.4	7.7	5.8
Philippines	14.0	7.1	5.3
Singapore	0.4	0.0	0.0
Thailand	20.1	16.1	10.0
Vietnam	12.0	15.1	11.7

Source: World Integrated Trade solutions (WITS), http://wits.worldbank.org/witsweb/.

Table 3.10   Southeast Asian trade with East Asia as a percentage of the total value of the region's trade

	East Asia	Of which		
		Japan	NIEs*	China
1992–94	28.0	70.0	22.5	7.5
1995–97	28.9	60.2	30.8	9.0
1998–2000	32.4	52.7	34.8	12.5
2001–03	31.0	45.8	35.2	19.0
2004–06	32.7	38.2	37.3	24.5
2007–08	33.4	34.7	32.3	32.8

Note: * South Korea, Taiwan and Hong Kong.

Source: Calculated from *ASEAN Statistical Yearbook*, various issues.

and increasing Japanese investment and trade links with China, which to a degree have replaced direct links with Southeast Asia while in turn direct Japanese trade with Southeast Asia has been increasingly supplanted by that of Taiwan and South Korea – a continuation of a process apparent before the crisis. This has involved both an increased range of products and the rapid expansion of trade with previously less important partners, most notably the Philippines, whose attraction has increased markedly given comparative political and economic stability, low costs and some rapid trade liberalization.

The expansion of interregional trade has not been as closely matched by investment flows as in the pre-crisis period (Gill *et al.*, 2007, 58–9). Indeed, while East Asia remains a major source of FDI for Southeast Asia, its relative share remains below the immediate pre-crisis level (Table 3.11), though changes in the source of the inflows do show some parallels

Table 3.11   East Asian FDI as a percentage of total net Southeast Asian inflows

	East Asia	Of which		
		Japan	NIEs*	China
1995–97	30.0	67.3	31.9	0.8
1998–2000	16.8	53.0	42.9	4.1
2001–03	22.5	64.9	32.4	2.7
2004–06	23.3	73.4	18.9	7.7
2007–08	21.4	57.9	31.7	10.4

Note: * South Korea, Taiwan and Hong Kong.

Source: Calculated from various issues of: *ASEAN Statistical Yearbook*; *Statistics of Foreign Direct Investment in ASEAN*.

with trade, with a decline in Japan's share and an increase in China's. The reduced importance of East Asian investment reflects the increased attraction of China, and the changes in the composition and volatility of flows discussed previously. However, the changes still leave Southeast Asia firmly linked with East Asia through trade, investment and regional production networks, though the latter have tended to become more fragmented and complex, with finer divisions of labour. This reflects a narrowing of regional income differentials, diversification and sophistication of production, and less distinctive export profiles (Gill *et al.*, 2007: 91). The result is higher levels of intra-industry trade in semi-finished products and components – the latter have increased their share of intra-regional trade from 35 per cent in 1990–94 to 50 per cent in 2000–04 (Gill *et al.*, 2007: 21, 55–6, 96).

For Pacific Asia as a whole, the most striking development is the rapid integration of China into regional trade and investment flows. In the long run this may well be *the* most significant development for all the Southeast Asian economies. The expansion of Chinese trade has been accompanied by a remarkable sophistication of products (Chaponniere, 2007: 10), such that it exports significant volumes of items that would be associated with economies with some three times the per capita GDP.[25] In part this reflects high levels of R&D expenditure.[26] However, China has not yet lost its advantage in more labour-intensive products. Cross and Tan (2004: 143) concluded that China has 'sufficient numbers of workers skilled at each stage in the value chain to satisfy the current needs of most investors, even in the more capital intensive and knowledge-intensive sectors'. Thus, China is increasingly competing at the more sophisticated levels as well

Table 3.12   Percentage of exports to the USA that compete with China's
              exports to the USA

	1990	1995	2000	2003
Japan	3.2	8.5	16.2	21.9
South Korea	24.8	28.5	37.3	40.9
Taiwan	27.5	40.2	49.5	68.8
Singapore	14.7	19.2	34.8	40.1
Indonesia	48.5	59.7	68.0	66.8
Malaysia	37.4	36.8	47.3	65.0
Philippines	41.9	45.6	45.9	60.7
Thailand	36.4	47.5	55.7	69.8

Source: Kwan (2006).

as the more labour-intensive (but perhaps no longer at *the* most labour-intensive).[27]

Since the latter part of the 1990s there seems to have been a general loss of Southeast Asian markets in Japan and the USA to China (Booth, 2007: 17). As can be seen from Table 3.12, there have been significant increases in the proportion of Southeast Asian exports to the USA that are directly competed with by China. Holst and Wiess (2004: 1263) found that Southeast Asia had lost competitive advantage to China in such major areas as electronics, electrical goods, engineering products, textiles, garments and footwear. They argued that the resultant loss of markets was not balanced by increased exports to China.

Some writers have been more positive about the impact of China on Southeast Asia (Lall, 2003: 30; Ng and Yeats, 2003: 63), suggesting that it has been important in the upgrading of production and export profiles. Certainly Southeast Asia exports to China have (with the exception of Cambodia and Vietnam) increasingly comprised intermediate goods which are assembled for export to the EU and USA (Anderson, 2006; Chaponniere, 2007: 9). However, the impact of this is likely to be extremely uneven and may not compensate for the loss of markets. Particular concern centres on Thailand, which, as before the crisis, is losing the advantage in labour-intensive activities to China – most strikingly in the electronics sector – while being unable to make any broad-based transition to more sophisticated production.[28] Thailand is perhaps the most likely candidate to be fully caught in the 'middle-income trap'. Similarly, there are concerns over the longer-term position of Indonesia, the Philippines and Vietnam. In the former two, low levels of investment in skills and R&D may make it difficult to break out of low-tech exports, while for Vietnam similarities to Chinese production profiles at the lower end of the technological range, but at higher costs, may prove a major stumbling block.

While China may be a threat to some Southeast Asian economic sectors, the region's development prospects remain linked to the still strikingly dynamic Pacific Asia region. As in the pre-crisis period, economic growth, trade and investment are closely tied to increasing regional integration,[29] a process for which China has become the principal driver. For the Southeast Asian economies this cannot be divorced from a whole range of regional and extra-regional concerns over the economic and strategic implications of the rise of China. While ASEAN has been remarkably successful in presenting a unified front to China in terms of trade negotiations and territorial disputes, very different views persist amongst the member states. The generally favourable views of Thailand, Singapore and Cambodia contrast markedly with the very much more cautious approach of Indonesia, Malaysia and Vietnam. While these different positions certainly reflect a historical legacy, they also reflect current economic reality, with Indonesia and Malaysia less directly connected with East Asia in general and China in particular, and Vietnam being most directly a competitor.

Regional integration, both before and after the 1997 crisis, has taken place through an informal process based on complementarities, facilitated by progressive liberalization of tariffs and controls over FDI. How much further integration can go without significant institutional structures remains a matter of serious debate. There are indications that China may well be thinking in terms of a major economic bloc (Lisbonne de Vergeron, 2007: 11). In this respect the signing of the ASEAN–China agreement in January 2007 (implemented on 1 January 2010) may be critical for Southeast Asia. However, while this could pave the way to a free trade area by 2015, it has also to be seen in the context of closer economic cooperation with Japan[30] and ongoing negotiations with India (Lisbonne-de Vergeron, 2007: 11). How far any of the regional economies may wish to go along with the construction of such a China-centred regional structure remains highly debatable. On the one hand, it may appear that, in the absence of the Chinese 'miracle' running into serious trouble, the Southeast Asian economies have little choice but much closer links, supported by an institutional framework.[31] On the other hand, this raises the question of whether deeper integration is *possible* given significant opposition and fragile political and administrative systems. It may be that liberalization of the Southeast Asian economies is beginning to press against national-level economic and political structures in such a way as either to preclude implementation or to render the measures ineffective. This certainly appears to be the case with foreign ownership. There is here the beginning of a basic contradiction: growth is driven by FDI, trade and regional integration, but this rests on further effective liberalization, which is negated by existing domestic structures. There are here some serious issues for the ASEAN Free Trade Area (AFTA), the ASEAN–China Free Trade Area, various bilateral treaties and WTO membership.

CONCLUSION

In terms of growth, trade and investment flows, the major Southeast Asian economies had by the early 2000s largely recouped the pre-1997 situation. However, growth remained much more uncertain and precarious, even before the onset of the 2007–08 global financial crisis. Of particular concern was the failure of domestic capital formation to return to pre-crisis levels (with the exception of Vietnam), a shift away from 'greenfield' investment, and a continuing loss of competitive 'edge' (Schwarz and Villinger, 2004). In addition, further liberalization had perhaps increased the vulnerability of most of the economies to external shocks and internal crisis, while further regional informal integration has increased the risk of such events becoming highly contagious. These developments, it can be argued, have not been accompanied by significant changes in Southeast Asian capitalism (Chaponniere, 2007: 13; Studwell, 2007). Business forms, ownership patterns, regulatory structures, state–business relations and general economic policies remain largely intact. The latter have been particularly commented on with respect to Indonesia and Thailand (Fajar and Prasetyantoko, 2007; McLeod, 2007: 29). Overall, there had been remarkably little of the 'Westernization' rapid liberalization and opening of the Southeast Asian economies advocated by the IMF and most Western commentators in the wake of the 1997 crisis. Certainly the relaxing of the foreign ownership regulations has not resulted in either a significant shift away from domestic control or changes in business forms and practice.

However, the above does need to be put into perspective. The recovery from the depths of the 1997 crisis, with the system, policies and general drivers of growth left in place, does suggest very considerable resilience, something that seems to have been confirmed in the face of the 2007–09 global crisis. Indeed, it could be argued that the limited nature of post-1997 reforms left Southeast Asian business still surprisingly insulated from the forces of economic globalization. In addition, increased dependence on the wider Pacific Asian region has, as before 1997, appeared to provide a degree of protection from events in the Western economies. However, it is important not to exaggerate this protection, because ultimately much of the intra-regional trade is driven by extra-regional flows. Perhaps more importantly, the 2007–09 crisis was centred in the Western banking sectors, with little direct resonance in Southeast Asia, where banking was both narrow in scope and principally domestic in orientation. This situation was reinforced by a degree of banking reform and the learning of some bitter lessons by both bankers and regulators, something that has perhaps received far too little attention outside of the Asian media (Dixon 2009a: 195; Xiao Gang, 2009). Indeed, in the light of the reaction of the Southeast Asian economies to the 2007–09 crisis, the whole question of post-1997 policy and domestic regulatory changes and the region's interaction with the global system demands further detailed appraisal.[32] That is not to say that the apparent comparatively successful weathering of the 2007–09 crisis endorses the nature and credibility of Southeast Asian systems, for there are clearly significant regulatory issues, if not major contradictions in the developmental forms. The latter is most apparent between domestic and regional imperatives. In addition, while the region seems to have been resilient in the face of a crisis that originated in the Western banking sector, it may prove less so in the face of problems that emerge closer to home, for which neither regulation nor policy changes have been prepared. It is apparent that there are (as of February 2010) a number of asset bubbles emerging in East and South Asia, for example in property, that could spark a major regional contagion. The question then would be how much more resilient have the Southeast Asian economies, regulatory systems and business forms become since 1997?

NOTES

1. Homi Kharas, Chief World Bank Economist for East Asia stressed in an interview that 'recovery could be dampened if the momentum of policy reforms slacken' ('East Asia increases integration outpaces the rest of the world in growth', 16 October 2003, http:/go.worldbank.org/4OT1EFZDW0).
2. See for example the summaries of conditions attached to IMF loans in Dash (2003: 274–9).
3. See Dixon (1995: 222) for a discussion of the link between FDI and export growth.
4. See Rasiah (2000: 951) for a discussion of the unusual nature of the link in these economies between growth and FDI.
5. It should be noted that in 2007 Asia remained significantly less open than all the other major regions except Sub-Saharan Africa (see the Index of Economic Freedom produced by the Heritage Foundation at www.heritage.org/index).
6. The provision of 'safety nets' and the elimination of 'moral hazard' are of course normal features of the international financial system and most national systems, illustrated most clearly in the UK in 2007 by the Northern Rock crisis.
7. While this business form has been perhaps most successful and persistent in Southeast Asia, it is certainly present elsewhere. See for example McCann (2000: 5051) on Italian capitalism.
8. The ease of access to funds was also increased by high debt/equity ratios. In Thailand

the average debt/equity ratio of companies was between 2:1 and 3:1 before the crisis as against the Western norm of 1:1 (Kasian Tejapira, 2002: 325).

9. At the end of 1999 the five Southeast Asian stock markets had a combined capitalization of US$ 465 billion – the equivalent of 3 per cent of all US listed stock and less than Microsoft alone (Freeman and Bartels, 2000: 2–3).

10. 'Dismantle an economic system based on collusion between state, banks and business, and the restrictive markets' (IMF Managing Director Michael Camdessus, cited in *Far Eastern Economic Review*, 18 December 1997: 64).

11. The Southeast Asian cross-border Chinese business network, with increasing links with China, Hong Kong and Taiwan, plays a significant, but far from clearly quantified or understood, role in regional integration.

12. However, it should be noted than some of the region's major companies – Renong (Malaysia), Salim (Indonesia) and Shinawatra (Thailand) – have expanded into Australia, Bangladesh, India, South Africa and Uruguay in telecommunications, the hotel industry, infrastructure finance and oil refining.

13. Between 1991 and 1996 Vietnam also become more dependent on FDI than Malaysia.

14. In some cases the lack of up-to-date lists of shareholders can be a major problem (see EIU, 2007a: 17).

15. Between 1998 and 2004, 66–75 per cent of the value of Thai corporate debt that was restructured was the result of 'informal workouts' (Pairyo Vongvipanond and Nuttanan Wichitakson, 2004: 58).

16. This was the brief of the Thailand Asset Management Company (TAMC) established to purchase non-performing loans (NPL) from the banking sector.

17. The impact of the crisis on such weak economies as Laos is one of its more neglected aspects.

18. The rapid recovery has to be seen in the context of a very different economic situation compared to those that prevailed in Indonesia and Thailand, particularly with respect to external debt (see Athukorala, 2000 for an excellent discussion).

19. If the M&A component of FDI is removed then inflows would be: 1991–96 US$ 18 863 million, 1997–2001 US$ 16 118 million and 2002–05 US$25 389 million.

20. In the absence of M&A, flows would have: remained negative for Indonesia throughout 2002–05; been negative for the Philippines during 1997–2001; and been for Thailand during 1997–2001 only a little above 1991–96.

21. Cross-border M&A has become increasingly significant in establishing 'deep integration' and increasing the TNC share of production (Kim Wan-Soon, 2000: 161).

22. See for example the review by Ozler and Taymez (2003). However, it should be stressed that, despite the major upsurge in M&A, there is still a lack of significant research that separates it out from other forms of FDI (see for example the comments by Reisen and Soto, 2000: 74, 76).

23. UNCTAD (2004: 321) suggests that the foreign share of assets was slightly higher, 6.8 per cent, but this is still one of the lowest levels in the world.

24. Where shares in major corporations have been sold, they have generally not involved controlling interests.

25. A World Bank study (Freud, 2006, cited by Gill *et al.*, 2007: 99) suggested that Chinese exports in 2000–04 were those of a country with a per capita GDP of some US$10 000.

26. In 2000–04 this was the equivalent of 1.3 per cent of GDP, the highest of any middle-income economy. In second place was Malaysia with 0.7 per cent. However, a significant proportion of high-tech production in China is produced by foreign investment enterprises, and there are doubts over the extent to which this is resulting in significant technology and knowledge transfers (Brown, 2008: 3).

27. In the earlier cases of Pacific Asian development, whether Japan, South Korea, Taiwan or even Thailand, rising costs led to industries being given up. This is not yet happening in China.

28. This reflects the lack of effective long-term policies towards R&D, education and training (Booth, 2000; Lauridsen, 2002: 175).

29. See Harvie and Hyun-Hoon Lee (2002: 138) on the need for closer integration and more intra-regional trade.
30. Repeated 'spats' over war shrines, history textbooks and offshore resources notwithstanding.
31. The establishment of an effective regional institutional framework would be expected to be highly conducive to the deepening of RDLs (see the comments in Legewie, 2000: 85).
32. See Dixon (2009b) for a brief overview of these changes.

REFERENCES

Abrenica, M.J.V. and G.M. Llando (2003), 'Services', in A.M. Balisacan and H. Hill (eds), *The Philippine Economy*, Oxford: Oxford University Press, pp. 254–82.
ADB (2005), *Asian Development Outlook 2005*, Manila: Asian Development Bank.
ADB (2007), *Asian Development Outlook 2007*, Manila: Asian Development Bank.
Ammar Siamwalla (2001), 'Picking up the pieces: bank and corporate restructuring in Post-1997 Thailand', paper presented at the Subregional Seminar on Financial and Corporate Sectors Restructuring in East and Southeast Asia, Seoul, Korea, 30 May–1 June.
Anderson, J. (2006), 'The return of Asia: de-linking or just recovering', UBS Investment Research, October, accessed at www.ubs.com/1/e/about/research.html.
Athukorala, Prema-chandra (2000), 'The Malaysian experiment', in P. Drysdale (ed.), *Reform and Recovery in East Asia: The Role of the State and Economic Enterprise*, London: Routledge, pp. 169–90.
Bartels, F.L. (2004), 'The future of intra-regional foreign direct investment patterns in Southeast Asia', in L. Freeman and F.L. Bartels (eds), *The Future of Foreign Investment in Southeast Asia*, London: Routledge, pp. 80–103.
Bartels, F.L. and L. Freeman (2000), 'Multinational firms and FDI in Southeast Asia: post-crisis changes in the manufacturing sector', *ASEAN Economic Bulletin*, **17**: 324–41.
Barton, D. (2007), 'Taking Stock: ten years after the Asian financial crisis', *McKinsey Quarterly*, Decemberaf, accessed at www.mckinseyquarterly.com/home.aspx.
Bello, W., S. Cunningham and Li Kheng Poh (1998), *A Siamese Tragedy: Development and Disintegration in Modern Thailand*, London: Zed.
Booth, A. (2000), 'Education and economic development in South East Asia: myths and realities', *Nordic Newsletter of Asian Studies*, **3** (October): 13–16.
Booth, A. (2009), 'The economic performance of the ASEAN economies from the Mid-1990s', Global Policy Institute research series no. 5, Forumpress, London, Paper presented at the session 'Ten Years after the Asian Financial Crisis', 7th EUROSEAS Conference, University of Naples, 12-15 September.
Brimble, P. (2002), 'Foreign direct investment: performance and attraction: the case of Thailand', paper presented at the Workshop on Foreign Direct Investment: Opportunities for and Challenges for Cambodia, Laos and Cambodia, Hanoi, 16-17 August.
Brown, K. (2008), 'Chinese overseas direct investment – what kind of opportunity?', Asia Programme paper, Chatham House, London.

Brown, R.A. (2000), *Chinese Big Business and the Wealth of Asian Nations*, London: Macmillan.

Buckley, P.J. (2004), 'The challenges of the new economy for multinational firms: lessons from Southeast Asia', in L. Freeman and F.L. Bartels (eds), *The Future of Foreign Investment in Southeast Asia*, London: Routledge, pp. 15–32.

Bullard, N. (2002), 'Taming the IMF: how the Asian crisis cracked the Washington consensus', in P. Masina (ed.), *Rethinking Development in East Asia: From Illusory Miracle to Economic Crisis*, Richmond: Curzon, pp. 144–60.

Chaponniere, J.-R. (2007), 'Ten years after the Asian crisis: retrospectives and perspectives', paper presented at the session 'Ten Years after the Asian Financial Crisis', 7th EUROSEAS Conference, University of Naples, 12-15 September.

Claessens, S., S. Djankov, J. Fan and L. Lang (1998), *Who Controls the Asian Corporations?*, Washington, DC: World Bank.

Claessens, S., S. Djankov and L.H.P. Lang, (1999), 'Who controls the East Asian corporations?', World Bank working paper, Washington, DC.

Crawford, D. (2000), 'Chinese capitalism: cultures, the South East Asian region and economic globalisation', *Third World Quarterly*, **21**: 69–86.

Cross, A. and H. Tan (2004), 'The impact of China's WTO accession on Southeast Asian foreign direct investment', in L. Freeman and F.L. Bartels (eds), *The Future of Foreign Investment in Southeast Asia*, London: Routledge, pp. 125–54.

Dash, K.C. (2003), 'The Asian economic crisis and the role of the IMF', in C.R. Goddard, P. Cronin and K.C. Dash (eds), *International Political Economy*, London: Palgrave Macmillan, pp. 269–90.

Dixon, C. (1995), 'Structural adjustment in comparative perspective: lessons from Pacific Asia', in W. Van Spengen, C. Dixon and A. Narman (eds), *Structurally Adjusted Africa*, London: Pluto, pp. 202–28.

Dixon, C. (1998), 'Regional integration in South East Asia', in J. Grugel and W. Hout (eds), *Regionalism Across the North–South Divide*, London: Routledge, pp. 115–33.

Dixon, C. (1999), *The Thai Economy*, London: Routledge.

Dixon, C. (2001), 'The Thai economic crisis: the internal perspective', *Geoforum*, **32**: 47–60.

Dixon, C. (2004), 'Post-crisis restructuring: foreign ownership, corporate resistance and economic nationalism in Thailand', *Journal of Contemporary Southeast Asia*, **26**: 45–72.

Dixon, C. (2006), 'Liberalisation of foreign ownership and cross-border M&A in South East Asia since the 1997 financial crisis', *Journal of Current South East Asian Affairs*, **5**: 5–41.

Dixon, C. (2009a), 'Global power shift: challenges and opportunities for the City of London', in S. Whimster (ed.), *Reforming the City: Response to Global Financial Crisis*, London: Forumpress, pp. 187–207.

Dixon, C. (2009b), 'The emerging Pacific Asian economies and the financial crisis', Global Policy Institute policy paper no. 9, accessed at www.global-policy.com/fileadmin/user_upload/GPI/Short_Policy_Docs/PP9_changing.pdf.

Economist (1999), 'The road less travelled', 1 May, p. 79.

Economist (2000), 'South-East Asia's problem trio', 2 December, pp. 93–4.

EIU (2003a), *Country Commerce: Thailand 2003*, London: EIU.

EIU (2003b), *Country Commerce: Indonesia 2003*, London: EIU.

EIU (2003c), *Country Commerce: Malaysia 2003*, London: EIU.

EIU (2004a), *Country Commerce: Singapore 2004*, London: EIU.
EIU (2004b), *Country Commerce: Malaysia 2004*, London: EIU.
EIU (2004c), *Country Commerce: Thailand 2004*, London: EIU.
EIU (2004d), *Country Commerce: Indonesia 2004*, London: EIU.
EIU (2007a), *Country Commerce: Indonesia 2007*, London: EIU.
EIU (2007b), *Country Commerce: Malaysia 2007*, London: EIU.
Fajar, M. and A. Prasetyantoko (2007), 'Indonesia's Ponzi economy: does financial crisis give lessons?', paper presented at the session 'Ten Years after the Asian financial crisis', 7th EUROSEAS Conference, University of Naples, 12-15 September.
Freeman, N.J. and F.L. Bartels (2000), 'Portfolio investment in Southeast Asia's stock markets: a survey of investors' current perception and practices', National University of Singapore economic and finance paper no. 3.
Freshfields Bruckhaus Deringer (2001), *Guide to Mergers and Acquisitions in Asia*, London: White Page.
Freshfields Bruckhaus Deringer (2004), *Guide to Mergers and Acquisitions in Asia*, London: White Page.
Freud, C. (2006), 'The effect of China's exports on East Asian trade with the rest of the world', unpublished paper, World Bank, Washington, DC.
Gill, I., H. Kharas and others (2007), *An East Asian Renaissance: Ideas for Economic Growth*, Washington, DC: World Bank.
Gilley, B. (1998), 'Buying binge', *Far Eastern Economic Review*, 20 August: 42–4.
Glassman, J. (2001a), 'Economic crisis in Asia: the case of Thailand', *Economic Geography*, **77**: 122–47.
Glassman, J. (2001b), 'From Seattle (and Ubon) to Bangkok: the scales of resistance to corporate globalisation', *Environment and Planning D: Society and Space*, **19**: 513–33.
Glen, J. and A. Singh (2004), 'Comparing capital structures and rates of return in developed and emerging markets', *Emerging Markets Review*, **5**(2): 161–92.
Hale, D. (1998), 'The hot money debate', *International Economy*, November/December, pp. 8–12, 66–9.
Harvie, C. and Hyun-Hoon Lee (2002), 'New regionalism in East Asia', *ASEAN Economic Bulletin*, **19**: 123–40.
Heritage Foundation (2001), 'Index of economic freedom', accessed at http://database.townhall.com/heritage/index/indextoffreedom.cfm
Hewison, K. (2000), 'Thailand's capitalism before and after the economic crisis', in R. Robison, M. Beeson, Kanishka Jayasuriya and Hyuk-Rae Kim (eds), *Politics and Markets in the Wake of the Asian Crisis*, London: Routledge, pp. 192–211.
Hihikawa, I. (2003), 'Financial sector FDI in Asia: a brief overview', a note prepared for the meeting of the Committee on Global Financial Services (CGFS) Working Group on FDI in the Financial Sector, CGFS publication no. 22, accessed at www.bis.org/press/p040330a.htm.
Hill, H. (2004), 'Foreign investment and Southeast Asian economic development: issues and challenges', in L. Freeman and F.L. Bartels (eds), *The Future of Foreign Investment in Southeast Asia*, London: Routledge, pp. 255–67.
Holst, D.R. and J. Wiess (2004), 'ASEAN and China: export rivals or partners in regional growth?', *World Economy*, **27**(8): 1255–74.
Ito, Takatoshi (2001), 'Growth, crisis, and the future of the region', in J. Stiglitz

and S. Yusuf (eds), *Rethinking the Asian Miracle*, Oxford: Oxford University Press, pp. 55–94.

Jansen, K. (1997), *External Finance in Thailand's Development: An Interpretation of Thailand's Growth Boom*, London: Macmillan.

Jayasuriyam, Kanishka and A. Rosser (2001), 'Economic crisis and the political economy of economic liberalisation in South-East Asia', in G. Rodan, K. Hewison and R. Robison (eds), *The Political Economy of South-East Asia: Conflicts, Crises and Change*, Melbourne, VIC: Oxford University Press, pp. 233–58.

Jomo, K.S. (2001), 'Rethinking the role of government in Southeast Asia', in J. Stiglitz and S. Yusuf (eds), *Rethinking the Asian Miracle*, Oxford: Oxford University Press, pp. 461–508.

Kasian Tejapira (2002), 'Post-crisis economic impasse and political recovery in Thailand: the resurgence of economic nationalism', *Critical Asian Studies*, **34**: 323–56.

Kawai, Masahiro (2000), 'Building institutions and resolution of the East Asian crisis', in P. Drysdale (ed.), *Reform and Recovery in East Asia*, London: Routledge, pp. 282–327.

Khan, H.A. (2002), 'Corporate governance of family-based business in Asia: which is right and which is wrong?', paper prepared for the Asian Development Bank Expert Group, Manila, January.

Kim, Wan-Soon (2000), 'Foreign direct investment in Korea: the role of the ombudsman', in ADB, *Development Resource Mobilisation in the Post-Crisis Period*, Manila: ADB, pp. 159–72.

Kim, Yun-Hwan (2000), 'Post crisis policy agenda for reforming the financial sector in Asia', in Asian Development Bank (ed.), *Development Resource Mobilisation in the Post-Crisis Period*, Manila: Asian Development Bank, pp. 19–42.

Krugman, P. (1998), 'Fire sale FDI', accessed 8 December at web.mit.edu/krugman/www/FIRESALE.htm.

Kwan, C.H. (1994), *Economic Interdependence in Asia-Pacific Region*, London: Routledge.

Kwan, C.H. (2006), 'The rise of China: challenges and opportunities for Japan', paper presented at the Japan Society in New York, 13 June, accessed at www.rieti.go.jp/en/china/index.html.

Lall, S. (2003), 'Foreign direct investment, technology development, and competitiveness: issues and evidence', in S. Lall and S. Urata (eds), *Competitiveness, Foreign Investment and Technological Activity in East Asia*, Cheltenham, UK and Northampton, MA,USA: Edward Elgar, pp. 12–56.

Lauridsen, L.S. (2002), 'Struggling with globalisation in South East Asia', *South East Asian Research*, **10**: 155–83.

Legewie, J. (2000), 'Production strategies of Japanese firms: building up regional production networks', in J. Legewie and H. Meyer-Ohle (eds), *Corporate Strategies for Southeast Asia after the Crisis*, New York: Palgrave, pp. 74–99.

Lim, R. (2002), 'External challenges facing the economy', in D. da Cunha (ed.), *Singapore in the New Millennium*, Singapore: ISEAS, pp. 26–49.

Lisbonne-de Vergeron, K. (2007), *Contemporary Chinese Views of Europe*, London: Chatham House.

Markland, R. (2001), 'Introduction', in Freshfields Bruckhaus Deringer, *Guide to Mergers and Acquisitions in Asia*, London: White Page, pp. 2–4.

McCann, D. (2000), 'Capitalism in Italy', *Modern Italy*, **5**: 47–61.

McLeod, R. (2007), 'Indonesia's vulnerability to a new balance of payments and banking crisis', paper presented at the session 'Ten Years after the Asian Financial Crisis', 7th EUROSEAS Conference, University of Naples, 12-15 September.

McLeod, R. and R. Garnaut (1998), 'Thailand', in R. McLeod and R. Garnaut (eds), *East Asia in Crisis: From Being a Miracle to Needing One*, London: Routledge, pp. 68–79.

Mody, A. and Shoko Negishi (2000), 'Cross-border mergers and acquisitions in East Asia: trends and implications', *Finance and Development*, **38** (March): 6–9.

Munakat, N. (2006), *Transforming East Asia: The Evolution of Regional Integration*, Tokyo: Research Institute of Economy, Trade and Industry.

Muscat, R.M. (1994), *The Fifth Tiger: A Study of Thai Development Policy*, Tokyo: United Nations University Press.

Nam, Il Chong, Yeongjae Kang and Joon-Kyung Kim (2001), 'Comparative corporate governance trends in Asia', in *Corporate Governance in Asia: A Comparative Perspective*, Paris: OECD, pp. 85–119.

Ng, F. and A. Yeats (2003), 'Major trends in East Asia: what are the implications for regional cooperation and growth?', World Bank policy research working paper no. 3084, Washington, DC.

Ozler, S. and E. Taymez (2003), 'Does foreign ownership matter for survival and growth?', paper presented at the 10th ERF Annual Conference, Marrakesh, December 2003.

Pairyo Vongvipanond and Nuttanan Wichitakson (2004), 'Thailand's corporate restructuring experience through formal bankruptcy procedures', *ASEAN Economic Bulletin*, **21**: 54–80.

Pasuk Phongpaichit and C. Baker (1995), *Thailand: Economy and Politics*, Singapore: Oxford University Press.

Piyanuj Ratprasatporn and Kobkit Thienpreccha (2002), *Foreign Investment in Thailand: Review of the Current Legislative Regime*, Bangkok: Tilleke and Gibbins International Limited.

Rasiah, R. (2000), 'Globalisation and private capital movements', *Third World Quarterly*, **21**(6): 943–61.

Regnier, P. (2000), *Small and Medium Enterprises in Distress: Thailand, the East Asian Crisis and Beyond*, Aldershot, Gower/Ashgate.

Reisen, H. and M. Soto (2000), 'The need for foreign savings in post-crisis Asia', in Asian Development Bank (ed.), *Development Resource Mobilisation in the Post-Crisis Period*, Manila: Asian Development Bank, pp. 65–86.

Robison, R. (2001), 'Indonesia: crisis, oligarchy, and reform', in G. Rodan, K. Hewison and R. Robison (eds), *The Political Economy of South-East Asia: Conflicts, Crises and Change*, Melbourne, VIC: Oxford University Press, pp. 104–38.

Rodan, G. (2001), 'Singapore: globalisation and the politics of economic restructuring', in G. Rodan, K. Hewison and R. Robison (eds), *The Political Economy of South-East Asia: Conflicts, Crises and Change*, Melbourne, VIC: Oxford University Press, pp. 138–77.

Rossi, S. and P. Volpin (2002), 'Cross-country determinants of mergers and acquisitions', EGGI finance working paper no. 25/2003.

Schwarz, A. and R. Villinger (2004), 'ASEAN and China', *Business Horizons*, **48**(2): 135–42.

Scott, J. (1997), 'Corporate business: comparative perspectives', revised version of a seminar presented at Ritsumeikan University in November 1996, accessed at http://privatewww.essex.ac.uk/~scottj/socscot3.htm.

Sender, H. (1998), 'Few takers so far at Asia's great firesale', *Far Eastern Economic Review*, 5 March: 52–4.

Sin, Jang-Sup (2002), 'Restructuring after the financial crisis in South Korea: corporate reforms, institutional transition and transitional costs', *Nordic Newsletter of Asian Studies*, **1** (May): 17–18, 31.

Sin, Jang-Sup and Ha-Joon Chang (2002), *Korea Inc.: Financial Crisis, Corporate Reform and Institutional Transition*, London: Routledge.

Studwell, J. (2007), *Asian Godfathers*, London: Profile Books.

Suehiro, Akira and Nateneapha Wailerdsak (2004), 'Family business in Thailand', *ASEAN Economic Bulletin*, **21**: 81–93.

Torres, M.-A. (2004), *The Tragedy that Didn't Happen*, Kuala Lumpur: ISIS.

UNCTAD, *World Investment Report*, Geneva: Annual.

Urata, Shujiro (2001), 'Emergence of an FDI–trade nexus and economic growth in East Asia', in J.E. Stiglitz and Shahid Yusuf (eds), *Rethinking the East Asian Miracle*, Oxford: Oxford University Press, pp. 409–60.

Wade, R. and F. Veneroso (1998), 'The Asian debt crisis: the high debt model versus the Wall Street – Treasury – IMF complex', *New Left Review*, **228**: 3–23.

Welsh, B. (2007), 'Malaysia at 50', *Current History*, April: 173–9.

Woo-Cumings, M. (2001), 'Economic crisis and corporate reform in East Asia', Council on Foreign Relations paper, Washington, DC.

World Bank (2001), *Thailand Economic Monitor*, Bangkok: World Bank.

World Bank (2005), *Thailand: Economic Monitor*, Bangkok: World Bank.

World Bank (2007), *World Trade Indicators*, Washington, DC: World Bank.

Xiao Gang (2009), 'Incremental banking reform proved best', Bank of China, accessed at www.boc.cn/en/bocinfo/bi1/200906/t20090622_756014.html.

Zhan, J. and T. Ozan (2001), *Business Restructuring in Asia: Cross-Border M&As in the Crisis Period*, Copenhagen: Copenhagen Business School Press.

4. Revisiting shared growth and examining horizontal inequality

Anis Chowdhury and Iyanatul Islam

Comparing communities in terms of inequality should not be performed in a vacuum; the study of income distribution and related issues cannot ultimately be divorced from the historical development of the social and economic system.

Champernowne and Cowell (1998: 49)

Wherever there is great property, there is great inequality. For one very rich man there must be at least five hundred poor, and the affluence of the few supposes the indigence of the many. . . . The affluence of the rich excites the indignation of the poor, who are often both driven by want, and prompted by envy, to invade his possessions.

Adam Smith (1976: 232)

The global debate on the role of inequality in the process of economic development has gone through several phases. A particular paradigm prevailed between the onset of the structural adjustment programmes (SAP) in the 1980s and the celebration of the 'East Asian economic miracle' in the early 1990s. The emphasis was on how market-friendly, export-oriented development strategies in a handful of economies in East and Southeast Asia produced the phenomenon of 'shared growth'. These economies were hailed by the World Bank for apparently being able to defy the so-called Kuznets inverted-U hypothesis that inequality first rises with growth before it declines.[1] The miracle was not about these countries' rapid and sustained growth, but that they could achieve it without worsening income distribution, and in some cases growth accompanied declines in inequality.

According to the World Bank (1993: 3), 'The HPAEs' low and declining levels of inequality are . . . a remarkable exception to historical experience and contemporary evidence in other regions.' The Asian Development Bank (ADB) (1994: 35) expresses a similar view: '[a] remarkable feature of economic growth in East Asia is that it has been accompanied by a reduction in income inequality'. Well-known scholars of development economics agreed. For example, Fields (1995: 84) observes, 'The most outstanding examples of broad-based economic improvements over a sustained period of time are the . . . NIEs. . . . Their income distribution experiences . . . present a picture of extraordinary improvements.'

The World Bank (1993) study summarizes the conventional wisdom when it notes that this 'miracle' was possible owing to export orientation based on labour-intensive industrialization, investment in human capital, prudent macroeconomic management and small states. The orthodoxy claimed that too much preoccupation with redistributive policies would lead to macroeconomic populism, which eventually harms growth and the very poor that these policies aim to help. Countries should concentrate on prudent macroeconomic policies and appropriate public expenditure allocations towards human capital in order to maintain sustained high economic growth. Labour-intensive industrialization, public investment in human capital and low inflation not only sustain growth, but also ensure that the benefits of growth reach the poor and thus lower inequality or prevent inequality from rising.

The celebration of the 'East Asian miracle' and its phenomenon of 'shared growth' came to an abrupt end with the 1997 financial crisis that swept through the East Asian region. The paradigm shifted from explaining 'shared growth' to seeking to understand how such success-ful economies became victims of a region-wide crisis. This circumspect literature paved the way for a global resurgence of interest in inequality and the central role that it plays in the process of development. This is evident from the fact that the World Bank's *World Development Report 2006* was on 'Equity and Development'. In the context of Asia, the Asian Development Bank's flagship publication, *Key Indicators 2007: Inequality in Asia*, also had inequality as its theme. Why is there this renewed interest in inequality?

To begin with, as recognized by both the World Bank and the ADB, increasing inequality slows the pace of poverty reduction and hence the achievement of Millennium Development Goals (MDG): 'for a given growth rate, a growth process in which inequalities are increasing sharply will be one in which the extent of poverty reduction is lower' (ADB, 2007: 1). On average, a 1 per cent growth in mean income generates a 1 per cent drop in the poverty head-count (see Bourguignon, 2003; Klasen and Misselhorn, 2007). Based on the WIDER Inequality Database, Jantii and Sandstrom (2005) have found that, in a majority of developing countries, inequality started rising significantly in the mid-1980s. This rise in inequal-ity seems to have lowered the growth elasticity of poverty reduction (Bourguignon *et al.*, 2008).

There is also the recognition that extreme inequality may impair human capabilities and the quality of institutions, which in turn adversely affects economic growth itself. 'Greater equity can, over the longer term, underpin faster growth' (World Bank, 2006: 17). There is a large volume of literature on the impact of initial patterns and the extent of inequality on subsequent growth and poverty reduction. Using a political economy approach, Alesina and Perotti (1993), Alesina and Rodrik (1994) and Alesina (1998) focus on the link between initial inequality and the political pressures for redistribution generated by the median voter. This results in increases in capital tax rates which discourage investment and future growth. Persson and Tabellini (1994) relies on the power of a wealthy elite to obtain differential treatment through lobbying and therefore over-investment in assets, for example land owned by the elite. The same logic applies in models which focus on the power of lobbies to thwart the implementation of stabilization reforms that might change the distribution of income. There is another strand which emphasizes the impact of asymmetric information on the supply of credit to the poor, who cannot offer collateral owing to a lack of any significant assets. Therefore, they are prevented from making productive investments in schooling and health to escape from the ranks of the poor (Bannerji and Newman, 1993). An implication of these models is that the economic system is caught in an inequality trap in which initial inequalities in income and wealth distributions are perpetuated into the future. This partially explains the stability in Gini coefficients in some economies over time.

The current literature also focuses on societal perceptions about inequality from the perspective of fairness and the impact of such perceptions on social cohesion. As the World Bank notes:

> Equity and fairness matter not only because they are complementary to long-term prosperity. It is evident that many people – if not most – care about equity for its own sake. Some see equal opportunities and fair processes as matters of *social justice* and thus as an intrinsic part of the objective of development.
>
> World Bank, 2006: 75, emphasis added

The Asian Development Bank expresses this issue in a more direct fashion:

> developing Asia's policy makers need to take the increases in inequality seriously. There are several reasons for this. First, income or expenditure inequality is only one dimension of inequality, as noted above. Indeed, when it comes to inequality in nonincome dimensions – including those in education and health outcomes *across socioeconomic population subgroups* – inequality remains stubbornly high in many parts of the region. . . . Among other things, high levels of

inequality can have *adverse consequences for social cohesion* and the quality of institutions and policies.

ADB, 2007: 1–2, emphasis added

The United Nations (2005) shares the same view on the importance of focusing on inequality when it notes in the *Report on the World Social Situation*:

Failure to address this inequality predicament will ensure that social justice and better living conditions for all people remain elusive, and that communities, countries and regions remain *vulnerable to social, political and economic upheaval*. . . . The violence associated with national and international acts of terrorism should be viewed in the context of social inequality and disintegration.

UN, 2005: 1, 5–6, emphasis added

There is now a growing body of literature that examines the link between horizontal inequality (between socio-economic population sub-groups and sub-national regions) and conflict. Internal social conflict, in this analysis, is a manifestation of the desire to right the wrong by those who lose out from unjust social and economic development processes.

In light of changing perspectives on the role of inequality in economic development, the chapter revisits the experiences of a group of Southeast Asian economies. Were they really worthy exemplars of 'shared growth'? How can one explain recent trends in inequality in the region? How important is the issue of horizontal inequality in terms of its impact on political and social cohesion? In order to delve into these issues, the chapter focuses on four countries, Indonesia, Malaysia, the Philippines and Thailand, which are diverse both regionally and ethnically. They are also facing social conflicts of varying degrees of severity. The chapter begins with a review of recent trends in inequality in the aforementioned countries. It then explores the various explanations that have been proffered to understand the trends. Finally, it proceeds to an examination of the issue of horizontal inequality and its political and social ramifications.

TRENDS IN INCOME INEQUALITY: IS SOUTHEAST ASIA A CASE OF 'SHARED GROWTH'?

Figure 4.1 presents the trends in Gini ratios for household income. Only Indonesia and Malaysia seem to defy the so-called Kuznets hypothesis. In the case of the Philippines and Thailand, the Gini coefficient increased from around 0.45 in the early 1970s to over 0.50 in recent years. These Gini coefficients are, in fact, comparable to those found in some Latin

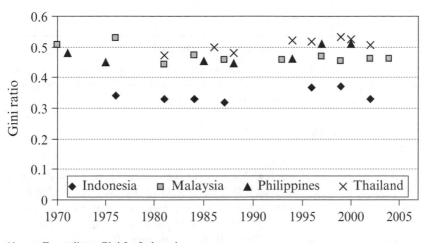

Note: Expenditure Gini for Indonesia.

Source: Medhi and Ragayah (2007).

Figure 4.1 Gini ratios for household income

American countries, such as Argentina (0.513), Brazil (0.570), Chile (0.558), El Salvador (0.508) and Mexico (0.531). Only Indonesia stands out, with a Gini ratio similar to those of the East Asian miracle economies – Korea (0.316) and Taiwan (0.339).[2] However, ADB (2007) reports slightly lower Gini ratios for Malaysia (0.403), the Philippines (0.440) and Thailand (0.420), and shows a decline in all except that of the Philippines since the early 1990s. The lower range of Gini ratios in the ADB report may be due to the fact that they are based on household expenditure not income. When measured with household income data, ADB finds Gini ratios of 0.487 and 0.523 for the Philippines and Thailand, respectively. As ADB (2007: 30) notes, 'inequality estimates based on income distributions are higher, sometimes considerably so, than those based on expenditure distributions'.[3]

The rise in inequality in the Philippines is particularly worrying given the high level of poverty in that country. Estimates by NSCB show that the poverty incidence of the population was close to 40 per cent in 2000.

Explaining Inequality

The Philippines
The Philippines has the highest concentration of land-holdings among the Southeast and East Asian countries. The Gini ratio for land-holdings in

Table 4.1   Land-holdings Gini

Indonesia	Malaysia	Philippines	Thailand	Korea	Taiwan
0.527 (1963)	0.68 (1960)	0.482 (1950)	0.444 (1963)	0.307 (1970)	0.539 (1920)
0.471 (1973)		0.488 (1960)	0.447 (1993)	0.372 (1990)	0.390 (1960)
0.454 (1993)		0.547 (1991)			

Source: Frankema (2006).

the Philippines rose from 0.482 in 1950 to 0.547 in 1991, which was among the highest in Asia (Table 4.1). With a land Gini of 0.547, the Philippines' land ownership concentration is about the same as what Taiwan had in 1920. According to Putzel (1992), about 72 per cent of rural families were landless in the late 1980s. Through the implementation of radical land reforms in the 1950s, Taiwan's land-holding Gini declined to 0.39 in 1960. Korea, too, implemented far-reaching land reform in the 1950s. There is a general consensus that, in the case of both Taiwan and South Korea, early land reforms played an important role in generating a relatively equitable distribution of income in the initial stages of their rapid economic growth. Unlike Taiwan and Korea, the Philippines was unable to implement land reform. A major source of inequality thus remained entrenched.

Public policy, especially investment in human capital (education and health), can go a long way in offsetting the impact of unequal wealth distribution (manifested in a high land-holdings Gini). Unfortunately, here, too, the Philippines failed. For example, public expenditure on education was only 1.7 per cent of GDP in 1980 as opposed to 2.9 per cent in Indonesia, 5.2 per cent in Malaysia and 3.7 per cent in Thailand. Although the ratio has increased in recent years, it still remains below that of Malaysia and Thailand. Owing to inadequate public expenditure, the share of private expenditure in total education expenditure is quite high (43 per cent in 1998) in the Philippines. This means a large number of poor households with few or no assets cannot afford to send their children to schools. In 1970, the Philippines' education Gini was 0.368, which declined to 0.309 in 1990. This is still quite high compared with Korea's education Gini of 0.22 in 1990 (Figure 4.2).

Thus, it is not surprising that a number of studies attributed inequality in the Philippines to education of household head.[4] They also found that a significant cause of wage inequality is the variations in educational attainments across the labour force. Income distribution turns unfavourably against workers with lower human capital endowments, who come mostly from poor households. This outcome may have been

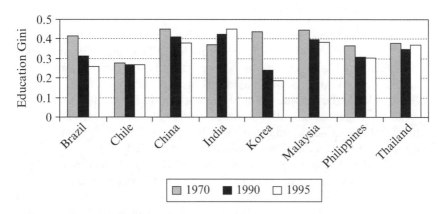

Source: Lopez, Thomas and Wang (1998); 1995 figures are based on projections.

Figure 4.2 Education Gini

compounded by the relative failure compared with the first-generation newly industrialized economies (NIEs) of East Asia in switching from earlier capital-intensive import-substituting industrialization to labour-intensive industrial activities.

The high rate of out-migration of skilled manpower from the Philippines in the last two and a half decades may also have contributed to the rise in inequality. It can happen through two channels. First, the out-migration of skilled labour creates a shortage of skilled human resources, whose pool is already quite small. As a result, the skill premium of those who stay back goes up, widening the wage gap. ADB (2007) indeed finds that wage differentials accruing to highly skilled occupations increased over time in the Philippines. Second, the skilled out-migration happens from a small section of the middle-class population, who have the ability to invest in education and training. The household income of these families rises disproportionately owing to remittances from members working overseas.

Finally spatial inequality accounts for a sizeable, although not overwhelming, portion of the national-level income inequality in the Philippines (Balisacan and Fuwa, 2004). The past development policy favoured the island of Luzon and discriminated against the peripheral islands of Visayas and especially Mindanao. The mean living standards for the Luzon regions are higher than for most of the regions in Visayas and Mindanao. Metro Manila, which accounts for about 14 per cent of the population, has the highest mean living standard. In 2000, its mean living standard was roughly 1.7 times the national average or about three times the mean living standard for Western Mindanao.

Thailand
One study finds that concentration of wealth among higher socio-economic classes is a key determinant of income inequality in Thailand.[5] The top decile, which accounts for 10 per cent of the population, owns over 40 per cent of total aggregated national household income. On the other hand, between 1986 and 1996, the income share of the bottom decile was less than 1 per cent of total aggregated national income across all socio-economic classes. The variable socio-economic class which explained nearly 25 per cent of overall income inequality dynamics in 1975 rose to nearly 35 per cent in 1992. Similarly, the geographical location variable which explained over 13 per cent of total income inequality in 1975 increased to 25 per cent in 1992.

The above study also finds that unequal access to education and formal credit markets explains the high Gini ratios in Thailand. Thailand lags far behind the other NIEs of East Asia in terms of performance in educational achievements. For example, in 1990, 83 per cent of workers had only primary education or less and, in 1994, only 20 per cent of the workforce had completed secondary school. The Thai gross enrolment rate in secondary-level education was only 57 per cent in 1996, well behind that of its neighbours.[6]

Thailand's education Gini is higher than that of the Philippines. It was 0.378 in 1980 and 0.348 in 1990. High education inequality is the result of unequal access caused by unequal wealth distribution, as manifested in a high land-holdings Gini (0.447). In Thailand, the private contribution to total education expenditure was found to be 44 per cent in 1998, making it nearly unaffordable for the poor families.

It is also possible that the IMF's structural adjustment programme in the 1980s contributed to the rise in inequality in Thailand. The Gini ratio in Thailand was 0.413 in 1962 and remained around that until the late 1970s. The Gini began rising from the early 1980s and reached 0.515 in 1992 (Lee and Rhee, 1999). Fofack and Zeufack (1999: 2) note: 'While the GDP grew at an average rate of 7.9 per cent between 1981 and 1992, income inequality increased steadily during the same period.' The study finds that:

> Despite the phenomenal growth rate recorded between 1986 and 1988, the growth rate of average real per capita income in the bottom decile increased by over 34 per cent, while that of the uppermost decile was over ten times much higher. Moreover, in subsequent years, where growth rates were much slower, the average real per capita income growth rate in the top decile continued to increase, while at the same time it declined in the bottom decile.
>
> Fofack and Zeufack (1999: 14)

One of the characteristics of Thai income inequality is high geographical concentration around Bangkok. As a consequence, there are large regional disparities in the spatial income distribution map – the gap between Bangkok, the wealthiest region, and the poorest Northeast is considerable.

Malaysia

In many ways, Malaysia is an enigmatic case (Chowdhury and Islam, 1996). Despite an ambitious affirmative action programme, its income inequality is still quite high compared with that of Korea and Taiwan – two of the most successful examples of 'shared' growth. Nonetheless, the high growth phase of Malaysia did not witness any significant rise in inequality; the Gini coefficient remained more or less stable around 0.46. The level of income inequality showed a rising trend until 1976, but fell systematically from 0.529 to 0.458 between 1976 and 1988. Critics have rightly pointed out the predictable microeconomic distortions of Malaysia's 'New Economic Policy' (NEP), aimed at addressing inter-ethnic inequality. The remarkable growth record of the Malaysian economy clearly suggests that such distortions either were short-lived or did not have significant systematic effects to deter the growth process.

The primary thrust of the NEP was to 'accelerate the process of restructuring Malaysian society to correct economic imbalance, so as to reduce and eventually eliminate the identification of race with economic function' (Second Malaysia Plan, 1971–75: 1). The state became the main instrument for this economic reorganization. With a view to increasing the Malay share in business and employment, a large number of state corporations were set up, along with the introduction of quotas on enrolments for different ethnic groups in public educational institutions. The government also used a preferential credit system to channel funds to Malay business and to preferred industrial sectors.

As can be seen from Figure 4.3, Malaysia has been quite successful in reducing inter-ethnic income disparity.[7] However, intra-ethnic inequality remained stubbornly high (Table 4.2). There have been only some marginal improvements in recent years.

Thus, the high overall Gini in Malaysia is due to within-group (intra-ethnic) rather than between-group (inter-ethnic) inequality. According to Ragayah (2008), within-group inequality explains 93.71 per cent of overall inequality. She also finds that the contribution of between-group inequality declined from 10.06 per cent in 1995 to 6.29 per cent in 2004. These findings are not much different from those of Anand (1983), who found that almost 90 per cent of the income inequality in Peninsular Malaysia in 1970 was due to intra-ethnic rather than inter-ethnic income differences.

While there have been secular declines in inter-ethnic income disparity, urban–rural income disparity has not changed much. After declining in

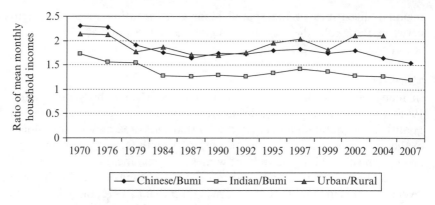

Source: Jomo (2006); Ragayah (2008).

Figure 4.3   Disparity ratio – Malaysia

Table 4.2   Gini coefficient by ethnic group – Malaysia

	1970	1987	2004	2007
Bumiputera	0.466	0.477	0.452	0.431
Chinese	0.455	0.430	0.446	0.430
Indians	0.463	0.402	0.425	0.411

Source: Ninth Malaysian Plan; Medhi (1994); Ragayah (2008).

the 1980s and 1990s, it returned to the level found in the 1970s. Despite very high land concentration at the time of independence, there has not been any major land reform in Malaysia. Instead, to address poverty among the rural Malays, new agricultural areas have been distributed through land development schemes managed by government agencies such as the Federal Land Development Authority (FELDA), the Federal Land Consolidation and Rehabilitation Authority (FELCRA) and the Rubber Industry Smallholders Development Authority (RISDA). From the trend in urban–rural income disparity, it seems that the impact of land distribution programmes has been limited (see Jomo, 1986; Halim, 1991).

   The rising rural–urban income disparity may also have been caused by the industrial strategy focused on foreign direct investment (FDI) and export processing zones. These are typically enclave-type activities and are located in urban areas. The rural land distribution programmes seem to have discouraged the large migration from rural areas seen in countries such as neighbouring Indonesia. As a result, the urban labour market has always been tight.

A puzzling phenomenon is the high education Gini despite significant public expenditure on education. Government expenditure on education rose from 7.9 per cent of total development expenditure during 1966–70 to 23.4 per cent during 2001–05. Yet it seems to have failed to improve access to education. One wonders whether the ethnic quota system on enrolment has had any adverse effect on education inequality. If this was indeed the case, then one can argue that, while the NEP succeeded in reducing inter-ethnic inequality, it adversely affected overall inequality by creating barriers to education, which was not offset by high public expenditure on education.

To some extent the NEP may have also contributed to intra-ethnic inequality and hence to overall inequality. The process of increasing the Malay shares in corporate ownership though privatization created a condition for state–government–party collusion (corruption, cronyism and nepotism). Only the upper class and well-connected people could benefit from such policies. It seems this phenomenon transcended ethnicity and enabled a select section of the Malaysian society to accumulate income and wealth very rapidly, thus accentuating inequality (Ragayah, 2008).

Indonesia

Among the four Southeast Asian countries, Indonesia is the only one with low inequality, regardless of whether the measures are based on household expenditure or income. Thus Indonesia probably fits the pattern of 'shared' growth as observed in the first-generation NIEs (Korea and Taiwan). However, there is considerable controversy as to whether the Indonesian household data accurately reflect the extent of inequality in that society.[8] This doubt arises in light of visible disparity of wealth in Indonesia. As can be seen from Table 4.3, Indonesia's wealth Gini is close to that of Argentina and Brazil, known for their high income inequality (Table 4.3). If Argentina, Brazil and Thailand are any guide, then Indonesia's income Gini should range between 0.5 and 0.57. This seems to be a reasonable conclusion given the entrenched corruption and cronyism leading to and feeding from acute wealth and asset concentration in Indonesia.

The high wealth Gini is consistent with high asset concentration in Indonesia. Claessens *et al.* (1999) estimate the extent of market capitalization by top ten families in selected Asian countries. Their data, summarized in Figure 4.4, illustrate the acute concentration of assets in Indonesia, which tops the list of the East Asian countries. Market capitalization in the hands of the top ten families accounted for as much as 57.7 per cent of the total in Indonesia, compared to 18.4 per cent in Taiwan.

Table 4.3   Wealth distribution in 2000 (PPP values)

Country	Wealth Gini	Income Gini	Expenditure Gini
Argentina	0.740	0.513 (2003)	
Brazil	0.783	0.570 (2004)	
Nigeria	0.735		0.436 (2003)
India	0.669		0.362 (2004)
Korea	0.579		0.312 (2004)
Taiwan	0.654		0.339 (2003)
Indonesia	0.763		0.344 (2002)
Thailand	0.709	0.523 (2000)	0.420 (2002)

PPP: purchasing power parity.

Source: ADB (2007).

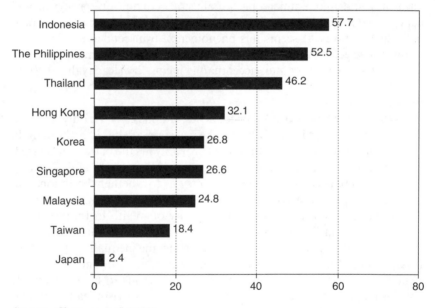

Source: Claessens et al. (1999).

Figure 4.4   Market capitalization controlled by top ten families, 1996

As Mishra (2008) notes, there is considerable uncertainty about the ownership and control structure of Indonesian corporations, which persists to the present day, as Indonesian conglomerates have been held together since their inception in a web of cross-holdings and inter-linked

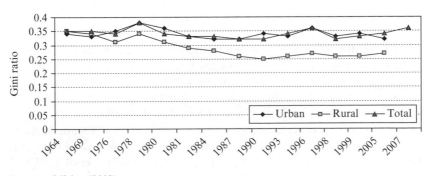

Source: Mishra (2008).

Figure 4.5   Rural–urban inequality in Indonesia

directorships. As a result, market capitalization data taken from capital market directories are frequently misleading and provide only a very approximate mapping of the structure of ownership and the concentration of assets. In addition,

> the well known interlocking of commercial, military and political interests in public and government favoured enterprises makes even a near accurate estimation of asset concentration during the New Order exceptionally difficult. Open capital markets simply make the problem of estimating asset concentration even more difficult since rich households and large businesses often invest in both financial and physical assets overseas.
>
> Mishra, 2008: 48

Despite the above reservations about the level of inequality in Indonesia, the falling rural inequality is worth noting (Figure 4.5). With the windfall gains from the oil price booms in the 1970s, the Soeharto government undertook massive rural infrastructure investment, aimed at rice self-sufficiency. This resulted in a rapid rise in agricultural productivity. Rising agricultural productivity, combined with declining land concentration in Indonesia (Table 4.1), may have contributed to declining rural inequality. Massive migration from rural to urban centres could be another factor that accounts for declining rural inequality and the near constancy of urban inequality.

Akita (1999) presents a decomposition of income inequality in Indonesia between and within urban and rural areas. They show that, in both categories, the contribution of between-group inequalities to total was significantly *lower* than for within-group inequality. For example, in 1993, only 24.5 per cent of the total income inequality was accounted for by differences between urban and rural areas, and the remaining 75.4 per cent was contributed by inequality within urban and rural households.[9]

Summing Up

The above discussion of inequality in the four Southeast Asian countries casts considerable doubt on the claim that these countries experienced shared growth. The root of their divergence from the East Asian miracle economies (Korea and Taiwan) lies in the fact that none of these countries addressed the initial inequality in wealth and land distribution. The initial inequality is perpetuated through a number of political economy channels, as noted earlier. They range from distributive politics and cronyism to resistance to reforms. The initial inequitable distribution of land and wealth also works through other channels. For example, landlessness deprives people of an important source of income, especially in an agrarian society. The poor also suffer from discrimination in the capital market owing to the lack of significant assets that can be used as collateral. These discriminations, to some extent, are manifested in the inequality of access to education as measured by the education Gini.

In the case of both Indonesia and Malaysia, it seems that the emphasis has been on the equality of outcomes rather than equality of opportunities. Indonesia tried to achieve equality of outcomes (in particular regional, for example rural–urban and inter-regional) by transfers, but did not pay much attention to equality of opportunities, such as education, by enhancing public spending. Although Malaysia did increase public spending on education, it created barriers to opportunities through an ethnic-based quota system.

HORIZONTAL INEQUALITY AND ITS IMPLICATIONS: REVISITING THE SOUTHEAST ASIAN EXPERIENCE

There can be different dimensions of horizontal inequality, such as urban–rural inequality, regional inequality, gender inequality and so on. The discussion of these dimensions generally remains confined within the context of decomposition of inequality (à la Theil's inequality index) and their contributions to overall inequality. The discussion of gender inequality and regional inequality also features prominently in the context of the human development index. Only a handful of researchers (e.g. Tadjoeddin, Suharyo and Mishra, 2001; Brown, 2008; Østby et al., forthcoming) in recent years have studied the phenomenon of horizontal inequality within the broader political economy context and have sought to examine the possible links between horizontal inequality and internal conflicts in Southeast Asia.[10] The emerging literature on the political economy of horizontal inequality in Southeast Asia follows the pioneering work of Stewart (2000, 2002), which suggests that 'horizontal inequalities', or inequalities that coincide with identity-based cleavages such as ethnic or religious fault lines, are important determinants of social conflicts.

As noted earlier, empirical research on inequality in Malaysia as well as in the Philippines finds a diminishing contribution of between-group inequality (inter-ethnic for Malaysia and spatial for the Philippines) to overall inequality. However, as the emerging literature shows, horizontal inequality should still be a cause of concern from the political economy perspective. We, therefore, provide a brief overview of horizontal inequality in Southeast Asia and highlight its political and social implications.

The Philippines

> . . . a considerable percentage of Filipinos (33% to 39% . . .) are biased against Muslims notwithstanding the fact that only about 14 per cent of them have had direct dealings with Muslims.
>
> UNDP, 2005: 58

There is a wide variation in the estimates of the Muslim population in the Philippines, as can be seen from Table 4.4. Despite the historical 'minorisation' policy, Muslims still remain the majority in the southwestern parts of the island of Mindanao, and in the Sulu archipelago – the province that now constitutes the Autonomous Region of Muslim Mindanao (ARMM).

It is quite evident from Table 4.5 that Mindanao in general, and the ARMM in particular, is the most underdeveloped part of the Philippines. They rank at the bottom of 77 provinces in terms of the human development index (HDI). The province of Sulu has ranked absolute bottom in every Human Development Report since 1994. Figures 4.6 and 4.7 show the disparity between Muslims and Christians in terms of per capita

Table 4.4   Muslim population (2000)

Area	Total (OMA)	Total (NSO)
Non-Mindanao	2 191 607 (3.8 per cent)	212 835 (0.4 per cent)
Mindanao	6 157 576 (34.0 per cent)	3 641 480 (20.1 per cent)
Philippines	8 349 183 (10.9 per cent)	3 854 315 (5.1 per cent)

OMA: Office of Muslim Affairs; NSO: National Statistical Office.

Source: UNDP (2005: 15).

Table 4.5 ARMM – socio-economic indicators

	Incidence of poverty (%), 2003	Per capita income (PPP), 2000	Life expectancy at birth, 2000	Percentage high school graduates (18+), 2003	Primary and high school enrolment rate, 2002	HDI (rank), 2003
Maguindanao	55.8	1052	52.0	28.9	81.2	0.498 (76)
Lanao del Sur	38.8	1221	57.9	45.9	81.1	0.601 (68)
Basilan	65.6	1074	60.6	31.6	83.9	0.578 (74)
Tawi-Tawi	69.9	1201	51.2	40.9	91.4	0.518 (75)
Sulu	88.8	1020	52.8	21.1	83.8	0.540 (77)
Philippines	25.7	2260	69.8	52.1	90.6	0.721

Total province = 77.

Source: UNDP (2005).

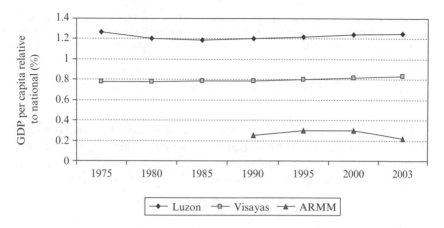

ARMM: Autonomous Region of Muslim Mindanao.

Source: Brown (2008).

Figure 4.6 GDP per capita of ARMM and Christian majority provinces (relative to national, %)

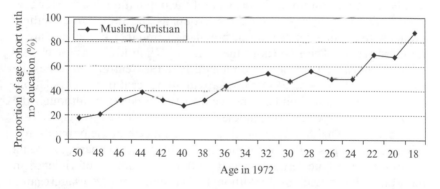

Source: Brown (2008).

Figure 4.7 Mindanao Muslim and Christian population without education by age, 1972

income and education. The per capita income of Christian Luzon is higher than the national level, whereas that of the ARMM is less than half and declining.

Commenting on the educational disparity between Christians and Muslims in Mindanao, Brown (2008: 270–72) notes:

while non-enrolment in at least one year of education was virtually eradicated among the Christian population by 1970, it remained a significant problem for the Muslim community. If we consider the specific population sector that might be considered the 'usual suspects' for recruitment to rebel organizations – males between ages of 15 and 30 (in 1972) – the situation is stark and clear: less than 4 per cent of Christians within this population had never attended school, but more than a third of their Muslim counterparts had no schooling.

The separatist movement in the Muslim Southern Philippines has a long history, rooted in colonization. But the socio-economic disparity has the potential for sustaining it. Violence itself can cause economic declines and socio-economic disadvantages, and create a vicious circle (see UNDP, 2005).

Thailand

Although Thailand has often been regarded as an ethnically homogeneous society, its ethnic structure is vastly more complex. The main ethnic group is the Central Thai, who constitute about 50 per cent of the population. The Central Thai are concentrated in the central region around the capital, Bangkok. The largest minority is the Isan, a Lao-speaking group populating the northeast region bordering the neighbouring country of Laos. The Isan account for about 23 per cent of the population. Khon Meuang, also predominantly a Lao-speaking group, is the third largest ethnic group, with about 9 per cent of the population, and they live mostly in the northern region. The Lao (both the Isan and Khon Meuang) are closely related linguistically, racially and religiously to the Central Thai. Thus the total Tai-speaking people constitute about 80 per cent of the population. Chinese make up just under 8 per cent of the population, although the Sino-Thai (Thai speakers of Chinese descent) would take this figure closer to 11 per cent. Thai Malays constitute only 2 per cent of the population.

There are signs that economic disadvantage is increasingly being interpreted in ethnic terms, especially after the eruption of violence in the Malay-dominated south. Although Thai data are not disaggregated according to ethnicity, we can glean the inter-ethnic inequality from regional data, owing to the concentration of major ethnic groups in particular regions. To reiterate, the northeast is mainly Isan, the north Khon Meuang, and the south Southern Thai and Malay (mainly Muslims). As can be seen from Figure 4.8, poverty is most severe in the northeast (mainly Isan area), followed by the south (mostly Muslim area), north and central regions respectively. Bangkok has the lowest incidence of poverty. The poverty rates in 2000 in the three Muslim southern provinces of Pattani, Yala and Narathiwat were, respectively, 25.5 per cent, 28.1 per cent and 35.1 per cent, well above the national rate of 14.1 per cent. The

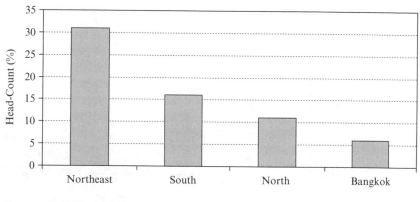

Source: Deolalikar (2002).

Figure 4.8   Regional poverty level, 1999 (Thailand)

poverty rates in the Lao-speaking (Isan) northeast provinces of Yasothon and Nong Bua Lam Phu were above 50 per cent (Brown, 2008).

According to the *Thailand Human Development Report 2007*, the north-eastern provinces dominate among the ten bottom-ranked regions. Using Thai census data, Selway (2007) finds that there is much less variation in per capita income among provinces with high minority populations than among provinces with small minority populations. Selway hypothesizes that having a large minority population (regardless of the identity of the minority group) is a barrier to high mean per capita incomes. However, having small minority populations is not necessarily associated with high per capita incomes. Figure 4.9 lends some support to this hypothesis. It shows that the per capita GDP of Bangkok and the central region, which is predominantly Thai-speaking Buddhist, exceeds the national per capita GDP, whereas the predominantly Lao-speaking north and northeast regions lag far behind. This is consistent with the variations in poverty rates as presented in Figure 4.8.

Figure 4.10 plots the per capita GDP of Thailand and the predominantly Malay southern provinces. It also includes the per capita GDP of Songkhla, a southern predominantly Buddhist province neighbouring Muslim provinces. As can be seen from Figure 4.9, the per capita GDP of the Muslim provinces is significantly below that of the neighbouring Buddhist province (Songkhla), whose per capita GDP is as high as the national per capita GDP.

Figure 4.11 reveals an almost identical picture for the Muslim provinces as for the Lao-speaking northeastern provinces. Their per capita GDP is significantly below the national average, and the gap appears to be rising.

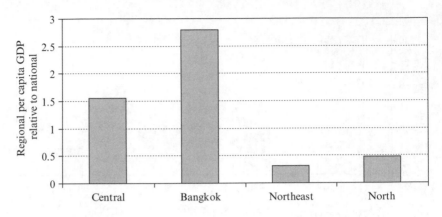

Source: Thailand Human Development Report 2007.

Figure 4.9   Regional per capita GDP (percentage of Thai national), 2004

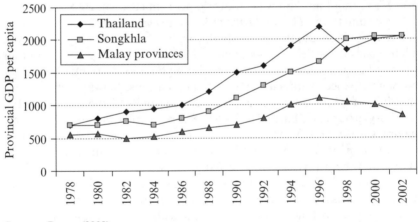

Source: Brown (2008).

Figure 4.10   Thai provincial GDP per capita (USD PPP, 2000)

Brown (2008) reports other dimensions of ethnic or horizontal inequality in Thailand. For example, Muslims in both rural and urban areas are far behind their Buddhist counterparts in educational attainment. The Buddhists have on average four to five years' extra education for both men and women, and their assets are also double the assets of Muslims. Central Thai Buddhists and assimilated Chinese dominate the socio-economic landscape of Thailand, as is reflected in the occupational distribution.

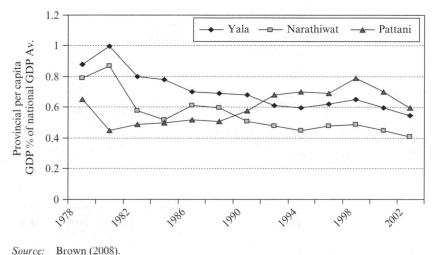

Source: Brown (2008).

Figure 4.11 Relative per capita GDP in Malay–Muslim provinces in Thailand

The fact that the socio-economic position of ethnic minorities, including that their income levels are much lower than among the Central Thai, lends support to the structuralist model of social exclusion. As Selway (2007: 60) notes:

> This model sees Thai society as hierarchical in nature, with the Central Thai as the dominant ethnic group controlling most of the resources. Furthermore, the Central Thai protect their spheres of influence against other ethnic and religious groups by constructing barriers to occupations, resources, and goods and services. To reinforce this exclusion, they promote solidarity within the ethnic group through nationalistic symbols. Thus, membership in Thai society is unequal, and exclusion buttresses the very structure of society.

Once again, as in the Philippines, this rising relative deprivation of the ethnic population (both Muslims and Lao-speaking northeasterners) may add fuel to the ethnic and regional discontent. It seems there is much potential for politicizing the ethnic dimension in Thailand.

Malaysia
Ethnic Malays constitute the majority ethnic group in Malaysia. Affirmative action policies of the NEP were designed to solve ethnic inequalities in wealth and educational attainment and in ownership of economic resources. As was noted earlier, these policies were largely successful in closing the horizontal inter-ethnic inequality of income.

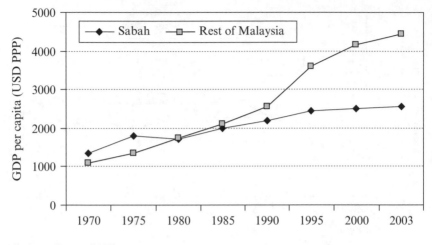

Source: Brown (2008).

Figure 4.12   GDP per capita (Sabah and the rest of Malaysia, USD PPP, 2000)

However, Malaysia still has substantial regional disparity, especially with the eastern state of Sabah. When Sabah joined the Malaysian federation in 1963, its socio-economic condition was well below that of Peninsular Malaya. For example, Sabah's poverty rate in 1976 was more than 50 per cent compared to around 25 per cent in Peninsular Malaya. On the other hand, owing to its abundant natural resources, Sabah's per capita GDP was about 20 per cent higher than the national average. However, Sabah's per capita GDP started falling behind in the early 1980s when Malaysia embarked on a market-oriented export and foreign-investment-led growth strategy (Figure 4.12). The gap between Sabah's and the rest of Malaysia's per capita GDP widened, and in 2003 Sabah's per capita GDP was more than a third below the national average.

With falling income, Sabah's poverty rate was about five times higher than West Malaysia's (Figure 4.13). By 2000, Sabah ranked bottom of all the Malaysian states in all socio-economic indicators (Brown, 2008: 275).

The Chinese in Sabah, who were significantly better off despite accounting for only 25 per cent of the population in the early 1970s, were to some extent marginalized as the migrant Malays took up high-ranking state government jobs. The Malays' influx also threatened Sabah's Christian Kadazans. By 1980, over 80 per cent of 'Echelon I' and 'Echelon II' civil servants in the state were Muslims (Brown, 2008: 276).

In mainland Malaysia, the narrowing of ethnic disparity did not cause

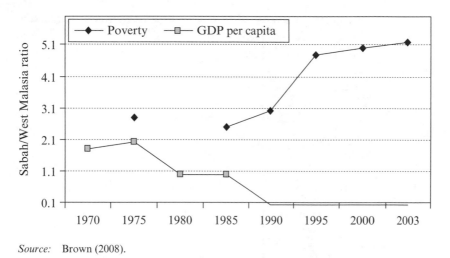

Source: Brown (2008).

Figure 4.13 Inter-regional horizontal inequalities

much ethnic tension, as it happened in the context of a growing economy (see Chowdhury and Islam, 1996). However, it was a different story in Sabah, whose per capita GDP in real terms grew at only 2.1 per cent per annum as opposed to 4 per cent for the Malaysian economy as a whole. When the native bumiputera (Christian Kadazans) saw that, through good government jobs, the migrant bumiputeras (Muslims) had on average doubled their per capita household expenditure, they might legitimately have felt aggrieved.

Indonesia

There are wide variations in Indonesia's regional or provincial per capita GDP. For example, the real per capita GDP of Jakarta and East Kalimantan is about four times the provincial average. On the other hand, the real per capita GDP of the poorest province, Gorontalo, is less than half the average (Figure 4.14). The provincial real per capita GDP in 2005 ranged from Rp 2.5 million (Gorontalo) to Rp 34 million (Jakarta).

Some broad geographical variations in per capita provincial GDP in Indonesia is presented in Table 4.6. It also shows the influence of oil and gas as a source of inter-provincial income variation. The ratio of the highest to the lowest provincial GDP was just over 17 in 1978 at the start of Indonesia's Green Revolution, falling to ten by the outbreak of the Asian economic crisis in 1997 and rising again to its 1978 mark by 2004.

Table 4.7 shows substantial difference in provincial rankings based on

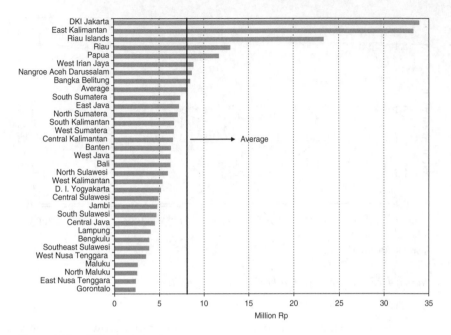

Note: Using 2000 constant prices.

Source: Mishra (2008).

Figure 4.14   Gross regional domestic product per capita, 2005

regional GDP per capita and those based on HDI ranks. The difference between the GRDP and the HDI ranks ranged from plus 17 to minus 26 among 30 Indonesian provinces in 2002. Papua was the third richest province in Indonesia in terms of regional per capita income. It was among the most disadvantaged Indonesian provinces, ranked 29 out of 30 on the human development scale. Aceh's rankings also differed significantly in terms of its per capita income and HDI. It was ranked fourth in terms of income, but fifteenth in terms of human development. To some extent, resource-rich East Kalimantan had a similar experience.

The failure to achieve social or human development commensurate with their resource wealth was partly due to the Soeharto government's equalization programme, which saw resource rent being used to uplift resource-poor regions, in particular Java. This can cause a 'rage of the rich', especially when the rent-sharing mechanism is not agreed upon through a democratic process. In the absence of a democratically derived social compact, resource-rich regions aspire to be unequal.[11]

Table 4.6   Regional output disparity in Indonesia, 1978–2004

	1978	1988	1993	1997	2000	2004
Ratio using GRDP per capita						
Highest to lowest	17.14	16.30	12.49	10.18	18.39	17.57
Java–Bali and						
Outer Islands	0.60	0.83	0.99	1.09		
Western to						
Eastern	0.79	1.09	1.11	1.12	0.99	1.12
Ratio using GRDP without Oil and Gas per capita						
Highest to lowest	4.55	7.50	9.61	9.37	13.92	15.83
Java–Bali and						
Outer Islands	0.93	1.13	1.24	1.30		
Western to						
Eastern	0.95	1.21	1.18	1.21	1.18	1.33

Note: Using current market prices; GRDP = gross regional domestic product.

Source: Mishra (2008).

CONCLUDING REMARKS

This chapter has navigated a wide and diverse terrain. One has reached an appropriate juncture where the various threads in the analysis offered so far can be woven together to provide a concluding narrative.

The chapter commenced by charting the evolution of the discourse on the role of inequality in the process of economic development. It noted how, during the 1980s and early 1990s, the literature was influenced by dominant interpretations of the 'East Asian miracle'. A handful of economies in East and Southeast Asia were seen by the World Bank and others as rare exemplars of 'shared growth'. They defied historical experience by combining equitable income distribution with rapid growth. Such an optimistic interpretation of the East Asian experience was abruptly terminated by the 1997 financial crisis that swept through the region. The circumspect literature that has emerged since then recognizes the central role that inequality can play in both retarding growth and impairing the capacity of the growth process to reduce poverty. One also has to pay much greater attention to the issue of horizontal inequality, in particular inter-regional and inter-ethnic inequality, because its perpetuation can be an important source of social conflict.

Given the emergence of the nuanced, post-1997 literature on the

Table 4.7   Comparison of per capita GRDP and HDI, 2002

	GRDP	GDRP rank	HDI	HDI rank	GRDP rank minus HDI rank
D.I. Yogyakarta	1581	20	70.8	3	17
Maluku	950	28	66.5	12	16
North Sulawesi	1695	17	71.3	2	15
Jambi	1270	23	67.1	10	13
Bengkulu	1188	24	66.2	14	10
Central Java	1340	22	66.3	13	9
Lampung	1085	27	65.8	18	9
Riau	2050	13	69.1	5	8
West Sumatera	1714	16	67.5	8	8
North Maluku	1094	26	65.8	19	7
Southeast Sulawesi	948	29	64.1	26	3
Central Kalimantan	2321	8	69.1	6	2
East Nusa Tenggara	756	30	60.3	28	2
DKI Jakarta	7705	2	75.6	1	1
West Java	1680	18	65.8	17	1
Gorontalo	1117	25	64.1	24	1
North Sumatera	2357	7	68.8	7	0
South Sulawesi	1340	21	65.3	21	0
South Sumatera	1769	15	66.0	16	−1
East Kalimantan	9242	1	70.0	4	−3
Bali	2497	6	67.5	9	−3
Banten	2727	5	66.6	11	−6
East Java	1641	19	64.1	25	−6
Bangka Belitung	2083	11	65.4	20	−9
Central Sulawesi	2053	12	64.4	22	−10
Nangroe Aceh Darussalam	3051	4	66.0	15	−11
South Kalimantan	2092	10	64.3	23	−13
West Kalimantan	1975	14	62.9	27	−13
West Nusa Tenggara	2290	9	57.8	30	−21
Papua	4180	3	60.1	29	−26

Source: BPS.

inequality–development nexus, the chapter revisited the experiences of four Southeast Asian economies – Indonesia, Malaysia, the Philippines and Thailand. The review of the evidence and the explanations of the evidence suggest that these Southeast Asian economies cannot really be regarded as exemplars of 'shared growth'. Land and other forms of wealth inequality are very high, and barriers to education persist. These sources of inequality can in turn unleash political economy forces that perpetuate the initial level of inequality. These countries do have a much higher income Gini than Korea or Taiwan.

Economic and social policies to rectify various forms of inequality in Southeast Asia have a mixed record. In Malaysia, for example, attempts to rectify inter-ethnic disparities since the 1970s have been accompanied by persistently high levels of intra-ethnic inequality. What is perhaps most germane to the political economy of inequality in Southeast Asian economies is the persistence of inter-regional and inter-ethnic inequality as a source of political and social tensions. These tensions cannot be captured in a statistical decomposition of inequality; such an exercise typically shows that horizontal inequality represents a modest proportion of aggregate inequality. In the Philippines and Thailand, inter-regional inequality is compounded by the fact that it coincides with inter-faith cleavages. In both countries, deprived Muslim minorities are concentrated in particular regions. In Malaysia and Indonesia, the tensions seem to be between resource-rich and resource-poor regions. The resolution of horizontal inequality in Southeast Asia is important for maintaining political and social cohesion.

NOTES

1. See Islam and Chowdhury (2001) for a discussion of 'weak' and 'strong' versions of shared growth and the role of policies.
2. The Gini ratios in parentheses for the Latin American countries are from WIDER, World Income Inequality database, as reported in ADB (2007).
3. ADB (2007) offers a brief review of the pros and cons of using expenditure distribution vis-à-vis income distribution data.
4. See ADB (2007); Balisacan and Fuwa (2004); Dacuycuy (2006); and Estudillo (2007).
5. See Fofack and Zeufack (1999).
6. In 1996, this rate was 69 per cent for China, 58 per cent for Malaysia, 72 per cent for Singapore, 102 per cent for Korea and 92 per cent for Japan (*sources*: UNESCO and World Bank, EdStats).
7. See Chowdhury and Islam (1996) for an evaluation of the NEP from a political economy perspective.
8. See Mishra (2008) for a comprehensive discussion of this issue.
9. See also Hughes and Islam (1981), Islam and Khan (1986) and Islam (2003) on spatial dimensions of inequality in Indonesia.
10. Brown (1988), Christie (1996). Taking a more horizontal approach, Christie (1996) emphasizes the process of decolonization where certain identity groups became dominant in the formation of new nation states, resulting in the alienation and undermining of other peripheral identities, which sow the seeds of ethnic conflicts in many post-colonized countries, Che Man (1990) and Chalk (2001) do not dispute the existence of socio-economic grievances among the separatist groups, but their overwhelming

emphasis is on the historical and political conditions. Some earlier studies of Malaysia, however, did explore the link between inter-ethnic inequality and the race riot of 1969, but the interest in the inter-ethnic inequality in Malaysia fizzled out with the apparent success of the NEP.

11. See Tadjoeddin, Suharyo and Mishra (2001), who have floated the concept 'aspiration to inequality' and identified this as a cause for continued centre–region conflicts in Indonesia. Interestingly, in the case of Indonesia, region–centre vertical conflict can be explained by the narrowing of the inter-regional inequality in socio-economic indicators, achieved through the equalization programme (see Tadjoeddin and Chowdhury, 2009).

REFERENCES

ADB (1994), *Asian Development Outlook*, Hong Kong: Oxford University Press.
ADB (2007), *Key Indicators 2007: Inequality in Asia*, Manila: ADB.
ADB (2005), *Poverty in the Philippines: Income, Assets, and Access*, Manila: ADB.
Akita, T. (1999), 'Spatial patterns of expenditure inequalities in Indonesia: 1987, 1990, and 1993', *Bulletin of Indonesian Economic Studies*, **35**(2): 67–90.
Alesina, A. (1998), 'The political economy of macroeconomic stabilizations and income inequality: myths and reality', in Vito Tanzi and Ke-young Chu (eds), *Income Distribution and High-Quality Growth*, Cambridge, MA: MIT Press.
Alesina, A. and D. Rodrik (1994), 'Distributive politics and economic growth', *Quarterly Journal of Economics*, **109**(2): 465–90.
Alesina, A. and R. Perotti (1993), 'Income distribution, political instability, and investment', NBER Working Papers 4486.
Anand, S. (1983), *Inequality and Poverty in Malaysia: Measurement and Decomposition*, Oxford: Oxford University Press.
Balisacan, A. and N. Fuwa (2004), 'Changes in spatial income inequality in the Philippines', UNU/WIDER Working Paper No. 2004/34.
Banerjee, A. and A. Newman (1993), 'Occupational choice and the process of development', *Journal of Political Economy*, April: 274–98.
Bourguignon, F. (2003), 'The growth elasticity of poverty reduction', in T. Eicher and S. Turnovsky (eds), *Inequality and Growth*, Cambridge, MA: MIT Press.
Bourguignon, F., A. Benassy-Quere, S. Dercon, A. Estache, J. Gunning, R. Kanbur, S. Klasen, S. Maxwell, J. Platteau and A. Spadaro (2008), 'Millennium development goals at midpoint: Where do we stand and where do we need to go?', European Report on Development.
Brown, D. (1988), 'From peripheral communities to ethnic nations: separatism in Southeast Asia', *Pacific Affairs*, **61**(1): 51–77.
Brown, G. (2008), 'Horizontal inequalities and separatism in Southeast Asia: a comparative perspective', in Frances Stewart (ed.), *Horizontal Inequalities and Conflict: Understanding Group Violence in Multiethnic Societies*, Basingstoke: Palgrave Macmillan, pp. 252–82.
Chalk, P. (2001), 'Separatism and Southeast Asia: the Islamic factor in southern Thailand, Mindanao, and Aceh', *Studies in Conflict and Terrorism*, **24**: 241–69.
Champernowne, D.G. and F.A. Cowell (1998), *Economic Inequality and Income Distribution*, Cambridge: Cambridge University Press.
Che Man, Wan Kadir (1990), *Muslim Separatism: The Moros of Southern*

Philippines and the Malays of Southern Thailand, Quezon City: Ateneo de Manila University Press.

Chowdhury, A. and I. Islam (1996), 'The institutional and political framework of growth in an ethnically diverse society: the case of Malaysia', *Canadian Journal of Development Studies*, **17**(3): 487–512.

Christie, Clive J. (1996), *A Modern History of South-East Asia: Decolonization, Nationalism and Separatism*, London: I.B. Tauris.

Claessens, S., S. Djankov, J. Fan and L. Lang (1999), 'Expropriation of minority shareholders: evidence from East Asian corporations', World Bank Working Paper 2088.

Dacuycuy, L. (2006), 'Explaining male wage inequality in the Philippines: non-parametric and semiparametric approaches', *Applied Economics*, **38**: 2497–511.

Deolalikar, Anil B. (2002), 'Poverty, Growth, and Inequality in Thailand', ADB, ERD Working Paper no. 8.

Estudillo, J.P. (2007), 'Income inequality in the Philippines, 1961–1991', *The Developing Economies*, **35**(1): 68–95.

Fields, G. (1995), 'Income distribution in developing economies: conceptual, data and policy issues in broad-based growth', in M. Quibria (ed.), *Critical Issues in Asian Development*, Hong Kong: Oxford University Press.

Fofack, H. and A. Zeufack (1999), 'Dynamics of income inequality in Thailand: evidence from household pseudo-panel data', Mimeo, World Bank.

Frankema, E. (2006), 'The colonial origins of inequality: exploring the causes and consequences of land distribution', Groningen Growth and Development Centre research memorandum GD-81, Groningen, Netherlands.

Halim, S. (1991), 'State capitalism in Malaysian agriculture', *Journal of Contemporary Asia*, **21**(3): 327–43.

Hughes, G. and I. Islam (1981), 'Inequality in Indonesia: a decomposition analysis', *Bulletin of Indonesian Economic Studies*, **17**(2): 42–71.

Islam, I. (2003), 'Dealing with spatial dimensions of inequality in Indonesia: towards a social accord', Paper presented at the Second Inequality and Pro-Poor Growth Spring Conference on the Theme of 'How Important is Horizontal Inequality?', World Bank, Washington, DC, 9-10 June.

Islam, I. and H. Khan (1986), 'Spatial patterns of inequality and poverty in Indonesia', *Bulletin of Indonesian Economic Studies*, **22**(2): 80–102.

Islam, I. and A. Chowdhury, (2001), *The Political Economy of East Asia: Post Crisis Debates*, Melbourne: Oxford University Press.

Jantti, M. and S. Sandstrom (2005), 'Trends in income inequality: a critical examination of evidence in WIID2', Mimeo, WIDER.

Jomo, K.S. (1986), *A Question of Class: Capital, the State and Uneven Development in Malaysia*, Oxford: Oxford University Press.

Jomo, K.S. (2006), 'Growth with equity in East Asia?', UN-DESA Working Paper, No. 33.

Klasen, S. and M. Misselhorn (2007), 'Determinants of the growth semi-elasticity of poverty reduction', Mimeo, University of Gottingen.

Lee Jong-Wha and Changyong Rhee (1999), 'Social Impacts of the Asian Crisis: Policy Challenges and Lessons', UNDP, Human Development Report Office, Occasional Paper 33.

Lopez, R., V. Thomas and Wang Yan (1998), 'Addressing the educational puzzle: the distribution of education and economic reform', World Bank Policy Research Working Paper No. 2031.

Medhi Krongkaew (1994), 'Income distribution in East Asian developing countries: an update', *Asian-Pacific Economic Literature*, **8**(2): 58–73.

Medhi Krongkaew and Ragayah Haji Mat Zin (2007), 'Income distribution and sustainable economic development in East Asia: a comparative analysis', IDEAs Working Paper, No. 02/2007.

Mishra, S. (2008), 'Economic inequality in Indonesia: trends, causes and policy response', Strategic Asia, Jakarta.

Østby, G., H. Urdal, M. Tadjoeddin, S. Murshed and H. Strand (forthcoming), 'Population pressure, horizontal inequality and political violence: a disaggregated study of Indonesian provinces, 1990–2003', *Journal of Development Studies*.

Persson, T. and G. Tabellini (1994), 'Is inequality harmful for growth?', *American Economic Review*, **84**(3): 600–621.

Putzel, J. (1992), *A Captive Land: The Politics of Agrarian Reform in the Philippines*, London, New York and Manila: Catholic Institute for International Affairs, Monthly.

Ragayah Haji Mat Zin (2008), 'Income distribution in Malaysia: old issues, new approaches', 11th International Convention of the East Asian Economic Association, Manila, 15-16 November.

Selway, J. (2007), 'Turning Malays into Thai-men: nationalism, ethnicity and economic inequality in Thailand', *South East Asia Research*, **15**(1), 53–87(35).

Smith, A. (1976 [1776]), *An Inquiry into the Nature and the Causes of the Wealth of Nations*, Volume II, Part II, Chicago: University of Chicago Press.

Stewart, F. (2000), 'The root causes of humanitarian emergencies', in W. Nafziger, F. Stewart and R. Väyrynen (eds), *War, Hunger and Displacement: The Origins of Humanitarian Emergencies*, Oxford: Oxford University Press.

Stewart, F. (2002), 'Horizontal inequalities: a neglected dimension of development', Queen Elizabeth House Working Paper Series 81.

Tadjoeddin, M. and A. Chowdhury (2009), 'Socioeconomic perspectives on violent conflict in Indonesia', *Economics of Peace and Security Journal*, **4**(1): 38–47.

Tadjoeddin, M., W.I. Suharyo and S. Mishra (2001), 'Regional disparity and vertical conflicts in Indonesia', *Journal of the Asia Pacific Economy*, **6**(3): 283–304.

UNDP (2005), *Philippines Human Development Report 2005: Peace, Human Security and Human Development*, Manila: Human Development Network and UNDP.

UNDP (2007), *Thailand Human Development Report 2007: Sufficiency Economy and Human Development*, Bangkok: UNDP.

United Nations (UN) (2005), *Report on the World Social Situation: The Inequality Predicament*, New York: UN-DEA.

World Bank (1993), *The East Asian Miracle: Economic Growth and Public Policy*, New York: Oxford University Press.

World Bank (2006), *World Development Report 2006*, New York: Oxford University Press.

5. Industrial relations and labour market conditions

Rene Ofreneo and Peter Wad

The Association of the Southeast Asian Nations (ASEAN) spans great unevenness in the development of the ten member countries of the ASEAN in GDP per capita. The GDP per capita of the oil-rich Brunei and Singapore, Southeast (SE) Asia's newly industrialized economy (NIE), is around US$30 000, and that is more than 50 times that of the Lao PDR, Cambodia and the militarized Myanmar, more than 20 times that of Vietnam and the Philippines, more than nine times that of Thailand and more than five times that of Malaysia, the third richest country in Southeast Asia GDP-wise (ASEAN Statistics, 2007).

This chapter not only outlines how this unevenness in economic development is reflected in the wage labour market and the system of industrial relations (IR) prevailing in the ten ASEAN countries. It also shows how the uneven and relatively weak IR and labour market institutions and conditions are shaping the accumulation process in Southeast Asia, particularly in the ASEAN developing economies[1] that have developed strong links with the global production and service chains of the transnational corporations (TNCs). These TNCs are generally averse or hostile to the formation of labour unions, especially in the so-called export economic zones (EEZs). And yet there are areas where the unions have managed to survive and remain viable despite the anti-union environment in the region. The challenge for a critical political economic analysis is to answer how these unions may be able to strengthen their ranks and collectively advance the workers' interests in a globalizing region marked by social and labour inequalities. The conclusion is that it is paramount that trade unions in SE Asia are able to forge national, regional and global alliances with like-minded civil society institutions in order to secure and broaden labour's social base in SE Asian society.

The chapter is structured as follows. The section 'IR concepts and systems in SE Asia' outlines the major trends in the IR systems and labour markets in SE Asia in the era of regionalization and globalization. The section 'Drivers of IR systems' analyses the drivers behind the evolving patterns of SE Asian IR systems. The next section is a case study of the IR situation in the auto industry of the ASEAN 4 (Indonesia, Malaysia, the Philippines and Thailand) as a result of the TNC-led regionalization–globalization processes. There follows another case study, this time on the impact of the twin technology revolution (information technology and information communication technology or the IT–ICT revolution) on the labour markets in the region and on the patterns of IR systems in the TNC-led IT, ICT and ICT-enabled industries. The chapter concludes by considering some options in IR theory and practice.

IR CONCEPTS AND SYSTEMS IN SE ASIA

Kaufman (2004) wrote that IR, as a field of study and as a system of institutions and rules governing the relations of industry and workers in a capitalist setting, developed in the decades of the 1920s and 1930s when the American government was groping for solutions to contain the labour unrest which had hit America and to stabilize the growing industrial capitalist system. Closely associated with institutional economics, IR focused on the harmonization of markets and the interests of the different production actors (employers and workers) and regulators (public authorities) through the development of institutions dealing with union recognition, settlement of industrial disputes and promotion of employee welfare, among others. In the 1960s, at the height of the industrial capitalist expansion in North America and Western Europe, IR gained global acceptance with the publication of the *Industrial Relations System* (1957), authored by US Secretary of Labor John Dunlop. The book popularized the IR model of rule making based on the tripartite relationship among the employers, unions and government.

In recent years, a growing number of management people have been using the term 'human resource management' or HRM instead of IR, to emphasize the enterprise focus on productivity, competitiveness and adjustments to global competition (De Silva, 1995). This preference for the use of the term HRM is reinforced by the crisis of traditional tripartite arrangements as a result of the general decline of unionism, decentralization of collective bargaining, and globalization of production systems. Until the 1970s, unions enjoyed a certain level of stability because of the stability of jobs in the industrialized countries and in the limited formal sector in developing countries. However, globalization has ushered in radical changes in the labour market, such as the 'atomization' of large workplaces and the outsourcing of work to so many units dispersed globally, the polarization of the workforce into a small elite group of skilled and educated and a large, malleable, non-regular, contingent segment, the increased hiring of women and migrants in EEZs and in varied production chains, the government retreat from Keynesian approaches to employment and the widespread adoption of external labour market flexibility measures such as temporary or casual hiring (Jose, 2002; Munck, 2002).

In general, however, IR is commonly understood today as the practices, laws and regulations governing employer–employee relations in the modern sector of the economy, including the dynamics of how groups of employees are able to form associations for collective bargaining purposes and to secure other labour and social concessions through pressure-group activities. Conceived in a comprehensive perspective, IR is also termed 'employment relations' (ER) or 'labour and employment relations' (LER) and comprises union as well as non-union organizations and networks of labourers and employees aiming to voice and collectively act upon their concerns, claims and rights.

Based on its Western and industrial sense as summarized above, IR is fairly 'underdeveloped' in SE Asia. First, the ASEAN countries are at varying stages of industrialization – a few have barely started (Cambodia, Laos and Myanmar), while others are late industrializers or are 'industrializing' in a narrow sense, such as reliance on the flow of foreign capital in controlled 'industrial enclaves' called export processing zones (EPZs) or in segments of industries attached to the global production and marketing chains of TNCs such as car parts assembly and garments sewing. As shown in Table 5.1, only the ASEAN 5 (Indonesia, Malaysia, the Philippines, Singapore and Thailand) and to a certain extent Vietnam have a substantial wage labour force, ranging from 25.6 per cent in the case of Vietnam to as high as 86.5 per cent in the case of Singapore. Malaysia, the second most industrially developed SE Asian country, has a wage labour force of 74.4 per cent. Not surprisingly, the least developed countries (Cambodia, the Lao PDR and Myanmar) are greatly dependent on agriculture for employment. Brunei, with its rich oil resources, is unique – its labour force is mainly in services.

Secondly, the IR system and institutions have evolved or developed in each of the SE Asian countries under different politico-historical circumstances (Sharma, 1985; Cooney *et al.*, 2002). The Philippines and Singapore–Malaysia have a fairly well-developed body of Anglo-Saxon-type labour laws and industrial relations practices. This is the legacy of American colonialism for the former and British colonialism for the latter. Additionally, the Philippines has a relatively long history of industrialization efforts and unionism dating back to the 1900s; however, the Philippines also has a long history of cycles of mild recoveries and deep crises, which have stunted its overall industrial development. In the rest of

Table 5.1   *Labour force, sectoral employment and wage workers in the*
                ASEAN (2006 where indicated, most recent year for the rest)

Country	Labour force (in thousands) (2006)	Sectoral shares in employment (as percentage of total employment) (most recent year)			Waged and salaried workers (as percentage of total employed) (most recent year)
		Agriculture	*Industry*	*Services*	
Brunei	167	1.4	21.4	77.2	NA
Cambodia	8 267	60.3	12.5	27.2	20.0
Indonesia	110 432	44.0	18.0	38.0	37.9
Lao PDR	2 427	82.7	8.7	8.6	14.4
Malaysia	11 288	14.8	30.1	52.5	74.4
Myanmar	27 954	62.7	12.2	25.1	NA
Philippines	38 294	37.0	14.9	48.1	51.7
Singapore	2 238	–	29.5	69.6	86.5
Thailand	36 136	42.6	20.2	37.1	43.7
Vietnam	45 628	57.9	17.4	24.7	25.6
ASEAN	282 831				

Source: ILO (2007).

the region, from the newly industrializing Thailand to the newly market-liberalizing Indo-China states of Vietnam, Cambodia and the Lao People's Democratic Republic, modern labour laws and labour institutions are still in their incipient level of development. In militarized Myanmar, there are hardly any.

Thirdly, the tripartite IR system and a number of protective labour laws had been adopted in the ASEAN 5 in the post-Independence periods of the 1950s up to the 1980s. However, this process took place not only in a highly uneven manner but also largely in the state-corporatist sense, that is, to allow governments to keep the small labour movement under their political control to 'maintain industrial peace' based on the requirements of the national accumulation projects and, later, as policies shifted from import substitution to export orientation, to sustain international competitiveness (Sharma, 1985; Kuruvilla, 1995). Corporatism in IR found expression in the 'one-party' system in Malaysia and Singapore, where the Internal Security Act (ISA) and the government's patronage became a powerful stick-and-carrot formula in keeping the union movement in check – mostly excluded from direct political influence in Malaysia and included but subordinated to the PAP regime in Singapore – while the state assiduously pursued the national development agenda of export-led growth. In Indonesia, General Soeharto's army, after crushing the Communist movement and their unions in the 1960s, promoted a state-led *Pancasila* IR system based on employer–worker partnership and belief in 'God the Almighty'. The Philippines, the only ASEAN country which ratified the ILO Convention No. 87 (Freedom of Association) in the post-Independence era, had a pluralistic IR system featuring a multiplicity of trade unions; however, in the 1970s, this system was disrupted when the country was placed under martial law by President Ferdinand Marcos, who also tried to promote a similar corporatist IR system. In Thailand, the business and military elites had always played a central role in shaping the IR processes such as the formation of unions, which were allowed mainly in select but large public corporations.

However, radical changes in the IR systems can also occur despite the corporatist wishes of SE Asia's strongmen, as seen in the Philippines in the mid-1980s, in Thailand in the 1990s, and in Indonesia in 1998 in the wake of the Asian financial crisis. In the Philippines, the martial-law regime was virtually impotent in containing the waves of strikes and protests which inundated the country's urban and industrial areas from 1981 to 1986 as a result of a multi-dimensional politico-economic crisis (Bacungan and Ofreneo, 2002). In Thailand, democratization since 1992 opened up a space for grassroots labour activism within and beyond a fragmented and partly co-opted trade union movement (Brown, 2001). In the case of Indonesia, the *Pancasila* IR system came tumbling down at the height of the 1997–98 Asian financial crisis, which subverted the politico-economic stability of the Soeharto regime and ushered in a shift towards IR pluralism. Indonesia also became the first Asian state to ratify all the seven ILO conventions on core labour standards – freedom of association, collective bargaining, abolition of forced labour, non-discrimination in employment and elimination of the worst forms of child labour (Lindsey and Masduki, 2002).

All in all, organized labour is a clear minority then and now in the SE Asian countries, and it is on the retreat virtually everywhere in spite of the decades-long industrial revolution, employment growth and even tight labour market conditions for selected and especially skilled groups of employees. Statistically, the weak and weakened state of unionism can be seen in the low density of unionism in SE Asia and the reported decline in union memberships almost everywhere. A 1998 study by Rasiah and Chua (1998) shows that union density was highest in corporatist Singapore (24 per cent), followed by the Philippines (12 per cent), Malaysia (8.5 per cent), Vietnam (7.6 per cent), Indonesia (2.7 per cent) and Thailand (1.1 per cent). The figures for the Philippines are on the high side, since union

membership statistics are based on 'claimed memberships' submitted by
a hundred or so quarrelling union federations which have been inflating
their respective strengths. If an assessement of 'union influence' factor-
ized by bargaining coverage and bargaining structure is added to union
density, as done by Sarosh Kuruvilla and associates (2002) for a sample
of Asian countries in the 1980s to 1990s, Singapore is again on top of the
SE Asian countries and on a par with the US labour organizations. The
Malaysian unions hold the position at the bottom, while the Philippine
unions outperform the Malaysian in terms of union density and slightly
in terms of union influence. Yet, Malaysia may be unfairly downgraded
in terms of bargaining coverage and bargaining structure. Its bargaining
coverage approximates to its level of union density, for example there
were 734 685 employees who were union members in 1996 while 722 830
employees were covered by a collective agreement, and the same figures
were 802 260 and 834 287 in 2002 (www.mtuc.org.my/ind_dispute.thm &
/total_union.htm, downloaded 20 August 2007; the figures are sourced
from the Industrial Court of Malaysia and the Ministry of Human
Resources Malaysia respectively). The bargaining structure in Malaysia
is not completely decentralized, as stated by Kuruvilla *et al.* (2002) as
it includes sectors with industry-level bargaining, for example in the
banking sector. A more valid estimation would provide Malaysian unions
with more union influence than, for example, the Chinese unions and the
Philippine unions, although both these labour organizations keep a higher
union density.

DRIVERS OF IR SYSTEMS

What are the major forces shaping IR trends in SE Asia since the 1970s?
There are six interrelated developments.

First, the uneven formation of an industrial working class in the
ASEAN is becoming more and more determined by the regional integration of the TNC global production chains in SE Asia. In a paper written
for the Asian Development Bank (ADB), Richard Baldwin (2007) noted
that the individual ASEAN member countries pursued unilateral liberalization from the 1980s onwards for two interrelated reasons – first, to get
a share of the 'Factory Asia' investments and, second, to compete with
China, which has also been attracting the same Factory Asia investments.
'Factory Asia' refers to the movement of the labour-intensive production
processes, for example electronic parts assembly and garments and textile
manufacture, from Japan, Europe, North America and Asian NIEs to
cheaper production sites in developing Asian countries. In the host Asian

countries, these investments are generally placed in the EPZ-based export-oriented industries (EOI).

Factory Asia is also referred to as the global production chain of the TNCs, which was described by Folker, Heinrichs and Kreye (1980) as the manifestation of the 'new international division of labour' (NIDL). Under the NIDL, developing countries, through the EPZs and other 'industrial sweatshops', have been transformed as export platforms for cheap sewn garments, assembled electronic products and manufactured automotive parts, while developed countries have specialized in high-tech, capital-intensive and skills-focused industrial processes. However, in the 1990s to the present, the NIDL has given way to the broader and all-encompassing process of economic globalization and a global division of labour (GDL) characterized by both intensive and extensive outsourcing of production processes and, lately, even of services, as countries in the region liberalize and deregulate virtually all sectors of their economies – industry, agriculture, finance and so on – in the name of global and regional integration.

In an official report to the ASEAN on the patterns of intra-ASEAN trade, Myrna Austria (2004) reaffirmed that the main driver of economic integration in the region is indeed the global production system of the TNCs 'made possible by the unilateral and multilateral reduction of barriers to trade and investment and the rapid development of transportation, and information and communication technology'. Austria also affirmed that the ASEAN Free Trade Area (AFTA) benefits primarily the TNC-led or 'FDI-driven production networks' in the region.

The problem, however, with this TNC-led integration process is the tendency of the TNCs to place investments in the relatively more developed SE Asian countries represented by the ASEAN 5. Thus, Thailand, with a large population with a growing disposable income, has become the auto hub in the region for the Japanese auto makers, while Malaysia and the Philippines have become the favourite assembly sites for electronic parts and components outsourced by the Japanese and American TNCs. Indonesia is a major production base for labour-intensive products such as shoes and garments. Singapore, an NIE, has become a major trader–investor in the region and, like the other Asian NIEs (Hong Kong, South Korea and Taiwan), a major facilitator of TNC investments in garments, electronics and other labour-intensive activities being outsourced by the TNCs under their 'global commodity chains' or GCCs (Gereffi, 2003).

Second, the industrial working class has been increasingly segmented into layers of primary regular blue- and white-collar jobs, secondary temporary yet formal jobs, and tertiary informal and immigrant jobs where national labour and employment regulations do not apply at all. The trend towards increased use by employers of 'labour-flexibility' measures, such as the wider use of casual or non-tenured workers in a liberalizing or integrating SE Asia, is an important explanation of this tendency. This is facilitated by the weak employment laws in most ASEAN countries and the corollary absence of protection against the arbitrary dismissal of workers and especially foreign migrant workers, as amply revealed at the height of the 1997–98 Asian financial crisis when hundreds of thousands in Indonesia, Malaysia and Thailand lost their jobs overnight without getting any social assistance (Rasiah and Hofmann, 1998; Athukorala 2006).

Under Factory Asia, capital is able to hop in and out of the region, pushing employers to keep regular workers at a minimum level and avoid unionism. Nike, Adidas, Benetton, Triumph and other global brand retailers can hop from one Asian country to another, in search of subcontractors which can deliver cheap and quality shoes and garments even while they preach about the importance of 'social corporate responsibility' on the part of their subcontractors. Supply-chain management also encourages TNCs such as Toyota and Mitsubishi to organize 'competition' among their own subsidiaries in SE Asia and China in order to produce cheaper and higher-quality auto parts, with the implied threat that jobs will be lost if productivity does not rise, as production will be shifted to the more 'productive' sites elsewhere.

At the same time, neo-liberal economists keep preaching about the importance of a 'flexible' labour market. The Asian Development Bank (1997), a major Official Development Assistance (ODA) partner of the ASEAN countries, warns that economies in the region will not realize maximum growth 'unless their labor markets are flexible' and if 'the minimum wage is too high'. ADB enumerated the sources of labour market flexibility as follows: employers' ability to hire and dismiss, the capacity of workers to accept wage cuts in economic downturns, international labour migration, government's hands-off policy and union support for national development goals.

With China dominating Factory Asia and India on the rise as a destination for international service outsourcing (Office Asia), SE Asian primary labour markets and trade unions are clearly under severe pressure in the early twenty-first century and substituted by secondary and tertiary labour markets. This pressure is characterized by several features (Ofreneo, 2002): restructuring towards more flexible employment practices; job-displacing and union-disrupting technological changes; reduction of public sector employment; extensive use of immigrant workers (especially in Malaysia and Singapore); and increased national, regional and global competition that is pushing employers everywhere to reduce labour cost.

Third, there has been an increased diffusion in the region of IR and HRM policies which keep unionism at bay. The old Western IR paradigm propounded by the likes of John Dunlop does not fit the realities of globalizing Asian labour markets, where there are less and less stability and continuity in the relationship between employers and workers. What is happening is that there is a diffusion and adaptation of HRM practices developed by the TNCs themselves in the different host economies. Some practices have positive impact on the workers, for example the development of 'employee caring programmes' (for example, recreation and sports facilities) or the improvement of the work environment (for example, safety consciousness programmes) as part of the company's commitment to 'corporate codes of conduct'.

However, most of the HRM practices are generally directed against the formation of unions. One approach, for example, is the pro-active HRM programme of surfacing employee problems well in advance and asking their supervisors and managers to understand how such problems can be resolved in the context of the vision, mission and values of the corporation. This approach is better known as the 'HRD approach', which is very strong in the use of employee communication, non-formal grievance machinery and labour–management consultation schemes in sorting out employee concerns and complaints, thus effectively preventing, in a soft manner, the formation of a formal union. A few companies even have what they call 'strategic alliances' between employees and employers on how the company, with the support of the employees, can win the global race.

Another approach is the more common outright 'union avoidance approach', which means either directly subverting any union organizing efforts through various means, fair or foul, or restructuring the company and relocating the unionized business in a non-unionized setting, often in an EPZ which promotes a covert policy of 'non-unionization' as a come-on to investors. In the first case, TNCs and local firms are increasingly using every legal means to avoid workplace unionization and collective bargaining, as was demonstrated in the Euromedical industrial dispute for organizing a foreign-controlled joint venture in Malaysia, which began in 1975 and ended with the legal victory of the union at the last legal resort of appeal, the Federal Court, in 2004 requiring the employer to recognize the union and initiate collective bargaining, which eventually took place in 2005 (Wad, 2007b). In the second case, companies which close shop only to reopen in another site of the city or country just to avoid a striking union or the demands of a militant union are – in the traditional IR systems – called 'run-away shops'. Today, these shops do not only run away; they fly away, literally.

Of course, there are 'hybrid approaches' combining not only the two union avoidance approaches above but also certain national IR practices of some global investors–locators with those they find in the host countries. There are also exceptional cases where some global investors–locators genuinely understand the interests of the workers and have no difficulty working with the unions, so long as the latter share or sympathize with the business vision and mission – or have learned the lesson and accepted the union after an intense industrial conflict which often must draw on international solidarity campaigns to succeed (see the Thai AAT case, page 187).

However, it is also clear that globalization has created new actors in the world of work who are not captured in the traditional IR paradigm, such as: global investors–locators, who are not visible in the 'national' tripartite system; outsourcing companies, who are also not 'visible' in the tripartite world because they are considered 'secondary' employers; and informal workers, who outnumber the formals in the formal labour market and yet hardly enjoy any labour rights under the law.

Fourth, unionization and union strength have been kept within narrow boundaries by governments if not prevented outright. The undeclared state policy in many ASEAN countries is to keep EPZs and other areas hosting TNC investments 'union free', which is a rehash of what the Asian NIEs did in the 1960s to 1980s. As documented by Deyo (1989), labour was subordinated during the NIEs' accumulation process, with the government imposing tight political and labour controls, especially in the EOI sector. Moreover, public sectors and essential services may have been prevented from unionization or, if allowed to unionize, their bargaining and striking rights may have been eliminated. Even in the private sector industrial actions are predominantly severed and almost impossible to carry out owing to legally sanctioned procedures for conciliation, mediation and arbitration. Finally, trade unions will not be allowed to engage in sympathy strikes and other actions, and they may be excluded from supporting political parties, or union leaders may be barred from holding positions in such parties. In the most extreme cases, state agencies intervene against organized labour by way of internal security legislation, secret police and military forces, if not using paramilitary groups to harass, intimidate or eliminate trade union leaders and activists. These kinds of atrocities are at present especially acute and widespread in the Philippines, as reported by ITUC's *Annual Survey of Violations of Trade Union Rights 2007*.

Fifth, although the SE Asian economies have been internationalized rapidly and the labour markets have been expanded and integrated across regional borders, the commodification of the labour market has not been countered by the evolution of new social security measures. No universal welfare institutions have been established and no welfare states have emerged which could have mitigated the loss of social protection enjoyed in the old rural and peasant economies. At best, 'workfare' systems have been developed, often targeting public sector employees and especially central administrative and security forces (SSA, 2007). Retrenchment benefits are the only entitlement which is captured by regular employees, if the company is not declared bankrupt. Unemployment insurance is not provided by the public or privately established by trade unions. Only sporadic and inefficient safety and health regulations began appearing in the 1990s but are far from being implemented and providing effective protection of workers. In short, and paraphrasing Gosta Esping-Andersen (1990), labour has not been de-commodified during the industrial revolution in SE Asia, putting employees at risk in volatile labour markets and leaving them with no other social security than returning to the rural areas and villages of their parents and extended families.

Sixth, the trade union movement has failed as an agency to expand, and has even declined, despite the so-called growth of the EOI sector. In fact, the multiplicity of unions in the Philippines, Indonesia and Thailand and the internal squabbles within the Malaysian Trades Union Congress (MTUC) tend to weaken further the labour movement in SE Asia. On the other hand, the unions in Singapore and Vietnam, despite their large membership base, are unable to provide regional leadership because of their special ties with the ruling parties in their countries.

However, there are pockets of trade union strongholds and growth despite the generally bleak situation for unions and the widespread use of flexible labour by capital. Some capable unions have survived despite the generally hostile anti-union environment. The unions in the banking, telecommunications, postal and other service industries have maintained their representation despite the technology-driven restructuring and globalization-induced mergers sweeping these industries. Unions in old but surviving import-substituting industries (ISI), for example steel, have also maintained their presence and collective contracts. Unions in the extractive mining and timber industries have declined, but there are survivors. Unions in government corporations and services have also been preserved, even in Thailand, which de-registered these unions in the 1990s. In Indonesia, the collapse of *Pancasila* IR ushered in a multiplicity of unions and fresh union organizing in various sectors. Despite its occasional internal conflicts, the MTUC remains the sole recognized national centre in Malaysia, and the squabbles can also be interpreted as part of the democratic governance system of the MTUC. Despite declining membership, the more radical unions in the Philippines have succeeded in electing representatives in the Philippine Congress under the country's 'party list' system. In Singapore, the National Trades Union Congress is able to use the corporatist IR system in preserving jobs, members and union rights in key industry lines (Rasiah and Chua, 1998).

In Factory Asia, one of the most unionized segments is the auto and auto parts industry, which is discussed in the following section. In the garments industry, there are only a few unions, except, ironically, in Cambodia, where a 'Better Factory' programme of the ILO is used by the government to promote Cambodian garment exports enjoying preferential tariffs in the developed countries.

In sum, we can say that the overall decline of the Western-style IR system follows the declining power of the SE Asian industrial classes of wage earners understood as independently organized communities with regional cross-border coordination. Moreover, the dominant transnational capital does not want centralized and collective bargaining, and the SE Asian states do not want to challenge the TNCS, for fear of FDI flight, nor do they want to pursue income policy in collaboration with trade unions, as was seen in the 1970s in Europe and even undertaken by Singapore in 1979–82. The employers' sway in each SE Asian society has never been so strong, and the unions' voice has never been so weak. Traditionally, employers, aside from their preference to deal directly with their individual employees alone, exercise stronger influence on the state, thus making the tripartite system generally skewed in their favour, whether the prevailing IR system is corporatist or not. With the neo-liberal deregulation policy ascendant and SE Asian governments abandoning or surrendering part of the power to regulate labour markets, except in times of economic and political crisis, labour protection and support for unionism are likely to wane further across the region, both in the ASEAN 5 and in the rest. Arresting and reversing this decline is a Herculean task for the unions in a liberalizing region and probably the most difficult one in the Philippines, where 33 trade unionists were killed in 2006 (ITUC, 2007).

A key to understanding the future of trade unionism in SE Asia is to grasp what is happening in the mature automobile industry and in the new ICT industry, which are industries where the value chain can be decomposed and recomposed into internationally dispersed configurations of business activities and therefore affected very much by the globalization processes.

THE DYNAMICS OF INDUSTRIAL RELATIONS IN THE SE ASIAN AUTOMOBILE INDUSTRY

The Political Economy of the Regional Automobile Industry

The automobile industry is one of the most globalized and unionized industries in the world. However, in Southeast Asia, although the auto industry was born as part of an international industry, it has traditionally been inward-looking, built behind protective barriers catering to import-substituting FDI or national auto projects aiming for the indigenization of the so-called 'industry of industries' (Malaysia, Indonesia) (Wad, 2007a). But, overall, the Japanese auto TNCs have captured the vast part of the regional auto market and control most of the production capacity directly or indirectly, through joint ventures and technology transfer agreements. The unionization of the auto industry has never reached the same level as in the Global North, probably with Malaysia as a temporary exception owing to its highly centralized IR system during the 1970s and early 1980s (Wad, 2004a). Yet the auto manufacturing industry in Southeast Asia is on average better unionized than most other industries (Wad, 2003, 2004b), although it did not employ more than 200000–250000 workers in 2000 with Thai auto workers amounting to around 100000 employees, Indonesia around 50000 and Malaysia around 35000 (IMF, 2007).

The protectionist auto industry policies started changing when Thailand switched to a TNC-oriented policy in the early 1990s, finally giving up local content requirements in 2000 (Abdulsomad, 2003). This policy has established Thailand as the 'Detroit of Southeast Asia' and a global production site for mini-vans (pickups) based on the global value chains of Japanese auto manufacturers and also US auto makers.

With the inclusion of the Malaysian auto industry into the AFTA and the accommodation of Malaysia to the AFTA auto policy, ASEAN is slowly moving towards a regional auto market with options for a regional division of labour and economies of scale. Auto TNCs may choose to locate single-model assembly plants and their core suppliers around the key AFTA countries, hence providing Malaysia (and the Philippines) with leverage in passenger car production and Thailand (and Indonesia) with strongholds in mini-van production. Yet, while the Malaysian national projects are causing opposition among Western auto TNCs (for example, Ford), Japanese auto makers like Toyota and Honda have adapted to the conditions of competition in Malaysia, improving their competitiveness and market share and forcing the Malaysian champion, Proton, to seek out new alliances and so far unsuccessfully targeting French PSA Peugeot Citroën, Korean Hyundai Motors, Chinese Chery, American GM and German VW. Proton's joint venture partner until 2004, Japanese Mitsubishi Motor Corporation (MMC), is stalled in its own problems.

Turning into a real auto free trade area, the AFTA market is interesting in its own right, with sales of vehicles around 1.3–1.5 million in the early 2000s, back to its pre-crisis level, and reaching sales of nearly 2 million vehicles in 2005, with a vehicle production of 2.1 million (IMF, 2007). However, if the ASEAN countries aim to foster a regional car industry with global reach and competitiveness, they face increasing competition in auto assembling and components manufacturing with China, which had become the third largest auto production site in the world by 2005. And employers take every opportunity to point out, as did Shinji Takeuchi, president of Denso International Thailand Co., one of the world's largest auto component makers, that, 'if Southeast Asian countries did not improve their competitiveness, their automobile industries would be swallowed up by China' (*Daily Yomiuri*, 8 September 2004). This statement is to be understood in the context that ASEAN also wants to establish a free trade area agreement with China from 2011.

Trade Unions, Organizing and Collective Bargaining

Trade unions in the auto industries of the ASEAN 4 are working in an environment hostile to unionism, with restrictive labour legislation or state practices on the one hand and more or less anti-union-oriented employers on the other hand. Most unions are constituted at the enterprise level as enterprise or in-house unions undertaking enterprise-based collective bargaining agreements (CBAs). Only Malaysia saw a centralized industrial relations system evolving in the 1970s, and, although centralized collective bargaining and agreement disappeared during the 1980s, the industrial union with jurisdiction in Peninsular Malaysia prevailed. Facing fallouts among assembling companies due to among other things the state-sponsored national automobile projects (Proton, Perodua and so on), the union again expanded its membership organizing in the automobile supplier sector. Moreover, the industrial union took over the chairmanship of the IMF Malaysia Council. An attempt to form a federation of the industrial as well as enterprise auto unions in Malaysia aborted, while the business associations of the manufacturers and traders of motor vehicles merged into the Malaysian Automotive Association (MAA) in 2000, establishing a business voice to the Malaysian government in the conjuncture of AFTA.

In the other three countries, auto workers' unions have formed federations affiliating to labour centres. Yet in none of the SE Asian countries have auto firms formed an employers' association. Employers prefer to tackle problems with unions in bilateral negotiations and/or coordinate their activities informally through personal networks or in federations of manufacturers. Employers' national associations only provide labour market services to their company members and do not act as collective bargaining units.

If the trade unions of the SE Asian automobile industries (except Vietnam's) are compared, the Malaysian automobile workers, unions seem to be the strongest and best organized in terms of union density and level of union centralization, with the Thai unions taking the second position. In all the countries, collective bargaining is taking place at the enterprise level, as the employers do not want to engage in centralized negotiations at the sector level. Except in Malaysia, auto workers are unionized at the enterprise level and form only loose union federations; they are not all united in one federation or industrial union. This situation is probably 'path dependent', conditioned by the British legacy in Malaysia and the dominance of Japanese auto makers in alliance with their home base of Japanese enterprise unions.

The Impact of the East Asian Financial Crisis on the Automobile IR System

The East Asian financial crisis of 1997–98 affected severely both the automotive industry and the economies and political structures influencing this industry, although the impact on unionism varied from country to country.

Indonesia underwent tremendous changes with the fall of the Soeharto regime in 1998. The Federation of Metal Workers Union of Indonesia (FSPMI) was established in 1999 (as Metal Workers Union of Indonesia, SPMI) and turned into a federation in 2001. FSPMI was composed of five metal workers' unions comprising 188 plant-level unions or branches in 2003. One of these affiliates was the Automotive, Machine and Components Workers Union (AMCWU), with 16757 members in 57 plant-level unions or branches, and this union had 10064 employees in the auto industry. Hence, the AMCWU had expanded since 2002, when it had 45 plant unions or branches with 15855 members (FSPMI, IMF Conference, Bangkok 2002). Japanese automotive companies have been involved in several severe disputes. At Honda Prospect Motor Indonesia, management–labour negotiations for wage improvements became deadlocked in 2002 and turned into a strike, against which the Honda management retaliated with a lockout of 208 workers.[2] A few months later, 160 workers were made redundant. The industrial conflict turned violent when police and former Honda employees met outside the factory in the early days of the strike. The Honda management seemed set on getting rid of the union by way of supporting a company union with 40 members and employing contract workers through an employment agency. The Honda headquarters and the Honda workers union in Japan insisted that the dispute was a local dispute and must be settled locally, while the IMF headquarters contended that the investment decisions, product choice and so on were decided by the head office of the transnational corporation and, hence, the industrial dispute was also international and should be solved by the head office.

In 2006, when the union of a Japanese–Indonesian joint venture, metal sheet manufacturer joined FSPMI, management dismissed all 45 union members and leaders and retaliated against the workers (ITUC, 2007). Both FSPMI and the Federation of Metal, Machine and Electronic Workers (Lomenik-KSBSI) are affiliated to IMF (Metal).

Malaysia faced political turmoil at the highest level of government during the financial crisis, but the old guard won the power battle. Rudiments of social corporatist political involvement of unions during the crisis of 1997–98 emerged but vanished with recovery, followed by a new split in the top ranks of the labour centre and the MTUC, and a shift of top leadership from a centre-right alliance to a centre-left alliance in 2005. Union density in the motor vehicle industry is estimated to be high. It stood at 34 per cent in 1997, rose to 40 per cent in 1999, fell to 39 per cent in 2000, when union membership was 15 726 out of 40 679 employees, and rose again to 41 per cent in 2004 with 20 355 members out of 49 264 employees (calculation based on DOS selected reports excluding firms below 30 employees, various MHR/DTUA annual reports). The industrial union (NUTEAIW), organizing non-national auto assemblers and auto suppliers, represented around 7700 employees in more than 40 companies in 2002. Today it is a 'pragmatic' union, having been more 'radical' in the past (the 1970s and 1980s) and even left the MTUC during the 1980s to work closely with grassroots movements. The union has been struggling to unionize upcoming assembly plants. For example, it tried to unionize Honda's new factory, but it lost the battle and could see an enterprise union emerging with the support of management.

However, the union has also recorded several successful actions. For example, it was able to organize the MTB (the 'national' truck and bus project), but the employer refused to recognize the union until the Industrial Court certified that the union should be recognized by the employer, and a collective agreement was concluded. In Associated Motor Industries (Malaysia) (AMI), a Ford-controlled auto manufacturer, a wild-cat industrial action took place in 2002 after four workers were suspended for not wearing safety glasses, and a domestic inquiry was called to decide whether they should be dismissed. The following day, 40–45 workers took medical leave and management selected 11 for suspension. When the workers left the factory gate the next day, the NUTEAIW, the industrial union, organized a 'briefing gathering', which looked like a picket and was to be understood as a message to the management. The picketing continued on the following days (observation and interview with the general secretary of NUTEAIW, May 2002). In the end the dispute was mediated by the Ministry of Human Resources, and the case was settled without management undertaking any dismissals.

Enterprise unions numbered around 13 600 members in national and non-national sectors of the Malaysian auto industry, or 64 per cent of total union members, down from 70 per cent in 2000 (own calculations based on DTUA 2001 and 2003). Proton Union and Perodua Manufacturing Union were big unions with around 5500 and 2400 members respectively in 2002. Perodua Union was split when the engine plant was incorporated as a separate company for tax reasons and the management insisted that a new Perodua Engine Union should be established and won the case after it was sent to the civil court. With the start-up of the new Proton factory in 'Proton City', the Proton Union also faced a potential split into two unions based on corporate boundaries. The industrial union and the two biggest in-house unions in the national sector negotiated the formation of a federation of auto workers' unions aiming to give auto unions and their members a united and public voice in relation to the upcoming auto-AFTA and the automobile policy pursued by the Malaysian government, but the negotiations stalled.

The Philippines was relatively less severely hit by the financial crisis of 1997, yet nearly 7000 employees lost their jobs in the auto industry in 1997–99. Only 10 per cent of the 290 companies are unionized, and 10 per cent of the 50 000 employees of the auto industry are union members (AIWA, 2002). The Auto Industry Workers Alliance (AIWA), founded in 2000 by non-affiliated union leaders, claimed to be the only independent national organization for auto workers with members in auto assembler and auto supplier firms (AIWA, 2002). AIWA was registered with the Department of Labour and Employment (DOLE) in 2002 and reported that the alliance had 2170 members, including members in core assembling companies: Mitsubishi Motors Workers Union Philippines (837), Mitsubishi Motors Philippines Corp. Salaried Union (150), Mitsubishi Motors Philippines Corp. Supervisor Association (170), Isuzu Philippines Corp. Workers Union (260), Toyota Motor Philippines Supervisors Union (300), Toyota Motor Philippines Corporation Labour Organization (TMPCLO[3]) (200), Nissan Independent Workers Union (123) and Nissan Motors Philippines Supervisor Union (130). AIWA includes several non-workers' unions with large memberships, and the MMC/Philippines members form the largest group of AIWA, holding the presidency of the federation. The Lakas ng Nanggagawang Nagkakaisa sa Honda Ind. (400 members) belonged to another federation (OLALIA) in 2002. Finally, the legitimate union of Toyota rank-and-file workers, the Toyota Motor Philippine Corporation Workers Association (TMPCWA), is not part of AIWA, but belongs to the CAR-AID auto workers alliance. The president of the TMPCWA contended that AIWA is a loose network of yellow unions among other Japanese-controlled companies in the Philippines (CEC/AMRC Conference 2003), while the president of AIWA holds that CAR-AID is a union without collective bargaining rights predominantly composed of terminated workers (interview, Quezon City, 19 August 2009). In fact, the TMPCWA has been engaged in a long struggle with Toyota for union recognition since 2000. Toyota managed to dismiss the social base of the TMPCWA in 2001, and, although the TMPCWA was recognized as the legal union of the TMPC workers by the Philippines authorities until 2006, the authorities gave in and certified the TMPCLO, which was established in late 2001, not as a 'yellow' union by TMPC management as held by the TMPCWA, but to prevent a management-supported union (TWLA) from taking control of the workforce (interview, Quezon City, 19 August 2009). In 2006 Toyota recognized the TMPCLO and concluded a collective agreement with the union by the end of the year, fending off a concerted local campaign of the TMPCWA in collaboration with the Metal Workers Alliance of the Philippines (MWAP) and the KMU (May First Labour Centre) as well as regional campaigns in Japan and Asia ('Protest Toyota Campaign') and a worldwide campaign by IMF (Metal) ('Reinstate Them Now!') (IMF Newsletter, 19 May 2006; Protest Toyota Campaign, Newsletter 10, 1 September 2007). However, the IMF Japan Council did not support the campaigns, and when the Toyota Union visited the TMPC in 2005 they took time to meet the TMPCLO and not the TMPCWA. The AIWA president argues that 'the ILO did not investigate the case properly. The same with IMF. We suspended our relationship with IMF because they did not consult us before they decided to support the TMPCWA claim. When you do not consult your members in such a case it is wrong' (interview, Quezon City, 19 August 2009). Finally, the TMPCWA and their Japanese allies complained to the OECD National Contact Point (NCP) in Japan in 2004, but this body, which is mandated to supervise TNCs' labour practices vis-à-vis the OECD codes of conduct for TNCs' did not act upon the complaint and has only recently initiated the assessment procedure (Protest Toyota, 26 October 2009). In an industrial dispute between a Malaysian industrial union and a Danish TNC, Danish trade union activists successfully used this novel institution to pressure the TNC headquarters in charge of the Malaysian-controlled joint venture factory (Wad, 2007b).

Thailand saw a shift in auto policy in early 1990, opening up to TNCs and finally abandoning local content requirements in 2000. These moves have boosted TNC investment before the crisis, and foreign direct investments are again picking up. Moreover, a democratic breakthrough came in 1997 in connection with the financial crisis, yet again followed by a setback with the government headed by Thaksin Shinawatra and a new military coup in 2006. The Federation of Thailand Automobile Workers' Union (TAW) was established in 1997 by five enterprise unions, including both assembling companies (Siam Nissan, Hino) and auto suppliers (NHK Spring, Siam Part, Denso Thailand) (TAW pamphlet, 2002). It dates back to 1992, when four auto workers' unions (Hino, Denso, NHK, Toyota) formed an association. Since 1997, Nissan workers' unions had stopped collaborating with the TAW unions, preferring to work in solitude based on their own federation of Nissan-related unions. In 2002, TAW had 24 enterprise unions, with a total of 15 672 members, among which are the affiliated companies of Toyota, Mitsubishi Motor, Isuzu, Hino, Kawasaki and Honda, and a year later the TAW federation claimed to have more than 20 000 members. The stated objectives of the TAW are: '1. To protect the benefit of trade unions and the workers' rights, 2. To promote good cooperation between trade unions and between workers and employers' (TAW pamphlet, 2002). In 2006, the management of a Japanese-owned supplier to several automobile assemblers tried to suppress the establishment of a union supported by TAW, but after TAW targeted a campaign at the company's customers the company gave up, reinstated the dismissed union leaders and concluded a collective agreement (ITUC, 2007).

At Ford/Mazda Auto Alliance Thailand (AAT), established before the East Asian financial crisis erupted in 1997, a union was formed around 2000 or 2001, and soon after a management–labour dispute arose. It escalated into a wider conflict when the management dismissed the union leadership, but Thai unionists informed unionists at Ford, Mazda and the IMF (Metal) and with concerted pressure the dispute was settled through negotiations. The AAT industrial relations improved quite a lot after this confrontation. Yet the AAT union was not affiliated with TAW in 2002. In 2006, the management of a Thai-owned supplier to AAT retaliated against the workers after they became members of the AAT union and locked out 230 union members (ITUC, 2007).

To sum up, auto workers' unions are not strong in the ASEAN 4 considering the political and legal obstacles unionism faces in general and the anti-union stand of TNCs and local employers. Yet they are probably stronger compared to unions in other industries in terms of union density and organization in the industry. Despite the problems posed by the financial crisis and industrial restructuring, which entailed downsizing, outsourcing, employment of temporary workers, rationalizations and so on, the unions have often been able to undertake collective bargaining at the bilateral, enterprise level and set a minimum standard of 'no retreat' in collective agreements (in local currencies and conditions) during crises and improved conditions during periods of growth. They have often achieved a higher-than-average income level in a protected industry. But auto TNCs try again and again in the region to lower the standards; they fight unions to the point of destruction. With national, regional and international union support, some conflicts can be won or at least not lost, and the concerns about union weaknesses and attempts to form more encompassing and stronger union networks, federations or industrial unions in the specific countries will certainly improve the 'union case'. However, it will take much more local inter-union collaboration, together with regional and global collaboration and support, to strengthen the auto workers' unions in the ASEAN 4. Yet, with the Japanese dominance of the ASEAN automobile industry, alliances with Japanese auto workers' unions are paramount, but mainstream Japanese auto unions are not eager to get involved in Southeast Asian problems, which they take to be local problems to be solved locally in the same way as their management do. Even global campaigning by the IMF (Metal) and regional NGOs have not forced Toyota to give up its resistance against TMPCWA and finally join hands with another enterprise union affiliated to the AIWA alliance. Probably, it will take a worldwide customer boycott and a coordinated campaign of several global union federations (GUFs), including the TWF (the transport workers' GUF), to get Toyota to the bargaining table.

CASE STUDY: SE ASIA IN THE GLOBAL PRODUCTION AND SERVICE CHAINS OF IT AND ICT TNCS

Information technology (IT), which has become part of a bigger telecom-based information communication technology (ICT), has revolutionized the world of work in the last three decades. Through IT/ICT, global and regional capital is able to simplify or atomize work, outsource work processes within and across national boundaries, and organize lean and mean business operations involving a flexible and insecure workforce everywhere. The resulting IT/ICT-driven globalization and outsourcing have also affected SE Asia's labour market, at least in four major ways.

1) Global Capital, IT/ICT Technology and Factory Asia

By expanding the capacity of the computer beyond simple computation, the advances in ICT have made it possible for global capital to introduce wide-ranging changes in the production, business and distribution processes. As defined, IT is '(i) the aggregation of information-related fields, such as computer hardware and software, telecommunication networks and equipment, and information-technology-based industries; and (ii) the application of these technologies in all economic sectors, publishing, broadcasting, libraries, data banks, and other information services industries' (Asian Development Bank, 2003). The fusion of IT with wireless and internet communications has made ICT a powerful instrument in reconfiguring industry and the economy. One major outcome of the ICT revolution in business and industry is the consolidation of the global supply-chain systems (GSM) or GCCs, which entail the global subcontracting by the TNCs of different aspects of work at the international, regional and national levels. This is what has given rise to Factory Asia, as discussed earlier.

In the 1970s and 1980s, advances in transport and the 'atomization' of production made it possible for the TNCs to break down production into high-tech and low-tech components and relocate the production of low-tech parts in low-cost, union-free sites in the developing world, usually free trade zones. The ICT revolution of the 1990s has strengthened this pattern. It has even intensified the effort of global capital to capture the maximum profits by exacting maximum returns out of every link in the chain of the global production units. This is exemplified by the behaviour of global garments retailers like Triumph, Liz Claiborne or Benetton, all of which are focusing on the design, branding and advertising of garments at their headquarters, while they try to squeeze productivity from the workers of their global subcontractors.

The ICT revolution itself has made it possible for some of these global producers to concentrate on service activities such as design, advertising and retailing, while leaving production or manufacturing to their global subcontractors under so-called supply-chain management (SCM). As two Nomura researchers put it (Masuyama and Vandenbrink, 2003), 'The overall outcome is that developing economies with abundant low-cost labour increase their share of manufacturing industries and advanced economies specialize in innovation activities and knowledge-intensive service industries.'

Much of Asia, SE Asia in particular, is involved in the numerous supply chains organized by either global or regional capital and operating across the region and beyond. A prime example of SCM is the garments industry, where global retailers and designers based in North America and Europe rely on their primary contractors based in the Asian NICs (South Korea, Taiwan, Singapore and Hong Kong), which, in turn, farm out various aspects of production to China and other developing Asian countries such as the Indochinese states (Vietnam, Kampuchea and Laos), the Philippines, Indonesia, Thailand and the South Asian countries of India, Pakistan, Bangladesh, Sri Lanka and Nepal. Exporters or contractors in the individual countries may also have their own subcontractors in the cities or the rural villages doing various aspects of work such as embroidery or attaching or sewing certain garment parts. In this seemingly complicated global–regional–national outsourcing chain or network, the global retailers and their Asian contractors are able to manage a seamless global–regional production process owing to the great facilitating role of the ICT revolution, complemented by modern communication and transportation and relatively open borders of nations.

2) Production of IT/ICT Electronic Products and Parts in Asia

The second major development is that SE Asia has become a major assembly site for the production of IT/ICT electronic products and parts such as PCs, notebooks, chips, transistors, diodes, routers and so on, which collectively have become the world's biggest manufacturing industry. Asia is the world's biggest producer of these electronic products, including chips or semiconductor devices and varied electronic and telecommunication parts. And, as with the SCM in most industries, electronics manufacturing has also developed based on some kind of global division of labour.

Japan and the Asian NICs – South Korea, Taiwan, Singapore and Hong Kong – are the biggest electronics parts producers. However, most of the chips or semiconductors and electronic or telecommunication parts are being produced under global outsourcing arrangements. The big chip and semiconductor producers from the United States, Europe, Japan, South Korea, Taiwan and Singapore have been farming out the labour-intensive process of manufacturing tiny electronic components (for example, resistors, capacitors, switches, connectors, wires and cables) and assembling the 'mini' semiconductors, integrated circuits and microprocessors (collectively dubbed as the 'semicon devices') to Indonesia, Malaysia, Thailand, the Philippines and China. In this global division of labour in the production of chips and parts, the developed countries concentrate on the more capital and technology-intensive processes such as the designing and fabrication of electronic wafers, as well as the testing of the wafers, the electronic parts and the assembled electronic devices. This global division of labour started in the 1970s and has deepened since then, with China now eclipsing other countries as the leading outsourcing destination for labour-intensive processes. Vietnam has also lately become another favourite destination site for electronics assembly work.

Within the ASEAN, electronics constitute the biggest export items traded within and outside the region. The electronics exports of the ASEAN 5 reached US$200 billion in 2000, with Singapore as the leading exporting country (Austria, 2005).

3) Contract Programming in Asia

The third major development is that the 'soft' side of the ICT industry – the programs running the computers and the telecommunication devices – has become one of the world's leading service industries, competing head to head with the banking and insurance industry. But, while the United States has huge success in doing large-scale software development, as exemplified by Bill Gates's Microsoft, most of its Fortune 500 companies have been contracting out their IT programming requirements outside America, mainly to India and other Asian countries.

As in the production of electronic products and parts, there is some kind of global division of labour taking place in the global IT service or software-programming industry, although the division of work is not as clear cut as in contract manufacturing, given the role of knowledge and skills in the decisions of global software companies to outsource programming and to scout for talent to do programming. The world's global companies have been outsourcing their software service requirements – programs, system development, program management, maintenance, training and so on – to India, the Philippines and other Asian countries. While there were records of outsourcing of software development as early as the 1970s, off-shored and customized software development became a big global commercial proposition only in the 1990s, again owing to the facilitating role of ICT.

Another aspect of outsourcing is 'body shopping', or the movement of IT professionals from one country, usually a developing one, to other countries in demand of such professionals. The Philippines has a fairly good number of IT professionals doing 'body shopping' in Singapore and Malaysia, both of which have assiduously marketed themselves as Asia's IT hubs.

4) Rise of ICT-Enabled 'Industries'

The fourth major development is the rise of the ICT-enabled services such as data encoding, customer service and business process outsourcing (BPO), and their outsourcing to developing countries in Asia, notably India and the Philippines.

The term 'ICT-enabled service' or ITES is most appropriate. The Asian Development Bank (2003) defines ICT 'as the set of activities that facilitate by electronic means the processing, transmission, and display of information'. ICT, or the fusion of IT and communication, means the use of information technology (represented by the PC), internet (represented by the web) and other modern communication media (wireless, satellite-based media and voice over the internet phone or VOIP). Without the growth, 'convergence' and relative decline in the cost of using these new technologies, it is unthinkable that a service job such as customer service could be 'off-shored' or outsourced outside a country's borders. In a way, even software development itself, especially its customized application for global customers, is part of the ICT-enabled services: hence the logic of putting a slash in the 'IT/ITES services'.

Impact on IR and Labour Markets

In 2003 and 2004, the outsourcing or off-shoring of customer service and BPO activities caused a backlash in the United States, Australia and a number of European countries, whose populist politicians complained about white-collar jobs fleeing their countries. How many American IT jobs are being lost? Job losses in the IT sector are guesstimates. *Newsweek* (1 March 2004) put the figure at anywhere between 300 000 and 600 000. In 2002, Forrester Research projected a job exodus of as many as 3.3 million up to 2015. However, a University of California study revised the job loss estimates, projecting the potential job losses to reach as high as 14 million for the same period (*Newsweek*).

However, jobs lost in the Northern (developed) countries as a result of global outsourcing or off-shoring do not necessarily translate into net job gains in Southern (developing) countries. This is so because participation in the global division of labour entails the adoption by the latter of market liberalization policies which can wipe out some of their own domestic industries and agriculture, for example, American rice, corn and wheat flooding SE Asia at the expense of grain producers in countries such as Indonesia and the Philippines. Also, the jobs created in the IT/ICT sector constitute a small percentage of the labour force. Because of the mobile character of TNC investments, jobs may also disappear overnight.

As to compensation, the wage differential is indeed a strong motivation for TNCs to outsource work. In the United States, a typical IT worker gets roughly $50 000 annually in wages and benefits. In India and the Philippines, a newly hired call centre employee gets starting pay of $200 to $300 a month ($2400–3600 on an annual basis), which is generally twice the minimum wage.

And yet the turnover rate is almost 50 per cent a year. Why? Because of the Fordist working conditions and the utter lack of voice of the workers on the work process. The majority of the workforce, who are young, female and educated employees, cannot stand for long the intensity of dedicated work in their ICT cubicles, processing as many as 300–400 calls a night, to service American and European clients in their waking hours.

The overall situation is aggravated by the fact that unionism in 'IT parks' is opposed vigorously by most employers. As one article put it, the voice workers are voiceless in their places of work (Ofreneo, Ng and Pasumbal, 2007).

In the electronics assembly plants, mostly located in EEZs, the situation is similar. McKay (2006), in a case study of several electronics companies, raised the question: are these firms 'silicon islands' or 'satanic mills'? He wrote that work in most of these IT assemblers has the following features: production standardization, strict quality control, management preroga-tive, various control measures (zone security, HR monthly consultation, local officials engaged in recruitment, surveillance within, and recruitment of single but meek women), and positive incentives or positive HRM for high performers.

The global outsourcing in IT-based industries has also made labour flexible in the service industries – distribution, banking, insurance and so on. Regular jobs are being phased out and transferred to in-sourcing companies using temporary workers, which includes those assigned to customer service, training, payroll, finance and accounting, information systems, legal services and so on. Outsourcing existing services means downsizing existing service departments and service jobs, preceded by some re-engineering exercise conducted by outside consulting firms.

To sum up, it is abundantly clear that the IT/ICT-driven outsourcing phenomenon sweeping the Asian labour market is making work flexible and jobs insecure for most workers, except for a few elite workers such as IT professionals. Neo-liberal economists argue that such labour flexibility is what is sustaining growth in the Asia-Pacific region, as in the US labour market. However, the quality of such growth, built on contract labour, is questionable and hides the collective worker anger seething beneath the surface of the seemingly expanding Asian labour market. There are indications that IT/ICT-driven outsourcing also generates jobless growth in SE Asia.

CONCLUDING OUTLOOK

Clearly, the world of work in SE Asia has changed radically under globali-zation. One major challenge to trade union leaders and members, labour NGO activists, scholars, researchers and students of IR is how to re-vision the meaning and content of IR in a globalizing labour market.

In theory and research on SE Asia, the IR issue has not been as highly prioritized a research issue as it was in the 1980s when the new interna-tional division of labour (NIDL) evolved bringing the first and second generation of newly industrializing countries (NICs) to the forefront of international concern regarding de-industrialization in the North, export processing zones with labour-intensive, low-paid jobs, and harsh working conditions, especially for young female workers in East and Southeast Asia. The NIDL spurred the New International Labour Studies (NILS), which widened the scope of labour studies to non-formal sectors and to developing countries, including Southeast Asia. Today, China is attracting very much attention, India is on the rise, and Southeast Asia seems to be suspended in mid-air, while a ghost of de-industrialization and global out-sourcing is passing not only the North once again but also SE Asia itself. In the wake of the SE Asian financial crisis of 1997–98, research on new forms of domestic and cross-border labour activism has voiced old claims for a more comprehensive understanding of organized labour beyond trade unionism (Ford, 2004). On a regional level, the Hong Kong-based AMRC has a long record of disseminating labour news, analysis and networking, with a recent initiative to disclose the activities and impacts of Asian TNCs (Chang, 2006). In a global perspective, efforts have been undertaken to form an alliance of unionists and researchers for the study of cross-border campaigns against violations of labour rights by TNCs, generating among other things a model for strategic corporate research from a labour angle (Bronfenbrenner, 2007).

But more importantly, however, is the challenge of practice. As long as SE Asian trade unions face intra-country fragmentation and a weak social basis in terms of union density and union influence, few resources are available or used for intra-regional interaction and coordination. Some unions are located in countries that are too affluent to benefit from inter-national NGO aid flows. Global union federations like the IMF (Metal), which has initiated global campaigns in support of local industrial dis-putes, have been weakened by the negative influence of the IMF Japanese Council and the distrust between some SE Asian trade unions and the IMF Southeast Asia and Pacific Office. In the pockets of union power, bilateral cross-border collaboration may seem to be a feasible option for trade union empowerment, as it was tried out recently by, for example, the Thai federation of automotive unions (TAW) and the Malaysian automo-tive industrial union (TEAIWU). Finally, trade unions and activists in the Global South established the 'Southern Initiative on Globalization and Trade Union Rights' (SIGTUR) in 1991 and what has been called the New Labour Internationalism sustained by national trade union organizations in Brazil (CUT), South Africa (COSATU) and South Korea (KCTU) and with affiliated organizations in Thailand, Indonesia, the Philippines and Malaysia in the beginning (Lambert and Webster, 2001; www.SIGTUR. com, accessed 17 October 2007[4]). Hence, there are several responses to the key question, and that is how to create a situation where the old values of justice, equity and fairness – the main reasons for the development of the old IR system, the formation of the ILO and the post-war expansion of the welfare and state socialist states – can be re-affirmed in a globalizing labour market of which the SE Asian labour markets are an integrated part.

NOTES

1. This chapter discusses the labour market and IR situation in SE Asia mainly in relation to the ASEAN 5 – Indonesia, Malaysia, the Philippines, Singapore and Thailand.
2. IMF Bangkok Conference 2002; Metal World No. 1, 2003.
3. The AIWA IMF report 2002 used the name Toyota Motor Philippines Corporation Labour Union (TMPCLU), which is the name of the first established workers' union of 1992, which defaulted in the 1990s (Haruhi, 2006).
4. For a critical comment on SIGTUR and the New Labour Internationalism, see Waterman (2009).

REFERENCES

Abdulsomad, K. (2003), *Building Technological Capabilities of Local Auto Parts Firms under Constrasting Industrial Policies: A Comparative Study of Malaysia and Thailand 1960–2000*, Ph.D., Lund Studies in Economic History 27, Lund: Lund University.
AIWA (2002), IMF report, Bangkok.
ASEAN Statistics, http://www.aseansec.org, accessed 30 June 2007.
Asian Development Bank (1997), *Emerging Asia: Changes and Challenges*, Manila: ADB.
Asian Development Bank (2003), *Toward E-Development in Asia and the Pacific*, Metro Manila: ADB.
Athukorala, P.-c. (2006), 'International labour migration in East Asia: trends, patterns and policy issues', *Asia-Pacific Economic Literature*, **20**(1): 18–39.
Austria, M. (2004), *The Pattern of Intra-ASEAN Trade in the Priority Goods Sectors*, REPSF Project 03/006e, Final Main Report, Jakarta: ASEAN-Australia Development Cooperation Program.
Austria, M. (2005), 'Recent development in the electronics production networks in Southeast Asia', paper submitted to the Asia Pacific Foundation of Canada (unpublished).
Bacungan, F. and R. Ofreneo (2002), 'The development of labour law and labour market policy in the Philippines', in S. Cooney, T. Lindsey, R. Mitchell and Y. Zhu (eds), *Law and Labour Market Regulation in East Asia,* New York: Routledge, pp. 91–121.
Baldwin, R. (2007), *Managing the Noodle Bowl: The Fragility of East Asian Regionalism*, Asian Development Bank working paper series on regional economic integration no. 7, Manila: ADB.
Bronfenbrenner, K. (ed.) (2007), *Global Unions: Challenging Transnational Capital*

through Cross-Border Campaigns, Ithaca, NY: ILR Press/Cornell University Press.

Brown, A. (2001), 'After the Kader fire in Thailand', in J. Hutchinson and A. Brown (eds), *Organising Labour in Globalising Asia*, London: Routledge, pp. 127–46.

Businessweek, 1 March 2004.

Chang, D.-o. (ed.) (2006). *Labour in Globalising Asian Corporations: A Portrait of Struggle*, Hong Kong: AMRC.

Cooney, S., T. Lindsey, R. Mitchell and Y. Zhu (2002), *Law and Labour Market Regulation in East Asia*, New York: Routledge.

De Silva, S.R. (1995), *Harmonizing Industrial Relations and Human Resource Management*, Geneva: ILO.

Department of Statistics (DOS) (selected years), *Annual Survey of Manufacturing Industries, Malaysia*, Kuala Lumpur: DOS.

Deyo, F. (1989), *Beneath the Miracle: Labor Subordination in the New Asian Industrialism*, Berkeley: University of California.

DTUA/MHR (various years), *Annual Report*, Kuala Lumpur: MHR.

Dunlop, John (1993 [1957]), *Industrial Relations System*, Cambridge, MA: Harvard University Press.

Esping-Andersen, G. (1990), *The Three Worlds of Welfare Capitalism*, Princeton, NJ: Princeton University Press.

Folker, F., J. Heinrichs and O. Kreye (1980), *The New International Division of Labor*, Cambridge: Cambridge University Press.

Ford, M. (2004), 'New forms of labour activism: a Southeast Asian perspective', Proceedings of Refereed Stream of the 2004 AIRAANZ Annual Conference, Noosa, 6-8 February.

Gereffi, G. (2003), 'The international competitiveness of Asian economies in the global apparel commodity chain', *International Journal of Business and Society*, **4**(2), pp. 71–110.

Haruhi, T. (2006), 'Toyota in the Philippines: drive your dream or drive to the bottom?', in D.-o. Chang (ed.), *Labour in Globalising Asian Corporations: A Portrait of Struggle*, Hong Kong: AMRC, pp. 247–71.

ILO (2007), *Labour and Social Trends in ASEAN 2007*, Bangkok: ILO Regional Office for Asia and the Pacific.

IMF (Metal), various newsletters.

IMF (2007), *Auto Report 2006/07*, Geneva: IMF.

ITUC (2007), *Annual Survey of Violations of Trade Union Rights 2007*, Brussels: ITUC.

Jose, A.V. (2002), *Organized Labour in the 21st Century*, Geneva: IILS.

Kaufman, B. (2004), *The Global Evolution of Industrial Relations: Events, Ideas and the IIRA*, Geneva: ILO.

Kuruvilla, S. (1995), 'Economic development strategies, industrial relations policies and workplace IR/HR practices in Southeast Asia', in K. Wever and L. Turner (eds), *The Comparative Political Economy of Industrial Relations*, Madison, WI: Industrial Relations Research Association.

Kuruvilla, S., S. Das, H. Kwon and S. Kwon (2002), 'Trade union growth and decline in Asia', *British Journal of Industrial Relations*, **40**(3), pp. 431–61.

Lambert, R. and E. Webster (2001), 'Southern unionism and the new labour internationalism', *Antipode*, **33**(3): 337–62.

Lindsey, Tim and Teten Masduki (2002), 'Labour law in Indonesia after Soeharto:

Reformasi or replay?', in S. Cooney, T. Lindsey, R. Mitchell and Y. Zhu (eds), *Law and Labour Market Regulation in East Asia*, New York: Routledge, pp. 27–54.

Masuyama, Seeichi and Donna Vandenbrink (eds) (2003), *Towards a Knowledge-Based Economy: East Asia's Changing Industrial Geography*, Tokyo: Nomura Research Institute.

McKay, S. (2006), *Satanic Mills or Silicon Islands? The Politics of High-Tech Production in the Philippines*, New York: Cornell University Press.

Munck, Ronaldo (2002), *Globalization and Labour: The New 'Great Transformation'*, London: Zed Books.

Ofreneo, R. (2002), 'Changing labour markets in a globalising Asia: challenges for Asian trade unions', *Asian Labour Update*, **45**.

Ofreneo, R., C. Ng and L. Pasumbal, (2007), *The Indian Journal of IR: A Review of Economic and Social Development*, Volume 42, No. 4, New Delhi: Shri Ram Centre, pp. 534–57.

Rasiah, R. and T.C. Chua (1998), 'Strength of trade unions in Southeast Asia', in R. Rasiah and N. Hofmann (eds), *Workers on the Brink: Unions, Exclusion and Crisis in Southeast Asia*, Singapore: Friedrich-Ebert-Stiftung, pp. 15–46.

Rasiah, R. and N. Hofmann (eds) (1998), *Workers on the Brink: Unions, Exclusion and Crisis in Southeast Asia*, Singapore: Friedrich-Ebert-Stiftung.

Sharma, B. (1985), *Aspects of Industrial Relations in ASEAN*, Singapore: Institute of Southeast Asian Studies.

SSA (Social Security Administration) (2007), *Social Security Programs throughout the World: Asia and the Pacific, 2006*, Washington, DC: SSA.

Wad, P. (2003), 'Auto Workers' Unions in ASEAN-4', *Asian Labour Update*, **49**.

Wad, P. (2004a), 'Transforming industrial relations: the case of the Malaysian auto industry', in R. Elmhirts and R. Saptari (eds), *Labour in Southeast Asia: Local Processes in a Globalised World*, London: RoutledgeCurzon, pp. 235–64.

Wad, P. (2004b), 'Autoworkers in ASEAN-4', in: D.-o. Chang and E. Shepherd (eds), *Automobile Workers and Industry in Globalising Asia*, Hong Kong: AMRC and CEC, pp. 3–27.

Wad, P. (2007a), 'Globalization and trade unions: transformation of automobile trade unions in Korea and Malaysia', in J.-S. Shin (ed.), *Global Challenges and Local Responses: The East Asian Experience*, London: Routledge, pp. 161–83.

Wad, P. (2007b), 'Due diligence' at APM-Maersk: from Malaysian industrial dispute to Danish cross-border campaign', in K. Bronfenbrenner (ed.), *Global Unions: Challenging Transnational Capital through Cross-Border Campaigns*, Ithaca, NY: ILR Press/Cornell University Press, pp. 40–56.

Waterman, P. (2009), 'Can the new global labour studies stimulate a new global labour movement?', Two discussion drafts, http://blog.choike.org/eng/tag/peter-waterman.

6. Urban and industrial environmental reform in Southeast Asia

David A. Sonnenfeld and Arthur P.J. Mol

INTRODUCTION

A majority of countries in Southeast Asia have been developing rapidly for several decades. With some notable exceptions,[1] Southeast Asia remains one of the high economic growth regions in the world. While economic development has been strong, growth patterns have differed significantly in the five countries studied in this chapter: Indonesia, Malaysia, Singapore, Thailand and Vietnam. Notwithstanding periodic ups and downs, including during the Asian financial crisis of 1997, all countries enjoyed sustained economic growth over several decades (see Figure 6.1). A wide range of growth histories and present performance are represented within these five countries: from Singapore, one of the most developed economies in the world, with a high level of industrialization and a large service sector, to Vietnam, which has only recently – but rapidly – begun to make the transition of its agriculturally based economy towards the industrial and service sectors (see Figure 6.2). Taken together, the five countries represent the diversity of growth and development in Southeast Asia.

Economic development has been paralleled by integration of individual countries into the Southeast Asian region, manifested by the Association of Southeast Asian Nations (ASEAN) and its ASEAN Free Trade Agreement (AFTA), and the world economy. Increasing foreign direct investment (FDI) inflows (and recently also outflows), growth in international trade, and increased regional and international political cooperation give evidence of that. In these respects, industrializing parts of Southeast Asia have been drawn increasingly into processes of globalization.[2]

Historically around the world, increased economic performance, industrialization (also of agriculture) and modernization have often been paralleled with deterioration of environmental quality and depletion of natural resources. Industrialization, modernization and economic growth severely deteriorated environmental quality in Europe and the United States, for instance, from the nineteenth century through at to least the 1970s.

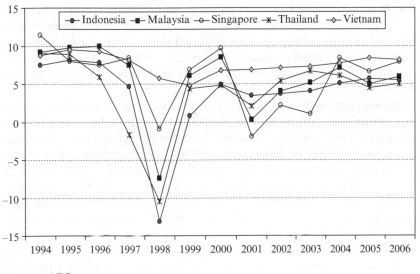

Source:　ADB.

Figure 6.1 Annual economic growth percentages, 1994–2006

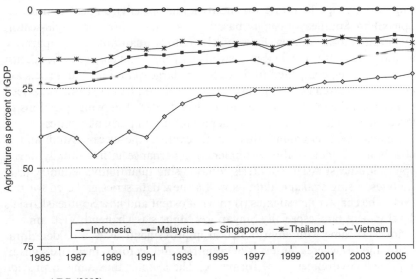

Source:　ADB (2002).

Figure 6.2　Level of industrialization

But these historical experiences by no means indicate a causal relationship with the status of an iron law. At least since the Brundtland report (WCED, 1987), policymakers have recognized that increased economic performance need not necessarily lead to environmental degradation and, indeed, that there are environmental imperatives for severing this negative co-relationship.

Within economics, and especially within the environmental or ecological subdiscipline, strong debates and broad research efforts have further elaborated this theme, for instance under the banner of the environmental Kuznets curve[3] (cf. Panayotou, 1993; Selden and Song, 1994; Antle and Heidebrink, 1995). Existing literature and debates on environment and development relations in Southeast Asia are large, but – especially compared to the same literature on OECD countries – limited in at least a couple of respects. First, up till now, Southeast Asian studies have been focused especially on development, management and, more recently, depletion of the region's rich natural resources, including forest, mineral and marine resources, and community involvement in natural resource management (cf. the excellent volumes edited by Brookfield and Byron, 1993; Parnwell and Bryant, 1996; and Hirsch and Warren, 1998). The urban and industrial sectors of Southeast Asia's modernization have been poorly analysed from an environmental perspective. Second, most English-language literature on the dynamics of environment and development in Southeast Asia is based on single-country or single-sector, quantitative case studies. Few multi-country, quantitative, comparative investigations of urban and industrial environmental change in Southeast Asia have been completed to date. Where large quantitative data sets are involved, research questions have been developed from existing data sets, rather than the other way around: collecting data following questions of (successes and failure in) environmental reform in particular states.

Against this background, this chapter explores the successes and failures of urban and industrial environmental governance in five rapidly developing Southeast Asian countries today, using quantitative, country-level analyses. Using available data as well as new data series gathered for this study, the chapter investigates (i) to what extent and how Southeast Asia's development (and especially Singapore, Malaysia, Thailand, Vietnam and Indonesia) came with environmental improvements as well as deteriorations, and (ii) where – in terms of countries and sectors – there are signs of improved environmental performance. The chapter thus aims to provide insights into the relation between economic development and environmental quality in urban industrializing Southeast Asia, and to identify mechanisms and dynamics which have positively influenced environmental quality.

The next section of this chapter surveys three theoretical perspectives on the relationship between environment and development in Southeast Asia; explores more closely various analytical approaches to the study of environmental reform; and then discusses methodological issues involved in an examination of environmental performance and reform in Southeast Asia. Subsequent sections examine the mechanisms, dynamics and results of environmental deterioration and reform with respect to air pollution, especially as related to traffic and industrial development; urban environmental infrastructure reform, with solid waste management used as an example; and industrial environmental management and reform, with particular reference to industrial development and industrial parks, respectively. The chapter concludes with a discussion of what can be learned from a quantitative assessment of environmental reform in these five Southeast Asian countries, for both the region itself and elsewhere.

ANALYSING ENVIRONMENTAL IMPROVEMENTS AND REFORMS

Up until now, most analyses of environment and development in Southeast Asia have taken either a developmentalist or a critical perspective related to governance of the region's natural resources and environment. Developmentalists have focused on increased investments, infrastructure development and other publicly supported measures to more fully capture and add economic value to Southeast Asia's rich base of natural resources (cf. Hill, 1996; ADB, 2000). For a long time this has been the main focus of governments in the region, as well as of international development banks and other intergovernmental institutions financially supporting them.

Others have critiqued the developmentalist approach, objecting to its perceived instrumental orientation towards exploiting Southeast Asia's 'natural capital', and pointing out the negative social consequences often paralleling short-term economic gains. Such critical perspectives go on to analyse structural and institutional factors contributing to environmental deterioration and the social costs of market-oriented economic development (cf. Hirsch, 1993; Carrere and Lohmann, 1996; Bello, Cunningham and Poh, 1998; Elliott, 2004; see also Sham, 1993). Local advocates, national and international non-governmental organizations (NGOs) and academic scholars have guided this latter type of analysis, with sometimes remarkable influence on development projects and national and international policies, such as the environmental conditionalities now standard for overseas development assistance and international development bank policies and practices (cf. Fox and Brown, 1998; O'Brien *et al.*, 2000; Goldman, 2004).

Following these two perspectives, a third, to some extent bridging or integrative, approach can be formulated and is taken up in this chapter: an analysis of environmental reform. This third approach aims to develop an understanding of how protection of natural resources and environmental quality became or can become institutionalized in development processes and practices in Southeast Asia. Neither pro- nor anti-development, such an approach aims to draw empirically based lessons on various successful and unsuccessful approaches to the environmental conditioning of economic development processes involving degradation of the sustenance base – for this chapter, especially with respect to the quality of urban and industrial environments.

The degree to which economic development no longer just degrades the natural environment, but results rather in environmental reform and improvements, differs according to time, place and environmental medium. Several models and theories have been formulated to further understand the time–space dependencies of environmental reform. The environmental Kuznets curve (World Bank, 1992) is one, much debated[4] quantitative model in which place–time dependencies on environmental reform are expressed, usually on one particular environmental issue (such as CO_2 or SO_2). Most simplistically, some argue that environmental improvements and reform are a function of 'level' of economic development. While economic modernization can contribute financial and social capital necessary for environmental improvement, institutional structures and political aspects of environmental governance play a key role as well.

Scholars working within the ecological modernization school of thought have explored, often in a more qualitative way, how and to what extent environmental reform and improvements accompany economic development, and what environmentally sound development might mean for the growth of a country, region or economic sector (cf. Weale, 1992; Mol, 1995; Weidner, 2002). Most environmental or ecological economists and ecological modernization theorists do not suggest an automatic unfolding of economic growth in sustainable directions. Rather, they argue that economic development must be actively and effectively governed to reduce environmental impacts. Such scholars have taken on the task of examining the effectiveness of various governance approaches for achieving more sustainable forms of economic development (cf. the various contributions in Mol and Sonnenfeld, 2000).

Analysing Environmental Reform

A review of literature on environmental reform in East and Southeast Asia (cf. Sham, 1993; Parnwell and Bryant, 1996; Hirsch and Warren, 1998;

Wehrmeyer and Mulugetta, 1999; Khondker, 2001; Lo and Marcotullio, 2001; Rock, 2002; Japan Environmental Council, 2003; Elliott, 2004; O'Rourke, 2004; and Sonnenfeld and Mol, 2006), and of ecological modernization processes more broadly, suggests that an analysis of urban and industrial environmental reform in Southeast Asia should distinguish three interdependent clusters of actors and institutional dynamics at work: those involving political institutions, civil society, and market actors and dynamics, respectively.

Political institutions

The first cluster of environmental governance and reform is made up of political institutions and governmental actors at the national level and below, increasingly connected to international political arrangements and institutions, such as multilateral environmental agreements (or MEAs, for example the Montreal protocol on ozone-depleting substances, the Kyoto protocol on greenhouse gas emissions), ASEAN, AFTA and Asia-Pacific Economic Cooperation (APEC). These political institutions and actors influence national economic and industrial development patterns via policies, legal standards and regulations, incentives, international pressures and assistance programmes, and contributions to global harmonization of standards and practices. National regulatory authorities and political institutions have been developed from the early 1970s onwards to safeguard the environment. These institutions have been based on the increasingly broadly accepted notion of the environment as a public good, together with the more conventional idea of addressing market failure in the provision of common goods. Subsequently, similar institutions have been established at the provincial and municipal levels and, from especially the 1980s onwards, at the international level.[5]

Civil society

The second cluster of environmental governance and reform includes environmental NGOs, civil society actors and the public domain as filled by media, legitimation and transparency institutions. Here as well, connections with international institutions and developments are common. National environmental NGOs are increasingly connected to global networks, and environmental information freely floats across borders (cf. Keck and Sikkink, 1998). Initially, this cluster of civic actors focused strongly on environmental agenda-setting and criticism of dominant political and economic actors and institutions for their inabilities to take the preservation of environmental goods sufficiently into account. More recently, in some countries, civil society actors and institutions have moved beyond that by taking up some environmental protection tasks conventionally carried out by state institutions, such as environmental education and information dissemination, environmental monitoring, environmental labelling, expert assessments and the building of trust. The prevailing political-institutional setting of a country strongly determines possibilities for an active civil society.

Market actors
The third cluster of environmental governance and reform encompasses market actors and dynamics. In the early years of modern environmentalism, in the 1970s and 1980s, economic actors and institutions were interpreted as the main antagonists in an ongoing deterioration of the sustenance base. More recently, with the broad, global advancement of environmental awareness, activism and institutions, economic actors and institutions have begun to play an increasingly significant role in environmental protection. In scholarship and debates on the limitations and in some cases failure of contemporary nation-states to effectively lead the making of environmental improvements (cf. Jänicke, 1990), and building as well on the wide, cross-sectoral support for the Brundtland report (WCED, 1987), economic actors and institutions have been given their place in environmental reforms. Internalization of environmental costs in market prices, corporate environmental management schemes (cf. Power, 1997), eco-labelling and certification organizations (such as those related to the ISO standards), the growth of the environmental industry and consultancies, and public–private environmental partnerships all give evidence of the market as more than just a place for short-term profits at the expense of the environment (cf. Wehrmeyer and Mulugetta, 1999). More than incidentally, these developments are internationally connected to the global market and market arrangements, global standardization schemes, foreign direct investments and transnational companies, and the like. Through transnational commodity chains and networks, demands of consumers and customers are communicated to producers and suppliers around the globe (see Gereffi and Korzeniewicz, 1994; Raynolds, 2004), no less with respect to the environment than other qualities.

Some parts of these clusters are more or less directly related to economic development, and thus would fit in and might support an environmental Kuznets curve type hypothesis. Others are independent of economic development, or levels of GDP per capita, providing a more full understanding of environmental improvement and reform. Each of the three clusters works at multiple geo-spatial levels or scales: local, national, regional and international.

Evaluating Environmental Performance

To answer if, to what extent and how each of these clusters of actors and institutions plays a role in environmental reform in contemporary Southeast Asia, it is necessary to be able to assess improvements (and degradations) in environmental performance in individual countries in the region. This in turn requires use of time-series data for various environmental indicators, rather than static information of one or another environmental parameter. Two broad types of time-series data can be used for these purposes: indicators of the transformation of environmental institutions, and of environmental outcomes, respectively.

Institutional indicators relate to (i) the capacity of social institutions with respect to the natural environment (including factors such as number and quality of environmental staff, number and quality of environmental authority organizations, environmental treaties signed and ratified, environmental laws; cf. Jänicke, 1997; Weidner, 2002); (ii) the development of civil society capacity to engage in environmental decision making (such as the number of environmental NGOs and their members, environmental journals and media coverage); and (iii) the capacity of economic institutions for environmental transformation (such as environmental investments, environmental research and development, the number of firms with ISO 14001 certification, market share for environmentally sound or eco-labelled products, development of environmental service industries, eco-industrial parks and so on).

Environmental outcome indicators include those referring to (i) various measures of environmental quality or deterioration (such as for air, water, forests, marine areas); and (ii) additions to and withdrawals from the natural environment (emissions and natural resource use, often standardized per unit of population, economic output or land area) (see Rogers *et al.*, 1997; Ballance, Biswas and Pattarkine, 2002).

As environmental monitoring and reporting in the Southeast Asian region as a whole are still in a relatively early phase of development,[6] reliable and consistent environmental time-series data on preferred indicators of environmental change are often lacking. This is even more true if we want to compare countries on their environmental successes and failures. Consequently, rather than designing an ideal set of indicators, we have used indicators (both environmental outcome and more institutional) for which quantitative time-series data are available to assess the progress (or lack thereof) of environmental reform in the region: those relating to air pollution, solid waste generation and recovery, and industrial environmental performance. For indicators of change in institutional factors, we utilize qualitative data derived from field research in the region, and quantitative data from secondary sources.

This chapter turns now to examine environmental performance and reform in Southeast Asia, in the areas of urban air quality, urban environmental infrastructure and services, and industrial environmental transformation.

URBAN AIR POLLUTION

Air pollution is often directly related to modernization and industrialization. It is especially in the rapidly growing urban metropolises that air quality is deteriorated by industrial production, transport, and energy and electricity production using fossil fuels.[7] While some Southeast Asian countries have set up policies to either radically reduce industrial air emissions or relocate major industrial polluters to peri-urban regions outside the city, for most, private car transport is increasingly becoming the main source of air pollution. To some extent, transport policies can reduce air emission, for instance by solving problems of urban traffic congestion, using more energy-efficient cars, switching to unleaded fuel, and stringent policies on car emissions to remove old vehicles. But 'relocation' is only an option if high-quality transport alternatives (for example mass transit) are available. With respect to electricity production, relocation and the switch to 'clean' fuels (solar, wind, hydro and to a lesser extent natural gas) are possible options – though used only to a limited extent today in Southeast Asia. All countries have started with air pollution policies, but the pollution and emission levels are clearly not the same.

As indicators of urban air pollution, we have gathered time-series data: on sulphur dioxide (SO_2) and nitrogen oxide (NO_x) emissions, as indicators of more local air quality problems; on carbon dioxide (CO_2) emissions, as an indication of the contribution to global warming; and on the largely industrial consumption of CFCs, indicating the contribution to atmospheric ozone depletion. Time-series data on emissions of additional toxic gases were not available over larger stretches of time in more than one country. In addition, data on passenger car ownership and the introduction of unleaded fuel are reported.

Local Air Quality

There are clear differences between countries with respect to local air pollution problems, both in relative improvements over time, and in absolute levels of emissions over the whole period. If the EDGAR database is used,[8] SO_2 emissions per unit of GDP seem to decrease especially for Malaysia and Vietnam during the 1990s, while the other countries show less clear

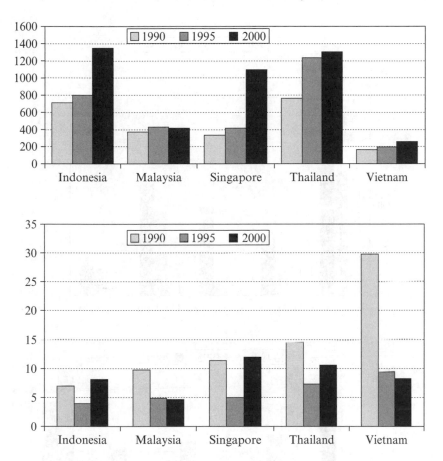

Note: In thousand metric tons, above; in kg/mln GDP, below.

Source: World Bank data.

Figure 6.3 SO$_2$ emissions, 1990–2000

tendencies of environmental improvement (see Figure 6.3). While data from Streets *et al.* (2000) show systematically higher levels of SO$_2$ emission per unit of GDP for Vietnam and Thailand (compared to the other three countries) over the period 1985–97, this is less clearly the case when entering the new millennium. We see also differences between countries with respect to NO$_x$ emissions per unit of GDP, where especially Malaysia shows steady decreases throughout the 1990s, but the other countries show increases towards the turn of the millennium (except for Vietnam) (see Figure 6.4).

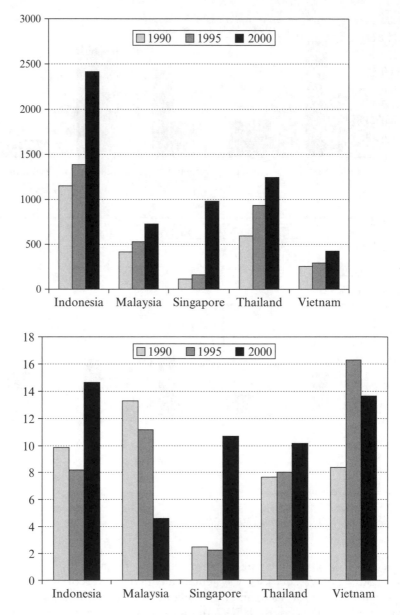

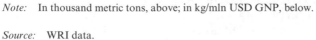

Note: In thousand metric tons, above; in kg/mln USD GNP, below.

Source: WRI data.

Figure 6.4   NO$_x$ emissions 1990–2000

Table 6.1 Introduction of unleaded petrol

	Unleaded introduced	Completely unleaded
Indonesia	1997/1998	1998/1999
Malaysia	1991	N/A
Singapore	January 1991	July 1998
Thailand	May 1991	January 1996
Vietnam	May 2000	January 2005

Source: ASEAN (2001).

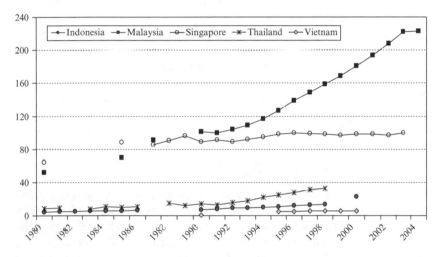

Source: IRF world road statistics; national data.

Figure 6.5 Automobile ownership (passenger cars per 1000 inhabitants)

The introduction of lead in the urban environment shows a decrease, although with different time scales for the distinct countries (see Table 6.1). Causal factors related to these environmental reforms of traffic-related emissions are to be found with national environmental policy, sometimes strongly linked to international policy networks (as in the case of the latecomers in unleaded petrol introduction, which was strongly pushed by international donor agencies). In the case of Singapore, we also see that active and interventional transport policies have slowed the growth of private passenger car ownership and use, helping to reduce or keep low various traffic-related emissions (see Figure 6.5).

Greenhouse Gas Production

CO_2 emissions per unit of GDP (at constant 2000 PPP USD) are often directly related to the energy intensity of economic processes, energy efficiency of the economy, and fuel composition (see Figure 6.6a). Thailand, Malaysia and Vietnam show hardly any decoupling of energy consumption from economic development between 1980 and 2002, but there are differences in fuel switch: Thailand started to use relatively larger amounts of coal and oil, and Malaysia moved heavily towards natural gas. Non-carbon-based fuel use was small, with only Thailand and Malaysia each obtaining some 10 per cent of electricity from hydropower – and that, too, not without its environmental controversies. Indonesia is comparable to Thailand on fuel composition, while Vietnam relies more strongly on natural gas. Singapore still relies heavily on oil, but seems to be the only country that succeeded in a relative decoupling.

The different trends in CO_2 emissions per unit of GDP can be explained by a combination of fuel composition and increase in energy efficiency of the economy. With respect to Malaysia, a sharp decline in CO_2 emissions per unit of GDP – coming from a high level – happened in the 1970s owing to a move to natural gas and later on a higher energy efficiency, but with more or less of a stabilization of such emissions occurring in the 1980s and 1990s. Thailand followed the Malaysian path of energy intensity of the economy in the 1970s, but saw its energy consumption (and CO_2 emissions) increasing during the 1990s. Singapore witnessed declining CO_2 emissions from the early 1990s onwards, Indonesia stabilized during the 1980s and 1990s, and Vietnam saw a sharp increase in CO_2 emissions from the second half of the 1990s onwards.

Comparing the countries by the early 2000s, in terms of CO_2 emissions per capita (Figure 6.6b), Singapore stands out as the most energy-intensive one, with Malaysia and Thailand rapidly increasing energy use per capita albeit at a considerably lower level. Vietnam and Indonesia are a factor 10 below the Singapore level of CO_2 emissions per capita. None of these countries have yet enacted an active greenhouse gas emission reduction policy, as they are all non-Annex 1 countries within the Kyoto protocol.[9]

Energy policies up till now thus have not been focused so much on reduction of emission of greenhouse gases (CO_2) as on related environmental problems (SO_2, NO_x, soot), national security in energy supply, and economic costs and energy prices. An increase in joint advanced and developing country projects such as the Activities Implemented Jointly (AIJ) and Clean Development Mechanism (CDM) programmes can be witnessed in several Southeast Asian countries, especially Thailand and

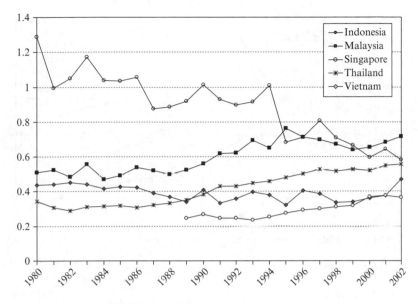

* = GDP at constant 2000 USD purchasing power parity rates.

Figure 6.6a   CO$_2$ emissions (kg per 2000 PPP \$ of GDP*)

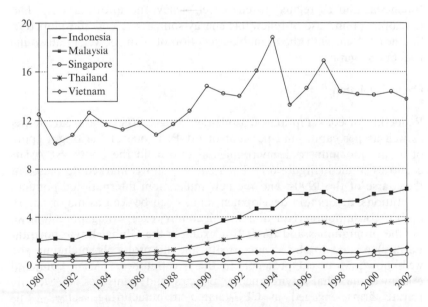

Figure 6.6b   CO$_2$ emissions (metric tons per capita)

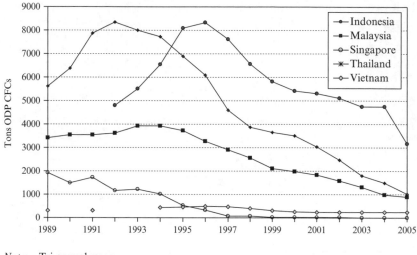

Note: Tri-annual mean.

Source: UNEP data.

Figure 6.7   CFC consumption

Indonesia, and as related to energy efficiency and afforestation.[10] The development and use of renewable energy sources are underdeveloped in Southeast Asia, with the arguable exception of hydropower in all countries but Singapore.

Ozone Depletion

Reduction of consumption of ozone-depleting CFCs (in absolute terms as well as per capita and per unit of GDP) is one of the bright spots of urban and industrial environmental reform in the Southeast Asian countries studied (Figure 6.7). Each country shows marked decreases in the course of the 1990s, and the new millennium international political institutions, actors and development banks can be seen as major actors in CFC consumption reduction in each country except Singapore, following the programmes and funds (for example the Global Environmental Facility) related to the Vienna treaty and its protocols, including the well-known Montreal protocol. In the five Southeast Asian countries examined, national environmental policies and ministries, as well as private firms engaged in CFC-related manufacturing, actively followed international political developments. Consumption of CFCs in

Indonesia remains at much higher levels than in the other countries studied.

URBAN INFRASTRUCTURE: SOLID WASTE

Solid waste can be distinguished in different categories, of which municipal and industrial solid waste are the most common.[11] With respect to the different categories of solid waste, relevant environmental indicators include (i) the total amount of solid waste (usually per capita for municipal waste, or per unit of GNP for industrial waste), and (ii) the amount and kind of recovery and recycling of various solid waste streams. With regard to the latter, there is a generally accepted ranking of environmental priorities: re-use in the same form, recycling (usually involving processing towards a low-value application), incineration with energy recovery, and landfilling. Recovery rates used in various countries can include the first three categories, but sometimes also only the first two. In general, re-use and recycling of industrial waste are easier and more profitable than for municipal waste. This is due to the more homogeneous streams of industrial wastes, the concentration of waste products at a few point sources, and possibilities to directly (re-)use industrial by-products ('waste') as inputs to other manufacturing processes (namely, some form of industrial ecology).

All countries show increases in the total amount of solid waste generated from the mid-1990s onwards (Figure 6.8), although Vietnam especially shows a remarkable growth, be it with still relatively low per capita amounts (Figure 6.9). Developments in Singapore and Thailand seem to show only limited increases, be it on a rather high level of per capita solid waste generation. Projections into the future, towards 2025 (Figure 6.9), show only a stabilization of per capita municipal solid waste generation in Singapore, while all other countries will witness increases.

Perhaps more interestingly in terms of environmental reform, rates of recovery and recycling of solid waste are high and increasing in Singapore (65 per cent), which includes incineration for energy recovery (Figure 6.10).[12] The government of Singapore has invested strongly in a large number of private–public incineration plants. Thailand also has a solid level of recycling of industrial solid waste (close to 50 per cent), though formal recycling of municipal solid waste is only starting, with rather low – though increasing – percentages. Malaysia is reported to have municipal waste recycling rates below 10 per cent (Japan Environmental Council, 2003). Recycling rates of municipal solid waste in Vietnam at the start of the new millennium ranged between 12 and 15 per cent (National Environmental Agency, 2003).

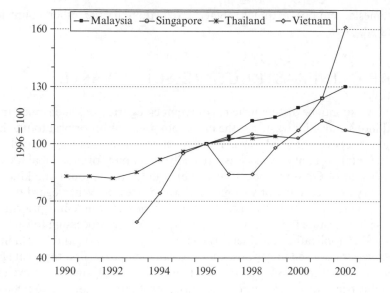

Source: National data, various local sources.

Figure 6.8   Solid waste generation, 1990–2003

In Vietnam and Indonesia, recovery and recycling of municipal wastes are done mostly by scavengers, waste pickers and other parts of what is often called the informal sector, as well as by local community groups (with percentages of 30 per cent and more being mentioned; Douglas and Ling, 2000); this occurs in Thailand, Malaysia and Singapore as well, though these countries have more fully developed formal waste collection and treatment systems. Even industrial waste recycling in Vietnam is to some extent part of the informal sector, for instance where communities collect unofficially waste from large pulp and paper industries, to sell it to small production units for second-quality board production (cf. Tran *et al.*, 2003).[13]

Discussion

In the countries studied, the main drivers towards less sharp increases in the generation of solid wastes and higher rates of waste recovery and recycling are diverse. Governmental policies often are the main drivers of modernization in the development of a municipal solid waste infrastructure. In Malaysia and Singapore, for instance, informal waste collection and recycling have completely vanished. While none of the

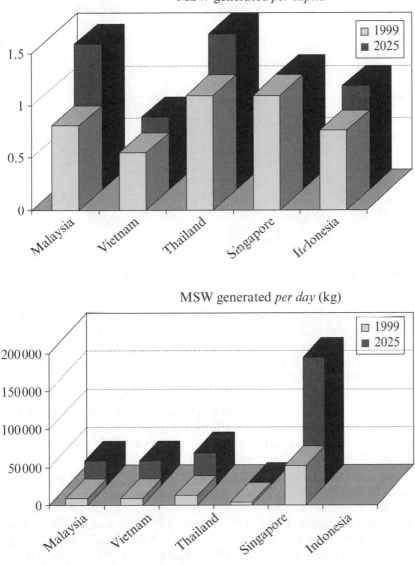

Source: Japan Environmental Council (2003: 285).

Figure 6.9 Municipal solid waste generation (kg)

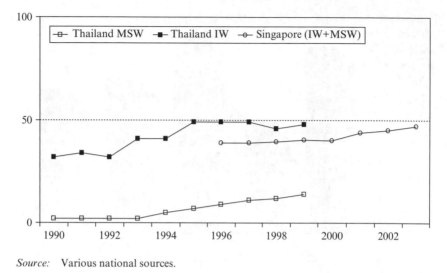

Source: Various national sources.

Figure 6.10   Recycling of industrial and municipal solid waste

countries examined have large-scale systems of separated waste collection, or composting of organic municipal solid waste, experiments have been held in Vietnam, Thailand and elsewhere. With the increasing amount of solid waste in the industrialized and industrializing Southeast Asian countries, finding appropriate landfill sites to dispose of that waste has become a major problem, especially since local communities often fiercely protest against nearby location of such sites. In that way civil society has become an actor in pushing governments into environmental reform of municipal and industrial solid waste collection and treatment systems.

Government agents are less dominant with respect to the generation, recovery and recycling of industrial solid wastes, though here too they are important rule-setting agencies and may play an important role in the collection and disposal of hazardous wastes, as well as some direct role through the management of industrial estates (cf. Phung, 2002). Firms and markets increasingly play major roles in waste reduction and increasing the levels of waste recovery, re-use and recycling. Governments can support that by introducing waste fees, which make waste reduction and waste recovery programmes profitable. Even without higher waste fees, firms' experiments with cleaner production methods and recently industrial ecology (cf. Rock, Angel and Feridhanusetyawan 1999; Tran, 2003) have resulted in waste reduction practices in each of the countries studied. Privatization in industrial solid waste collection and treatment is rather the rule than the exception, although the organizational schemes differ between the countries. In Vietnam and Indonesia, small local firms and individuals are still often involved in industrial solid waste collection, treatment and re-use, while in the more developed countries the majority of industrial solid waste collection is carried out by larger national private companies.

Having addressed environmental performance and reform dynamics related to air pollution and solid waste management, the third and final area of transformations examined here concerns industrial environmental practices.

INDUSTRIAL TRANSFORMATIONS

Since the launching of the International Human Dimensions Programme (IHDP) on Global Change, 'industrial transformation' has been used as a common term in the examination of environmental reform in industrial sectors (and even agro-industrial and service sectors). In assessing industrial environmental transformations in Southeast Asia, we collected nation-wide data on three indicators: industrial solid waste recovery and recycling, discussed in the previous section; industrial organic water pollution; and adoption of industrial environmental management systems; and discuss as well the dynamics related to variation among firms, the engagement of state environmental agencies, cleaner production programmes, experiments in industrial ecology, and the role of NGOs and civil society.

Water Pollution

Total quantities of organic water pollution from industry have been more or less stable in Singapore since the mid-1980s, and increasing in Indonesia and Malaysia, at least till the mid-1990s, to stabilize from then onwards.[14] In terms of industrial organic water pollution per unit of industrial GDP (Figure 6.11), all countries show decreasing tendencies over this period, although at different levels (and sometimes with limited data). More local and sectoral data indicate that this decreasing tendency can be confirmed for Thailand. For Vietnam, it is less easy to provide an overall picture. Increasing efficiencies in modernized industries and stringent environmental policies and enforcements are to be found at the source of the success story in Singapore, a path that seems to have been followed by Malaysia and Thailand more recently.

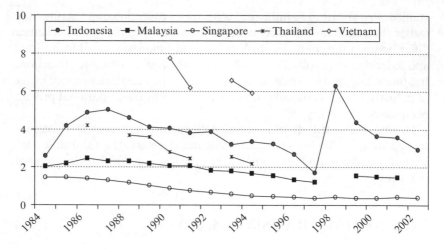

Note: 10^3kg/10^6 USD industrial GDP/yr.

Source: World Bank indicators; WRI data; own calculations.

Figure 6.11   Industrial water pollution: biological oxygen demand (BOD)

Industrial Environmental Management Systems

The development and certification of corporate environmental management systems (EMS) conforming to the International Standards
Organization (ISO) 14001 standards are widely referenced as an indicator
of industrial environmental reform throughout the world. Figure 6.12
illustrates trends in corporate ISO 14001 certification in the countries
studied. In just ten years, Thailand had over 1100 firms with certified ISO
14001 environmental management systems, followed by Singapore with
over 800 firms, Malaysia with just under 700, Indonesia with more than
400 and Vietnam with over 100. While clearly with a great deal of unevenness, the adoption of internationally recognized and certified industrial
environmental management system standards in Southeast Asia indicates
the promising influence of 'green' global markets and the 'greening' of
global supply chains (see Mol, 2001).

Variation among Sectors and Firms

While differences in the push towards more environmentally sound production methods and products exist between countries, there are also

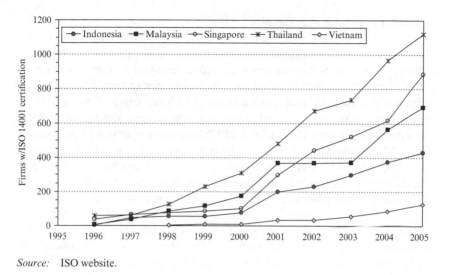

Source: ISO website.

Figure 6.12   ISO 14001 certified firms

many differences between industrial sectors and between firms within
industrial sectors. Generally, for large internationally oriented companies
producing for a world market, major incentives can be found in economic
dynamics, sometimes strongly supported by national policies and authorities. The rapidly expanding palm oil sector in Malaysia witnessed a major
improvement in environmental performance (especially water pollution)
between 1975 and 1985, caused by a combination of economic incentives,
stricter pollution standards, government-induced technology programmes
and a growing internationalization of the palm oil industry (Vincent and
Ali, with Rahim, 2000; Rock, 2002). In general, the more open and international integrated economies are more influenced by international standards on products and production circumstances. But even in Vietnam,
with rather weak governmental environmental authorities, these global
economic pressures and mechanisms are felt, as can be seen by the major
differences in environmental performance between large state-owned
companies producing basically for the domestic market, and major FDI
companies producing for the world market (cf. Mol, 2001; Tran, 2003).
For domestically oriented industries and the thousands of medium-sized
and small industrial firms, economic drivers, actors and mechanisms play
a minor role in environmental reforms. Here local authorities and community complaints are the most vital mechanisms in bringing about environmental improvement.

Cleaner Production Programmes

In all five countries examined, state governmental agencies have started cleaner production programmes to move industries from end-of-pipe abatement approaches to more preventive cleaner technology strategies. Especially in Vietnam and Indonesia, and to a lesser extent Thailand, these cleaner production centres and programmes have been supported strongly by international donor agencies and ODA programmes of OECD countries. While starting in the larger companies of the most polluting sectors (textiles, pulp and paper, palm oil, chemicals, metal, electronics), currently the emphasis has switched to small and medium-sized companies, also in the lesser polluting branches of industry. In the poorer countries, the willingness of the domestic industries to cover the initial costs in starting with cleaner production is usually low, and cleaner production programmes still heavily rely on external support. Recently, this cleaner production approach has been supplemented in a number of countries with research and pilot studies or projects on what is now popularly called industrial ecology (e.g. Graedel and Allenby, 1995; Ayres and Ayres, 1996).

Experiments in Industrial Ecology

Benefiting from the structure of industrial parks, even less developed countries such as Vietnam and Thailand have started experiments in which waste streams of companies are linked to natural resources use and needs of neighbouring firms.[15] Even more than with cleaner production, governmental involvement is essential, as market organizations are ill fitted for designing and implementing such geographical systems of natural resources dependencies. This government dependency is less relevant in chain- and network-oriented industrial ecology systems, where the dominant actors (often multinational firms) in a value chain can coordinate environmental improvements through cooperation.

Role of the State, NGOs and Civil Society

The above examples notwithstanding, especially in countries with a relatively poor environmental capacity of state authorities, we witness limited incentives towards broad-based environmental reform. In countries such as Indonesia and Vietnam, environmental NGOs (cf. Sonnenfeld, 1998a, 1998b, 2002) and community-driven regulation (O'Rourke, 2004) are the only real incentives that force domestic industries into environmental transformations. In countries with much stronger environmental states, such as Malaysia and Singapore, it is especially the relative autonomy of the state embedded in social relations with industrial sectors which results in efficient and successful arrangements in cleaning up industrial practices.[16]

But these strong states, and also Vietnam, lack a major push from environmental NGOs engaged in relation to the industrial sector. Lack of openness and transparency, limited public pressure and the difficulties of international NGOs in entering these countries result in restricted incentives from civil society to move towards more sustainable production patterns. Even in Thailand, where NGOs are more present and have greater room for manoeuvre, their impact on greening the industrial sector is limited. Perhaps most effective are those NGOs such as the Thailand Environmental Institute and the Thailand Business Council for Sustainable Development which are supported by government agencies and the business community. Opportunities for more adversarial and pressuring activities towards polluting industries in Thailand are restricted (cf. Rock, 2002, p. 139; but see also Sonnenfeld, 2000).

CONCLUSION

In drawing conclusions from this comparative research on five countries and three environmental sectors, we note a number of methodological findings, draw several substantive conclusions, and end with two more general recommendations for policy research and analysis on urban and industrial environmental reform in Southeast Asia.

Methodological Findings

In bringing together quantitative evidence on the environmental performance of five countries on a number of environmental indicators over a decade or so we ran into problems of data availability and data reliability. Data on air pollution and air emissions are more readily available than data on solid waste or water pollution, for instance. The selection of indicators and environmental issues therefore is driven more by data availability (and to some extent reliability) than methodological considerations of representativeness, generalizability and indication of change. The current state of monitoring and reporting of environmental data in the Southeast Asia region is poor and non-standardized, especially when compared to, for instance, the EU. There is hardly any harmonization in environmental monitoring, data collection and reporting, recent initiatives of the ADB and APEC notwithstanding. While international data sets (for example those on CO_2 emissions, CFC consumption, ISO 14001 and automobile use) appear to make countries' environmental practices comparable, the difficulties of collecting comparable national data sets lead to doubts regarding the comparability of country data published by international organizations.

Given these methodological concerns, it makes little sense to try to integrate all country data into one indicator and list the countries accordingly, as has been done for instance in Columbia University's widely cited Environmental Sustainability Index (ESI).[17] Under such conditions, comparing issue-specific environmental performance over specific time trajectories remains for the present the best basis for working conclusions about the relative successes and failures of efforts to transform urban and industrial environments in Southeast Asia. The set of environmental issues and indicators we were able to work with seem not too biased with respect to local versus global problems, different media, or problems typically for rich countries versus those typically for poor countries.

Substantive Findings

Based on the above methodological qualifications, we find that at this time drawing conclusions about comparative, overall national environmental performance makes little sense. Rather, comparisons of environmental reforms between countries should be done in a disaggregated manner, for example urban waste management infrastructure, industrial production, energy use and energy-related pollution (see the data sets for that). Sometimes an environmental Kuznets curve type relationship between economic development and environmental deterioration seems to be supported (for example on CO_2 emissions or on CFC consumption). For other indicators, however, there is little evidence of an environmental Kuznets curve type dynamic (for example ISO 14001, municipal solid waste).

The most interesting conclusions may be found by combining the analysis of quantitative data with qualitative analysis of the actors and institutions involved in more and less successful environmental reforms over time. While similar actors and institutional arrangements are involved in improved environmental performance on a number of environmental issues (for example on CFC reduction, on industrial pollution by large TNCs), on other issues the mechanisms, actors and institutional arrangements are quite different (for example on solid waste recycling, on industrial pollution by SMEs, on CO_2 emissions). The local, national and international institutional arrangements (with respect to state, market and civil society) 'govern' the environmental issues at stake. It is here that further explanations must be found: strong versus weak regulatory states (Singapore versus Indonesia), active versus limited environmental movements (Indonesia versus Vietnam), and highly internationalized versus local issues (TNC industrial production or CFC, versus municipal solid waste). Country- and issue-specific reform trajectories should be explained as well as designed based on such characteristics, building on and strengthening various actors' respective policy styles and environmental capacities.

Recommendations for Policy Research and Analysis

At least two more general conclusions and recommendations may also be made. First, with the possible exception of Singapore, the other Southeast Asian countries studied show similar tendencies of a combination of high economic growth and – on most environmental indicators – increasing absolute environmental deterioration. These similarities suggest a basis for increased environmental cooperation in the region. Until now, however, ASEAN – the logical institution to start such cooperation – has been focused primarily on trade liberalization and economic agendas, leaving environmental issues largely untouched.[18] Lessons from other regional institutions, such as the EU and NAFTA (cf. Mol, 2001; Sanchez, 2002), show not only that the environment can profit from regional cooperation, but also that regional economic institutions can be strengthened and legitimized by environmental cooperation, albeit with new relationships between various social actors.

Second, the differences in absolute and relative environmental performance and improvements (over time) between countries raise important questions for further scholarly research and policy analysis. While automatic transfer of environmental reform practices between countries is often unwise owing to great differences in national environmental conditions, institutional arrangements and capacities, countries nevertheless can learn from each other. Thailand's successes in encouraging adoption of ISO 14000 environmental management system standards, Singapore's accomplishments in restraining growth of private car ownership and generation of solid waste, Vietnam's success in the relative decrease in SO_2 emissions in the 1990s, and Malaysia's achievements in the relative decline in NO_x emissions in the 1990s, are some examples. Much remains to be learned about the actors, institutions and contingent factors responsible for these apparent successes in urban and industrial environmental policy-making in Southeast Asia.

NOTES

1. Myanmar/Burma, Laos and Cambodia have developed markedly less than their neighbours; neither they nor the Philippines and Brunei are addressed in this chapter.

2. Even while industrializing areas of Southeast Asia are increasingly articulated with national, regional and global economies, other areas remain relatively marginal, outside at least formal economies and modes of development; this is the case for vast regions within some Southeast Asian countries, as well as some countries in their entirety.
3. Economist Simon Kuznets (1955, 1963) observed that social inequality declined in certain countries following lengthy periods of sustained economic growth. Others have attempted to generalize these observations, positing the existence of what has become known as 'Kuznets' U-shaped curve' or, more simply, the 'Kuznets curve', named after the shape of the projected graphic form of the relationship between economic growth and social inequality. In recent years, analysts have hypothesized a similar dynamic with respect to economic development and environmental quality, namely that, after a period of worsening environmental quality, with sustained growth eventually environmental quality will 'turn the corner' and improve. This hypothesized relationship has become known as the 'environmental Kuznets curve'.
4. Several authors have – with good arguments – questioned the empirical validity of this curve and the extrapolation that implies that the same process will occur in all cases and countries. They have pointed at the selective use of environmental indicators (only some emissions and no resource stocks are involved in the empirical studies), limited and unreliable data, contradictions between studies and a bias towards 'best fit' curves (cf. Arrow *et al.*, 1995; Ekins, 1995; Stern, Common and Barbier, 1996; Wallace, 1996; Stern, 2004; for empirical studies, see the references in these publications).
5. Singapore established its major national environmental authority in 1972, to be followed by Malaysia in 1974. Malaysia was first in establishing a comprehensive environmental framework law, also in 1974, followed by Thailand in 1975.
6. See for instance the project supported by the Asian Development Bank (see: http://www.adb.org/) in setting up region-wide environmental monitoring and reporting and to harmonize existing schemes between states, to be able to compare monitoring data (e.g. ADB, 1999, 2002). See also the web-based APEC Virtual Center for Environmental Technology Exchange, for most of the Southeast Asian countries (see: http://www.apec-vc.or.jp/world_e/index.html).
7. As well as by haze from field or forest burning in upwind rural areas.
8. EDGAR stands for Emission Database for Global Atmospheric Research, and data are available at http://www.mnp.nl/edgar/.
9. Thailand (1999, 2002), Malaysia (1999, 2002) and Vietnam (1998, 2002) have signed and ratified the Kyoto protocol, however; Indonesia is a signatory (1998) as well; only Singapore is a non-participant.
10. AIJ and its successor CDM are systems under the Kyoto protocol, where developed (Annex 1) countries finance CO_2 emissions reduction projects in developing (or non-Annex 1) countries, with the idea that the emissions reductions can be added to the national greenhouse gas performance of the developed countries.
11. Most countries also classify hazardous waste, though definitions vary; hazardous waste is for the most part not addressed here.
12. Compare the incineration rates for other countries: Indonesia 5 percent, Malaysia 5 per cent, Thailand 5 per cent, and Vietnam less than 1 per cent (Japan Environmental Council, 1999, p. 164, using ESCAP data).
13. While the environmental benefits and the economic importance for the poor of informal recycling schemes have often been celebrated (cf. Japan Environmental Council, 1999, p. 165), the health effects are often considerable (cf. Weinberg, Pellow and Schnaiberg, 2000; and Pellow, 2004).
14. The total amounts of organic pollution by industry only partly correspond with data from other sources. For instance, Sham (1993), Vincent, Rozali and Khalid (1997) and Department of Environment Malaysia (1998) report significant improvement of the water quality of the major Malaysian rivers between 1980 and 1989, with a slight deterioration at the end of the 1990s, especially owing to non-industrial sources.
15. In Vietnam, for instance, the semi-governmental industrial development organization

SONADEZI is involved in industrial ecology projects within its industrial zones Bien Hoa I and Bien Hoa II in Dong Nai province. In Thailand, the Industrial Estate Authority of Thailand (IEAT) is involved in various industrial ecology projects within its estates. See also the Eco-Industrial Estate Network Asia (http://www.eieasia.org/).

16. In analysing the role of voluntary initiatives taken by industrial firms in Singapore and Malaysia, Perry and Singh (2001) indeed conclude that the overall contribution of voluntary measures is rather meagre. Only corporate pressure to standardize the environmental performance of affiliates in different foreign locations makes some impact, especially with respect to larger TNCs in Singapore.
17. See http://www.ciesin.columbia.edu/indicators/ESI/.
18. Recently, discussions on regional environmental cooperation have been centred on the haze problem, especially between Indonesia, Singapore, Malaysia and Vietnam (Mayer, 2006). For a more general overview of regional environmental cooperation in Southeast Asia, see Badenoch (2002).

REFERENCES

ADB (1999), *Development of Environmental Statistics*, Manila: Asian Development Bank

ADB (2000), *Environments in Transition: Cambodia, Lao PDR, Thailand, Viet Nam*, Manila: Asian Development Bank.

ADB (2002), *Handbook on Environmental Statistics*, Manila: Asian Development Bank

Antle, J.M. and G. Heidebrink (1995), 'Environment and development: theory and international evidence', in J.B. Opshoor, K. Button and P. Nijkamp (eds), *Environmental Economics and Development*, Aldershot, UK and Brookfield, VT, USA: Edward Elgar.

Arrow, K., B. Bolin and R. Constanza *et al.* (1995), 'Economic growth, carrying capacity, and the environment', *Science*, **268**: 520–21.

ASEAN (2001), *Second ASEAN State of the Environment Report*, Jakarta: ASEAN.

Ayres, R.U. and L. Ayres (1996), *Industrial Ecology: Towards Closing the Materials Cycle*, Cheltenham, UK and Brookfield, VT, USA: Edward Elgar.

Badenoch, N. (2002), *Transboundary Environmental Governance: Principles and Practice in Mainland Southeast Asia*, Washington, DC: World Resources Institute.

Ballance, R., B. Biswas and V. Pattarkine (2002), *Handbook on Environment Statistics*, Manila: Asian Development Bank.

Bello, W., S. Cunningham and L.K. Poh (1998), *A Siamese Tragedy: Development and Disintegration in Modern Thailand*, London: Zed Books.

Brookfield, H.C. and Y. Byron (eds) (1993), *Southeast Asia's Environmental Future: The Search for Sustainability*, Tokyo: United Nations University Press.

Carrere, R. and L. Lohmann (1996), *Pulping the South: Industrial Tree Plantations and the World Paper Economy*, London: Zed Books.

Department of Environment Malaysia (1998), *Malaysian Environmental Quality Report 1998*, Kuala Lumpur: MoSTE.

Douglas, M. and O.G. Ling (2000), 'Industrializing cities and the environment in Pacific Asia', in D.P. Angel and M.T. Rock (eds), *Asia's Clean Revolution: Industry, Growth and the Environment*, Sheffield, UK: Greenleaf, pp. 104–27.

Ekins, P. (1995), 'The Kuznets Curve for the Environment and Economic Growth: Examining the Evidence', Mimeo, Birkbeck College, University of London.

Elliott, L. (2004), 'Environmental challenges, policy failure and regional dynamics in Southeast Asia', in M. Beeson (ed.), *Contemporary Southeast Asia: Regional Dynamics, National Differences*, Hampshire, UK: Palgrave Macmillan. pp. 178–97.

Fox, J.A. and L.D. Brown (1998), *The Struggle for Accountability: The World Bank, NGOs, and Grassroots Movements*, Cambridge, MA: MIT Press.

Gereffi, G. and M. Korzeniewicz (eds) (1994), *Commodity Chains and Global Capitalism*, Westport, CT: Praeger.

Goldman, M. (2004), *Imperial Nature: The World Bank and the Making of Green Neoliberalism*, New Haven, CT: Yale University Press.

Graedel, T.E. and B.R. Allenby (1995), *Industrial Ecology*, Englewood Cliffs, NJ: Prentice Hall.

Hill, H. (1996), *The Indonesian Economy since 1966: Southeast Asia's Emerging Giant*, Cambridge, UK: Cambridge University Press.

Hirsch, P. (1993), *The Political Economy of Environment in Thailand*, Manila: Journal of Contemporary Asia Publishers.

Hirsch, P. and C. Warren (eds) (1998), *The Politics of Environment in Southeast Asia*, London and New York: Routledge.

Jänicke, M. (1990), 'Erfolgsbedingungen von Umweltpolitik im internationalen Vergleich', *Zeitschrift für Umweltpolitik und Umweltrecht*, **3**, 213–32.

Jänicke, M. (1997), 'The political system's capacity for environmental policy', in M. Jänicke and H. Weidner (eds), *National Environmental Policies: A Comparative Study of Capacity Building*, New York and Berlin: Springer-Verlag, pp. 1–14.

Japan Environmental Council (ed.) (1999), *The State of the Environment in Asia, 1999/2000*, Tokyo: Springer-Verlag.

Japan Environmental Council (ed.) (2003), *The State of the Environment in Asia 2002/2003* (trans. Rick Davis), Tokyo: Springer-Verlag.

Keck, M.E. and K. Sikkink (1998), *Activists Beyond Borders: Advocacy Networks in International Politics*, Ithaca, NY: Cornell University Press.

Khondker, H. (ed.) (2001), Special issue on 'Politics and the environment', *Asian Journal of Social Science*, **29**(1).

Kuznets, S. (1955), 'Economic growth and income inequality', *American Economic Review*, **35**: 1–28.

Kuznets, S. (1963), 'Quantitative aspects of the economic growth of nations', *Economic Growth and Structural Change*, **11**: 1–92.

Lo, F.C. and P. Marcotullio (ed.) (2001), *Globalization and the Sustainability of Cities in the Asia Pacific Region*, Tokyo and New York: United Nations University Press.

Mayer, J. (2006), 'Transboundary perspectives on managing Indonesia's fires', *Journal of Environment and Development*, **15**(2): 202–23.

Mol, A.P.J. (1995), *The Refinement of Production: Ecological Modernization Theory and the Chemical Industry*, Utrecht: Jan van Arkel/International Books.

Mol, A.P.J. (2001), *Globalization and Environmental Reform: The Ecological Modernization of the Global Economy*, Cambridge, MA: MIT Press.

Mol, A.P.J. and D.A. Sonnenfeld (eds) (2000), *Ecological Modernization Around the Globe: New Perspectives and Critical Debates*, London: Frank Cass.

National Environmental Agency (2003), *State of the Environment Viet Nam 2002*, Hanoi: MoSTE.

O'Brien, R., A.M. Goetz, J.A. Scholte and M. Williams (2000), *Contesting Global Governance: Multilateral Economic Institutions and Global Social Movements*, New York: Cambridge.

O'Rourke, D. (2004), *Community-Driven Regulation: Balancing Development and the Environment in Vietnam*, Cambridge, MA: MIT Press.

Panayotou, T. (1993), *Empirical Tests and Policy Analysis of Environmental Degradation at Different Stages of Economic Development*, Geneva: ILO.

Parnwell, M.J.G. and R.L. Bryant (1996), *Environmental Change in South-East Asia: People, Politics and Sustainable Development*, London and New York: Routledge.

Pellow, D.N. (2004), *Garbage Wars: The Struggle for Environmental Justice in Chicago*. Cambridge, MA: MIT University Press.

Perry, M. and S. Singh (2001), *Corporate Environmental Responsibility in Singapore and Malaysia: The Potential and Limits of Voluntary Initiatives*, Technology, Business and Society Programme Paper no. 3, Geneva: UN Research Institute for Social Development.

Phung, P.T. (2002), 'Ecological Modernisation of Industrial Estates in Viet Nam', Ph.D. thesis, Environmental Policy, Wageningen University, the Netherlands.

Power, M. (1997), *The Audit Society: Rituals of Verification*, Oxford, UK: Oxford University Press.

Raynolds, L.T. (2004), 'The globalization of organic agro-food networks', *World Development*, **32**(5): 725–43.

Rock, M. (2002), *Pollution Control in East Asia: Lessons from Newly Industrializing Economies*, Washington, DC and Singapore: Resources for the Future/Institute of Southeast Asia Studies.

Rock, M.T., D.P. Angel and T. Feridhanusetyawan (1999), 'Industrial ecology and clean development in East Asia', *Journal of Industrial Ecology*, **3**(4): 29–42.

Rogers, P.P., K.F. Jalal and B.N. Lohani et al. (1997). *Measuring Environmental Quality in Asia*, Cambridge, MA: Harvard University Press.

Sanchez, R.A. (2002), 'Governance, trade and the environment in the context of NAFTA', *American Behavioral Scientist*, **45**(9): 1369–93.

Selden, T.M. and D.S. Song (1994), 'Environmental quality and development: is there a Kuznets curve for air pollution emissions?', *Journal of Environmental Economics and Management*, **27**: 147–62.

Sham, S. (1993), *Environment and Development in Malaysia: Changing Concerns and Approaches*, Kuala Lumpur: Centre for Environmental Studies, Institute of Strategic and International Studies (ISIS) Malaysia.

Sonnenfeld, D.A. (1998a), 'From brown to green? Late industrialization, social conflict, and adoption of environment technologies in Thailand's pulp industry', *Organization and Environment*, **11**(1): 59–87.

Sonnenfeld, D.A. (1998b), 'Social movements, environment, and technology in Indonesia's pulp and paper industry', *Asia Pacific Viewpoint*, **39**(1): 95–110.

Sonnenfeld, D.A. (2000), 'Contradictions of ecological modernization: pulp and paper manufacturing in Southeast Asia', in A.P.J. Mol and D.A. Sonnenfeld (eds), *Ecological Modernization Around the Globe: New Perspectives and Critical Debates*, London: Frank Cass, pp. 235–56.

Sonnenfeld, D.A. (2002), 'Social movements and ecological modernization: the transformation of pulp and paper manufacturing', *Development and Change*, **33**(1): 1–27.

Sonnenfeld, D.A. and A.P.J. Mol (2006), 'Environmental reform in Asia:

comparisons, challenges, next steps', *Journal of Environment and Development*, **15**(2): pp. 112–37.

Stern, D.I. (2004), 'The rise and fall of the environmental Kuznets curve', *World Development*, **32**(8): 1419–39.

Stern, D.I., M.S. Common and E.B. Barbier (1996), 'Economic growth and environmental degradation: the environmental Kuznets curve and sustainable development', *World Development*, **24**(7): 1151–60.

Streets, D.G., N.Y. Tsai, H. Akimoto and K. Oka (2000), 'Sulfur dioxide emissions in Asia in the period 1985–1997', *Atmospheric Environment*, **34**: 4413–24.

Tran, T.M.D. (2003), 'Greening food industry in Vietnam: putting industrial ecology to work', Ph.D. thesis, Environmental Policy, Wageningen University, the Netherlands.

Tran, T.M.D., P.T. Phung, J.C.L. van Buuren and V.T. Nguyen (2003), 'Environmental management for industrial zones in Vietnam', in A.P.J. Mol and J.C.L. van Buuren (eds), *Greening Industrialization and Asian Transitional Economies: China and Vietnam*, Lanham, MD: Lexington Books, pp. 39–59.

Vincent, J.R., M. Rozali and A.R. Khalid (1997), *Environment and Development in a Resource Rich Economy*, Cambridge, MA: Harvard University Press.

Vincent, J.R., R.M. Ali, with K.A. Rahim (2000), 'Water pollution abatement in Malaysia', in D. Angel and M.T. Rock (eds), *Asia's Clean Revolution: Industry, Growth and the Environment*, Sheffield, UK: Greenleaf, pp. 173–93.

Wallace, D. (1996), *Sustainable Industrialization*, London: Royal Institute of International Affairs/Earthscan.

WCED (World Commission on Environment and Development) (1987), *Our Common Future*, ed. G.H. Brundtland, Oxford, UK: Oxford University Press.

Weale, A. (1992), *The New Politics of Pollution*, Manchester: Manchester University Press.

Wehrmeyer, W. and Y. Mulugetta (eds) (1999), *Growing Pains: Environmental Management in Developing Countries*, Sheffield, UK: Greenleaf.

Weidner, H. (2002), 'Capacity building for ecological modernization: lessons from cross-national research', *American Behavioral Scientist*, **45**(9): 1340–68.

Weinberg, A., D.N. Pellow and A. Schnaiberg (2000), *Urban Recycling and the Search for Sustainable Community Development*, Princeton, NJ: Princeton University Press.

World Bank (1992), *World Development Report 1992: Development and the Environment*, New York: Oxford University Press.

7. Civil society and distributional conflicts in Southeast Asia[1]

Johannes Dragsbaek Schmidt

For too long Western rights advocates have tended to equate social progress with the growth of a welfare state, measuring commitment by gross social spending

FEER, 23 June 1994: 5

There is no such thing as society, only individuals and their families.

Margaret Thatcher, 1987

With the end of the Cold War, civil society together with democracy and the market became the new global denominators for neo-liberal change and more or less a panacea for virtually all the problems in both South and North: 'In the world of ideas, civil society is hot. It is almost impossible to read an article on foreign or domestic policy without coming across some mention of the concept' (Zakaria, 1995). The sentiments of euphoria about civil society were almost omni-present in the new international ideological agenda and in most cases presented as a new type of 'anti-politics': it became part and parcel of the doublespeak intended to impose a mental and ideological colonization of the world by introducing new categories intended to present a harmonious world and depoliticize social change (Bourdieu and Wacquant, 2001: 2–5; Hersh, 2004: 3–19). Aiding in the rise in popularity of civil society was the movement from authoritarian to more democratic regime forms all over the globe. This was observable not only in the former Soviet-type socialist societies, but also in Taiwan, South Korea, Brazil and Central America, and in almost all of sub-Saharan Africa, where unions, women's organizations, student groups and other forms of social and popular activism provided the empirical foundation for stirring accounts of the role played by resurgent and often rebellious civil societies in triggering the demise of many forms of dictatorship.[2] These transformations, in turn, encouraged the rise of the alluring but problematic notion that, if an invigorated civil society could force a

229

democratic transition, it could consolidate democracy as well (Hedman, 2001: 921–51; Encarnaci, 2003), and this gave renewed almost universal prominence to the mainstream view that democratization relying on a strong civil society is good for development and may be a causal factor in its own right.

What does it mean in Southeast Asia? Prominent scholars in the region also hold the rather linear and anti-statist view that 'democracy arises as a direct result of the strength of civil society' (Anek, 1997: 17). Although the authoritarian Suharto regime in Indonesia collapsed in conjunction with the aftermath of the financial crisis in Southeast Asia, it seems that the dictatorship in Myanmar (Burma) and one-party rule in Vietnam and Laos have been experiencing only gradual or virtually no sign of opening up access to other political forces' potential influence on decision making and the political system in general. The region is composed of a diverse mosaic of various types of regimes and might together with China and North Korea be considered one of the last strongholds of non-democratic or illiberal political systems, although with important variations between what some scholars refer to as soft authoritarianism (Singapore, Malaysia and Indonesia) and guided democracy in Thailand or American-style democracy in the Philippines. The overall benchmark of the political evolution and governance of the region in the past two or three decades shows that the situation is fluid and could change tomorrow!

Strong government vested with the responsibility of upholding collective needs, an absence of many liberal democratic practices, and the longevity of traditional and conservative political elites seem to be the norm. Singapore, for example, has been ruled by the People's Action Party since independence, and under the leadership of Lee Kuan Yew between 1959 and 1990. The ruling Golkar party of Indonesia, with the support of the military, won all the elections from 1975 until the Suharto regime was toppled in 1997. A similar longevity of power has been experienced by the United Malays National Organization (UMNO) in Malaysia, and the recruitment of the elite in Thailand has come from the same feudal and royalist networks surrounding the royal family, the Privy Council and King Bhumipol himself. The harsh anti-democratic measures performed by the Thaksin government showed signs of a renewal of autocratic policies,[3] and the mob violence instigated by the middle class and civil society in alliance with the conservative elite against the poor peasants and workers illustrates in a genuine way the hollowness and hypocrisy of the mainstream view in political science that the middle class and civil society are the preconditions for democracy. In fact, Thai politics illuminate that the middle class and civil society can be precursors to autocracy and authoritarian regimes as well.

Even if Southeast Asian societies are legally considered democratic, there has not been complete freedom for opposition parties, freedom of speech, a separation of powers, or civil and political rights.[4] In societies where the emphasis is upon consensus and harmony, especially as an ideologically legitimizing device with reference to economic growth, it has proved possible to deem opposition subversive. Cultural values have been used as a tool to control dissent, and the role of civil society has in many cases been curtailed to marginalization or co-opted for various elite objectives. It has been widely argued by some Asian leaders that economic growth precedes democracy and civil rights, as indeed it did in the West, and these arguments became a platform for agitation against Westernization – meaning social welfare, laziness, social movements and trade unions, but interestingly to a lesser degree against right-wing illiberal agents from civil society.

The rhetoric about Asian values,[5] which temporarily seemed to fade away in the aftermath of the 1997 financial crisis, is being recycled to legitimize authoritarian tendencies, for instance in relation to the so-called war on terror. The former prime minister of Malaysia, Mahathir, referred in 1996 to the debate being defensive in nature, and then actually reinforced it by declaring: 'It was right and about time that Asia too was accorded the regard and high esteem that was its due.' He went on to say 'that there was a belief among many in the West that their values and beliefs were universal; that the advocates and champions of Asian values were merely justifying oppression, dictatorship and uncivilized behaviour'.[6] This was reinforced in late summer 2001 with reference to the infamous Internal Security Act (ISA), when the Malaysian police arrested ten members of the Kumpulan Mujahiddeen Malaysia (KMM). They were accused of having links to the Taliban regime in Afghanistan and to have connections in Ambon, Indonesia, where they were said to be fighting with local militants. 'The fact that six of the detainees were also members of PAS was utilized as evidence against the biggest opposition party, in an attempt to unveil its hidden and subversive political agenda.'[7]

However, 'the people whose political and other rights are involved in this debate are not citizens of the West, but of Asian countries. The fact that individual liberty may have been championed in Western writings, and even by some Western political leaders, can scarcely compromise the claim to liberty that people in Asia may otherwise possess' (Sen, 1997; Robison, 1999; Rodan, 1999). What is important here is the strange alliance between the supporters of Asian values and conservatives in the West, which implies a convergence between the illiberal social agenda of the post-Washington consensus and the specific type of benevolent autocracy which seemingly has been reinvented as a response to 'terror'. The re-emergence of authoritarian practices in the region might prove to have serious consequences for progressive NGOs and labour and social movements which challenge the status quo and the hegemony of traditional elites.

This contribution examines the debate about civil society in a comparative political economy perspective (Cox, 2000; Schmidt and Hersh, 2000; Underhill, 2000). Its main approach relies on two inspirations. One is the famous assertion by Karl Polanyi that markets do not evolve organically but are instead the creations of vested interests (Polanyi, 1944; Strange, 2000: 82). Another is the dictum by Karl Marx, 'that free competition is the final form of the development of productive forces, and thus of human freedom, means only that the domination of the middle class is the end of the world's history – of course a quite pleasant thought for yesterday's parvenus' (Marx, 1970 edn; cf. Gills, 2000: 52). The first section of the chapter focuses on the competing theoretical definitions and assumptions about civil society, democratization and social change; the second section explores the attempts by civil society actors to affect conflicts over resources and distribution of welfare in Southeast Asia; the third section focuses on the conflictual relationship between civil society organizations (CSOs)[8] and the state and various types of social and labour market regulations, laws and contractual relationships; and finally the need for progressive social reform is emphasized as one important type of social resistance against the downsizing of the social and public sector's provision of collective goods.

LINKING CIVIL SOCIETY, DEMOCRATIZATION AND SOCIAL CHANGE

Civil society and democratization are often presented by liberal theorists as a separate positive category opposing dictatorship and protectionist markets. However, the distinction of state, market and civil society is implausible. The market is constructed and constrained by the state and the civil society. The state is a reflection of both the market and the civil society. And the civil society is defined by the state and the market. One cannot separate these three modes of expression of actors' interests, preferences, identities and wills into closed arenas in which different groups of people will make scientific statements. There are no clear demarcations between the three analytical categories. On the contrary there are clear overlaps, and it is in the borderlands between the three that conflict occurs.

However, the concepts of civil society and democratization are also the history of social meaning in practice. It has been the history of social invention, both at a scholarly level and in practice, of the twin concepts as a continual process and of the modification over time of what civil society and democratization mean. In some cases ideas about civil society are being used for specific goals, as clearly demonstrated in the post-Cold War anti-politics device accomplished by the international financial institutions (IFIs) and the Washington consensus (Wade, 2002), but also by the launching of the anti-globalization movement, where there have been tendencies to lump together all segments of society and organizations into one category as long as they resist globalization.

Scholars differ considerably in their assessments and ideas of the forms and extent of civil society's influence in politics and economic policy-making, but it is clear that in one way or another civil society matters. They also seem to differ in their conceptualizations and theorizing about the location of civil society in broader social analysis and how to define and distinguish civil society from market-based actors and state-related institutions.

To be sure, confusion about the precise meaning of civil society is part of the allure and lore of the concept's long history (Mouzelis 1994, 1995; Fine and Rai, 1997). Over the years, philosophers as diverse as Ferguson, Tocqueville and Gramsci have appropriated the concept of civil society to articulate particular points of view about the relationship between state and society (Encarnaci, 2003). It is possible to trace its origins back to the philosophical writings of political economists like Locke and Hegel and also more contemporary scholars like Gellner and Habermas.

It has been suggested that present-day thought on civil society should be divided into four competing views: the associational school, the regime school, the neo-liberal school and the post-Marxist school (Hyden, 1997: 8–13).

The associational school's definition of civil society refers to 'that arena where manifold social movements . . . and civic organizations from all classes . . . attempt to constitute themselves in an ensemble of arrangements so that they can express themselves and advance their interests' (Stepan, 1988: 3–4). This is inspired by Tocqueville, as it indicates a growing consensus among scholars about civil society as part of democratization but also understood as a conflictual process. The definition also deviates from the classical liberal notion by either assuming or hiding that civil society is a highly politicized space occupied by actors from all social classes. 'The gulf that separates classical liberal and modern notions of civil society suggests that one must make choices in defining and deploying the term, especially when it comes to integrating it into actual policy making' (Levin, 1995).

Critics from the regime school who draw inspiration from Locke and the neo-liberal angle, however, making civil society synonymous only with moralizing civilized organizations, debate the concept by stripping it of its analytical utility. Equating civil society with high-minded groups renders the concept a theological notion, not an analytical category. Against this background the concept might potentially include the mafia, the triads and semi-fascist movements, who then would belong to civil society, since they also claim to advance citizens' values. To further complicate the picture we could also include: tribal and kinship groups, name groups (as with the Chinese), guru-oriented groups and traditional secret societies (Judge, 1997: 124–32). Take also a number of Islamic groups who reject the rule of law and support violence,[9] or the movement that supported former President Estrada's return to power in Manila by trying to take over the Malacanang presidential palace, unmasking 'the dark side, the dark twin' of the much-vaunted Philippine-style 'people power' which had earlier inspired democratic political movements around the world. The protests, which some analysts say brought the Philippines to the brink of civil war, prompted Arroyo on 1 May 2001 to declare a 'state of rebellion' (Sison, 2001).

Against this background it seems that both liberal and conservative writers on civil society who see civil society as a non-political zone of social intercourse based in the free market and dominated by the bourgeoisie have failed to provide an adequate account of how poverty and the welfare state affect civic and political engagement, and their argument that economic freedom automatically produces democracy and prosperity has not been empirically verified. The experience from East and Southeast Asia suggests that a weak civil society in many cases was a precondition for the insulated developmental state and the concomitant high economic growth. The neo-liberal version of civil society, and social capital for that matter, fails to address properly either capital or the social, and it tends to set aside issues of power and conflict (Fine, 2001: 136–54). There is furthermore a tendency in the literature to romanticize civil society as the ideal on behalf of its counterpart the state, and this relationship is often presented as a zero-sum game (Guan, 2004).

The problems inherent in post-Marxist notions of civil society are not that different from the critique of the neo-liberal theorists. Many scholars have tended to see economic growth and development as a precondition for a vibrant civil society and democracy. There are significant exceptions in the writings of Gramsci, who introduced the concept of hegemony and who saw civil society as a sphere occupied by struggle for material, ideological and cultural control over all of society, including the state. Therefore passive or moral resistance becomes an inherent part of civil society's battle for and against capitalism. What matters is ideology, power and political and legal institutions.

It leaves us with a number of interesting conclusions. First of all, whatever the relationship between democratization and civil society it remains a contextual and empirical issue to judge its potential impact on the polity and also whether it might be able to mobilize resources that the state is unable to do. Second, it can co-exist with authoritarian state structures and also can or cannot be an impediment for the development of markets. Third, the 'global demand for democratization' emanating from progressive parts of civil society is an inescapable part of popular discourses and not a specific European phenomenon or invention exported by the West. This popular demand for citizens' rights is not only related to the state and its institutions, nor is it simply a demand for the rights to organize in trade unions or to strike, or a matter of gender equality, but part of a global discursive process directed towards a more egalitarian distribution of resources (Schmidt, 2000a: 158–77). It is: 'the organized efforts to increase control over resources and regulative institutions on the part of groups and movements of those hitherto excluded from such control' (Wolfe, 1982) and '[a] belief that democratic ideas and practices can only in the long run be protected if their hold on our political, social and economic life is deepened' (Held, 1987: 4). Fourth, the question about civil society and democratization is related not only to national citizens or civil rights, but also to the question about autonomous political representation. In the end, this cannot be reduced to a purely legalistic issue, although as will be shown below civil society is always legally sanctioned by the state, but must be put in conjunction with the legitimacy devoted to the rights of civil society organizations to engage in political activity.

Throughout history 'the present almost universal and inclusionary concept of citizens' rights was only brought about through pressure and agitation by and on behalf of those who were initially excluded or marginalized from the territorial political community' (Whitehead, 1997: 95). Therefore efforts at social 'levelling' will be met with stiff resistance, even if attempted through democratic institutions. This is the theme of one seminal work on the ebb and flow of political opposition in Southeast Asia. The authors are clear about the Left as a force which has been significant in 'giving much momentum to the development of non-state political space' (Hewison and Rodan, 1994, 1996: 236). They furthermore make the important point that civil society is not a new phenomenon but rather a historical product of political struggles mainly performed by leftist forces which were curtailed or blocked through the actions of repressive governments and military force.

The following attempt to link these observations with Jayasuriya and

Hewison's discussion about the new social policy of the post-Washington consensus deliberately 'uses the liberal language of participation and empowerment as a strategy of "anti-politics" that marginalises political contestation. Unlike earlier governance programmes identified with structural adjustment, this new governance discourse envisages a more active role for the state as a regulator for civil society seeking to promote the disciplines of the market.' With examples from the aftermath of the financial crisis in Thailand, the maintenance approach developed by the IFIs was to devote a specific and strengthened role to civil society organizations and the ideological imperative as the pre-eminent measure to ameliorate the social impacts of crisis, along with 'flexible' labour markets (Jayasuriya and Hewison, 2004: 1–2, 9). It leaves us with the important question of whether civil society is undermining the key functions and social responsibilities of the state in terms of delivering public collective goods. The fact that the IFIs' policy of dumping social services on to voluntary organizations means they should take over the work without a corresponding transfer of funding and the development of a mutual relationship with the state denotes a peculiar situation almost without any corresponding elaboration in theory (Van Rooy and Robinson, 1998: 41–2).

These issues lead to the challenge of examining the intricate links between civil society, democratization and attempts to affect existing socioeconomic policies on privatization of social sectors and deregulation of labour markets in Southeast Asia. In addition, the chapter investigates the links between labour and civil society understood as the competing interests at stake and the coalescence of social forces forming around policy-making. In the end it is a struggle over societal control over resources as they are performed by 'the locus of range of inequalities based on class, gender, ethnicity, race, and sexual preference' (Rodan, 1996: 22).

CIVIL SOCIETY AND ITS IMPACT ON SOCIO-ECONOMIC POLICY-MAKING

It is not easy to encompass all of Southeast Asia, as the region is extremely heterogeneous, in terms of its historical evolution, its geographical size (ranging from a small city-state to the fourth most populous country in the world), its historical perspective and accordingly each country's colonial legacy, and not least its concomitant composition of the relationships between the state and civil society. Likewise, economic parameters denote a very diversified picture in terms of the region having a country belonging to OECD standards to some of the poorest societies in the world.

As a result of the reliance on export orientation for several decades, the incorporation into the world market of capitalist countries in Southeast Asia has been extremely rapid, although the 1997 financial crisis clearly illustrated the vulnerability of heavy dependency on external markets, actors and institutions. Together with the expansion of increasingly complex social structures, the region has also experienced profound social inequalities, uneven development and poverty, which increased to such an extent that there are both external and domestic pressures on the political system and economic policy makers to take action.[10]

As noted in Chapter 1, the historical role for academia, critical theory and sociology in the region did not play a decisive role in terms of the radicalization of social movements up to the 1960s, when the Left and social democratic forces finally were eliminated in tandem with the end of the Vietnam War and the influence of anti-communist laws and repression. The emergence of CSOs in the 1980s and 1990s should be understood in light of the end of the Cold War and the de-radicalization of the Left. Subsequently civil society in non-socialist Southeast Asia is a product of and a response to the decline of the old Left and the student movement and the dissolution of 'real-existing socialism'. This way, civil society should be seen as filling the gap where weak, repressed and co-opted social movements and trade unions have been unable to gain major victories in terms of influencing the policy-making process or gaining from distributional conflicts. This highlights the necessity of focusing on distributional issues and the links between formal unionism and labour activism on the one hand and CSOs on the other. Conflict and control over resources, not only environmental, but also agrarian change and land ownership, are linked to injustice and political and human rights, which are also closely related to democratization and recently the so-called war on terror. This leads to an examination of how identity politics, ideology, ethnicity and gender-related issues shape the new emerging NGOs and other movements and class representation in civil society in the Southeast Asian region.

That there is a close relationship between the role of academia, intellectuals and the radicalization of students, and the organization of civil society makes it necessary to do a brief historical detour to explain the views of the scholarly community and critical studies on social change and civil society. The middle class, especially its intellectual and educated strata, has privileged access to the institutional bases of civil society and mobilization of popular forces in democratization, which makes it necessary to understand their role (Hirsch and Warren, 1998: 19; Hutchison and Brown, 2001: 13).

In his seminal work on the role of sociology understood as the description, analysis and understanding of social relations, King notes that, compared to that of other regions of the world, sociology in Southeast

Asia has not in historical perspective been particularly extensive or distinguished (King, 1996: 148). Also Taylor and Turton note that the region is of utmost importance and is socially complex, yet local contributions have lacked in their broader horizon and explanations (Taylor and Turton, 1988).

Although the reasons might be pretty straightforward, as King mentions, war and conflict in Indo-China and Myanmar have limited access for foreign scholars, and critical studies were almost non-existent until recently, when slowly it has become possible to gather data and do field work and collect empirical information. But also, in capitalist Southeast Asian countries, we had to wait until a few decades ago before critical commentary entered the agenda (Higgott and Robison, 1985); indeed radicalism and critical thinking only took shape in the aftermath of communism at the end of the 1970s and beginning of the 1980s (Anderson, 1993).

As one of the mavericks of Southeast Asian studies noted in 1995, 'It is a curious phenomenon, by no means limited to Southeast Asia, that as a system becomes successful and entrenched it also becomes more subject to question' (McVey, 1995: 7). This was exactly what happened as the situation changed considerably in the 1970s and 1980s when there was a virtual explosion in the expansion and diversification of civil society, and also the academic community became vigorous and engaged in terms of taking the initiative and supporting the rise of new social movements and NGOs.

> They are almost always based on educated and very often on university-connected cadres. These NGOs have generally aimed at establishing or supporting moral communities whose boundaries do not mirror those of the state apparatus, which is seen as a source of repression rather than the font of legitimacy. At one level, this is part of a transnational movement away from faith in the state, which is no longer seen as willing or able to safeguard basic social and economic concerns (as well of course, as a loss of faith in political parties as a source of remedy). At another level, the emergence of NGOs is a response to the failure of Southeast Asian states to dominate the vast changes over which they preside, and in particular to adjust to the rapid expansion and changing priorities of the middle classes. The current appreciation of the virtues of private over public ownership reflects the same attitude, however different its social sympathies may be.
>
> McVey, 1995: 37

Especially after the financial crisis, there are clear tendencies that social movements and NGOs have attempted to re-create an independent political space outside the reach of the state entities as an attempt to gain autonomy and create new alliances among social actors, with the sole purpose of confronting the elite-based political and economic systems. In connection to this it is important to stress that the old Left did have a relatively strong intellectual base among students and scholars, and did receive moral and ideological support, and in many cases they even participated in the armed struggle, but there was a lack of pertinent and critical scholarship on a larger scale.

One of the implications of this discussion is that 'the historical evidence contradicts the assumption that the development of civil society in capitalist societies is a progressive and incremental outcome of economic growth. Rather, civil society has ebbed and flowed in the region throughout this century' (Hewison and Rodan, 1996: 253). A similar proposition is raised by Deyo in his attempts to examine the role of working-class organizations in historical perspective. Labour influence on economic politics, at least in Thailand, was more important up to new political reforms and less influential in the institutionalization phase (Schmidt, 1996: 63–81; Deyo, 1997, 2000).

That there are links between trade unions and civil society illustrates the point made above about the blurring of lines between state, market and society. There are incidences where labour in conjunction with CSOs, even under authoritarian regimes, has been able to influence policy-making and implementation, 'in many cases through community-based political mobilization only loosely linked to trade unionism. Labour's oppositional potential became especially evident during interludes of political crisis and government transition' (Deyo, 1997: 207–8).

Although they share a sceptical view of civil society, Hutchison and Brown (2001) do ask the potent question: 'What effects does the NGO involvement in the labour arena have on workers' capacities to self-organise in the region?'[11] The answer varies from country to country, but in Indonesia NGOs can act outside the legal constraints applied to trade unions through legal advice, training and funding. What is of interest, however, is the involvement of international NGOs, social movements and trade unions, which in a number of cases have had a determining impact on issues related to labour in Southeast Asia. In the Philippines the KMU social movement unionism has made attempts to articulate commitment beyond narrow workers' interests and devote attention toward social change at the societal level. This has been done through alliances with other sectors of society and international solidarity networks and touched upon a whole series of issues, from campaigning against US bases to resistance against the World Bank and the IMF conditionalities on Filipino economic policy-making, and strikes against the accompanying privatization and deregulation measures. It is safe to say that, 'while not all NGOs are politically radical, in Southeast Asia, many have experienced a degree of radicalization' (Hewison and Rodan, 1996: 256).

In the years after the financial crisis there are several examples of collaboration between labour and popular sector groups in Thailand. In the private sector, blue-collar workers have been able to obtain agreements with the Ministry of Labour and Social Welfare for redundant workers and improved severance pay legislation under the Labour Protection Act. Accordingly, as the consequences of the crisis unfolded, NGOs and academics have played an important role in agitating for improved health and safety regulations, especially for female workers. 'In part too, academics and NGOs have helped to consolidate a more unified opposition to reforms, denationalization, and austerity. A case in point was the United Front to Return Privatization to the People to evoke a referendum on the Enterprise Corporations Act' (Deyo, 2000: 6). There are also many examples of successful campaigns, at least indirectly, with external partners such as the ILO and INGOs, but in other cases there have been major disagreements on political vision and interests, for instance with regard to the issue of migrant labour where the NGOs traditionally uphold a supportive role while trade unions tend to see migrants as threats to wages and jobs.

In this way, there is a tendency showing that the political influence of labour in the region has been and is still dependent on cross-sectional support in civil society. For instance, in Thailand it was primarily community activists who lobbied for improved health and safety regulations at the workplace after the tragic fire at the Khader factory in 1995 where 188 workers lost their lives (Brown, 2001: 132–3). One explanation for this is the weak level of labour organization and that civil society is able to get access to the media or collaborate with foreign NGOs and thereby create pressure on the government while trade unions are constrained by strict laws and regulations.

In-house unionism in Malaysia, strongly encouraged by the Malay government, has not led to democratization of labour legislation, but nevertheless in some cases workers in firms with in-house unions have enjoyed better work conditions than workers organized in national unions (Rasiah, 2001: 95, 104). The most important aspect of the popular sectors' interest in labour issues has been attempts to provide protection for migrant labour. There have been joint campaigns between the MTUC and several NGOs for a minimum wage, but as with the Thai situation there are significant disagreements as well. There are instances where the trade unions have argued against the government's policy of keeping the door open for migrants, who number approximately one million mainly Indonesian workers, while NGOs are more supportive.

After years of human rights abuses and widespread corruption during the time of the Suharto government, Indonesian unions are now playing a more active role. A diverse number of 67 independent national unions and NGOs across Indonesia launched a campaign to promote the ILO

Declaration on Fundamental Principles and Rights at Work. At the national level, the trade union agenda has been dominated by the issue of law reform. More important than legislation is the ability of workers and their organizations to ensure that legislation is enforced. This is in a country where the 1997 GNP contracted by 50 per cent and where all sorts of communal violence erupted in the aftermath of the crisis. About 100 million people were scaled back into third world level poverty after being drawn out of it during 30 years of growth. Furthermore the democratic transitions have been controlled by the middle class and elite, opening space for the collaboration and influence of civil society and the labour movement.

The instances of full trade union rights have yet to be realized, as most countries have not yet ratified the core conventions of the ILO. In the guise of so-called labour market flexibility, the security of the livelihood of workers is being threatened through contractualization, sub-contracting, informalization and other innovations in working arrangements, such as work sharing, individualized production quota and incentives systems, and rotating contracts. Of all Southeast Asia, only the Philippines, Myanmar and Indonesia ratified ILO Convention No. 87, which respects the right to self-organization. ILO Convention No. 98, which provides for the right to collective bargaining, was ratified only by the Philippines, Indonesia, Malaysia and Singapore. Even as these ILO conventions are ratified, the labour legislation is inadequate and in most cases circumvented to promote the interest of employers and the governments as well.

The role of civil society in terms of influencing social issues has, as illustrated above, in many cases led to increased social control. Labour and independent trade unions' attempts to increase the proportion of collective goods for the benefit of workers and the poor have been met with outright suspicion at best, but worse they have also led to repression or more sophisticated types of inclusion. The situation in 2009 is not very different from that of the mid-1990s, when: 'The institutionalized incorporation of labour into the structures of the state is now well advanced throughout the region, and the existence of independent labour organizations is everywhere threatened' (Hewison and Rodan, 1996: 255). Not only is the weak collective bargaining strength of the labour movements a consequence of political restraint, but these controls are 'natural' requirements of the heavy reliance on export orientation (EOI) and the neo-liberal downsizing of the public sector all over the region.

Labour has had some success in campaigning against economic liberalization and privatization, especially at the beginning of the 1980s in Thailand and the Philippines, although the latter case compares more with Latin America, where developmental sequencing resulted in a shift from corporatism to non-unionized labour markets. The 1997 financial crisis also acted as a catalyst for renewed attempts to increase social insurance programmes and other benefits for workers and the poor. However, social coverage in the region is still well below the level predicted by the region's better-off countries' GDP per capita, urbanization rate and development of the formal sector. Unemployment insurance is virtually absent (Cornia, 2001: 3). The only country which differs from this is Malaysia, where social coverage is broader and more diversified compared to the other countries, but this is not because of pressures from trade unions and NGOs but rather part of UMNO's strategy.

The reasons are well known. The race-to-the-bottom thesis indicates that global competition and especially competition from low-wage countries in China, Cambodia and Vietnam, together with the new social policy of the IFIs, led to the introduction of flexible labour markets, but without government investment in collective goods like training, R&D, physical infrastructure and social insurance. Lack of effective government support for minimal labour standards, adequate wages and benefits and fair employment practices encourages companies to compete through labour-cost reduction and union avoidance.[12] Static flexibility ensures the existence of a floating workforce, and labour market deregulation has in this way become a more effective policy than direct repression to avoid labour unrest and grievances regarding social welfare benefits from the public sphere.

Now to turn briefly to the role of advocacy groups, it is probably not a coincidence that, until the September 11, 2001 incident, US development aid had gone primarily to this sector. USAID's main focus has been on advocacy NGOs, less on other parts of civil society, such as religious organizations, labour unions, social and cultural groups, associations based on identity (such as clan or ethnic associations), or service delivery NGOs. Perhaps most insightful is USAID's uncritical romance with the 'benevolent Tocquevillean vision' of civil society as an idealized, inordinately American perspective that is not widely shared even in other Western democracies: a civil society characterized by 'the earnest articulation of interests by legions of well-mannered activists who play by the rules, settle conflicts peacefully, and do not break any windows' (Carothers, 1999; cf. Baron, 2002).

This kind of 'transnational benevolence' is where NGOs advocate 'greater public accountability and transparency in government who seek to eradicate official corruption and other obstacles to a modern, efficient capitalist economy' (Rodan, 1996: 7). Even business can benefit from the existence of advocacy groups, since it at least indirectly legitimizes their entry into politics. 'The structurally rooted elimination of labour from democratic politics under regimes of "exclusionary democracy" has enhanced the usefulness to business of parliamentary institutions, thus creating a critical political base for those institutions' (Deyo, 1997: 221).

On the other hand, the environmental NGOs in Southeast Asia have been greatly strengthened and have been able to gain major victories in a number of important cases (Mitchell, 1998: 84). Together with rapid industrialization, competition for the rural resource base and the decline in agrarian unrest, the region has opened up spaces for political activity and expression among the 'hitherto excluded' (Turton, 1987). During the past few decades, environmentally inspired NGOs and people's organizations in Thailand have been active in political movements, were a major force together with workers in the opposition to the Suchinda military junta in 1992 (Amara and Nitaya, 1997: 173; Schmidt, 2000a: 158–77) and formed the backbone in the initial phases of Thaksin's successful Thai Rak Thai movement and its populist support for the rural masses. Institutional bases of a transnational environmentalism have multiplied in the region and in Indonesia, Thailand, Malaysia and the Philippines they have mushroomed and diversified in character.

The anti-large-dam movements in Indonesia and Thailand have conducted fierce resistance together with national and transnational NGOs and local inhabitants in Kedungombo against the dams built or supposed to be constructed in the Mekong river delta. Resistance has been rooted in the soil of material struggles over the means of livelihood (Hirsch and Warren, 1998).

NGOs along ethnic and religious lines have also emerged. As described in Hirsch and Warren (1998), examples are legion all over the region, where loggers or the state in the name of nation-building threatens the livelihoods of indigenous people. The Dayak forest-dwellers in Sarawak and in Mindanao, the Philippines are cases in point, where the internationalization of civil societies has blossomed with INGOs' direct intervention and collaboration with indigenous groups. This has also happened in Laos and Vietnam, where it is the impact of INGOs that has stimulated debate and public discourse over various contentious issues. In the Philippines, basic Christian community movements seek to establish a self-sustaining economy based on local agriculture and supported by local industry, and in Thailand Buddhist-based movements have established CSOs working for self-reliance and self-sufficiency and have in some cases had a direct influence on Thai politics.

A final aspect concerns the diasporic Chinese communities in Thailand, the Philippines, Malaysia and Indonesia. They have established Rotary and Lions clubs which are almost exclusively ethnic Chinese. Together with clan associations they exert a tremendous influence on economic policy-making, and in some cases they have determined the outcome of national elections (Callahan, 2003: 502–03, 506).

The ideological underpinnings of broadening involvement range from notions of social justice to various middle-class-based movements, and in some cases, especially in Thailand, Indonesia and the Philippines religious symbols and representations serve as a focal point not only for environmental NGOs but also for ethnic and religious CSOs.

STRUCTURE OF THE LEGAL FRAMEWORK

As suggested in the previous sections, governments have traditionally exerted strong legal controls over the establishment and oversight of NGOs in the region. Statist law is still the dominant mode of control and management of civil society. Managerial and regulated rules mean that actors in civil society are not autonomous but are both in and out of the state, 'and therefore, it may be said that the state manages civil society. The key to understanding the emergence of this managerial civil society is seen in the vertical linkages between state and other civil actors' (Jayasuriya, 1999: 18). With the important exception of the Philippines, the state has been able to exclude those who are considered unacceptable, but, as illustrated above, a new type of socio-economic regulation has emerged where the state virtually delegates power and competence to NGOs and thus produces 'an organizational hybrid of state and civil society' (White, 1996; cf. Jayasuriya, 1999: 18).

East and Southeast Asian regimes have been characterized by having 'their qualities of governance in common irrespective of motley constitutional characteristics. Whatever regime title, whatever the legal structures, whatever the voting arrangements if any, whatever citizen rights might be formally laid down, all have in practice functioned as exercises in "top down consensus" by persuasion and/or imposition' (Jones, 1993: 203). In practice it means that the question about either co-optation or exclusion of CSOs by governments cannot be overestimated either historically or in the present period. In comparison, and in parallel with basically the same reasons, this is illustrated by the low level of organized labour unions, which have been either excluded from policy-making by the state, as in Malaysia, Indonesia and Thailand, or incorporated into the state and party realm, as in Singapore, Vietnam, Laos, Cambodia and Myanmar (Frenkel, 1993: 310–20). The situation in the Philippines differs from that of the rest of the region in the sense that legislation has been more liberal, especially after the ousting of the Marcos regime, and there has been more political space for autonomous action and organization (Hutchison, 2001: 71–89).

The legal and fiscal environment in which labour and civil society operate varies greatly between countries in the region. In recent years, the governments of the Philippines and Thailand have moved toward creating a more supportive or, in the latter case, inclusionary environment. This means that, in the Philippines, CSOs in some instances have been able to influence public policy, partner with government in the implementation of development programmes and design a system for the self-regulation of the sector. CSOs in Indonesia, Malaysia and Singapore, in comparison, have been subject to close supervision and guidance by the state. This has limited the scope of their actions (Winder, 1998), but changed in Indonesia after the 1997 crisis, when CSOs virtually exploded and became more politicized. The military regime in Myanmar crushed the re-emergence of civil society in March 1988, when a spontaneous protest against perceived injustice erupted into a popular upsurge against authoritarianism during the next four months. The ban on independent unions and political organizations was breached, and this was followed by a plethora of student unions, trade unions, associations, and class and mass organizations (Than, 1997: 185). It ended in September 1997 with a military coup and a return to repression and later on the brutal clampdown on the Buddhist monk-led uprising in Rangoon in 2007.

Today there are more than 500 NGOs in Cambodia, including six major human rights NGOs. They are responsible for dispersing more than 50 per cent of technical assistance from external donors and have in many cases taken on quasi-government functions. It illustrates that the regional borderline between what are state and public sector responsibilities and what is the prerogative of private institutions is at best blurred.

The weakness of CSOs in Laos and Vietnam is a function less of state repression and more because of the events that have enveloped the historical trajectories of these countries. The national project for consolidating society is now focused on rebuilding the polity and economy after years of war and violence. The state rebuilding policies in these countries have led to the adoption of reformist policies as well as the emerging important role of external donors. In Vietnam, civil society is re-emerging and, while the state has attempted to limit its growth, there is evidence that it is not very successful. In Laos, there are strong community structures but no legal framework that enables the registration of CSOs.

In Myanmar and Laos, INGOs are collaborating with local development CSOs in poverty alleviation programmes aimed at increasing food production and improving health and education. These transnational organizations are also involved in strengthening the capacity of local organizations and micro-credit projects. No legislation exists, and the relationship between the NGOs, the development CSOs and the state is unclear.

This is further exacerbated, because the majority of CSOs in the region rely on external funding for their activities. The former prime minister in Thailand, Thaksin, for instance, tried to discourage foreign donors from funding civil society (*The Nation*, 10 May 2002). This move was reportedly blocked by the Ministry of Foreign Affairs officials, and in the end the government did not attempt to dissuade foreign donors. Amnesty International was concerned that these government statements about NGOs could be construed as veiled threats against their legitimate peaceful activities.

On the other hand, as this chapter has suggested, trends towards lessening of controls are occurring at least superficially, although occasionally CSOs are accused of fifth-column activities, sometimes with reference to their links with transnational forces, which in many cases are determining their activities. There are very large numbers of CSOs in the Philippines, Thailand and especially Indonesia, which lost their funding from US and Australian donors, who shifted aid to terror-related activities overnight and to funding of conflict prevention, human security projects and the like.

Under section 88 of the Corporation Code of the Philippines, non-stock (not-for-profit) corporations may be formed. Although a plethora of informal organizations exist, they do not have full legal status. A not-for-profit corporation is the only type of legal entity permitted as a CSO in the Philippines.

Much of the legal framework for CSOs in Vietnam is in regulations or administrative practice and not in laws. The 1957 Law on Association and the later Civil Code (1996) regulate the sector with scant detail. The Civil Code recognizes three types of entities: social and socio-professional organizations; social and charitable funds; and other organizations. In the main, these are closely connected with the Party or with mass organizations, such as the Vietnam Women's Association.

In Thailand, the National Police Office Bureau has responsibility for establishment and oversight of associations, and the Ministry of the Interior has responsibility for foundations under the Civil and Commercial Code established in 1992. One ministry, the Cultural Commission, oversees and approves the substantive activities of CSOs, and another agency, the Ministry of the Interior or the National Police Office Bureau, regulates all other aspects of their activity. At the beginning of 2002, Thai NGOs tried to work with the Thaksin government to devise a new and more appropriate set of regulations for the sector, but after various attempts Thai civil society is still as of 2009 under a double pressure from both the government and right-wing forces within civil society itself. The paradox seems to be that conservative and even anti-democratic forces within civil society have been successful in pressurizing various governments to step down and create more space for unelected forces in Thai politics.

Throughout the region, governments retain the right to dissolve CSOs and foundations for vague and politically determined reasons, such as 'operating against the interests of the state' (Vietnam), 'for being managed in a manner contrary to public order, good morals, or the security of the state' (Thailand), or 'being used for purposes prejudicial to public peace, welfare, or good order' (Singapore) (Baron, 2002).

This means that regulation of both associations and foundations has been highly subject to government discretion. In a recent survey, the major problems with the general legal framework for CSOs in Southeast Asia (except in the Philippines) are the following (Simon, 2002):

- Dual authority for establishment and oversight, which results in: (a) excessive government control over which types of NGOs are permitted to exist (resulting in the virtual exclusion of advocacy organizations in many cases); and (b) excessive bureaucracy for NGOs seeking to carry out their activities.
- Intrusive regulation and administrative discretion, which results in: (a) arbitrary treatment of NGOs that seek to carry out activities that the government does not like; and (b) lack of independence for NGOs.

Gradually, however, this situation is changing. The lack of a requirement for permission from a relevant ministry in the Yayasan law in Indonesia seems clearly preferable to a mandatory two-track system. In addition, the initial negotiations between government and NGO leaders in Thailand indicated that governments are beginning to listen to NGO representatives about the need for legal reform that will allow the sector to operate more freely (Simon, 2002). This is contradicted by several commentators who see 'intellectuals' close to the state who "eat" oppositional forces by appropriating, influencing and developing potentially progressive ideas in order to sideline radical projects and reconstruct national ideology' (Connors, 2003: 1). Suddenly the term 'civil society' is everywhere in government plans, in journals of line ministries and even in quasi-NGOs which act more or less on behalf of the state. In tandem with the heavy involvement of the IMF and the World Bank in Thai planning and economic policy-making, the state has changed its vocabulary and discourse by now officially relying on Good Governance, including 'people's participation' and social policy. Suddenly, CSOs have become instruments through which national development should be implemented through partnership and potential co-optation. This is essentially the anti-politics agenda, where the IFIs and the Washington consensus appropriate discourses on participation, empowerment, social capital and civil society and redefine them into their own discourse and interest. What we have seen in Thai policy-making is a spill-over effect of the anti-politics agenda by the establishment of a new social contract which initially was supported by progressives and labour. 'The new social contract involves the protection of domestic capital by the government of the remaining rich, while delivering increased social protection to the poor' (Hewison, 2004: 13). Some elements of the contractual relationship between the former Thaksin government, continued by the present Abhisit government, and the poor were housing projects, loans for the poor, and the 30-baht health scheme to go to hospital if people were not covered by private insurance. It turned out to be expensive to implement, with the consequence that the government merged the scheme with other programmes, such as the Workers' Compensation and Social Security funds, which led to major protests by workers, but in reality it was a very modest percentage of the government's budget.

The limited and circumscribed nature of civil society in East and Southeast Asia has meant that private law plays a less significant role than in Western Europe. The circumscribed role of private law has meant that law has been identified with the operation of public law, and the consequence is 'that law is associated with the extension and management of state power rather than providing a framework for private contractual relationships', that is, a statist form of legalism (Jayasuriya, 1996: 93).

Even though the enabling environment for 'giving' and benevolence has improved in some countries in Southeast Asia in recent years, a culture of giving to organizations beyond religious institutions is little developed. What's more, with tax avoidance still a problem in most countries, tax incentives do little to influence the decisions of the wealthy on their philanthropic contributions.

In the end, civil society groups are neither fully understood nor entirely trusted by the government and business sectors in Southeast Asia. There is a challenge as yet unmet by civil society to strengthen public understanding and acceptance of CSOs and their roles in society. In Indonesia, foundations are still figuring out how best to position themselves given that the term 'Yayasan' became somewhat tainted in the public's eyes under the rule of Suharto, who, along with his family and cronies, was accused of using foundations to launder money (Amott, 2003–04).

It appears that the liberal dictum of law and legalism requires a liberal state and an autonomous civil society, which is on the defensive at the time of writing also at the regional level. One scholar notes that, 'Civil society in Southeast Asia serves the dual purpose of providing logic for resistance in the face of the onslaught of the state, or logic for coping in the face of its absence or neglect' (Contreras, 2002: 3). Also, at the regional institutional level there is scepticism toward civil society, as can be seen by the lack of reference to CSOs and institutions by ASEAN in its declarations and statements. The guidelines for achieving accreditation are limited, and the parameters for consultation and participation available to civil society are restricted.[13] Again the Philippines tend to have an advanced approach, as seen in the suggestion in 2000 of key civil society spokespersons to reinvigorate ASEAN with a social dimension. Whether this will lead to a more equal relationship at the regional level remains to be seen, but the vibrant, active and dedicated regional civil society networks have been able to push forward a People's Charter but were not consulted when the ASEAN Charter was changed in 2007 to promote, protect and respect human rights and to establish a regional human rights body.

EMERGING RESISTANCE FOR SOCIAL REFORM

Some of the key findings of this chapter are related to the new strategies of anti-politics originally developed by the IFIs in an attempt to appropriate progressive concepts and sensitive political projects. The meaning of privatization of social policy management is to remove functions traditionally performed by the state, placing them in the private sphere. The World Bank and the IMF have co-opted the language of progressive civil society and locked it inside the neo-liberal discourse as a strategic move against the current, which consists of the vocal and powerful anti-globalization movement which many progressive Southeast Asian civil society organizations identify with. On the other hand, the 1997 and 2008 financial crises are challenging the hegemony of neo-liberal globalization, and today the IFIs are under increased double pressure from transnational and regional civil society forces and from neo-conservative anti-multilateralist right-wing forces in the United States.

At the moment this cleavage does not lead to significant increases in social welfare benefits in Southeast Asia. What might prove more important then is factors which have not been touched upon in this chapter, for example changing demographics, changing gender perceptions and roles, and social atomization of the family, including more divorces and more individualism. All this means that the family, or women to be more precise as the last-resort social safety net, is under retrenchment and rapidly being reconfigured to a new type of social institution (Schmidt, 2000b, 2007, 2008).

On the political agenda, social policy is not as relevant as other public policies and is still being subordinated to the economic growth imperative. Reforms have been initiated only because of the pressure and conditionalities from the IFIs, which acted on behalf of international capital's fear that social chaos and havoc would put their investment into jeopardy.

Although there are encouraging examples of victories won by CSOs, especially in Thailand and the Philippines, there is also considerable fragmentation of civil society. The new demands of flexible production and labour markets have decreased the strength of workers. This has implicitly meant that CSOs in a number of situations either act on behalf of labour or collaborate with non-unionized workers or more informally with the established trade unions.

Finally, there is a tendency towards CSOs either taking over state and public sector responsibilities, but always with a significantly lower budget, or even acting against the interests of those who support increases in collective goods and social redistribution. In a way they tend to deflect responsibility from the state, and as long as workers don't have any political representation in accordance with their class interests this might not be a sustainable strategy in the long run. The very act of defining themselves as 'non-governmental' explicitly rejects any ambition for establishing an alternative hegemonic project, which would, by its nature, have to include states and governments as the means through which political and economic power is articulated in modern societies (Sader, 2002).

A weak and fragmented civil society also tends to alienate people from their political institutions. People lose confidence in politicians not only from evidence of widespread corruption and arrogance but also (and more specifically linked to the IFIs' new social policy and the globalization effect) from a conviction that politicians do not understand and cannot resolve the major problems confronting their societies, such as unemployment and decline of public services (Cox, 1997: 66). The old civil society was formed in large part around interest groups like industrial and professional associations and trade unions, and also around co-operatives and charitable or self-help organizations. More recently, these older components of civil society have been diluted by a greater emphasis on 'identities' defined by religion, ethnicity and gender, and also on 'locality' rather than wider political authorities.

The integration of the vast majority of countries of the world into a single economy represents at once the self-justifying reversion of capitalism to its own nature, and its intensifying penetration of the whole world. All the reasons for dismantling social security, for the neglect of welfare nets and for the further marginalisation of the poorest are now justified, not in the name of 'capitalism', but under the banner of 'integration', the institutionalising of a partnership in which the participants are profoundly unequal and destined to remain so.

Seabrook, 1997: 81

NOTES

1. The author would like to thank participants at the workshop on the Political Economy of Southeast Asia in Kuala Lumpur, 29-30 October 2004, co-organized by IME, Malaysia and DIR, Aalborg University, funded by the Danish Development Agency Danida, Ministry of Foreign Affairs. A revised version was presented at the XXV Congreso De La Asociación Latinoamericana De Sociologia, 'Desarrollo, Crisis Y Democracia en America Latina: Participation, Movimientos Sociales Y Teoria Sociológica', 22-26 August 2005 in Porto Alegre, Brazil.
2. There were other factors, not least the dissolution of the Soviet system itself by its own creator, the Communist Party. The end of the Cold War also had a spill-over effect on regime change which should not be underestimated.
3. According to human rights organizations and Amnesty International, the Thaksin regime ordered the police and military to crack down on criminal elements in Thai society. This left more than 2500 people killed at gunpoint, and 50000 arrested in the southern, predominantly Muslim provinces, with hundreds killed and more wounded. Observers claim that several political activists have been killed or jailed, and Pradit Chareonthaitawee, the head of Thailand's official human rights commission, received death threats after saying, 'People are living in fear all over the kingdom.' The atrocities continue under the Abisith government, but this time the purge has been turned against Thaksin and his supporters.
4. Asia is also the only region in the world without a regional charter for human rights or other regional arrangements for the protection of rights and freedoms. And in many countries websites, newspapers and other media outlets are censored and constantly under threat of closure.
5. For some of the arguments presented by prominent advocates for Asian values see Tong (1994); Yew (1994); Mahbubani (1995).
6. Dr Mahathir Mohamad, at the 29th International General Meeting of the Pacific Basin Economic Council in Washington, delivered a paper and a speech on 'The Asian Values Debate'.
7. Filipino President Arroyo and President Megawati also claimed the existence of such networks, and they therefore formed a committee tasked with the activation of a 1997 bilateral defence and security accord to address arms smuggling. Megawati, in her turn, lamented the infiltration of Malaysian Muslim militants in Indonesia with the objective of causing political destabilization. Those elements were blamed, among other things, for the series of bombings in the capital around the end of 2000. Mahathir subsequently clamped down on the culprits. See Mezzera (2002).
8. Note that in this chapter I use the terms NGOs, CSOs and popular sector groups interchangeably.
9. In Indonesia, for instance, after the overthrow of Suharto (see He, 2004: 241).
10. For instance the World Bank notes that income inequality usually decreases as poverty rates fall. It said Malaysia was one of the few countries in East Asia where inequality had fallen over the past few decades, but where, despite the long-term reduction in poverty rates, the trend has reversed itself since 1990. 'Overall, Malaysia remains among the most unequal countries in East Asia' (Heong, 2004).

11. For this and the following see the introduction and various chapters in Hutchison and Brown (2001: 14).
12. Again Singapore and Malaysia are the exceptions (Deyo, 1997: 215).
13. Only five out of 56 NGOs have a relationship with social issues, and the most recent NGOs accredited to ASEAN are a chess confederation, a cosmetic association and the Academies of Science (International Council on Social Welfare, 2001: 16).

REFERENCES

Amara, Pongsapich and Nitaya Kataleeradabhan (1997), *Thailand Nonprofit Sector and Social Development*, Bangkok: CUSRI, Chulalongkorn University.
Amott, Natasha (2003–04), 'The Quest for Financial Sustainability: Foundations in Southeast Asia. Introduction to Financing Development in Southeast Asia: Opportunities for Collaboration and Sustainability', accessed at www.synergos.org/globalphilanthropy/04/asiafinancingintro.htm.
Anderson, Benedict (1993), 'Radicalism after communism in Thailand and Indonesia', *New Left Review*, 1/202 (November–December).
Anek, Laothamatas (1997), 'Development and democratization: a theoretical introduction with reference to the Southeast Asian and East Asian cases', in Anek Laothamatas (ed.), *Democratization in Southeast and East Asia*, Singapore: ISEAS.
Baron, Barnett F.F. (2002), 'The legal framework for civil society in East and Southeast Asia', *International Journal for Not-for-Profit Law*, 5(4) (July).
Bourdieu, Pierre and Loïc Wacquant (2001), 'Neoliberal newspeak: notes on the new planetary vulgate', *Radical Philosophy*, **105** (January).
Brown, Andrew (2001), 'After the Kader fire', in Jane Hutchison and Andrew Brown (eds), *Organising Labour in Globalising Asia*, London: Routledge.
Callahan, William A. (2003), 'Beyond cosmopolitanism and nationalism: diasporic Chinese and neo-nationalism in China and Thailand', *International Organization*, **57** (Summer).
Carothers, Thomas (1999), *Aiding Democracy Abroad: The Learning Curve*, Washington, DC: Carnegie Endowment for International Peace.
Connors, Michael Kelly (2003), 'The reforming state: security, development and culture in democratic times', Southeast Asia Research Centre working paper series no. 42, April, Hong Kong.
Contreras, Antonio P. (2002), 'Role of civil societies in transboundary common property resource governance in Southeast Asia', paper presented at the Conference of the International Association of Common Property (IASCP), 17-21 June.
Cornia, Giovanni Andrea (2001), 'Social funds in stabilization and adjustment programmes: a critique', *Development and Change*, **32**.
Cox, Robert (1997), 'Democracy in hard times: economic globalization and the limits to liberal democracy', in Anthony McGrew (ed.), *The Transformation of Democracy?*, Cambridge, UK: Polity Press.
Cox, Robert (2000), 'Political economy and the world order: problems of power and knowledge at the turn of the millennium', in Richard Stubbs and Geoffrey Underhill (eds), *Political Economy and the Changing Global Order*, Ontario: Oxford University Press.

Deyo, Frederic (1997), 'Labour and industrial restructuring in South-East Asia', in Garry Rodan, Kevin Hewison and Richard Robison (eds), *The Political Economy of South-East Asia*, Oxford, UK: Oxford University Press.

Deyo, Frederic (2000), 'Reform, globalization and crisis: reconstructing Thai labor', *Journal of Industrial Relations*, **42**(2).

Encarnaci, Omar G. (2003), 'Beyond civil society: promoting democracy after September', *Orbis*, Foreign Policy Research Institute's quarterly journal of world affairs, **47**(4) (Fall).

Far Eastern Economic Review (*FEER*) (1994), 'Asia's welfare: learning from the West's forgotten values', Editorial, 23 June.

Fine, Ben (2001), 'The social capital of the World Bank', in Ben Fine, Costas Lapavisas and Jonathan Pincus (eds), *Development Policy in the Twenty-first Century*, London: Routledge.

Fine, Robert and Shirin Rai (eds) (1997), *Civil Society: Democratic Perspectives*, London: Frank Cass.

Frenkel, Stephen (ed.) (1993), *Organized Labor in the Asia-Pacific Region*, Ithaca, NY: ILR Press.

Gills, Stephen (2000), 'Knowledge, politics, and neo-liberal economy', in Richard Stubbs and Geoffrey Underhill (eds), *Political Economy and the Changing Global Order*, Ontario: Oxford University Press.

Guan, Lee Hock (2004), 'Introduction: civil society in Southeast Asia', in Lee Hock Guan (ed.), *Civil Society in Southeast Asia*, Singapore: ISEAS.

He, Baogang (2004), 'Transnational civil society and the national identity in East Asia', *Global Governance*, **10**(2) (April–June).

Hedman, Eva-Lotta E. (2001), 'Contesting state and civil society: Southeast Asian trajectories', *Modern Asian Studies*, **35**(4): 921–51.

Held, David (1987), *Models of Democracy*, Cambridge, UK: Polity Press/Basil Blackwell.

Heong, Chee Yoke (2004), 'Anti-poverty moves: old wine, new bottles', *Asia Times*, 27 May.

Hersh, Jacques (2004), 'Oldspeak/newspeak of (neo)liberalism on development', *Interdisciplinary Journal of International Studies*, **2**(1) (also accessed at www.ijis.auc.dk/).

Hewison, Kevin (2004), 'The Politics of Neo-Liberalism: Class and Capitalism in Contemporary Thailand', Southeast Asia Research Centre working paper series no. 45, May, Hong Kong.

Hewison, Kevin and Garry Rodan (1994), 'The decline of the left in South East Asia', *Socialist Register*, **1994**.

Hewison, Kevin and Garry Rodan (1996), 'The ebb and flow of civil society and the decline of the left in Southeast Asia', in Garry Rodan (ed.), *Political Oppositions in Industrialising Asia*, London: Routledge.

Higgott, R. and Richard Robison (eds) (1985), *Southeast Asia: Essays in the Political Economy of Structural Change*, London: Routledge & Kegan Paul.

Hirsch, Philip and Carol Warren (1998), 'Introduction: through the environmental looking glass', in Philip Hirsch and Carol Warren (eds), *The Politics of Environment in Southeast Asia: Resources and Resistance*, London: Routledge.

Hirsch, Philip and Carol Warren (eds) (1998), *The Politics of Environment in Southeast Asia: Resources and Resistance*, London: Routledge.

Hutchison, Jane (2001), 'Export opportunities: unions in the Philippine garments industry', in Jane Hutchison and Andrew Brown (eds), *Organising Labour in Globalising Asia*, London: Routledge.

Hutchison, Jane and Andrew Brown (eds) (2001), *Organising Labour in Globalising Asia*, London: Routledge.

Hyden, Goran (1997), 'Civil society, social capital, and development: dissection of a complex discourse', *Studies in Comparative International Development*, **32**(1) (Spring).

International Council on Social Welfare (2001), 'Civil society and the ASEAN', ICSW briefing paper, November, London.

Jayasuriya, Kanishka (1996), 'Review essay: legalism and social control in Singapore', *Southeast Asia Research*, **4**(1) (March).

Jayasuriya, Kanishka (1999), 'Introduction', in Kanishka Jayasuriya, *Law, Capitalism and Power in Asia*, London: Routledge.

Jayasuriya, Kanishka and Kevin Hewison (2004), 'The Anti-Politics of Good Governance: From Global Social Policy to a Global Populism?', Southeast Asia Research Centre working paper 59, January, Hong Kong.

Jones, Catherine (ed.) (1993), *New Perspectives on the Welfare State in Europe*, London: Routledge.

Judge, Anthony (1997), 'Presentation to a World Bank workshop on civil society in the FSU and East/Central Europe', Washington, DC, 16 October published in *Transnational Associations*, **49**(3).

King, Victor T. (1996), 'Sociology', in Mohammed Halib and Tim Huxley (eds), *An Introduction to Southeast Asian Studies*, London: I.B. Tauris.

Levin, Andrew S. (1995) 'Civil society and democratization in Haiti', *Emory International Law Review*, **9**(2) (Fall).

Mahbubani, Kishore (1995), 'The Pacific way', *Foreign Affairs*, **74**(1) (January/February).

Marx, Karl (1970 edition), *Grundrisse*, ed. David McLellan, St Albans: Paladin.

McVey, Ruth (1995), 'Change and continuity in Southeast Asian studies', *Journal of Southeast Asian Studies*, **26**(1) (March).

Mezzera, Marco (2002), 'In the name of terror', accessed at http://focusweb.org/publications/2002/in-the-name-of-terror.htm.

Mitchell, Michael (1998), 'The political economy of Mekong Basin development', in Philip Hirsch and Carol Warren (eds), *The Politics of Environment in Southeast Asia: Resources and Resistance*, London: Routledge.

Mouzelis, Nicos (1994), 'The state in late development: historical and comparative perspectives', in D. Booth (ed.), *Rethinking Social Development: Theory, Research and Practice*, Essex: Longman.

Mouzelis, Nicos (1995), 'Modernity, late development and civil society', in J.A. Hall (ed.), *Civil Society: Theory, History, Comparison*, Cambridge, UK: Polity Press.

Nation (2001), 'Donations: PM fobs off govt move to hurt NGOs', 10 May.

Polanyi, Karl (1944), *The Great Transformation*, Boston, MA: Beacon Press.

Rasiah, Rajah (2001), 'Labour and work organisation in Malaysia', in Jane Hutchison and Andrew Brown (eds), *Organising Labour in Globalising Asia*, London: Routledge.

Robison, Richard (1999), 'The politics of Asian values', *Pacific Review*, **9**(3).

Rodan, Garry (1996), 'Theorising political opposition in East and Southeast Asia', in Garry Rodan (ed.), *Political Oppositions in Industrialising Asia*, London: Routledge.

Rodan, Garry (1999), 'The internationalisation of ideological conflict: Asia's new significance', *Pacific Review*, **9**(3).

Sader, Emir (2002), 'Beyond civil society – The left after Porto Alegre', *New Left Review*, **17** (September–October).

Schmidt, Johannes Dragsbaek (1996), 'Paternalism and planning in Thailand: facilitating growth without social benefits', in Michael Parnwell (ed.), *Uneven Development in Thailand*, Aldershot, UK: Avebury, Ashgate.

Schmidt, Johannes Dragsbaek (2000a), 'Globalization, democratization and labour social welfare in Thailand', in J.D. Schmidt and J. Hersh (eds), *Globalization and Social Change*, London and New York: Routledge.

Schmidt, Johannes Dragsbaek (2000b), 'Restructuring social welfare in East and Southeast Asia: corporatism with or without labor', paper for the International Conference of ASEM/World Bank/KSSA: 'Flexibility versus Security? Social Policy and the Labor Market in Europe and East Asia', Seoul, South Korea.

Schmidt, Johannes Dragsbaek (2007), 'Globalizing social welfare and labor markets in East and Southeast Asia', in Woontaek Lim (ed.), *Diversity and Dynamics of Globalization: Socio-Economic Models in Global Capitalism*, Seoul: Korean Sociological Association.

Schmidt, Johannes Dragsbaek (2008), 'Finanzkrise, Sozialkrise und ungleiche Entwicklung in Südkorea und Thailand', in Karin Küblböck and Cornelia Staritz (eds), *Asienkrise: Lektionen gelernt? Finanzmärkte und Entwicklung*, Hamburg: VSA Verlag.

Schmidt, Johannes Dragsbaek and Jacques Hersh (2000), *Globalization and Social Change*, London: Routledge.

Seabrook, Jeremy (1997), 'Convergence, welfare and development', *Race and Class*, **39**(1) (July–September).

Sen, Amartya (1997), 'Human rights and Asian values', *New Republic*, 14–21 July.

Simon, Karla W. (2002), 'NGO regulation in East and Southeast Asia: a comparative perspective', accessed at www.thailawforum.com/articles/ngo.html.

Sison, Marites (2001), 'Filipinos jolted as "people power" bites back', *Asia Times*, 4 May.

Stepan, Alfred (1988), *Rethinking Military Politics: Brazil and the Southern Cone*, Princeton, NJ: Princeton University Press.

Strange, Susan (2000), 'World order, non-state actors, and the global casino: the retreat of the state', in Richard Stubbs and Geoffrey Underhill (eds), *Political Economy and the Changing Global Order*, Ontario: Oxford University Press.

Taylor, John G. and Andrew Turton (eds) (1988), *Southeast Asia*, Sociology of Developing Societies series, Basingstoke and London: Macmillan.

Than, Tin Maung Maung (1997), 'Myanmar democratization: punctuated equilibrium or retrograde motion?', in Anek Laothamatas (ed.), *Democratization in Southeast and East Asia*, Singapore: ISEAS.

Tong, Goh Chok (1994), 'Social values, Singapore style', *Current History*, December.

Turton, Andrew (1987), *Production, Power, and Participation in Rural Thailand: Experiences of Poor Farmers' Groups*, Geneva: UNRISD.

Underhill, Geoffrey (2000), 'Conceptualizing the changing global order', in Richard Stubbs and Geoffrey Underhill (eds), *Political Economy and the Changing Global Order*, Ontario: Oxford University Press.

Van Rooy, Alison and Mark Robinson (1998), 'Out of the ivory tower: civil society and the aid system', in Alison Van Rooy (ed.), *Civil Society and the Aid Industry*, London: Earthscan.

Wade, Robert Hunter (2002), 'US hegemony and the World Bank: the fight over people and ideas', *RIPE*, **9**(2) (Summer).

White, Gordon (1996), 'The dynamics of civil society in post-Mao China', in B. Hook (ed.), *The Individual and the State in China*, Oxford, UK: Clarendon Press.

Whitehead, Laurence (1997), 'Bowling in the Bronx: the uncivil interstices between civil and political society', in Robert Fine and Shirin Rai (eds), *Civil Society: Democratic Perspectives*, London: Frank Cass.

Winder, David (1998), 'Civil society resource organizations (CSROs) and development in Southeast Asia', accessed at www.synergos.org/globalphilanthropy/98/csrosinasia.htm.

Wolfe, Marshall (1982), UNRISD PPP. Quoted from *Assignment Children*, **59/60**, UNICEF, Geneva.

Yew, Lee Kuan (1994), 'Culture is destiny', *Foreign Affairs*, **73**(2) (March/April).

Zakaria, Fareed (1995), 'Bigger than the family and smaller than the state: are voluntary groups what make countries work?', *New York Times Book Review*, August.

8. Rationale for free trade agreements (FTAs) in Southeast Asia

Sanchita Basu Das and Aekapol Chongvilaivan

INTRODUCTION

With regionalism gaining strength, free trade agreements (FTAs) have emerged to be a reality world-wide. They are seen as an action by governments to liberalize or facilitate trade and investment on a bilateral basis through detailed negotiations. FTAs are thus the first building blocks for regional economic integration. Initially, FTAs focused on providing preferential treatment for trade in goods among the members, but later they became more complex and covered negotiations on trade regulation and customs cooperation as well as those on labour standards, safeguard provisions and so on, besides negotiations on market access for trade in services. Thus FTAs are being regarded by policymakers as being effective and expeditious instruments for achieving economic cooperation and trade liberalization among 'like-minded' trading partners (Sen, 2007), while concomitantly pursuing multilateral trade liberalization through the World Trade Organization (WTO). These agreements, largely providing preferential market access to its signatory members on a reciprocal basis, are discriminatory by definition against non-members.

The number of FTAs and regional trade agreements (RTAs) has grown rapidly since the creation of the WTO in 1995 (Figure 8.1). As of 2008, out of more than 400 FTAs notified to the GATT/WTO, almost 300 arrangements were established after January 1995. Among these FTAs, over 225 are currently in force, with the remaining ones expected to be operational soon. The WTO estimates that, by the end of 2010, about 400 FTAs might come into force all over the world, provided FTAs reportedly planned or already under negotiation are concluded by then.

But what does a country expect to gain from these FTAs? FTAs broadly have two main welfare effects: (1) trade creation – an expansion of trade volume when inputs from high-cost domestic industry are replaced by imports from lower-cost member countries; (2) trade diversion – reduced imports from non-FTA nations, which occurs when there is a shift from

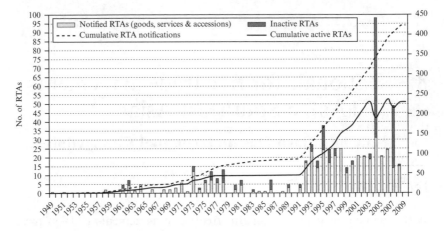

Source: World Trade Organization, 'Regional Trade Agreements: Facts and Figures',
accessed at www.wto.org/english/tratop_e/region_e/regfac_e.htm.

Figure 8.1   *Evolution of regional trade agreements in the world,
                1948–2008*

a more efficient supplier (low-cost, non-FTA nations) to a less efficient
supplier (higher-cost, FTA nations). The former improves the welfare of
a country owing to the elimination of tariffs and other non-tariff barriers
(NTBs), whereas the latter is welfare-deteriorating since discriminatory
tariff reduction induces private agents to import from a supplier that is not
the most efficient source. Thus, the net impact of FTAs is ambiguous. If
the positive effects from trade creation are larger than the negative effects
from trade diversion, then the FTA will generate net welfare gains (Viner,
1950).

By definition, FTAs eliminate trade barriers between contracting parties.
However, FTAs are discriminatory in nature and may not necessarily
promote smooth economic transactions. The FTA web often complicates
the tariff rates and rules on new areas like trade in services, investment,
competition policy, government procurement and migration. This raises
the costs and may impede the trade liberalization process through creation
of NTBs. In this case, FTAs have been viewed as being a stumbling block
for multilateral liberalization. It is further argued that FTAs could undermine the efforts undertaken by the WTO for global free trade and could
exclude some sectors from negotiations, which is inconsistent with the
WTO rules. Despite these arguments against FTAs, promoters of FTAs
argue that trade liberalization avoids protectionism. Moreover, the FTAs,
which are WTO-plus, provide a demonstration effect that motivates future

rounds of multilateral agreements under the auspices of the WTO. Hence, whether a country gains from an FTA is very much an open debate and depends very much on the way an FTA has been negotiated.

This chapter attempts to investigate the rationale of FTAs proliferating among the six leading ASEAN countries – Indonesia, Malaysia, the Philippines, Singapore, Thailand and Vietnam – with an emphasis on the comparison of their trade policy measures. The review of trade policies in those Southeast Asian nations reveals that closer economic linkages stand them in good stead, notwithstanding their slow, painstaking pace of trade liberalization. This chapter addresses several concerns – such as infant, stagnant stages of FTA negotiations and complex, multiple rules of origin – that will make the burgeoning FTAs in this region a stumbling block for regional economic integration. The discussions regarding ASEAN's roadmap to the ASEAN Economic Community (AEC) and East Asian integration, particularly with China, Japan and Korea, argue that there remains room for future improvement. This includes appropriate institutionalization that advocates intra- and extra-regional trade and FDI flows, better legal and financial infrastructure that facilitates international allocation of capital resources and labour movement, and well-designed compensatory schemes that ensure smooth adjustment and mitigate the negative effects of economic integration.

The remaining part of this chapter is organized as follows. The section 'Southeast Asia and FTAs' discusses the origin of FTAs in Southeast Asian countries. It starts with the emergence of AFTA and later discusses the initiation of bilateral FTAs by individual ASEAN countries. Then this section further discusses some of the current trends of ASEAN FTAs. The section 'Trade policies in, Southeast Asia' provides the motives of bilateral FTAs for countries to actively pursue trade negotiations. A general stocktake of bilateral trade liberalization initiatives of ASEAN as a whole is presented in the section 'Bilateral initiatives of ASEAN'. The section 'Regional economic integration' provides an assessment of regionalism, with particular mention of the ASEAN Economic Community (AEC) and East Asian integration. The final section concludes.

SOUTHEAST ASIA AND FTAs

Frustrated with the slow pace of the Doha round, lacklustre momentum in the Asia-Pacific Economic Cooperation (APEC) and growing FTA networks in the US and the EU, Southeast Asian countries joined the FTA bandwagon. The countries started as a regional grouping establishing the

Association of Southeast Asian Nations (ASEAN) in 1967. But this made limited progress in reducing trade barriers.

Thus, in 1992 the ASEAN leaders launched the ASEAN Free Trade Area (AFTA) with the signing of a common effective preferential tariff (CEPT) scheme, which requires member countries to reduce their tariff rates on a wide range of products traded within the region to 0–5 per cent. AFTA was fully operative in January 2003 with respect to the original six ASEAN members, with different dates of full implementation applicable to the four new ASEAN members of Cambodia (2010), Myanmar (2008), Laos (2008) and Vietnam (2006). To date, 99.7 per cent of products in the CEPT Inclusion List of the ASEAN 6 countries have been reduced to 0 to 5 per cent. However, AFTA is not fully functional yet, as NTBs remains problematic. Intra-regional trade remains low, and the utilization rate of CEPT is below 10 per cent. In November 1999, ASEAN economic ministers went further in their efforts to realize the vision of a regional free trade area by agreeing to adopt a target of zero tariffs by 2010 for the ASEAN 6 and 2015 for Cambodia, Laos, Myanmar and Vietnam (CLMV). For products in the priority sectors,[1] tariffs were targeted to be eliminated for the ASEAN 6 by 2007 and 2012 for the CLMV. Hence, a fully operational AFTA by 2015 was believed to provide a solid foundation for the ASEAN as a region.

But, since the Asian crisis, some changes have happened globally, and there have been rising concerns about the competitiveness of Southeast Asian countries. Regionally, until 2001, AFTA was the only trade agreement involving the ten ASEAN member countries. However, the agreement was restricted only to trade in goods, and some of the older ASEAN members were not agreeable to fully complying with AFTA guidelines. The agreement also involved a phased elimination of tariffs on intra-ASEAN trade, thus setting a slow pace of liberalization. Internationally, economic fundamentals have been undergoing dramatic and rapid changes. The Southeast Asian countries were concerned about the challenges of trade blocs by the consolidation of the Europe market in the Treaty of the European Union in 1992 and the completion of the North American Free Trade Agreement (NAFTA) in 1994. More closer to home, China, with its accession to the WTO, was rapidly opening up its economy, and this gave the private sector an incentive to invest in the huge Chinese market. The economic emergence of another large developing economy in Asia, namely India, was further putting pressure on ASEAN economies to remain competitive in the global market and be an attractive destination for FDI. This led to the proliferation of FTA initiatives in the region. Individual ASEAN economies started to pursue bilateral agreements with a number of countries and regions.

Singapore, which is a highly trade-dependent country in ASEAN, embarked on this new wave of regionalism as a means of enhancing its free trade agenda. This was soon followed by Thailand and Malaysia so as to actively pursue this strategy to enhance economic and strategic cooperation among 'like-minded' trading partners.

With new FTA initiatives being regularly announced by ASEAN or its individual countries, it is increasingly becoming difficult to track the exact number and features of existing and proposed agreements. Sen (2007) provides details on the progress of all the FTAs in ASEAN over the period 2001–06 that are being proposed or negotiated by these countries. He observes that, among all the FTA initiatives launched so far in ASEAN since 2001, the ones that have been mostly implemented and are currently in force are Singapore's FTAs (involving New Zealand, Japan, EFTA, Australia, the US, Jordan, India and Korea), ASEAN–China and ASEAN–Korea (trade in goods only) and Thailand's FTAs (involving Bahrain, Australia and New Zealand).[2] Apart from these, most of the other initiatives either are at the stage of being studied before formal negotiations or are being currently negotiated. Thus, the likely content and coverage of many of these agreements and their possible impacts on regional and global trading patterns cannot be comprehended.

It is also observed that current FTA activities in ASEAN range from that of limited FTAs on trade in goods to that of highly comprehensive bilateral agreements, like those of Singapore, that cover trade in goods and services, investments, and elimination of non-tariff barriers, besides including other complex issues of government procurement, competition policy and intellectual property protection, thus making it a 'WTO-plus' FTA.

Further, varieties of rules of origin (ROOs) have been applied or are currently being negotiated across ASEAN's FTAs. It is observed that, while the value-added (VA) rule is generally applied across Singapore's FTAs, a mix of other criteria, such as the change in tariff classification (CTC) and other restrictive rules, has also been applied.

There is also a lot of overlap among the FTA partners of ASEAN and the individual member countries. For example, while Singapore has already implemented its agreements with New Zealand, Australia, India, Korea and Japan, it is also a negotiating member in ASEAN-wide FTA initiatives with these countries. If these existing agreements and negotiations are happening in the absence of a common framework, there is a danger that ASEAN may end up with various inconsistent frameworks, thus negating the maximum gains for the region. This can have further negative implications such as higher costs of doing business and discriminatory trade owing to the 'noodle bowl' effect of regulations (Baldwin, 2006).

Many of these agreements have been implemented or are being negotiated without being notified to the WTO. Most of those ASEAN FTAs
that have been formally notified to the WTO either under GATT Article
XXIV or GATS Article V are those of Singapore's bilateral FTAs with the
developed members, namely New Zealand, Australia, EFTA, the US and
Japan. This implies that most of the ASEAN FTAs are currently unable
to be screened for WTO consistency.

These features raise concerns that FTAs currently proliferating in
Southeast Asia may become a stumbling block to regional economic
cooperation. But there is also a possibility that the perceived benefits from
greater liberalization and stronger strategic links may override these concerns. Thus, while FTAs could be a useful tool for promoting economic
cooperation in the region, not only do they need to be well designed and
implemented, but they also need to be supported by unilateral liberalization
and important domestic economic reforms. As observed by Sally and Sen
(2005), the engine of liberalization and regulatory reform by ASEAN countries has to be home-driven, with FTAs playing at best a supportive role.

TRADE POLICIES IN SOUTHEAST ASIA

As discussed earlier, while remaining committed to the trade liberalization
process under AFTA, the Southeast Asian countries have also begun bilateral free trade negotiations with distant partners like the United States,
South Asia, the Middle East, and the Australia–New Zealand markets.
The said motives for these cross-regional agreements are economic gains.
However, some of these markets have a very low share in the country's
total trade and investment basket. This is especially true for New Zealand
or some Middle Eastern countries, which are very popular partners among
Southeast Asian governments. This leads to some alternative rationales
that could account for these FTA initiatives.

Singapore

Being a city-state and a vastly open economy, Singapore is highly integrated with the world economy. Especially since the Asian crisis, Singapore
has aggressively pursued liberal economic and trade policies with the rest
of the world (ROW). In 1999, Singapore began its free trade negotiations
with New Zealand and thereafter completed FTAs with Japan, Australia,
the US, South Korea, India, Jordan and Panama. Seven other FTAs are
under negotiation, and many others are under consideration.

As for the motive, Singapore has a strong market access focus. It is

Table 8.1   Singapore exports to FTA partner countries, 2006

FTA partners	Export value (US$ million)	Share of total exports (%)
USA	27 621	10.15
China	26 513	9.75
Japan	14 854	5.46
Australia	10 186	3.74
South Korea	8 736	3.21
India	7 673	2.82
UAE	3 194	1.17
Panama	2 696	0.99
New Zealand	1 393	0.51
Mexico	1 009	0.37
Sri Lanka	922	0.34
Canada	820	0.30
Pakistan	771	0.28
Qatar	182	0.07
Kuwait	121	0.04
Bahrain	56	0.02
Jordan	43	0.01
Peru	15	0.006
World	272 049	100

Source: International Monetary Fund, *Direction of Trade Statistics Year Book 2007.*

believed that Singapore's leaders were frustrated by the failure of global and regional trade to produce substantial liberalization, and sought alternative ways to advance Singapore's economic interests, notably by negotiating FTAs (Rajan, Sen and Siregar, 2003). The city-state looked for the first-mover advantage, wanted to avoid future protectionist measures (such as quantitative restrictions) and wanted to secure the advantage of dispute settlement mechanisms.

However, the export figures in Table 8.1 suggest that trade access was not the only driver of Singapore's FTA initiatives. It should be noted that 13 out of the 18 current and prospective partners accounted for less than 3 per cent each of Singapore's exports in 2006. Clearly, the Singapore government has a political and security imperative for its main FTAs: to cement long-term strategic alliances with major powers and trading partners (Sally and Sen, 2005). This was also voiced by Singapore's chief negotiator, Tommy Koh, while detailing the benefits to arise from the FTA with the US:

Singapore's interest in the U.S., however, transcends business and economics. Singapore wishes to entrench the presence of the U.S. in the region because it underpins the security of the whole Asia-Pacific region. Singapore regards the U.S.-Singapore FTA as a symbol of continued U.S. commitment to the region. . . . the USSFTA . . . is about enhancing the prospects of peace and stability in the region.

Koh, 2004

Besides, Singapore views 'WTO-plus' FTAs as a building block for regional cooperation, which will eventually facilitate the multilateral liberalization process through the WTO. That said, Singapore has already set a precedent in terms of FTA standards that other countries in the region feel compelled to follow.

Thailand

Thailand was the first Southeast Asian country to follow Singapore on its FTA track. Its FTA talks started in early 2000 by the then prime minister, Thaksin Shinawatra, as he promoted the export-led growth and focused on liberalization initiatives. Thailand's first bilateral FTA came into being in 2002 with Bahrain, soon followed by agreements with China, India and Peru. Thailand further negotiated free trade arrangements with Australia, New Zealand, Japan and the US, along with the BIMSTEC[3] group and the EFTA[4] countries. In 2005, not only were most of these FTAs implemented, but Thailand also considered talking with Russia and South Africa.

The objectives of these FTAs were varied. Although, broadly, Thailand wanted better access to big markets for its agricultural and manufacturing products, it was also trying to secure oil from the Middle East and promoting its tourism industry. But, as with Singapore's policy, Thailand's FTA policy cannot be attributed solely to market strategy. One might question Thailand's economic benefits from agreements with small distant trade partners such as Bahrain, Croatia, the Czech Republic, New Zealand and Peru. As shown in Table 8.2, none of these countries figure prominently as a trade partner of Thailand. Hence there were other reasons for the Thai FTAs.

Thailand was not satisfied with the GATT Uruguay round. Notwithstanding its completion in 1994, it did not offer much for agricultural exports. In addition, there was also an alteration in government policy from import substitution to export promotion. Thailand shifted its economic centre of gravity from rural agriculture to urban manufacturing with the emergence of internationalized entrepreneurs (Pasuk and Baker, 1995, 1998). Hence, Bangkok elites in manufacturing and information technology (IT) wanted sectoral access to complementary economies, many of which lay outside Asia.

Table 8.2   Thailand exports to FTA partner countries, 2006

FTA partners	Export value (US$ million)	Share of total exports (%)
USA	19 674	15.04
Japan	16 571	12.67
China	11 806	9.03
Australia	4 384	3.35
India	1 818	1.39
South Africa	1 097	0.84
Myanmar	761	0.58
New Zealand	531	0.41
Russia	391	0.30
Sri Lanka	297	0.23
Czech Republic	355	0.27
Bahrain	79	0.06
Peru	58	0.04
Croatia	4	0.003
World	130 790	100

Source: International Monetary Fund, *Direction of Trade Statistics Year Book 2007.*

However, the more powerful motives lay with raising the country's international standard and avoiding trade diversion. The Thai government was eager to raise its overall diplomatic status by pursuing trade diplomacy, and FTAs were considered to be an integral component of the Thaksin administration's 'forward engagement diplomacy'. Thus, Thailand signed numerous FTAs in order to establish broader relations of cooperation with key partners.[5] Another driver for Thailand's FTA policy was the avoidance of trade diversion caused by the formation of trade blocs world-wide. As Thai trade officials became worried about economic regionalism and the proliferation of FTAs around the world, they became committed to either neutralizing or joining such arrangements.

It was also suggested that, through FTAs, Thailand wanted to build up its administrative and negotiating capabilities. As observed by Nagai (2002), 'Supachai initiated FTAs with small states like the Czech Republic and Croatia so that Thailand can gain access to the European Union (EU). The Czech Republic and Croatia are located at the "backdoor" of the EU.' But another important reason was 'the flexibility for subsequent policy adjustment that entering into FTAs with small states allows. Since Thailand cannot know the impact that FTAs may have, it might have picked small countries as experimental cases to guide later FTA policy.'

All of this suggests that, in the case of Thailand, political will and symbolism are the important motives, with little economic strategy in place. In general, FTAs are viewed as catalysts of domestic reforms. But Thai FTAs displayed poor quality and sought concessions in selected sectors, while otherwise preserving the domestic-protectionist status quo. There was little idea of how FTAs fitted into the broader national economic framework. This 'trade-light' approach is expected to make little positive difference to competition and efficiency in the Thai economy, but it is likely to create complications in the process (Sally, 2005).

Malaysia

Compared to Singapore and Thailand, Malaysia was a late entrant on the FTA bandwagon. It was a promoter of Southeast Asian regionalism, but at the same time refused to remove automobile products from the exclusion list of the AFTA protocol. In this way, though Malaysia is one of the most liberal countries in the region, it also practised peak tariffs, tariff escalation and non-tariff barriers in politically sensitive sectors.

While, in 2002, some interest was shown in the bilateral FTA between Malaysia and Japan, it was only in 2005 that the Ministry of International Trade and Industry (MITI) announced that it was negotiating FTAs with Japan, Australia, New Zealand, India and Pakistan. The country signed the Japan–Malaysia Economic Partnership Agreement (JMEPA) in 2006, initiating Malaysia's first bilateral FTA. However, there was not much enthusiasm about the FTAs. This was partially attributed to the fact that Malaysia may not be able to sign comprehensive FTAs, as the government shows no signs of negotiating away protection of the state-mentored automobile and steel industries, the Bumiputra (Malay) enterprises and the services sector generally, government procurement, and regulation of foreign direct investment.

In general, Malaysia's objectives in seeking FTAs are straightforward. They include: (a) better market access by addressing tariffs and non-tariff measures, (b) facilitation and promotion of trade, investment and economic development, (c) enhancement of the competitiveness of Malaysian exporters and (d) strengthening of capacity in specific targeted areas through technical cooperation and collaboration.[6] As portrayed in Table 8.3, Malaysia tends to explore advantageous opportunities economically. The regional market of Japan accounted for 8.86 per cent of Malaysia's exports in 2006; if the ASEAN markets of around 20 per cent were added, the East Asian total was approximately 29 per cent. But the cross-regional markets of the US, Australia, New Zealand, India and Pakistan were nearly as attractive, totalling 25.76 per cent.

In addition to these market-oriented reasons, one may discern strategic

Table 8.3   Malaysia exports to FTA partner countries, 2006

FTA partners	Export value (US$ million)	Share of total exports (%)
USA	30 191	18.79
Japan	14 241	8.86
Australia	4 553	2.83
India	5 129	3.19
Pakistan	843	0.53
New Zealand	674	0.42
World	160 664	100

Source: International Monetary Fund, *Direction of Trade Statistics Year Book 2007.*

reasons, such as avoidance of exclusion from proliferating preferential trade agreements (PTAs) in the European Union (EU) and the US, maintenance of a leadership role in Southeast Asia and keeping up a diplomatic pace with Singapore and Thailand. Other plausible reasons for the links with Australia, New Zealand, India and Pakistan could be the long-standing Commonwealth and security ties with Australia and New Zealand, sympathy on Islamic grounds with Pakistan, and large markets and technology opportunities in India. The latter motives could also be applied to the FTA with the US.

On the whole, while Malaysia stands to its commitment to maintaining relatively open trade and investment policy regimes, its main challenge is to liberalize pockets of protection and come out with significant domestic regulatory reforms. As posited by Athukorala (2005), the future of Malaysia's international trade diplomacy 'is still shrouded in uncertainty and ambiguity' otherwise.

Indonesia, the Philippines and Vietnam

Other Southeast Asian countries are not as active as the other three in the arena of FTAs. These countries are more concerned about their domestic reforms and are struggling to meet the AFTA commitments. Most of these countries suffer from a weak domestic regulatory and institutional environment and hence present a bigger obstacle for trade and investment liberalization. For example, though Indonesia views FTAs as a way to foster cooperation between two countries, it remains questionable whether Indonesia's participation in such trade agreements will produce much positive result. This is especially because Indonesian domestic industrial and agricultural sectors are still behind in terms of competitiveness and efficiency, and lack the necessary infrastructure to support any form of

FTAs. Nevertheless, Indonesia has indicated interest in negotiating bilateral FTAs with the US, Australia, New Zealand and EFTA. But this is more as a reaction to other governments in the region.

Similarly, the failure of the two successive rounds in the WTO as well as the rise of Asian bilateralism has prompted the Philippines to jump on to the bandwagon of FTAs. The Philippines has initiated efforts to forge FTAs with Japan, China and the US. However, the government has no concrete strategies or deliberate policies toward FTAs. The Philippines appears to be more of a passive negotiator or participant in FTAs (Medalla and Lazaro, 2004). Hence, as with Indonesia, the Philippines' FTA policy appears reactive and ad hoc, with little sense of economic strategy.

Finally, Vietnam has also been involved in bilateral negotiations since the Asian crisis. Vietnam reached a milestone when it signed the bilateral trade agreement with the US in July 2000. This was regarded as an important step towards Vietnam's membership in the WTO. However, currently the country is more focused on domestic market-based reforms and is in a process to devise a national strategy for future involvement in free trade deals with countries and trade blocs.

BILATERAL INITIATIVES OF ASEAN

Besides individual countries' interest in negotiating bilateral FTAs, ASEAN is also involved with several region-wide FTAs/RTAs. This started soon after the crisis, when various proposals were laid out on East Asian regional cooperation. However, none of these proposals has been very successful. This led to a number of proposals to achieve an RTA with ASEAN. It is in this context that ASEAN's FTA negotiations with its five major regional partners, that is, Australia and New Zealand (CER), China, India, Japan and Korea, assume importance. Currently, all these agreements are at various stages of negotiation (Table 8.4).

The above suggests that, to facilitate economic cooperation, ASEAN is following the ASEAN+1 framework. This, combined with several bilateral FTAs, may place ASEAN as a 'hub' for East Asian regional cooperation. However, it should be noted that several ASEAN+1 arrangements may pose some difficulties in terms of limited resources in the region.

A closer look at these RTA agreements indicates that the coverage of most of these initiatives is far more comprehensive than that of just a free trade agreement and pertains to liberalization of goods, services and investment. In this sense, all these are 'WTO-plus' agreements. However, much will be revealed once the negotiations are completed.

On a bilateral basis, these FTAs are beneficial to ASEAN, as they

Table 8.4   ASEAN's ongoing RTA initiatives

RTA	Status	Coverage area	Timeframe
ASEAN–China Comprehensive Economic Co-operation Agreement	Early Harvest Programme (EHP) in force; FTA under negotiation	Economic partnership agreement and FTA for trade in goods	Duty-free status to all commodities by 2010
ASEAN–India Comprehensive Economic Co-operation Agreement	FTA for trade in goods concluded	FTA for trade in goods	Implemented from 1 January 2009
ASEAN–Japan Comprehensive Economic Partnership Agreement	Framework agreement signed	FTA for trade in goods	In force from 1 December 2008
ASEAN– Australia and New Zealand Free Trade Area	Framework agreement concluded	FTA for trade in goods and services, and investment in a single undertaking	Signed in December 2008
ASEAN–Korea Comprehensive Co-operation Partnership	Agreement in force	FTA for trade in goods and services, and investment, including 'WTO-plus' issues	Eliminate tariffs for 80 per cent of all products by 2010

Source: Authors' compilation.

will provide a bigger market access for goods and services as a result of lower tariff barriers, more investment opportunities and more efficient costs of doing business. Most of these FTAs also have political significance. For instance, the ASEAN–China FTA may allay fear on Chinese competition.

It has often been argued that FTAs in ASEAN have the potential to promote regional economic development and particularly help newer ASEAN members to build up production networks, thereby strengthening their economic integration within ASEAN and East Asia (Sen, 2007). However, there are fears that multiple hubs and spokes may deter regional economic cooperation. For example, there is no single hub for ASEAN FTAs, as both ASEAN as a group and Singapore and Thailand are pursuing several FTA negotiations. At the same time, China and India are creating their own FTA hubs, thus creating a 'noodle bowl' of FTAs in the Asian context (Baldwin, 2006). This reduces the overall welfare impact, especially as each of them enters into a bilateral deal with the same trading partner.

Further, as observed by Sen and Rajan (2005), with individual ASEAN members having already enforced some of their own bilateral deals with 'like-minded' trading partners, an important issue that comes up is how these countries are supposed to treat the ASEAN-wide agreements with the same trading partners. It is not yet clear whether regional agreements would subsume these bilateral deals and therefore raise concerns about their applicability and consistency in the negotiating framework.

One last consideration regarding the RTAs is the extent to which these will complement the ongoing integration process in ASEAN. This issue is particularly pertinent because, although AFTA has been implemented and tariff barriers have been reduced, it is not fully functional yet, as NTBs remain a problem. Intra-regional trade remains low at around 25 per cent, and the utilization rate of CEPT is below 10 per cent. Similarly, for the ASEAN Framework Agreement on Services (AFAS), the pace of services sector liberalization is not very significant. In this regard, comprehensive FTAs involving goods, services and investment may encourage individual ASEAN countries to undertake domestic reforms and hence improve their global and regional competitiveness.

On the whole, what can be said for ASEAN-wide FTAs is that, while most of these initiatives are of major political and economic significance to both parties, they are also a drain of scarce administrative and negotiating resources. They could divert ASEAN's attention from the WTO. However, as ASEAN governments have yet to realize this as a problem, the group will continue with its bilateral trade liberalization initiatives with its major regional partners.

REGIONAL ECONOMIC INTEGRATION

The past decade has seen a rapid proliferation of regionalism among the Asian economies. But in the aftermath of the 1997–98 financial crisis and with the inability of the WTO to further the multilateral trade liberalization agenda, there has been growing attention given to formalizing regional cooperation in East Asia. In general, there has been less progress on regional integration in East Asia compared to the European Union

(EU) or the North American Free Trade Agreement (NAFTA). This could be the result of competition and antagonism between Japan and China and an absence of any major geopolitical challenge that helped post-war Europe to integrate. The EU experience, however, cannot be totally applied to Asia, as the scope, depth and character vary across regions. It is also observed that, in comparison to the case in Europe, Asian regionalism is not well institutionalized, since it operates by governments' consensus. Nevertheless, one of the major factors giving rise to increasing interest in regionalism is the development of intra-regional trade, and this may witness remarkable increases in the international production network. Thus, what is currently evident is the initiative on East Asian integration or the ASEAN+3 arrangements.

ASEAN Economic Community

ASEAN member countries are also undertaking deeper economic integration among themselves. At the 2003 ASEAN summit in Bali, ASEAN leaders agreed to integrate their economies and establish an ASEAN Economic Community (AEC) by 2020. This was later brought forward to 2015. The end-goal of the AEC is the creation of a single market and a production base where there is a free flow of goods, services, investments, capital and skilled labour. Although the approach towards achieving this end-goal was not elaborated in the Bali Concord II, what seems clear at the start was the need to have a significantly higher degree of regional economic integration and institutional development.

The loss of economic competitiveness to emerging markets such as China has been the major driving force in ASEAN's efforts to accelerate economic integration. Furthermore, China has now overtaken ASEAN as the world's prime location for FDI. This may have serious repercussions for ASEAN's economic well-being over the medium to long term, as FDI has long played an important role in the region's economic development (Freeman and Hew, 2002). Therefore, economic integration will provide the means to revitalize ASEAN's economies. Given that ASEAN countries are at very different levels of economic development, this diversity can be an advantage, as it maximizes the complementarities among its member countries.

The AEC concept builds on three existing building blocks: the AFTA, the AFAS and the ASEAN Investment Area (AIA). While AFTA requires all its member countries to adopt zero tariff rates by 2015, AFAS aims to enhance cooperation in the services sector among ASEAN countries by eliminating intra-regional trade restrictions and facilitate free flow of services by 2015. Lastly, the AIA aims to attract FDI flows from both

ASEAN and non-ASEAN investors and binds member countries to reduce or eliminate investment barriers and grant national treatment to ASEAN investors by 2010 and to all investors by 2020. Hence, having a fully operational AFTA, AFAS and AIA should provide a solid foundation for the AEC.

That said, the AEC initiative is a roadmap to an economically integrated ASEAN market. To strengthen ASEAN integration and to eliminate the economic divide among member countries faster, ASEAN leaders launched an Initiative for ASEAN Integration (IAI) in 2000, which mostly concentrated on studies and training on human resources, technology development and infrastructure provided by the older members or financed with funds mobilized by ASEAN from the international financial organizations. This further emphasizes three things: ASEAN's commitment to regional economic integration, the notion that integration would not exclude the newer members, and the association's determination to integrate the newer members into the ASEAN mainstream (Severino, 2007). This is very important, as, without uplifting the poorer ASEAN countries (Cambodia, Myanmar, Laos and Vietnam), further trade liberalization and other forms of FTAs would not be successful. This would not only dilute the agreements, but also reduce their regional political, economic and social significance.

Thus, the AEC is viewed as more of an 'FTA-plus' arrangement that includes some elements of a common market, such as the free movement of capital and skilled labour. However, the AEC needs to involve a better institutional and legal infrastructure to facilitate greater economic integration (Sally and Sen, 2005).

East Asian Integration

Economic integration through liberalization of trade and FDI in East Asia has contributed enormously to the region's economic growth and development. In the last two decades, the East Asia economies – ASEAN, China, Japan and Korea – have gained their growing significance in global trade, with the share of world exports nearly doubled from 14.2 per cent in 1980 to 23.9 per cent in 2003.

Several regional institutions that constituted intra- and extra-regional economic linkages have been established in East Asia, including ASEAN, ASEAN+3 (Japan, China and Korea), APEC and Asia–Europe Meeting (ASEM). Among these groupings, ASEAN+3, institutionalized in 1999 in the aftermath of the Asian financial crisis, seems to be the most prominent in terms of trade and investment cooperation. It deepened East Asia's cooperation at various levels in various areas, including economic, trade, financial, political and security cooperation. The long-term objective of ASEAN+3 adopted by the signatories at the ASEAN Plus Summit in 2002 in Cambodia is to materialize an 'East Asia community' through various mechanisms, namely economic, monetary and finance, political and security, tourism, agriculture, environment, energy and ICT.

A number of fundamental factors rationalize closer economic linkages among the East Asian economies. First of all, anecdotal evidence indicates substantial surges in the amounts and volumes of intra-regional trade and FDI flows. The share of intra-regional trade among the East Asian countries persistently increased from 37 per cent in 1980 to more than 50 per cent in 2007. The strength of the trade relations among the East Asian economies is attributable to the prevalence of intermediate inputs procurement in the manufacturing sectors (Urata, 2004).[7] This implies that economic integration in East Asia has a pivotal role to play in fortifying a nexus that vertically and horizontally ties firms through production and procurement networks.

Second, financial market integration, like trade liberalization, has been an increasingly imperative aspect of economic integration in East Asia owing to its rapid expansion of FDI flows. To date, the ASEAN+3 economies are the world's largest recipient of FDI, sharing approximately 15 per cent of the world FDI inflow. Furthermore, the share of intra-regional FDI flows also exhibits an increasing trend, with more advanced economies like Japan, Korea and Singapore as major FDI suppliers and middle-income economies like Malaysia, Thailand and Vietnam as major FDI recipients. These trends of FDI in East Asia shed light on potential benefits from capital transactions facilitation and improved efficiency of capital allocation that resulted from regional economic integration.

Third, the motivation for regional collaboration is politics-driven (Schott, 2004). This argument seems plausible given the knowledge that world trade is for the time being dominated by two mega-blocs – namely, the EU and NAFTA – burgeoning since the early 1990s. This gave rise to political concerns that the developing East Asian countries would be laggards in the new era of globalization. These concerns were exacerbated by the Asian financial crisis in 1997–98, during which East Asian policymakers were forced to restructure their financial institutions and strengthen regional collaboration. In addition, the opening up of China after its WTO accession in 2001 has been a political catalyst of East Asia's emphasis on economic integration and thus provided a strategic tool for its governments to thrive on regionalism prevalence.

Last but not least, the diversity of social, economic and political structures accounts for unprecedented propagation of East Asia's economic integration. East Asian countries are greatly heterogeneous in terms of economic and financial development levels, ranging from highly developed economies like Japan, Korea and Singapore to less developed economies like Cambodia, Indonesia, Myanmar, the Philippines and Vietnam. These fundamental differences have made mutual benefits – such as skilled labour movement, technological spillovers and institutional infrastructure development – from tightened economic collaboration in East Asia highly feasible.

Economic integration among the East Asian nations, nonetheless, raises two major concerns the policymakers are supposed to be aware of. The first is the perilous 'noodle bowl' effect prompted by the proliferation of FTAs in this region. With an ongoing process of East Asia's formation of an economic bloc, inconsistency and complication of ROOs that emanate from overlapping FTAs will increase transaction costs. A complicated tariff structure that emanates from overlapping FTAs may hamper gains from trade because of rising trade costs (for example through complicated customs procedures and costly product customization), low utilization of the FTA preferences, and poorly established regional production networks.

The other is concerned with distortions of resources allocation spurred by trade liberalization. Paving the way toward zero tariffs inevitably entails domestic production adjustment as a result of a shift in terms of trade (TOT). In this regard, the benefits from economic integration are unlikely to be equally shared among economic sectors – some sectors may gain, but others may lose. These conflicts of interests across sectors imply that the success of FTAs would not have been viable without the assumption that the winners from the policy shift are able and willing to compensate the losers who are suffering the income losses that result.

Therefore the challenge of economic integration in East Asia is how to ensure that the gains from economic integration outweigh the losses stemming from multiple ROOs and the trade adjustment costs. The East Asian economic partnership as a welfare-enhancing economic grouping is achievable in two ways. First, consolidation of the noodle bowl into a single, East Asia-wide FTA, perhaps in the form of an East Asia Free Trade Area or Comprehensive Economic Partnership in East Asia (Kawai and Wignaraja, 2008), helps mitigate the negative impacts of the complex and overlapping tariffs, standards and ROOs. Second, a crucial negotiation agenda is to minimize trade adjustment costs in transit to expand East Asian economic integration. Several compensatory schemes may facilitate smooth adjustments, such as relocation expenses, unemployment benefits, training, construction of infrastructure, and technology support, among many others.

CONCLUSION

This chapter provides the rationale for Southeast Asian bilateralism – a stepping stone toward regional, and perhaps multilateral, integration. The ASEAN nations have demonstrated many encouraging signs of successful economic regionalism, such as rapid expansions of intra- and extra-regional trade and capital flows that reflect improved regional resource allocation, deeper, wider trade facilitation that trims tariff and non-tariff barriers, ceaseless proliferation of 'WTO-plus' FTAs that transform East Asian bilateralism into a building block of multilateralism, materialized institutionalization of AFTA, AFAS and AIA, which serve as the key milestones of the integrated East Asia, namely AEC, and strengthened production networks and industrial clusters that result in productivity improvement through production sharing and specialization among regional firms.

Nevertheless, the review and analysis of FTA initiatives and progress in Southeast Asia reveal that trade liberalization is largely limited. In this regard, the bilateralism way the ASEAN members have paved toward regional economic integration remains patchy. There are still concerns, including policy uncertainty, multiple, inconsistent ROOs, conflicts among signatories and interest groups within countries, and overlapping FTAs (a hub-and-spoke problem), which may not only prevent the ASEAN economies from fully tapping benefits from the moves toward an integrated economy, but also make ASEAN's economic block stumbling.

ASEAN has potentially flourished on the formation of closer economic linkages with well-functioning organizations of an integrated market. The obstacles that appeared in the roadmap toward AEC as well as an East Asia community imply that the hasty efforts to accomplish a regional free trade area without a thorough understanding of its economic and political consequences are highly detrimental. Fine-tuned, more collaborative trade and investment policies are therefore needed.

NOTES

1. In 2003, the ASEAN High-Level Task Force on Economic Integration recommended fast-track integration of 11 sectors. One more sector was added in 2007.
2. Thailand entered into a framework agreement for an FTA with India in 2004, which currently involves tariff elimination only on 82 selected goods. Although the framework agreement indicates this FTA will be comprehensive, there has not been significant progress since the Early Harvest Scheme.
3. BIMSTEC stands for Bangladesh, India, Myanmar, Sri Lanka and Thailand Economic Cooperation. Sometimes it is also called the Bay of Bengal Initiative for Multi-Sectoral Technical and Economic Cooperation.

4. European Free Trade Association (EFTA), with members Iceland, Liechtenstein, Norway and Switzerland.
5. Speech by former prime minister Thaksin Shinawatra, 'Forward Engagement: The New Era of Thailand's Foreign Policy', delivered at the Inaugural Lecture of the Saranrom Institute for International Affairs, 12 March 2003, Bangkok, Thailand; available at http://www.thaiembdc.org/pressctr/statemnt/pm/sifa031203.html.
6. Malaysia, 'Malaysia and Free Trade Agreements' (Kuala Lumpur: Ministry of International Trade and Industry, 2005), available at http://www.miti.gov.my.
7. In East Asia, Japan has emerged as a source or hub of production networks and industrial clusters, as it accounts for approximately one-third of all intermediate inputs exports by the East Asian countries (Ng and Yeats, 2003).

REFERENCES

Athukorala, P. (2005), 'Trade policy in Malaysia: liberalization process, structure of protection, and reform agenda', *ASEAN Economic Bulletin*, **22**(1): 19–34.

Baldwin, R. (2006), 'Managing the noodle bowl: the fragility of East Asian regionalism', Centre for Economic Policy Research discussion paper no. 5561.

Freeman, N. and D. Hew (2002), 'Introductory overview: rethinking the East Asian development model', *ASEAN Economic Bulletin*, **19**(1): 1–5.

Kawai, M. and G. Wignaraja (2008), 'EAFTA or CEPEA? Which way forward?', *ASEAN Economic Bulletin*, **25**(2): 113–39.

Koh, T. (2004), 'The USSFTA: a personal perspective', in Tommy Koh and Chang Li Lin (eds), *The United States Singapore Free Trade Agreement: Highlights and Insights*, Singapore: Institute of Policy Studies, p. 8.

Medalla, E.M. and D.C. Lazaro (2004), 'Exploring the Philippine FTA policy options', Philippine Institute for Development Studies policy notes no. 2004–09.

Nagai, F. (2002), 'Thailand's trade policy – WTO plus FTA?', IDE APEC Study Center working paper series 01/02, no. 6, p. 10.

Ng, F. and A. Yeats (2003), 'Major trade trends in East Asia: what are their implications for regional cooperation and growth?', World Bank policy research working paper no. 3084.

Pasuk Phongpaichit and C.J. Baker (1995), *Thailand, Economy and Politics*, New York: Oxford University Press, pp. 162–7.

Pasuk Phongpaichit and C.J. Baker (1998), *Thailand's Boom and Bust*, Chiangmai: Silkworm Books, pp. 67–72.

Rajan, R.S., R. Sen and R.Y. Siregar (2003), 'Singapore and the new regionalism: bilateral trade linkages with Japan and the US', *World Economy*, **26**(9): 1325–56.

Sally, R. (2005), 'Analysis/Thailand's trade policy: too many free trade agreements, far too little domestic reform', ISEAS Viewpoints, 21 September, accessed at www.iseas.edu.sg/viewpoint/rs21sep05.pdf

Sally, R. and R. Sen (2005), 'Whither trade policies in Southeast Asia? The wider Asian and global context', *ASEAN Economic Bulletin*, **22**(1): 92–115.

Schott, J.J. (2004), 'Assessing US FTA policy', in Jeffrey J. Schott (ed.), *Free Trade Agreements: US Strategies and Priorities*, Washington, DC: Institute for International Economics (IIE).

Sen, R. (2007), 'Bilateral trade and economic cooperation agreements in ASEAN:

evolution, characteristics, and implications for Asian economic integration', ISEAS working paper in economics and finance no. 1.

Sen, R and R. Rajan (2005), 'The new wave of FTAs in Asia: Implications for ASEAN, China and India', in ADB, *Asian Economic Cooperation and Integration*, Manila: Asian Development Bank.

Severino, R.C. (2007), 'The ASEAN developmental divide and the initiative for ASEAN integration', *ASEAN Economic Bulletin*, **24**(1): 35–44.

Urata, S. (2004), 'The shift from "Market-led" to "Institution-led" regional economic integration in East Asia in the late 1990s', RIETI Discussion Paper No. 12.

Viner, J. (1950), *The Custom Union Issues*, New York: Carnegie Endowment for International Peace.

Index